D1248264

The Killing Zone

*The United States Wages Cold War
in Latin America*

The Killing Zone
The United States Wages Cold War in Latin America

STEPHEN G. RABE
University of Texas at Dallas

New York   Oxford
OXFORD UNIVERSITY PRESS

Oxford University Press, Inc., publishes works that further Oxford University's
objective of excellence in research, scholarship, and education.

Oxford   New York
Auckland   Cape Town   Dar es Salaam   Hong Kong   Karachi
Kuala Lumpur   Madrid   Melbourne   Mexico City   Nairobi
New Delhi   Shanghai   Taipei   Toronto

With offices in
Argentina   Austria   Brazil   Chile   Czech Republic   France   Greece
Guatemala   Hungary   Italy   Japan   Poland   Portugal   Singapore
South Korea   Switzerland   Thailand   Turkey   Ukraine   Vietnam

Copyright © 2012 by Oxford University Press, Inc.

For titles covered by Section 112 of the US Higher Education
Opportunity Act, please visit www.oup.com/us/he for the latest
information about pricing and alternate formats.

Published by Oxford University Press, Inc.
198 Madison Avenue, New York, New York 10016
www.oup.com

Oxford is a registered trademark of Oxford University Press

All rights reserved. No part of this publication may be reproduced,
stored in a retrieval system, or transmitted, in any form or by any means,
electronic, mechanical, photocopying, recording, or otherwise,
without the prior permission of Oxford University Press.

Library of Congress Cataloging-in-Publication Data
Rabe, Stephen G.
    The killing zone : the United States wages Cold War in Latin America / Stephen G. Rabe.
      p. cm.
    Includes bibliographical references and index.
    ISBN 978-0-19-533323-7 (pbk. : acid-free paper)
1. Latin America—Foreign relations—United States.   2. United States—Foreign relations—
Latin America.   3. Cold War—Diplomatic history.   4. Intervention (International law)
5. Latin America—Politics and government—1948–1980.   6. Latin America—Politics
and government—1980-   7. United States—Foreign relations—1945–1989.
8. Regime change—Latin America—History—20th century.   9. Espionage,
American—Latin America—History—20th century.   I. Title.
    F1418.R235 2011
    327.7308—dc22   2010036008

ISBN 978-0-19-533323-7 (paper)

Printing number: 9 8 7 6 5 4

Printed in the United States of America
on acid-free paper

For the Hamilton College History Faculty (1966–1970)

Charles C. Adler
David M. "Spoolie" Ellis
Edgar Baldwin "Digger" Graves
Edwin B. "Asian Ed" Lee, Jr.
David R. Millar
James F. Traer

Dedicated scholars and teachers

CONTENTS

ACKNOWLEDGMENTS

I express my gratitude to Dr. B. Hobson Wildenthal, the academic vice president and provost at the University of Texas at Dallas, and Dr. Dennis M. Kratz, the dean of the School of Arts and Humanities. Both men have consistently supported my research over many years. These two academic leaders have provided me with the generous Arts and Humanities Endowed Chair and have granted me released time for my writing. I also thank Brian Wheel, my editor at Oxford University Press, for supporting this project, and Danniel Schoonebeek, the editorial assistant for American and Latin American history at Oxford, for guiding me through the production process. Finally, I thank the attorneys in my family, Genice A. G. Rabe, the renowned civil rights and labor law lawyer, and Elizabeth R. Rabe, the soon-to-be-famous federal prosecutor, for their support.

I also wish to express my thanks to the professors who reviewed *The Killing Zone* in its various stages of development: Mark T. Gilderhus, Texas Christian University; Mark Lentz, University of Louisiana, Lafayette; Alan McPherson, University of Oklahoma; Stephen Irving Max Schwab, University of Alabama; James Siekmeier, West Virginia University; Jeffrey Taffet, United States Merchant Marine Academy.

THE UNITED STATES AND LATIN AMERICA: COLD WAR CHRONOLOGY

1945

- Meeting in Mexico City, the United States and Latin American nations issue the Act of Chapultepec, pledging collective security. The meeting represents the highpoint of inter-American wartime cooperation.
- President Franklin Delano Roosevelt dies in April and is succeeded by Vice President Harry S. Truman. President Roosevelt has been associated in Latin America with the Good Neighbor Policy and the principle of nonintervention.
- World War II ends with the surrender of Germany in May and Japan in August.

1946

- The Unites States unsuccessfully tries to persuade Argentines not to elect Juan Perón as president of Argentina.
- The Truman administration declines to schedule an economic conference with Latin Americans to discuss economic aid.

1947

- In March, President Truman pronounces his "Truman Doctrine." The policy is established that the United States will assist anticommunist forces.
- Secretary of State George Marshall delivers a speech in June calling for economic assistance for postwar Europe. The "Marshall Plan" will ensue the next year.
- George Kennan publishes an article in *Foreign Affairs* that will serve as the basis for the U.S. policy of "containing" the Soviet Union and communism.
- The United States concludes in September the Rio Treaty with Latin America. Western Hemisphere nations will form a military alliance against aggression.

1948

- In a policy paper, NSC 16, the State Department concludes in March that communism is not a threat in Latin America.
- At an inter-American meeting in April in Bogotá, Secretary of State Marshall informs delegates that there will not be a "Marshall Plan for Latin America." Delegates establish the Organization of American States, which incorporates the non-intervention principle.
- In November, military officers in Venezuela overthrow a constitutional government. The military action seemingly signals the end of the movement toward democracy and social reform throughout the region.
- On 10 December, the United Nations adopts the Universal Declaration of Human Rights. Eleanor Roosevelt, widow of President Roosevelt, had led the movement to adopt the declaration.

1949

- In September, the United States announces that the Soviet Union has successfully tested an atomic weapon.
- Communist leader Mao Zedong proclaims on 1 October the People's Republic of China.

1950

- In February, Senator Joseph McCarthy makes sensational allegations about Communist influence within the U.S. government.
- George Kennan tours Latin America and subsequently submits report recommending support for anti-Communists in Latin America even if they are authoritarian and undemocratic.
- In April, President Truman secretly approves the policy paper NSC 68/2, which calls on the United States to confront the Soviet Union globally with awesome military power.
- In April, Assistant Secretary of State for Latin America Edward Miller delivers his "Miller Doctrine" speech, suggesting that in the fight against communism the United States could not abide by the non-intervention principle.
- In May, the Truman administration adopts the policy paper NSC 56/2, authorizing military aid for Latin America to fight the Cold War. Aid to Latin American militaries begins in 1951.
- In June, the Korean War begins when North Korea invades South Korea.

1951

- The Washington Conference concludes in April, with the Truman administration unable to persuade most Latin American nations to contribute troops for the Korean War. The failure signals the end of the cooperation that characterized inter-American relations during World War II.

1952

- In March, Fulgencio Batista seizes power in Cuba.
- In June, Guatemala issues Decree 900, expropriating large landholdings, including properties of the United Fruit Company.
- President Truman recognizes the Bolivian Revolution in June. Assured of the non-Communist nature of the revolution, both the Truman and Eisenhower administrations provide economic assistance to Bolivia.
- In July, President Truman approves PBFORTUNE, a covert plan to overthrow the Guatemalan government.
- In October, Secretary of State Dean Acheson halts PBFORTUNE.

1953

- President Dwight D. Eisenhower takes office.
- In March, President Eisenhower approves policy paper NSC 144/1 that confidentially notes that the United States cannot observe the non-intervention principle in the Cold War.
- On 26 July, Fidel Castro leads Cuban rebels on an assault on Moncada army barracks in an unsuccessful attempt to overthrow the government of Fulgencio Batista.
- In August, President Eisenhower approves PBSUCCESS, a covert plan to overthrow the Guatemalan government.
- With U.S. approval, the United Kingdom overthrows in October the elected government of Cheddi Jagan in British Guiana.

1954

- With CIA backing, Colonel Carlos Castillo Armas overthrows in June the constitutional Guatemalan government of President Jacobo Arbenz Guzmán.
- In September, U.S. analysts, operating under PBHISTORY, report that they can find no evidence in Guatemalan archives of links between President Arbenz and international communism.
- A presidential panel, the Doolittle Commission, recommends that the United States improve its abilities to intervene covertly in other nations.
- The Eisenhower administration awards the Legion of Merit to Marcos Pérez Jiménez, the dictator of Venezuela.

1955

- In September, President Juan Perón is overthrown by the Argentine military. Three decades of political instability ensue in Argentina.

1956

- On 2 December, Fidel Castro and supporters land in Cuba on a small boat, the *Granma*. Cuban forces kill most of the invaders. Castro and the survivors seek refuge in Cuban mountains in the eastern part of the island.

1957

- In July, President Castillo Armas of Guatemala is assassinated.

1958

- In January, Colonel Marcos Pérez Jiménez, the dictator of Venezuela, is overthrown by a popular movement. His overthrow marks a movement toward constitutional regimes throughout the region.
- With the Castro insurgency spreading, the United States cuts off arms shipments to Batista in March.
- Vice President Richard Nixon travels to South America and is threatened with physical harm during a riot in May in Caracas, Venezuela.
- The Marxist political leader, Salvador Allende, nearly wins Chilean presidential election held in September.

1959

- In January, Fidel Castro assumes power in Cuba.
- In April, the revolutionary government of Cuba adopts an extensive agrarian reform law.
- In April, Castro meets with Vice President Nixon in Washington.
- In December, Colonel J. C. King of the CIA calls for the "elimination" of Castro.

1960

- In February, Cuba signs a commercial agreement with the Soviet Union.
- In March, President Eisenhower authorizes a program to overthrow Castro.
- President Eisenhower announces the Social Progress Trust Fund for Latin America. The July announcement breaks with the fifteen-year U.S. policy of not providing extensive economic assistance to the region.
- The MR-13 Rebellion breaks out in Guatemala in November. The rebels protest both social injustice and the U.S. role in their country. More than three decades of political violence in Guatemala will ensue.

1961

- On 3 January, President Eisenhower breaks diplomatic relations with Cuba.
- On 6 January, Soviet Premier Nikita Khrushchev's delivers his "Wars of National Liberation Speech."
- On 19 January, President Eisenhower warns President-elect John F. Kennedy that the United States cannot live with Fidel Castro. Kennedy takes office the next day.
- On 1 March, President Kennedy creates the Peace Corps. Between 1961 and 1969, more than 19,000 U.S. citizens serve in Latin America.
- In March, President Kennedy announces his Alliance for Progress economic aid program.

- On 17–19 April, Cuban exiles invade at the Bay of Pigs. Castro's forces easily rout the invaders.
- On May 30, Dominican dissidents assassinate Rafael Trujillo, dictator of the Dominican Republic. The dissidents had received weapons from the United States.
- In early June, President Kennedy meets with Soviet Premier Khrushchev in Vienna. Kennedy concludes that Khrushchev will support revolution in Latin America.
- The United States meets in August with Latin American nations at Punta del Este, Uruguay, to plan the Alliance for Progress.
- In October, President Kennedy hosts Prime Minister Cheddi Jagan of British Guiana in the White House. Kennedy decides that Jagan must not be allowed to be the leader of an independent Guyana.
- In November, President Kennedy authorizes Operation Mongoose, a covert plan to destabilize Cuba.
- The Kennedy administration employs diplomatic and military pressure to force the remaining members of the Trujillo family out of the Dominican Republic.

1962

- In late March, the Argentine military overthrows President Arturo Frondizi. Frondizi had angered the Kennedy administration by maintaining relations with Cuba.
- Attorney General Robert Kennedy receives a briefing in May on U.S. efforts to assassinate Castro.
- In August, the Kennedy administration begins to provide extensive aid to Latin American police forces through the Office of Public Safety (OPS).
- The Cuban Missile Crisis erupts in October.
- On 20 November, President Kennedy announces the end of the Cuban Missile Crisis but continues covert efforts to destabilize Cuba.
- In December, Attorney General Kennedy journeys to Brazil to inform President João Goulart of U.S. displeasure with his domestic and international policies.

1963

- In March, the Kennedy administration encourages a military seizure of power in Guatemala to prevent former President Juan José Arévalo from returning to office.
- In June President Kennedy, using the rubric of "Higher Authority," authorizes a sabotage campaign against Cuba.
- On 30 June, President Kennedy meets with Prime Minister Harold Macmillan in England and demands that the United Kingdom prevent Jagan from leading an independent Guyana.
- In September, President Juan Bosch of the Dominican Republic is overthrown by the military.

- In November, Venezuela announces it has discovered a cache of Cuban arms on the Venezuelan coast.
- On November 18, President Kennedy gives his last speech on inter-American affairs, pronounces the "Kennedy Doctrine," and says that Castro is a "barrier" to be removed.
- On 22 November, President Kennedy is assassinated. On the same day, the CIA continues the assassination plots against Castro, meeting with "AM/Lash" in Paris.
- In December, Venezuela conducts a successful presidential election, despite threats from Cuban-inspired insurgents.

1964

- In January, riots break out in Panama over U.S. policies in the Canal Zone. Negotiations will ensue to change the U.S. control over the Panama Canal and lead to the Canal Treaties of 1977–78.
- In March, Assistant Secretary of State Thomas Mann pronounces his "Mann Doctrine." The United States will work with military regimes to prevent communism.
- In April, the Brazilian military, with U.S. encouragement, overthrows President Goulart. Two decades of military dictatorship ensues.
- Eduardo Frei, the U.S.-supported candidate, defeats Salvador Allende in the September Chilean presidential election.
- Cheddi Jagan is denied power in December in a proportional representation election system in British Guiana. Forbes Burnham takes power and creates a dictatorship in independent Guyana that will last two decades.

1965

- In March, President Johnson begins his massive buildup of U.S. ground forces in Vietnam.
- In late April, the United States invades the Dominican Republic.
- On 2 May, President Johnson pronounces his "Johnson Doctrine," vowing to prevent communism in the hemisphere.
- In June, President Johnson shuts down covert war against Castro.

1966

- The Guatemalan military, with U.S. assistance, launches in March *Operación Limpieza*, a counterinsurgency campaign.
- In April, Senator J. William Fulbright, chair of the Senate Foreign Relations Committee, delivers his "Arrogance of Power" speech. Fulbright denounces President Johnson's invasion of the Dominican Republic and his Vietnam policy.
- Joaquín Balaguer, the U.S.-backed candidate, wins in June the presidential election in the Dominican Republic.

- In October, Che Guevara enters Bolivia with the goal of leading a revolutionary movement.

1967

- In October, Bolivian military forces, trained by the United States, capture and execute Che Guevara.

1968

- In September, the Conference of Latin American Bishops, meeting in Medellín, Colombia, issues a statement calling for the organization of the poor at the local level.
- The United States helps Forbes Burnham of Guyana rig the election, which is held in December.
- In December, Brazil's military rulers issue Decree 5, which outlaws dissent in the country.

1969

- President Richard Nixon takes office and makes Henry Kissinger his chief foreign-policy advisor.
- In May, Latin American delegates issue the Consensus of Viña del Mar. They call for fairer terms of trade for Latin America. The delegates tacitly concede that the Alliance for Progress has not transformed the region.
- In July, the Nixon administration adopts its policy paper for Latin America, NSSM 15. The United States should respond to Latin America's trade concerns.
- Governor Nelson Rockefeller submits in August his report to President Nixon. Rockefeller agrees that the United States should address trade issues. Rockefeller also suggests that the Latin American military will "modernize" the region.
- On 31 October, President Nixon delivers his only major address on inter-American affairs. He pledges a new attitude toward the region.

1970

- Salvador Allende wins a plurality of votes in the September presidential election in Chile.
- On 15 September, the Nixon administration initiates Project FUBELT to block Allende from becoming president.
- On 22 October, General René Schneider, a constitutionalist, is assassinated by Chilean military men.
- On 24 October, the Chilean legislature ratifies the results of the presidential election. Salvador Allende takes office in November.
- On 9 November, President Nixon adopts policy paper NSDM 93. The United States will pursue a policy of hostility toward Allende.

1971

- President Nixon hosts Emílio Garrastazú Médici, the military dictator of Brazil, in Washington in December. The leaders agree to cooperate in opposing Allende.

1972

- An earthquake devastates Managua in December. The Nicaraguan government of Anastasio Somoza Debayle embezzles international relief aid.

1973

- In January, the United States signs the Paris Accords, ending the U.S. war in Vietnam.
- In March, Allende's political coalition, *Unidad Popular*, increases its strength in legislative elections.
- In June, the military seizes effective power in Uruguay, ending the country's long history of constitutionalism.
- In August, Chilean truckers launch a strike. The CIA funds groups that support strikers. Political and economic chaos spreads throughout the country.
- On 11 September, the Chilean military, led by General Augusto Pinochet, overthrows Allende. President Allende commits suicide.
- On 13 September, the United States rushes aid to Pinochet and grants him diplomatic recognition on 24 September. Chile will have seventeen years of military rule under General Pinochet.
- After eighteen years of exile, Juan Perón returns to Argentina, wins a presidential election, and becomes president in October. His wife, Isabel Martínez Perón, is elected vice president.

1974

- In July, Argentine President Juan Perón dies in office and is succeeded by Isabel Perón.
- In August, President Nixon resigns, after being impeached for "high crimes and misdemeanors" by the House of Representatives. Gerald Ford becomes president.
- In September, Chilean General Carlos Prats and his wife, who are living in exile in Buenos Aires, are assassinated by Chilean intelligence agents.
- The U.S. Congress abolishes the Office of Public Safety in response to reports of human rights abuses carried out by U.S.-trained police officers in countries such as Uruguay.

1975

- In November, Chile organizes Operation Condor, a form of state-sponsored international terrorism. The military dictatorships of Southern Cone counties will cooperate to hunt down political leftists in exile.

- A congressional committee, the Church Committee, releases reports documenting the U.S. involvement in the assassination efforts against Fidel Castro, Rafael Trujillo, and General Schneider and the U.S. involvement in the overthrow of President Allende.

1976

- In March, Argentine generals overthrow President Isabel Perón, seize power, and launch their "dirty war" against political leftists.
- In June, Secretary of State Kissinger meets with General Pinochet in Santiago and assures him of U.S. support. Kissinger also delivers a speech defending human rights principles.
- In September, Orlando Letelier, the former Chilean ambassador to the United States, and Ronni Moffitt, a U.S. citizen, are assassinated in Washington, D.C., by Chilean agents.
- Secretary Kissinger meets in October with the Argentine foreign minister in Washington and assures him of U.S. support for Argentina's war against radicals.

1977

- President Jimmy Carter takes office. He emphasizes his commitment to human rights principles in a speech to the United Nations in March.
- The Mothers of the Plaza de Mayo begin to march, protesting the disappearance of their children in Argentina.
- In September, the United States and Panama sign treaties giving Panama control over the Panama Canal by the end of the century. The U.S. Senate ratifies the treaties the next year.

1978

- In January, Pedro Joaquín Chamorro, the editor of *La Prensa* and a critic of the Somoza dynasty in Nicaragua, is assassinated. The civil war in Nicaragua intensifies.

1979

- Anastasio Somoza Debayle, the dictator of Nicaragua, flees in July. The revolutionary organization, the Sandinistas, take power.
- In September, the Argentine military, responding to U.S. pressure, releases Jacobo Timerman, a publisher and human rights activist, from prison.
- In October, General Carlos Humberto Romero, the dictator of El Salvador, is overthrown by a military-civilian coalition that pledges to bring reform to the country.

1980

- In March, Óscar Romero, the archbishop of San Salvador and a human rights crusader, is assassinated while celebrating Mass.

- In December, four Roman Catholic nuns, who are U.S. citizens, are murdered by Salvadoran military forces.

1981

- President Ronald Reagan takes office in January.
- In February, the Reagan administration issues a White Paper, alleging Sandinista interference in El Salvador.
- In March, President Reagan approves military aid for El Salvador that will eventually amount to over $1 billion in the 1980s.
- In April, the Reagan administration suspends the Carter administration's economic aid program for Nicaragua.
- In November, President Reagan authorizes a program, NSDD 17, to overthrow the Sandinista government of Nicaragua.
- In November, Salvadoran security forces massacre more than eight hundred civilians in the village of El Mozote.

1982

- In April, the military rulers of Argentina launch an invasion of the Falkland Islands (Malvinas). The United Kingdom's defeat of Argentine forces and recapture of the Falklands in June hastens the end of the military dictatorship.
- In July, the Guatemalan military begins to execute Operation Sofía, an attack on Mayan communities.
- In December, Gabriel García Márquez, the Colombian novelist, gives his Nobel Prize speech lamenting the violence in Latin America.
- At a news briefing in December, President Reagan defends the Guatemalan leader, General Efraín Ríos Montt, who is overseeing the destruction of Mayan villages.
- In late December, Congress passes and President Reagan signs the first of the Boland Amendments, which restricts U.S. aid to Nicaraguan opponents of the Sandinistas.

1983

- In July, Latin American leaders, the Contadora Group, call for the end of foreign intervention in Central America.
- In October, the United States invades Grenada and overthrows the leftist regime.
- Democracy is restored in Argentina with inauguration in December of President Raúl Alfonsín.

1984

- In January, a U.S. commission headed by Henry Kissinger issues a report calling for both economic and military aid to Central America.

- In May, the U.S.-backed candidate, José Napoleón Duarte, wins the presidential election in El Salvador.
- The study *Nunca Mas* is published in Argentina. It exposes the atrocities committed by the Argentine military during the dirty war.

1985

- Democracy is restored in Brazil with the election in January of Tancredo Neves as president.
- At a February news conference, President Reagan admits that it is U.S. policy to overthrow the Sandinista government of Nicaragua.
- Democracy is restored in Uruguay with the inauguration in March of President Julio María Sanguinetti.

1986

- In June, the World Court finds the United States guilty of violating Nicaragua's sovereignty.
- In November, U.S. citizens learn of the Iran-contra scandal. The Reagan administration has been violating the Boland Amendments, illegally funding the Nicaraguan counterrevolutionaries or *contras*.
- The archbishop of São Paulo publishes *Nunca Mais*, documenting atrocities committed by the Brazilian military.

1987

- In August, Central American presidents sign a peace agreement.
- President Óscar Arias Sánchez of Costa Rica wins the Nobel Prize for Peace for his efforts to mediate the conflicts in Central America.

1988

- In a plebiscite held in October, Chileans vote to reject the continuation of General Pinochet in office.

1989

- In January, President George H. W. Bush takes office.
- In November, the Berlin Wall is toppled, signaling the end of the Cold War.
- In November, military forces in El Salvador murder six Jesuit priests on their university campus.
- In December, U.S. military forces invade Panama and arrest Manuel Noriega.

1990

- In Chile, democracy is restored in March, with General Pinochet relinquishing power and the election of Patricio Aylwin as president.

- The Sandinistas relinquish power in April in Nicaragua, with Violeta Chamorro becoming president.
- In May, Arthur M. Schlesinger publicly apologizes to Cheddi Jagan for U.S. hostility toward him during the Kennedy administration.

1991

- In February, the Rettig Report is released, documenting political murders in Chile during the Pinochet regime.
- The Soviet Union collapses in August, and the new leader, Boris Yeltsin, subsequently abolishes the Communist Party in Russia.
- In September, the Bush administration and the new government in Nicaragua settle the World Court judgment against the United States.

1992

- In January, the civil war in El Salvador ends, with the government and leftist groups signing a peace accord.
- In October, Cheddi Jagan is elected the head of state of Guyana. Former President Carter supervises the election.
- Rigoberta Menchú, a Guatemalan human rights activist and representative of indigenous communities, is awarded the Nobel Prize for Peace.

1993

- In January, President Bill Clinton takes office.
- Russia withdraws troops from Cuba. Soviet troops had been in Cuba since 1962.

1996

- In December, the civil war in Guatemala ends with the signing of a peace accord between the government and leftist groups.

1998

- In April Bishop Juan José Geradi of Guatemala is murdered two days after the release of his study, *Nunca Mas*, which documents human rights abuses by security forces.
- In October, General Pinochet is arrested in London. A judge in Spain has requested his extradition to stand trial for human rights abuses.

1999

- In February, an international commission releases a report, *Guatemala: Memory of Silence*, which documents human rights abuses in Guatemala from 1954 to 1996.
- President Clinton apologizes for the U.S. role in the Guatemalan civil war.
- President Clinton orders the declassification of records relating to the U.S. role in the overthrow of Salvador Allende and subsequent support for General Pinochet.

2000

- In March 2000, General Pinochet is released on medical grounds by the United Kingdom and returns to Chile.
- In December, the Clinton administration closes the School of the Americas. It had trained Latin American military officers for five decades. It reopens the next year as the Western Hemisphere Institute for Security Cooperation.

2001

- In January, President George W. Bush takes office.

2002

- In April, Venezuelan President Hugo Chávez survives an attempt to overthrow him. The George W. Bush administration approved of the attempt.

2003

- Secretary of State Colin Powell apologizes for the U.S. role in the overthrow of Allende in Chile.

2004

- In November, in Chile the first part of the Valech Report is released, detailing human rights abuses by security forces during the Pinochet regime. A second part of the report is released in 2005.

2006

- In March, Patricia Derian, who served as assistant secretary of state for human rights during the Carter administration, receives an award from Argentina for her defense of human rights during Argentina's military rule.
- In July, an ailing Fidel Castro transfers his duties as president and head of he Communist Party to his brother Raúl Castro.
- In December, General Pinochet dies in Chile, having never stood trial.

2008

- In June, Manuel Contreras, the head of Operation Condor, receives two life sentences from a Chilean court for the assassination of General Prats and his wife.
- In September, Michelle Bachelet of Chile presents an award to Senator Edward M. Kennedy for his defense of human rights during the Pinochet years.
- In October, an Argentine court resentences General Jorge Videla to military prison for human rights abuses. General Videla had previously been convicted in 1985.

2009

- In October, an Uruguayan court sentences the nation's last dictator, General Gregorio Alvarez, to twenty-five years in prison.

- In December, a Chilean judge rules that former President Eduardo Frei had been poisoned in the early 1980s by agents of the Pinochet regime.

2010

- In April, Reynaldo Bignone, the last leader of Argentina's dictatorship, receives a twenty-five-year sentence for human rights abuses from an Argentine court.

INTRODUCTION

The Cold War is over. The momentous battle between the United States and the Soviet Union for the hearts, minds, even "the soul of mankind" that dominated international life from 1945 to 1991 ended suddenly, with little warning. During the period between 1989 and 1991, the world witnessed some of the most breath-taking developments in human history—the breaching of the Berlin Wall, the collapse of the Soviet Empire first in Eastern Europe and then in the Baltic Republics, the overthrow of the Communist system itself in Russia, and finally the breakup of the Soviet Union. The end of Soviet tyranny meant that millions of Europeans, from Estonians to Hungarians to Ukrainians, had the chance to fulfill their national aspirations and enjoy their freedom. History seemed to work out in the way that diplomat and Soviet expert George F. Kennan predicted in his 1946 "Long Telegram" and in his "The Sources of Soviet Conduct" article published in 1947. Kennan had called on the Harry S. Truman administration to develop measures to "contain" the Soviet Union. Kennan reasoned that if the United States remained steadfast that eventually the Soviet Union would falter and then implode. The architects of U.S. Cold War policies—President Truman, Secretaries of State George Marshall and Dean Acheson, and foreign-policy experts like Kennan and Paul Nitze—are celebrated as visionaries. Their handiwork—the Truman Doctrine (1947), the Marshall Plan (1948), the North Atlantic Treaty Organization (1949), and National Security Council Memorandum 68/2 (1950)—served as the framework for Cold War victory.[1] President Truman, spectacularly unpopular with the U.S. public during his time in office, is now ranked as one of the "greatest" presidents in U.S. history. Other presidents who are perceived as effectively waging Cold War, like John F. Kennedy and Ronald Reagan, also enjoy great historical prestige.

My teaching and scholarly experiences have led me to accept, in part, this congratulatory view of U.S. Cold War policies. Over the past two decades, I have had the honor and privilege of teaching or lecturing in fourteen countries in Europe and the Western Hemisphere, under the auspices of programs like the Council for the

International Exchange of Scholars (Fulbright Program). This has included living for two years in Europe, first teaching at University College, Dublin in Ireland and then at the University of Helsinki and the University of Turku in Finland. Finnish universities offer courses taught in the English language and attract students from all over the world. Students from twenty countries enrolled in my course on the history of U.S. foreign relations. Such wonderful opportunities are voyages of personal discovery and enlightenment. When I teach abroad, I know that I always learn more from colleagues and students than I can offer them.

My academic journeys have led to encounters with the residues of Soviet tyranny. I have toured the chilling Museum of Occupation of Latvia (1940–91) in Riga and seen the grim interrogation rooms of the Soviet secret police, the KGB, in Tartu, Estonia. In Berlin, near the Brandenburg Gate, one can view the photographs of East Berliners who were shot and killed in their desperate attempts to surmount the Berlin Wall. At a Fulbright conference in Sofia, I heard professors describe the dishonesties that characterized academic life in Bulgarian universities under the Soviet Communist system. Finland, which had been invaded by the Soviet Union in 1939–40 and remained quietly neutral during the Cold War, has oriented its society and culture toward the West and has created one of the most serene societies on the face of the earth. While teaching in Europe, I also noted that students from Eastern European counties unfailingly brought me gifts at the end of the semester. The gifts seemed to symbolize their appreciation for the resolute U.S. support for their respective countries' freedom.

Perhaps my most profound encounter, however, was with Dr. Miloš Calda, a political scientist and the engaging Chair of the Department of American Studies at Charles University (1348) in Prague in the Czech Republic. A Czech student, whom I had taught at the University of Helsinki, had facilitated my coming to lecture at Charles University. The Communist authorities banned Dr. Calda from university teaching for fifteen years. He had to scrap together a living by teaching language courses. Dr. Calda's crime was that he was "a non-party member with no perspective." The forthright scholar apparently found it difficult to wax eloquently about the 1968 Soviet invasion of the jewel of a city that is Prague. Dr. Calda's suffering (and ultimate triumph) provided living testimony to the themes presented in the Academy-Award-winning film *The Lives of Others* (*Das Leben der Anderen*) (2006), which explored the nefarious activities of the East German secret police, the *Stasi*.

History and life do not, however, readily lend themselves to facile generalizations. As a scholar who focuses on the history of U.S. relations with Latin America, I have traveled to many Latin American countries and have had extended teaching assignments in Argentina, Brazil, and Ecuador. The Latin American students whom I have taught do not share the enthusiasm for U.S. Cold War policies expressed by my Czech, Lithuanian, and Polish students. Memories of the Cold War in Latin America are bitter, without much sense of appreciation for the U.S. triumph over the Soviet Union. In Buenos Aires, every Thursday afternoon, the mothers and grandmothers (*las madres y las abuelas*) silently march in the central plaza, the Plaza de Mayo. They have been marching for more than three decades. It is a moving experience to watch their procession. The women wear photographs stitched to their clothing of the children and grandchildren who vanished at the hands of the Argentine military. A dramatic account of the mothers' agony can be viewed in the great film *Official Story* (*La Historia Official*) (1985). In the southern cone countries of Argentina, Brazil, Chile, and Uruguay, tens of thousands of people disappeared in the 1960s and 1970s, earning the sobriquet *los desaparecidos*, "the disappeared ones." In Argentina alone, perhaps thirty thousand disappeared in *la guerra sucia* ("the dirty war"). My Argentine students have told me about their parents fleeing for their lives during that awful time. One student's parents encountered a human torso that washed ashore on the Argentine coast. A retired Argentine naval officer calculated that armed forces dropped as many as two thousand people from aircraft into the Atlantic Ocean on weekly flights over a two-year period. The officer, Adolfo Scilingo, admitted to shoving thirty prisoners who were still alive out of aircraft. In Chile, President Michelle Bachelet (2006–10) surely thinks of her father who died of cardiac arrest in 1974 after being tortured by military thugs under the command of General Augusto Pinochet (1973–90). As a young woman, President Bachelet was also abused by Chilean military men. The suffering endured by the Bachelet family was not unique in Chile. In the aftermath of the Pinochet regime, thirty-five thousand Chileans submitted testimonies of their torture to Chilean

The Mothers of Plaza de Mayo (*Asociación Madres de Plaza de Mayo*), wearing their characteristic white head scarves, march on a Thursday afternoon in Buenos Aires. The Mothers want to know the fate of their children, who were abducted by Argentine security forces during the "dirty war" (*la guerra sucia*). The Mothers also demand that the kidnappers face justice. These weekly demonstrations began in 1977 and have continued into the twenty-first century. (Stephen G. Rabe)

fact-finding commissions. The United States aided and abetted these ferocious anti-Communist military regimes.

Horror and savagery also characterized the Cold War in Central America. The covert U.S. intervention in Guatemala in 1954 against a suspected Communist government sparked a four-decade-long cycle of violence that led to the death of two hundred thousand Guatemalans. Right-wing death squads and the Guatemalan military executed over 90 percent of these murders. The military massacred indigenous communities of Mayan people. During the last decade and a half of the Cold War, civil war between the political right and left raged in the tiny countries of El Salvador and Nicaragua. When the violence wound down at the end of the Cold War, the body count was seventy-five thousand in El Salvador and perhaps seventy thousand in Nicaragua. The economies of both countries were in shambles, and vast numbers of people had fled their homelands. By 2000, more than eight hundred thousand native-born Salvadorans resided in the United States. The death toll in Nicaragua relative to population was more than the casualties the United States suffered in the Civil War of the 1860s and in its international wars of the twentieth century combined. As in Guatemala, anti-Communist forces did most of the killing in El Salvador and Nicaragua.

The story of Suzanne Marie Berghaus captured the depravity of the Cold War in Latin America. In April 2007, Berghaus, twenty-six, returned home to the tiny village of Cacaopera in the hills of El Salvador near the border with Honduras. Through the efforts of *Asociación Pro-Bósqueda*, a Salvadoran group founded by families seeking their lost children, Berghaus had a bittersweet reunion with the Sáenz family, including her aged birth parents and some of her siblings. She could embrace but not converse with them, because Berghaus did not speak Spanish. In 1982, Salvadoran soldiers had stolen the bright-eyed fourteen-month old with the happy smile, then known as María, and passed her on to an orphanage. The Salvadoran military stole children in order to terrorize the peasant population to insure that they did not support leftist guerrillas. The military also made money by stealing babies. A couple in Massachusetts adopted and raised little María. The Berghaus family was unaware that their Suzanne had been kidnapped in El Salvador in the name of anticommunism. Suzanne Berghaus graduated from college and earned a master's degree in social work from Salem State College.[2]

Stealing babies was a pastime of anti-Communist forces in Latin America. The Argentine military imprisoned pregnant women suspected of leftist tendencies and allowed them to give birth in prison hospitals. Thereafter, the military slaughtered the mothers, dropped their bodies from aircraft into the South Atlantic, and gave the babies to families who supported their "dirty war" tactics. The women who march in the Plaza de Mayo estimate that this happened to five hundred of their daughters and grandchildren. By the early twenty-first century, *las abuelas* had been able to locate less than one hundred of their missing grandchildren. Little wonder that humane U.S. political leaders have reacted with dismay to this Cold War history. President Bill Clinton publicly apologized for the

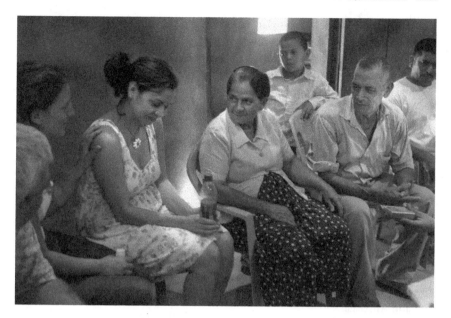

Suzanne Marie Berghaus of Massachusetts meets with her birth parents in April 2007 in Cacaopera, El Salvador. This was Berghaus's first meeting with her parents since she was kidnapped at age fourteen months by Salvadoran security forces. The woman with her hand on Ms. Berghaus's shoulder translates for her. (Redux Pictures/Monica Almeida/New York Times)

U.S. intervention in Guatemala in 1954 and its subsequent support for right-wing death squads. Secretary of State Colin Powell expressed regret for the U.S. intervention in Chile during the Salvador Allende years (1970–73).

Historians of the U.S. role in Latin America during the Cold War largely share the sentiments expressed by President Clinton and Secretary Powell. They take a critical stance toward inter-American relations. They criticize the United States for its repeated covert and overt interventions in Latin America. During the period from 1945 to 1989, the United States destabilized governments in Argentina, Brazil, British Guiana (Guyana), Bolivia, Chile, the Dominican Republic, Ecuador, El Salvador, Guatemala, and Nicaragua. These interventions helped perpetuate and spread violence, poverty, and despair within the region. El Salvador, Nicaragua, and Guatemala are wrecked societies. The southern cone countries, Argentina, Brazil, Chile, and Uruguay, have made economic progress in the post-Cold War period. Nonetheless, decent Latin Americans are scarred by the horrific memories of the past and must come to terms with those who perpetrated the monstrous crimes and still live among them. Guyana has not been be able to move past the racial hatred and tensions between Guyanese of African and Indian descent that the U.S. intervention in the 1960s inflamed and exacerbated.

In the views of inter-Americanists, U.S. Cold War leaders committed several grave errors. These leaders failed to distinguish between the Soviet Union and indigenous forms of political and economic nationalism in Latin America. Throughout most of the Cold War, the Soviet Union judged the Western Hemisphere to be the traditional U.S. sphere of influence and, other than in Fidel Castro's Cuba, wielded little influence in the region. The Cold War was a global war, expanding from Central Europe to the "Third World" of Asia, Africa, Latin America, and the Middle East. The Soviet Union created more than its share of havoc, approving the North Korean invasion of South Korea in 1950, invading Afghanistan in 1979, and arming insurgent groups like the Congolese in the early 1960s and the Angolans in the 1970s. The Soviet Union also invested heavily in Cuba for thirty years and supplied significant military and economic assistance to the Sandinista government of Nicaragua in the 1970s. And the Cuban Revolution proved a powerful attraction to many Latin Americans. But the Soviet Union did not direct events in Guatemala in the early 1950s, nor in Brazil, Guyana, and the Dominican Republic in the 1960s, nor Chile in the early 1970s. The brilliant scholar Piero Gleijeses, who has conducted archival research in Cuba, has further demonstrated that Castro's Cuba focused on making revolution in Africa rather than Latin America, because Cuban leaders feared directly confronting U.S. power.[3] Compared to their activities in Asia, Africa, and the Middle East, Communist nations played minor roles in Latin America.

Throughout the Cold War, U.S. officials presumed that the Soviet Union promoted subversion in the region and were often surprised when they could not find evidence to sustain their fears. Secretary of State John Foster Dulles expressed disappointment that his agents could not find, after the overthrow of the Guatemalan government in 1954, evidence of a direct link between Moscow and Guatemala City. The Central Intelligence Agency (CIA) planted arms with markings from Communist nations on the coasts of Nicaragua in 1954 and Venezuela in 1963. Attorney General Robert F. Kennedy, President Kennedy's brother, once recommended that the United States bomb its military base at Guantánamo Bay and use the bombing as pretext to invade Cuba. President Lyndon Johnson released lists of Communists in the Dominican Republic in 1965 that included people who had been long dead. The Reagan administration issued various "White Papers" on an international Communist conspiracy in Central America that generated international ridicule because the documents were replete with factual errors.

Despite lacking hard evidence of international ties between domestic radicals and the Soviet Union, the United States relentlessly opposed leftist political leaders in Latin America. Both Democrats and Republicans feared the domestic political repercussions of "losing" a Latin American nation to communism. After 1959, the apparition of "another Cuba" haunted U.S. officials. Being charged as "soft on communism" proved lethal within the context of U.S. domestic politics. Such political weapons wounded both the Truman and Jimmy Carter administrations. U.S. presidential administrations, from Truman to George H. W. Bush, further believed that they had to keep the region secure and stable so that they could wage Cold War elsewhere. Latin America was in the "backyard" of the United States, and U.S. leaders were determined to keep its Western Hemisphere home tidy and orderly. Secretary of State Dean Rusk explained to an Argentine official that the

U.S. credibility to defend West Berlin would be undermined if Latin American nations did not support the aggressive U.S. policies toward Communist Cuba. President Johnson thought his Vietnam policy would be questioned if he did not display his resolution by invading the Dominican Republic in 1965.

Scholars assess this "backyard" mentality as a reflection of a patronizing, condescending attitude that has traditionally informed U.S. attitudes toward Latin America. President Theodore Roosevelt labeled Colombians as "crazy Dagos," and President Woodrow Wilson famously vowed to "teach South American republics to elect good men." During the Cold War, the United States sponsored right-wing military dictatorships, reasoning that such regimes could best prevent communism. According to aides, Secretary Dulles would have been happy to see "flourishing little democracies" in Latin America but thought it "not in the nature of things." Latin American democrats might allow "instability and social upheaval, which would lead to Communist penetration."[4] When such regimes engaged in grotesque violations of human rights, U.S. officials excused them, suggesting that violence and inhumanity characterized Latin American life, history, and culture. In 1968, Viron P. Vaky, who served as deputy chief of mission in Guatemala City, reported to Washington that his colleagues, including Ambassador John Gordon Mein, argued that "murder, torture and mutilation are all right if our side is doing it and the victims are Communists." Indeed, Ambassador Mein had suggested to Guatemalan security forces that when they carried out summary executions they bury the bodies. The ambassador advised that leaving bodies to be found created a bad impression with the international press.[5] A 1986 State Department study on state terror in Guatemala dismissed it by observing that "Guatemala is a violent society." U.S. officials often implicitly judged Latin Americans as marked at birth for lives of wickedness and degeneracy. As historian Greg Grandin has aptly noted, U.S. officials judged Latin Americans as "the children of Cain."[6]

Caveats must be attached to a thesis that lists the people of Latin America as casualties of U.S. Cold War policies. Deep socioeconomic inequities characterized Latin American societies. Latin American elites who held power, wealth, land, and prestige fought tenaciously to hold on to their privileges. They marked their opponents as "Communists" and eagerly accepted U.S. support in the form of weapons and military and police training. Latin American security forces, who usually resisted thoroughgoing social reform, carried out the killings, terrorized peasants, and stole the babies. Cold War fears became entwined with Latin American struggles over issues surrounding race, gender, and sexual orientation. Traditionalists labeled as "communistic" the women's movement that became a global phenomenon beginning in the 1960s. The Brazilian military dictators dispatched troops to attack urban female students who called for sexual liberation. Elite and middle-class Chilean women demanded the overthrow of Salvador Allende, because they were terrified that a socialist Chile would undermine the mother's role in the traditional family. The racist Forbes Burnham, the leader of Afro-Guyanese, encouraged the covert U.S. intervention in British Guiana as a way of depriving the majority Indo-Guyanese led by Cheddi Jagan from holding power. Historians of Latin America appropriately insist that the Cold War had local, national, and international dimensions in the region.[7]

Right-wing forces also did not carry out all atrocities and gross violations of human rights. Inspired by the Cuban Revolution or some other dubious vision of a Marxist-Leninist heaven, left-wing groups launched armed insurgencies throughout the region. In Venezuela, the "Movement of the Revolutionary Left" threatened to shoot any Venezuelan citizen who participated in the December 1963 democratic elections. In the 1970s, urban guerillas created havoc in the streets of Montevideo with shootings and bombings. Argentine military officers claimed that subversives killed 495 uniformed personnel, military and police, between 1960 and 1989. In the 1980s, the Sandinistas of Nicaragua persecuted the indigenous population of Moskito Indians. Leftists also targeted U.S. officials in the region. An insurgent group assassinated Ambassador Mein in Guatemala City in August 1968, and political leftists kidnapped U.S. Ambassador Charles Burke Elbrick in Rio de Janeiro in 1969.

Appalling incidents committed by political leftists might suggest that an immoral equivalency existed between the extreme right and left in Latin America or that fanatics engaged in a bizarre dialectic, with leftist insurgency making necessary rightist atrocities. By such reasoning, the conduct of something like *la guerra sucia* by Argentina's military dictators becomes the logical, albeit exaggerated, response to leftist threats. The Reagan administration gave voice to this way of thinking when it ascribed political violence in Guatemala to a "cycle of provocation from the left and overreaction from the right."[8] Such questionable reasoning, also known as the "theory of the two demons," ignores historical chronology and trivializes the methodical abuse of human rights and the campaign of state terror perpetrated by anti-Communists in Latin America. The Guatemalan right, for example, had systematically stamped out non-violent civil and political dissent for decades, eliminating the possibility of moderate opposition and making radicalism a near certainty. Leftist political violence in Brazil followed the overthrow of a constitutional government by the Brazilian armed forces and the suppression of peaceful politics. In Chile, political leftists were participating in a constitutional democracy when the Allende government was overthrown. In Guatemala, Brazil, and Chile, the United States encouraged the military to strike against constitutional systems. The theory of two demons also ignores the reality that the Latin American military and their friends in paramilitary groups and death squads unleashed their violence against society, not just rural guerrillas or urban terrorists. Democracy was perceived as incompatible with national security because open political systems gave voice to subversive political elements. The political right labeled suspect political activities as "Communist" and attacked leftist thought whether by priests, nuns, trade unionists, students, or peasants. In an incident known as "The Night of the Pencils," Argentine security forces abducted seven high school students in La Plata and murdered six of them, because the students had the temerity to protest the elimination of subsidies for student fares on the city's buses. Argentine security forces also murdered a paraplegic, José Liborio Poblete, because he wrote a petition calling on companies to hire a fixed percentage of disabled workers. Poblete, who had lost both legs in a car accident, was taunted with the nickname *cortito* or "shorty" by his torturers.[9] Whatever the merits of a thesis that finds historical justification for torture, the killing of mothers and the kidnapping of their infants, the slaughter of high-school student petitioners, and the humiliation of the disabled, a fundamental verity cannot be dismissed. Fact-finding and "Truth Commissions" set up in the various countries after the Cold War established that leaders and security forces supported by the United States carried out 90 percent or more of the killings in every Latin American country.

Historians must also be conscious of the limits of U.S. power. Relative to Latin America, the United States exercised enormous diplomatic, economic, and military power. Per capita income in any Latin American country was one-eighth to one-tenth that of the United States. Latin American militaries deployed obsolete U.S. equipment. As a political scientist would have it, "asymmetries of power" existed between the United States and its southern neighbors. Nonetheless, the United States did not always have its way in the region. During the 1960s, the United States repeatedly failed to overthrow the corrupt dictator of Haiti, François "Papa Doc" Duvalier (1957–71). The wily Duvalier criticized U.S. foreign policies and stole U.S. humanitarian aid intended for the nation's desperate poor. Jimmy Carter, the one president troubled by the ghastly nature of Latin America's Cold War, found that his human rights policy moderated but did not end violence in South America. The United States also fell short of overthrowing Fidel Castro. The Bay of Pigs invasion of 1961 turned into a disaster, and the various CIA plots to assassinate the Cuban leader failed. The United States had to content itself with the policy of strangling the Cuban economy with an economic embargo that has lasted nearly fifty years.

Coordinate to the "limits to power" thesis is the defensible case that Latin American leaders knew how to manipulate the United States. Decent democrats like Rómulo Betancourt (1959–64) of Venezuela and José "Pepe" Figueres, who served three times as president of Costa Rica, solicited additional economic aid from the United States by exaggerating international threats to their countries. Eduardo Frei Montalva (1964–70) of Chile received several million dollars of covert U.S. financial assistance to conduct his presidential campaign against Salvador Allende in 1964. In a conversation with U.S. diplomats in May 1964, Frei expressed "unusual optimism" concerning his electoral prospects, although he "jokingly observed that his selfish interests should lead him [to] paint a bleaker picture to the US authorities for obvious reasons."[10] When he visited the White House in 1966, Forbes Burnham lauded President Johnson for his support of civil rights and his effort in Vietnam. The Johnson administration aided Burnham in rigging the 1968 election in Guyana.

The United States was not omnipotent, and Latin American leaders were not mere puppets of the United States. But historians can go too far in denying the realities of the global distribution of power or the active U.S. role in fomenting chaos in the region during the Cold War. Rafael Trujillo (1930–61), the vicious dictator of the Dominican Republic, skillfully manipulated U.S. officials and public opinion. During World War II he proclaimed his anti-fascist sympathies, and after 1945 he pronounced himself the world's most dedicated anti-Communist. Trujillo also advertised the glories of his regime in U.S. newspapers and bribed U.S. legislators. But when the Dwight D. Eisenhower and Kennedy administrations decided that Trujillo had created the pre-conditions for Communist revolution in the Dominican Republic, they informed him he must leave his nation. The administrations answered Trujillo's rejection of the demand to abdicate the throne by passing arms to Dominicans who riddled the old dictator with twenty-seven bullets in May 1961. In the aftermath of the Cuban Missile Crisis, the Soviet Union secured for Cuba a pledge that the United States would not invade the island. The pledge did not stop President Kennedy from approving sabotage and terrorism projects against Cuba. Assassination plots also continued. U.S. officials probably did not know about the kidnapping of the little María who became Suzanne Marie Berghaus. Reagan administration officials covered up, however, the massacre of nine hundred residents in the village of El Mozote in El Salvador by the U.S.-trained Atlacatl battalion in late 1981. The soldiers raped females before machine-gunning them and tossed babies in the air and caught them on bayonets.[11] President Reagan deflected international criticism of the blood-thirsty Efraín Ríos Montt (1982–83), the Guatemalan military dictator who may have overseen more political murders in a shorter time than any tyrant in Latin American history. After meeting with the general at a conference in Honduras in December 1982, Reagan vouched that "President Ríos Montt is a man of great personal integrity and commitment" who wanted to promote "social justice" in his country. Reagan added that the Guatemalan dictator was getting "a bad deal" from international critics.[12]

What follows is a concise, interpretative history of the U.S. drive to win the Cold War in Latin America. It focuses on the U.S. effort to eradicate the real and perceived threats of communism in the region. Beyond highlighting the critical crises and events of the period between 1945 and 1991, the study analyzes the discussions and debates among U.S. officials as they waged Cold War in the region. What motivated U.S. officials to act? How did they assess Latin America in the context of the Soviet-American confrontation? What did officials fear? How did they justify their decisions? What did they willfully choose to ignore? Beyond evaluating decision-making, the study asks a bigger question about the conduct of Cold War in Latin America. How did U.S. actions in the region contribute to the defeat of the Soviet Union? Had the United States chosen not to destabilize popularly elected governments in Guatemala, British Guiana, Brazil, or Chile, would the global balance of power have been fundamentally altered? Did the collapse of the Soviet Union hinge on keeping leftist politicians out of power in Latin America? Latin Americans suffered widespread death and devastation during the Cold War. Did the Cold War triumph that freed Czechs, Latvians, and Poles depend on Latin Americans paying such a costly price?

The study does not pretend to be a comprehensive examination of U.S. relations with Latin America in the postwar period. Significant issues of trade, immigration, narcotics trafficking, environmental degradation, popular culture, and globalization are not addressed in detail. The outstanding historian Alan McPherson has recently labeled the Cold War as a "temporary event" in the history of inter-American relations. In Professor McPherson's view, "unequal interdependence" characterizes inter-American relations in the postwar period. The Cold War had been "hiding many integrative trends in the post-World War II era."[13] Latin Americans shop at Wal-Mart, and U.S. citizens have developed an enduring fondness for "Tex-Mex" food. U.S. residents now buy more jars of zesty salsa at supermarkets than bottles of tangy ketchup, the condiment associated with the traditional favorite, the hamburger. In 2008, Latinos comprised about 15 percent of the U.S. population and flexed their voting power in the presidential election. U.S. residents also sent money back to their relatives in Latin America. Remittances from the United States represented the largest source of income, excepting oil revenues, for Mexico. In small countries such as El Salvador, Haiti, and Honduras remittances accounted for 18 to 30 percent of the national income. McPherson may be right in emphasizing harmony, consensus, and interdependence over conflict. But the Cold War ravaged Latin America. The legacies of the Cold War are woven into the fabric of contemporary Latin American life.

This analysis draws on many fine monographs on the U.S. role in Latin America during the Cold War. Michael Grow, for example, has recently written a solid study on "regime change" in Latin America, investigating presidential decisions to overthrow Latin American governments during the Cold War. Grow thinks that historians have operated within an inadequate analytic framework, debating whether national security concerns or economic interests motivated U.S. presidents to authorize interventions. He argues that the respective presidents did not act to protect the homeland from attack or to safeguard the interests of capitalists. Offering a "fresh interpretation," the author argues that presidents ordered the CIA or the U.S. Marine Corps into action to enhance their domestic and international credibility as tough, decisive leaders. Presidents fought in "symbolic battlefields" and engaged in "exercises in imagery." In presenting his intriguing thesis that the Cold War in Latin America had little to do with the Soviet Union or the global balance of power, Grow makes the jarring statement that he acknowledges but declines to evaluate the horrific results of regime change.[14] Historical inquiry mandates that both the causes and consequences of decisions be analyzed. Latin America was not just a symbolic arena for the Cold War. The fate of Latin Americans merits study.

Keeping in mind that the Cold War in Latin America had local and national dimensions and that Latin Americans also tried to entangle the United States in their political and cultural struggles, this study of the United States, Latin America, and the Cold War proceeds chronologically. Chapter 1 provides historical background by outlining relations between 1895 and 1945. The United States established a sphere of influence in the region and repeatedly intervened in the internal affairs of Latin American counties. An important question is whether the approach the United States took toward Latin America in the Cold War differed substantially from the policies of the previous fifty years. Chapter 2, which covers from 1945 to 1952, concentrates on the ideas of George Kennan. Kennan, who made a controversial tour of Latin America in 1950, concluded that in the context of the Soviet–American confrontation the United States could not respect the sovereignty of Latin American nations or abide popularly elected leaders who did not outlaw domestic political radicals. Kennan's conclusions became U.S. policy, as evidenced in Chapter 3 on the 1950s. Covert intervention became the preferred U.S. method of destabilizing suspect regimes. The CIA intervention in Guatemala in 1954 represented a defining moment both for U.S. policy and for the political milieu within Latin America.

The Cuban Revolution reverberated throughout the Western Hemisphere. Fidel Castro's radical turn terrified U.S. policymakers and revealed new possibilities for systematic change for Latin Americans. Chapter 4 analyzes the relentless U.S. war against Fidel Castro's Cuba, especially during the period from 1959 to 1969. Chapter 5 focuses on the efforts of the Democrats, John Kennedy and Lyndon Johnson, to prevent the spread of "Castro-communism" throughout the region. Through his Alliance for Progress economic program, Kennedy sought to immunize Latin Americans against the appeals of communism by transforming the traditional socioeconomic structure of the region within one decade. Kennedy also changed U.S. military aid to the region, emphasizing counterinsurgency and police training to combat rural and urban guerrillas. Vowing also not to permit "another Cuba," in the region, Kennedy authorized numerous covert interventions. President Johnson followed the "Kennedy Doctrine" with his "Johnson Doctrine," invading the Dominican Republic in 1965 to prevent a takeover of the government by presumed Communists. The invasion of the Dominican Republic was preceded by a consequential covert intervention—the destabilization of the Brazilian government in 1964. The Johnson administration finished the work started by the Kennedy government. The Brazilian military dictators became models for other authoritarians. By the mid-1970s, military men dominated political life in much of South America.

Chapter 6 recounts how the Richard Nixon administration tried to forestall the election of Salvador Allende in Chile and thereafter examines the administration's drive to destroy the Allende presidency. The chapter also analyzes U.S. programs to assist Latin American security forces to eliminate leftist groups in Argentina, Brazil, and Uruguay. The bloodbaths perpetrated by the South American military and their associates in paramilitary outfits and death squads appalled many U.S. citizens and helped contribute to the rise of a human rights movement and the election of Jimmy Carter as president.

The Ronald Reagan administration's support for mercenary wars in Central America represents the last Cold War crusade in Latin America. After briefly addressing the efficacy of President Carter's human rights efforts in Latin America in the late 1970s, Chapter 7 considers the Reagan administration's efforts to unseat the leftist Sandinista regime in Nicaragua by organizing and funding the so-called "contras." The chapter further examines the administration's decision to promote civil war in El Salvador. The final section looks at the aftermath of the Cold War. It assesses how Latin Americans have struggled to come to terms with their Cold War history. It also explores how the United States has interpreted its Cold War victory.

No one, least of all Latin Americans, misses the Cold War. Civilized, rational people do not lament the collapse of the Soviet Union and the relegation of Soviet-style communism to the dustbin of history. I am pleased that my colleague, Dr. Miloš Calda, has resumed his teaching at Charles University. U.S. sacrifice and steadfastness contributed to the undermining of the Soviet empire. But joy and relief over the liberation of Eastern Europeans cannot be used as an excuse for ignoring the devastating consequences of U.S. interventions in Latin America both for the region as a whole and for individuals like the elderly women who march in the Plaza de Mayo in Buenos Aires every Thursday afternoon and Suzanne Marie Berghaus of Massachusetts and her birth mother in El Salvador.

CHAPTER 1

Roots of Cold War Interventions

In his award-winning study, *The Global Cold War*, historian Odd Arne Westad asserts that "the Cold War was a continuation of colonialism through slightly different means."[1] Much as the European imperial powers had done for several hundred years, the United States and the Soviet Union sought control and domination over people in Asia, Africa, and Latin America. Prior to 1945, the United States had not colonized Latin American nations. But in the previous fifty years, the United States had created a sphere of influence within the Western Hemisphere. The United States tried to maintain peace and stability, exclude foreign influences, expand U.S. trade and investment, and shape Latin America's political, socioeconomic, and ideological development. The anti-Communist crusade that the United States pursued in Latin America during the Cold War was rooted in that tradition.

THE ROOSEVELT COROLLARY

The United States extended control and domination over the Caribbean region between 1895 and 1904. During that brief period, the U.S. officials achieved momentous diplomatic and military victories. In the Venezuelan Boundary Crisis of 1895, U.S. leaders forced the United Kingdom, the world's preeminent power, to accede to U.S. domination of the region. The United States thereafter defeated Spain in the War of 1898, established a protectorate over Cuba, secured a naval base at Guantánamo Bay, and annexed Puerto Rico. With its military position enhanced in the Caribbean basin, the United States bolstered the province of Panama's fight in 1903 to win independence from Colombia. The United States easily secured a treaty to give the United States the exclusive right to build an interoceanic canal through the new nation of Panama. President Theodore Roosevelt (1901–09) locked up these conquests by announcing in late 1904 that the United States would exercise "international police power" in the region. The so-called Roosevelt Corollary to the Monroe Doctrine served to justify more than thirty armed interventions in the Caribbean during the following three decades.

The United States ostensibly believed in the principles of the Monroe Doctrine. In 1823, President James Monroe, with the assistance of his able Secretary of State, John Quincy Adams, issued his striking policy statement. The United States looked sympathetically on the struggle by its southern neighbors to secure their independence from colonial Spain and Portugal. The United States opposed either colonization by any European power or re-colonization by the Iberian nations. Subsequent presidential administrations would add that the United States further opposed the transfer of colonies between imperial powers. Monroe added to his pledge to defend Latin America his ringing affirmation of the distinct, harmonious nature of the "New World." The Americas were "eminently and conspicuously different" from old, imperial Europe. "Our southern brethren," if left to "their own accord," would never adopt the political systems of Europe. Independent Latin Americans would adopt U.S. models of governance, "under which we have enjoyed unexampled felicity."

Historians have long been fond of pointing out that rhetoric did not match reality when it came to the Monroe Doctrine. For a good part of the nineteenth century, the United States lacked the military muscle to confront the Europeans. Between 1823 and 1826, Latin American nations made five direct requests for U.S. assistance to help protect their independence. All were turned down. Washington did not protest when the United Kingdom seized in 1833 the Malvinas (Falkland Islands) of Argentina. Latin American nations largely maintained the independence they won during the period from 1808 to 1825, but not because of the Monroe Doctrine. The United Kingdom saw economic opportunity in free trade and investment in the region and used its navy to block the return of Spain and Portugal. Throughout the nineteenth century, the British exercised authority over the region's domestic and international policies. British diplomats attended constitutional conventions in Latin America. The British navy shut down the Brazilian slave trade with Africa in 1850. In the second half of the nineteenth century, British warships also shelled Latin American countries, such as Honduras, when they failed to pay international debts, and the British established a protectorate on the Caribbean or "Moskito" coast of Nicaragua.

The United States did not always adhere to the noble sentiments expressed in the great doctrine. U.S. officials and citizens judged Latin Americans to be backward, with "crazed and narrow minds." Latin Americans allegedly had inferior racial heritages, practiced the wrong (Roman Catholic) religion, and became indolent in their tropical homelands. Beyond being intolerant, nineteenth-century U.S. citizens apparently were "geographically challenged," for most Latin American nations fall within the temperate zone.[2] Despite these shortcomings, the land of Latin America seemed alluring to U.S. leaders. Thomas Jefferson prophesied the vast expansion of the United States into an "Empire of Liberty." It was U.S. destiny to take Canada, Mexico, and Central America "piece by piece." With his purchase of the Louisiana Territory in 1803, Jefferson hastened what he considered the inevitable historical process of U.S. expansionism. In terms of Cuba, the dominant island in the Caribbean, Secretary of State Adams wrote in 1823 that "it is scarcely possible to resist the conviction that the annexation of Cuba to our federal republic will be indispensable to the continuance and integrity of the Union itself." Cuba was like a ripe fruit, "an apple severed by the tempest from its native tree," that inevitably would fall into the lap of the United States.[3] The United States reached for its dreams in the pre-Civil War era. It bullied Spain into relinquishing Florida, annexed the independent republic of Texas, and defeated Mexico in the 1840s, securing California and the future states of Arizona and New Mexico. The vision of U.S. territorial expansion persisted into the late nineteenth century. In 1893, at the dazzling Colombian Exposition held in Chicago, seventy-four national leaders contributed essays on "America in 1993." These futurists predicted a "United States of the Americas," under the U.S. flag. The imagined nation would stretch from Alaska to Patagonia. Citizens of the Americas would travel on railroads that linked Chicago to Buenos Aires.[4]

The United States developed the power to work its will in the Western Hemisphere. The debate over slavery had hindered the nation's ability to conduct a vigorous foreign policy. Whereas the Civil War and Reconstruction failed to create a racially just society, the epic struggle over the place of African-Americans in U.S. life had the effect of strengthening the power of the federal government. Washington found itself in a stronger position to conduct international affairs than before the Civil War. The material demands of the war also gave a great boost to the industrial process. During the late nineteenth century, the United States surpassed the United Kingdom, France, and Germany and became the leading industrial power in the world. Immigration fueled population growth, with the country's population more than doubling between 1865 and 1900. Migration into the Great Plains, combined with the mechanization of farming, also spurred vast increases in agricultural output. Late nineteenth-century economic growth was uneven, with several sharp economic collapses. But by 1895, the United States was a wealthy, powerful nation, producing surpluses of agricultural and industrial products for export to global markets.

An obscure diplomatic incident, the Venezuelan Boundary Crisis, proved a watershed event in the history of U.S. relations with Latin America. Venezuela shared a boundary with the British colony of Guiana (Guyana) in South America. For more than fifty years, the British and Venezuelans had haggled over the proper boundary lines. In the 1870s and 1880s, Venezuela implored the United States to support its boundary claim. The United States made, however, only mild representations to the British. In 1895 the United States surprised the Venezuelans and the British by entering the dispute. In a stridently worded note, President Grover Cleveland (1893–97) and Secretary of State Richard Olney demanded that the United Kingdom state whether it would submit the disputed territory issue to arbitration. Citing the Monroe Doctrine as moral authority, Secretary Olney claimed the right to speak for Latin Americans. He boasted that "to-day the United States is practically sovereign on this continent, and its fiat is law upon the subjects to which it confines its interposition." The two powers heatedly debated the issue for several months. British officials appropriately pointed out that the Monroe

Doctrine, a unilateral declaration, had no standing in international law. But the British ultimately agreed to arbitration. They concluded that it was foolish to contest U.S. power over a few thousand square miles of land, and they had enough difficulties with the Boer War in South Africa.

Though supposedly aiding a neighbor, the United States ignored Venezuela's desires. Cleveland and Olney never consulted Venezuelan leaders about their July 20 protest, and they excluded Venezuela from the arbitral commission. The U.S. ambassador in London, Thomas F. Bayard, a former secretary of state, thought Latin America represented a "lower civilization." After vehement protests, including street rioting in Caracas, Venezuela gained the right to appoint one arbitrator, but not a Venezuelan. In any case, U.S. and British officials had agreed beforehand to exempt from arbitration those areas settled by British subjects for fifty years. These were the very areas that the Venezuelans had hoped to secure from arbitration.

The Cleveland administration used the boundary dispute to achieve economic and diplomatic goals. Beset by the economic depression of the mid-1890s and hopeful of marketing surplus products, the administration wanted to insure Venezuela's control of the mouth of the Orinoco River. The river drained deep into northern South America. U.S. investors had also recently shown interest in developing the Orinoco region. The Orinoco's mouth was the only key area that the United States won for Venezuela through the arbitral process. More important, by bringing the British to arbitration, the United States demonstrated its hegemony over the Caribbean basin. U.S. officials were uncertain where the European imperialists might encroach next. The British had seemed aggressive in their recent relations with Nicaragua. The Cleveland administration, flexing the new industrial muscle, wanted to serve notice that the United States now had the right and responsibility to settle regional disputes. As Olney put it in speaking of his country, "its infinite resources combined with its isolated position render it master of the situation and practically invulnerable as against any or all other powers." The United States had the power to enforce the Monroe Doctrine as never before.[5]

Significant consequences flowed from the U.S. diplomatic victory over the British and the Venezuelans. The United Kingdom agreed to the Hay-Pauncefote Treaty, which the U.S. Senate ratified in 1901. The British conceded that the United States had the exclusive right to build and fortify an inter-oceanic canal. The two countries had agreed in a previous treaty (1850) not to build a canal without the other's consent. The world took greater note, however, of the new U.S. diplomatic and military resolve in its confrontation with Spain. Cleveland and Olney had declared that the United States had the right to determine the course of history in the Western Hemisphere. The new William McKinley administration (1897–1901) made good on that claim by driving Spain out the last remnants of its colonial empire, Cuba and Puerto Rico, in the War of 1898.

Cubans, who called for a free Cuba or *Cuba Libre*, had risen in rebellion against Spanish colonial authority in 1895. It marked the second major uprising in the recent past. Between 1868 and 1878, Cubans had fought for their freedom. The

McKinley administration found a variety of reasons why the United States needed to declare war against Spain. The Spanish seemed incapable of maintaining law and order. Their "reconcentration" or "pacification" policy of forcing Cuban citizens out of their homes and villages into "secure" areas spread disease and destruction, with over two hundred thousand Cubans perishing. Official fact-finding teams and energetic journalists constantly reminded the U.S. public of Cuba's suffering. The violence imperiled the substantial U.S. trade and investment on the island. U.S. citizens had property worth $50 million in Cuba. Cuban exports to the United States fell from $79 million in 1892 to $15 million in 1898. The hullabaloo that followed the sinking of the U.S. warship *Maine* in Havana harbor in February 1898 intensified the crisis. The official inquiry into the ship's sinking asserted that a mine attached to the bottom of the ship's hull caused the explosion. The administration and the public assumed that Spain bore responsibility for the tragedy. Historians have also argued that President McKinley asked for a congressional authorization to intervene in Cuba, because he feared that Cubans would defeat the Spanish, without U.S. assistance.[6] The insurgents controlled two-thirds of the island by April 1898. These reasons for action supplemented the basic U.S. desire to shape the region's future.

With the assistance of Cubans, U.S. forces routed the Spanish on land and sea in 1898. U.S. troops occupied the island from 1898 to 1902. The Theodore Roosevelt administration (1901–09) withdrew U.S. forces, only after Cuban leaders accepted the Platt Amendment (1901–33) to their new constitution. Cuba became a protectorate of the United States, enjoying only quasi-independence. The Platt Amendment gave the United States the right to supervise Cuba's finances and internal development and to intervene militarily to enforce order and stability. As General Leonard Wood, who served as Governor-General of Cuba during the military occupation observed, "there is, of course, little or no independence left Cuba under the Platt Amendment."[7] The spoils of victory also included a naval base at Guantánamo Bay and the annexation of Puerto Rico. Through the War of 1898, the United States had won the strategic ability to dominate the Caribbean. A powerful U.S. Navy patrolled the area. In 1898, the United States had four battleships. From 1899 to 1906, sixteen new battleships were commissioned. With twenty battleships, the United States tied with Germany as the world's second leading naval power, after the United Kingdom.

U.S. power waxed with the acquisition of the right to build a canal in 1903–04 and the opening of the Panama Canal in 1914. When Colombia refused in 1903 to accept the terms that President Roosevelt offered to build a canal through Colombia's province of Panama, he intervened in a manner that foreshadowed subsequent U.S. interventions in the Cold War. His administration encouraged Panamanians to rise in rebellion against the central government in Bogotá. Panamanians had long wanted an independent country. A U.S. naval task force arrived off Panama's Atlantic Coast to hinder Colombia from landing troops to suppress the rebellion. The United States immediately granted diplomatic recognition to the new nation of Panama and then signed and ratified a favorable treaty. Beyond gaining the right to build, fortify, and operate a canal, the United States gained exclusive privileges in the Canal Zone, the ten-mile-wide, fifty-mile-long region that bisected Panama. Panama, like Cuba, became a protectorate of the United States. Six decades later, President Lyndon Johnson adopted, perhaps unknowingly, Theodore Roosevelt's intervention model. His delegates encouraged Brazilian generals to overthrow the constitutional government of President João Goulart (1961–64), and the president readied material and naval support for the generals. The Johnson administration recognized the new military dictatorship within hours after it seized power. The military dictators showed their appreciation for Johnson by backing his invasion of the Dominican Republic in 1965. In justifying his violation of Colombia's sovereignty and international law, Roosevelt claimed that he possessed "the mandate of civilization." During the Cold War, U.S. leaders would similarly claim that they acted with high intentions when they overthrew popularly elected governments.

President Roosevelt consolidated the stunning regional gains that the United States had made in less than a decade with the pronouncement in late 1904 of the "Roosevelt Corollary to the Monroe Doctrine." Perhaps like many U.S. citizens, Roosevelt had trouble admitting the new U.S. role in Latin America. The United States did not act "eminently and conspicuously different" from European imperial powers in the international arena. In 1901, he wrote to his German friend, Hermann Speck von Sternberg, that the United States still subscribed to the principles of the Monroe Doctrine and believed in an "open door" policy. The United States did not claim exclusive investment, trade, or treaty rights with South America. An outside nation might even engage in "transitory intervention" in the region to redress a grievance. In fact, Roosevelt initially approved a joint Anglo-German naval maneuver against Venezuela in 1902–03. The colorful Venezuelan president, Cipriano Castro (1899–1908), refused to pay the country's international debts, and he harassed foreign investors and diplomats. But subjected to sharp criticism from military advisors and U.S. citizens and beset by personal doubts, President Roosevelt reconsidered his position and informed the Europeans that he wanted a peaceful arbitration of the debt issue. Roosevelt accepted the logic inherent in the Olney memorandum of 1895, the Platt Amendment, and the Panama Canal Treaty of 1904. The United States claimed a sphere of influence in the Western Hemisphere. In his 6 December 1904 message to Congress, Roosevelt twisted the meaning of the Monroe Doctrine. According to Roosevelt, Monroe's and Adams's handiwork required the United States "to the exercise of international police" to redress "chronic wrongdoing" in the hemisphere. The United States would intervene in a country that misbehaved. U.S. intervention would forestall foreign intervention and protect Latin America. Roosevelt had extended the Platt Amendment to the entire region. Indeed, he claimed that, under the Platt Amendment, Cuba was now progressing toward a "stable and just civilization." As historian David F. Healy has noted, "what had been a declaration that European powers must keep their hands off the independent states of the Americas [the Monroe Doctrine] became the justification for unilateral United States intervention in the hemisphere at its own discretion. In the name of security, the nation now claimed regional hegemony."[8]

In the brief period from the Olney Memorandum to the Roosevelt Corollary, the United States had created a sphere of influence, defined by political scientists as "a determinate region, which limits the independence or freedom of action of political entities within it." Within its sphere of influence, a great power assumes exclusive responsibility for peace. Cubans, Dominicans, Panamanians, and other Latin American leaders had to keep uppermost in their minds potential U.S. reactions to critical international and domestic policies and decisions. Put another way, the United States had become the Western Hemisphere's imperial power. Definitions of imperialism can be tricky. The key to imperialism is power—the power to make others move as the imperial state dictates. As the British historian Tony Smith has noted, imperialism exists "when a weaker people cannot act with respect to what it regards as fundamental domestic or foreign concerns for fear of foreign reprisals." Imperialism can take several forms, both formal (annexation,

In this bravura photograph taken in 1906, President Theodore Roosevelt operates a steam shovel that is digging the Panama Canal. Roosevelt was the first sitting U.S. president to travel outside the United States. The photograph reveals the president's obvious pride in detaching Panama from Colombia and securing a canal treaty with Panama. With his "Roosevelt Corollary to the Monroe Doctrine," Roosevelt further established the U.S. domination of the Western Hemisphere that would last through the twentieth century. (Corbis Images)

colonialism, or military occupation) and informal (economic penetration, political subversion, or the threat of intervention).[9] During the period from 1895 to 1945, the United States brought to bear against Latin Americans both the "formal" and "informal" powers inherent in definitions of imperialism.

During the Cold War era, the United States held on to its sphere of influence and acted like an "imperial" power. If U.S. officials offered a historical justification for covert and overt interventions in Latin America, they mumbled something about the Monroe Doctrine and nothing about the Roosevelt Corollary. But as the great Walter LaFeber, the dean of historians of U.S. foreign relations, has observed, it was the "Roosevelt Doctrine, not Monroe's," that "justified U.S. unilateral intervention in the internal affairs of Latin American states."[10] The Guatemalans, the Cubans, the Guyanese, the Chileans, and others had engaged in "chronic wrongdoing" by pursuing leftist policies and flirting with the Soviet Union. The United States exercised "international police power" to protect them, the region, and, of course, the interests of the United States.

PATTERNS OF INTERVENTION

In the aftermath of the Roosevelt Corollary, the United States rapidly expanded its influence in Latin America. During the first third of the twentieth century, the United States carried out thirty armed expeditions in the Caribbean basin. U.S. military forces occupied Cuba, the Dominican Republic, Haiti, and Honduras. U.S. military forces were stationed in Nicaragua almost continuously from 1909 to 1933. The United States also supervised the financial affairs of these small nations, collecting their export/import taxes and then paying off their international debts. The security and stability that U.S. marines and bankers created in Central American and Caribbean nations gave confidence to U.S. entrepreneurs to set up shop in the region. U.S. enterprises, like the United Fruit Company of Boston, produced vast quantities of tropical foods such as bananas and sugar. Cuba became a U.S. playground, as U.S. citizens flocked to Cuban clubs, casinos, and beaches for fun, sun, and sin. U.S. investors also became a major presence in South America, rapidly expanding U.S. holdings in extractive industries like Chilean copper and Venezuelan oil. U.S. financial advisors proffered advice to South American governments on how to conform to the dictates of the international capitalist economy.

U.S. presidents—Republicans and Woodrow Wilson, the one Democrat—dispatched U.S. troops to Central American and Caribbean lands for many reasons. All gave high priority to protecting the Panama Canal. The canal opened in 1914, with more than one thousand ships passing through the intricate lock system during its first year of operation. The canal facilitated the deployment of the two-ocean navy that the United States had built in the industrial era and served as a vital strategic asset during World War I. The new nation of Panama nominally retained its independence and title to the Canal Zone. Panama had "titular sovereignty," although the United States exercised the "equivalent of sovereignty."

As William Howard Taft, the Secretary of War and future president and Supreme Court justice noted, the United States could agree that Panama had "titular sovereignty," because the term "had a poetic and sentimental appeal to the Latin mind." But U.S. officials created a replica of the United States in the Canal Zone, with U.S. schools, a U.S. judicial system, and the dollar as the legal currency. The flying of the U.S. flag over the Canal Zone made clear to Panamanians and the world who was in charge. With U.S. military forces in the Canal Zone, the United States supervised Panama's political and diplomatic affairs. U.S. investors and banks controlled economic affairs and tied Panama to the U.S. economy. By 1929, the United States provided Panama with 67 percent of its imports and bought 94 percent of its exports. Pan American Airways had a monopoly on international flights to Panama, and the United States operated Panama's railroad.[11]

Preserving such a valuable asset became a justification for regional intervention. As the canal was being built, Secretary of State Elihu Root observed in 1907 in a letter to his boss, President Roosevelt, that "the inevitable effect of our building the Canal must be to require us to police the surrounding premises."[12] Caribbean countries had importance, because they lay "in the front yard of the United States." Wilson administration officials justified the landing of U.S. marines in Haiti in 1915 as a way of excluding Germany from the region. U.S. financial supervisors quickly paid off Haiti's international debt, including German creditors, and the marines shipped German citizens and investors back to Germany. During the interventions, U.S. officials gave high priority to using local tax revenues to pay off foreign bondholders. They wanted Latin Americans to obtain credit from New York, not from London or Berlin. In 1917, the United States also purchased the Virgin Islands for $25 million from Denmark to insure that Germany did not obtain a base in the Caribbean. In 1927, Henry L. Stimson, the future secretary of state, summarized the consistency of U.S. policy on the Panama Canal. The Monroe Doctrine honored "the principle of national self-determination." But when it came to the canal, the United States had to bend its principles. As Stimson concluded, "the national safety of our country had, however, imposed upon us a peculiar interest in guarding from foreign influence the vital sea route through the Caribbean Sea and the Panama Canal, and therefore in seeing to it that no cause for foreign intervention may arise along the borders of that route."[13]

Beyond excluding extra-continental influences from the region, the U.S. exercise of international police power involved upholding its definition of law and order. Venezuela's irrepressible Cipriano Castro continued to harass foreigners and infuriate President Roosevelt. Castro also reneged on his promise to pay his international debts and expropriated U.S. property. He posed as a nationalist, defending Venezuela's honor and integrity. Foreigners, including U.S. investors, had indeed meddled in the country's domestic affairs. A furious President Roosevelt proposed to Secretary of State Root that U.S. marines land on Venezuelan shores and occupy a customs house. Roosevelt would "show those Dagos they will have to behave decently." Root shared the president's contempt for Castro, calling him a "crazy brute," but he counseled against war. On 13 June 1908, the United States broke relations with Venezuela.

Six months later, General Juan Vicente Gómez (1908–35) solved the Castro problem for Roosevelt. In late November, Castro left the country for Europe for medical treatment. On 19 December, Gómez, the vice president, usurped the presidency and quickly announced that he would resolve Venezuela's international obligations. The *North Carolina*, a U.S. battleship, soon thereafter called at the Venezuelan port of La Guiara and dispatched a State Department envoy to negotiate with Gómez. The United States restored relations with Venezuela in early March 1909. Gómez was free to consolidate a dictatorship that lasted twenty-seven years and turned out to be unusually venal and vicious.

The Roosevelt administration had conspired with General Gómez. Roosevelt alerted his team to be ready to act two days before Gómez seized power. The *North Carolina* had been readied for its mission. Gómez thought the battleship "a convenient presence." It was, as the journal of opinion, the *Nation*, jibed, "a nicely timed revolution." Roosevelt had learned from his Panama embarrassment of 1903 to wait until the revolution began before dispatching the navy. Thereafter, the U.S. navy blocked Castro's return to Venezuela, and U.S. intelligence agents kept Castro under surveillance, until he died in exile in 1924.[14]

President Woodrow Wilson (1913–21) had less success punishing General Francisco "Pancho" Villa of Mexico. In March 1916, Villa led a band of his followers across the border and attacked the town of Columbus, New Mexico, killing seventeen New Mexicans. Villa resented that the United States supplied arms to his opponent in the Mexican Revolution, Venustiano Carranza. Villa apparently hoped to emerge victorious from the international chaos. Germany also saw diplomatic advantages to be gained in a clash between the United States and Mexico. President Wilson ordered General John J. "Blackjack" Pershing and seven thousand U.S. troops to capture Villa. The U.S. forces penetrated 350 miles into Mexico chasing after the elusive Villa. The "Punitive Expedition" had its comic and tragic aspects. Villa made fools of Pershing and his men and enhanced his reputation as a folk hero to Mexicans. Recognizing the nationalist backlash that the invasion was generating, General Carranza denounced Wilson, and his forces clashed with Pershing's expedition in June 1916. With war looming in Europe, Wilson withdrew U.S. troops from Mexico in February 1917. He recognized Carranza as the legitimate government of Mexico to ensure Mexican neutrality in the fight against Germany.

The failure of the Punitive Expedition pointed to key interpretative issues in the history of U.S. relations with Latin America. Despite its immense power, the United States did not always get its way, especially with the larger, more populous nations like Mexico. That Pancho Villa baited the United States into invading Mexico also demonstrated that Latin Americans could manipulate the mighty United States. Both General Gómez and the United States cooperated in 1908–1909 for their own purposes. Under the aegis of the Platt Amendment, the United States sent troops back into Cuba for periods of time in 1906, 1912, and 1917. In 1906, for example, warring Cuban politicians on both sides urged a U.S. intervention. President Tomás Estrada Palma (1902–06) asked that the United States to send two warships to Cuba. His rival, José Manuel Gómez, traveled to New York and called on the United States "to intervene and guarantee a fair election." Roosevelt unenthusiastically decided he must end "misrule and anarchy" on the island.[15] In Nicaragua, Adolfo Díaz (1911–17, 1926–28), the leader of the Conservative Party, relied on the U.S. marines to suppress his Liberal Party opponents and buttress his power and legitimacy. During the Cold War, conservative and elitist groups reliably played on U.S. Cold War fears to protect their privileged lives. They labeled Latin American social progressives as "Communists."

The repeated U.S. interventions in the Caribbean flowed from strategic and diplomatic imperatives. The United States wanted to transform the region into a calm, placid "American Lake." Presidents did not dispatch U.S. marines to protect the investments of corporate barons or the dividends of Wall Street brokers, per se. But as Louis A. Pérez, Jr., the preeminent historian of Cuba's history under the Platt Amendment, has aptly argued, "intervention is not an event, it is a process."[16] U.S. officials did not relish occupying foreign lands; they told themselves that the United States did not act like the European imperialists. U.S. leaders wanted to achieve the goals of security and stability without resort to force. They thought that U.S. credit, investment, and trade would create peace, prosperity, and happiness in the Caribbean region and forestall future interventions. Exposed to U.S. largess, Latin Americans would presumably adopt the sober values of "Main Street, USA." U.S. financiers, investors, and traders eagerly sought opportunities in Caribbean and Central American nations, because they understood that the overwhelming presence of the United States provided security for their money. Some even ventured that the United States could establish a symbiotic relationship with Latin America that had economic and psychological aspects. The United States would export manufactures and finished goods and import Latin America's raw materials and tropical foods. In Secretary of State Elihu Root's view, this trade would reflect complementary personalities. Root opined that "where we accumulate they spend. While we have less of the cheerful philosophy which finds happiness in the existing conditions of life, as the Latins do, they have less of the inventive faculty which strives continually to increase the productive power of men."[17]

During the era of armed intervention, the economic presence of the United States in the Caribbean region expanded. Under the reciprocity treaty of 1903, Cuba gained a guaranteed market in the United States for its sugar and, in turn, gave U.S. traders a privileged position in Cuba. By 1929, U.S.–Cuban trade amounted to over $300 million, the largest U.S. trade with any Latin American country. U.S. direct investments in Cuba, which stood at $50 million in 1895, grew to $220 million by 1913 and to over $900 million in 1929. U.S. investments in Haiti, which amounted to $11.5 million in 1915, the year the U.S. marines invaded, rose to $29 million by 1929. By 1929, U. S. capitalists controlled over 50 percent of Central America's trade and had over $200 million invested there.[18] United Fruit owned the coastal area of Honduras and had substantial holdings in Costa Rica,

Guatemala, and Nicaragua. The company also operated steamship lines, railroads, and radio and telegraph communication facilities. Honduras and Guatemala had become vast plantations of United Fruit or in the pejorative vernacular of the time, "banana republics."

Beyond promoting the expansion of U.S. capital, U.S. officials, especially the Wilson administration, tried to reform Latin American nations. President Wilson had denounced the Taft administration's efforts to stabilize the economies of countries like Nicaragua by having New York financiers buy up defaulted bonds and extend new credit. Wilson charged that such policies, dubbed "dollar diplomacy," assisted bankers more than Latin Americans. Wilson warned in a notable speech in Mobile, Alabama, in 1913 that "it is a very perilous philosophy thing to determine the foreign policy of a nation in the terms of material interest."[19] Wilson, a progressive reformer at home, saw his philosophy at work in Haiti and Dominican Republic. Much like urban progressives in the United States who passed legislation to improve unhealthy living conditions in tenement buildings, U.S. marines tried to clean up impoverished Haiti, which they considered a "pigsty." The marines improved water and sanitation facilities and built hospitals, schools, bridges, and roads for the Haitians. "Progressive interventionism" did not, however, win the favor of Haitians. Haitians were fiercely nationalistic people, proud of their little nation's history of liberating itself from the French and abolishing slavery in the early nineteenth century. When Haitians resisted occupation, the marines slaughtered them. Between 1914 and 1920, the marines killed 3,250 Haitians, while taking only 16 casualties. The marines built roads by impressing Haitians into forced-labor or *corvée* gangs. The oppression reminded Haitians of slavery. Critical U.S. observers compared the *corvée* to a southern prison chain gang.[20] The intense racism of U.S. officials and military men further alienated the Haitians. Secretary of State William Jennings Bryan, after receiving a briefing about Haiti, remarked: "Dear me, think of it. Niggers speaking French." Bryan's successor, Robert Lansing, defended the occupation by claiming that the "African race are devoid of any capacity for political organization and [have no] genius for government." Colonel Littleton W. T. Waller, the marine commander who governed Haiti, lamented to his military superiors that he felt humiliated having to work with light-skinned, mulatto Haitians. Colonel Waller complained: "They are real nigger and make no mistake—they are some very fine looking, well educated polished men here but they are real nigs beneath the surface."[21] A mass uprising by Haitians in 1929, fourteen years after the occupation, highlighted the loathing Haitians held for the U.S. model of development.

The United States eventually created stability in the Caribbean region but in an ironic and tragic way. In the Dominican Republic, occupied from 1916 to 1924, the marines first crushed the armies of local strongmen and then disarmed the population. The marines seized 53,000 firearms and innumerable knives and machetes from a population of less than one million people. Prior to 1916, political life had been chaotic in the Dominican Republic, but tyrants did not last long because Dominicans had the ability to organize against them. In 1917, the marines established a national constabulary, *Guardia Nacional*, and a military academy in 1921 to train officers for the guard. The marines wanted an apolitical military force loyal to the constitution that could maintain political order and stability and move swiftly to any part of the country to suppress rebellion. As in Haiti, the marines built roads and telecommunications systems that radiated from the capital. The marines had created the conditions that fostered a lasting dictatorship. The Dominican Republic lacked features of a civic society—a free press, business organizations, agricultural cooperatives, labor unions, teacher and student organizations—that could balance the power of the military. The *Guardia Nacional* had a monopoly on arms, munitions, and power in the nation. Rafael Leonidas Trujillo Molina, an ambitious, talented Dominican with a criminal past, enlisted in the guard in 1919. A favorite of the marines, who admired his command of presence and martial spirit, Trujillo rose through the ranks, attended the military academy, and became commander of the Dominican guard in the late 1920s.[22] In 1930, Trujillo (1930–61) seized power and used his control of the *Guardia Nacional* to buttress his odious, three-decade-long dictatorship. Appalled international observers compared the murderous Trujillo to Adolf Hitler and Josef Stalin. What happened in the Dominican Republic was replicated throughout the Caribbean region. Cuba's Fulgencio Batista and Nicaragua's Anastasio Somoza García used national constabularies, which had been created by the marines, to enforce their respective dictatorships.

The patterns of intervention woven during the early twentieth century were refashioned during the Cold War. Like Woodrow Wilson, President John F. Kennedy judged U.S. policies in Latin America to be both unproductive and immoral. In 1961, he designed a grand economic aid program, the Alliance for Progress, for Latin America. Also, like Wilson, he intervened for democracy. In the Dominican Republic, for example, he forced the Trujillo family out, sponsored a democratic election, and awarded the Dominican Republic with substantial economic assistance. But Kennedy and his advisors quickly lost faith in the Dominican Republic's democratic reformers, taking the patronizing attitude that they lacked the toughness and skill necessary to be effective Cold Warriors. President Lyndon Johnson subsequently sent U.S. marines into the Dominican Republic to prevent suspect political leftists from gaining power. In 1966, the Johnson administration helped rig the presidential election to guarantee that its candidate, the archconservative Joaquín Balaguer, won. Balaguer, an acolyte of Rafael Trujillo, thereafter provided the Dominican Republic with the anti-Communist stability that the United States desired.

U.S. influence in South America also spread, especially in the period after World War I. The major European powers—the United Kingdom, France, and Germany—emerged from the war with ravaged economies and horrific population losses. The British and French had also borrowed billions of dollars from U.S. banks to finance the war. Between 1914 and 1919, the United States went from being a net debtor nation to a creditor nation. New York replaced London, Paris, and Berlin as the international center of finance. Europeans, especially the

British, had traditionally been the chief traders, investors, and bondholders in South America. In the postwar period, U.S. investors came to dominate the region, investing billions in extractive industries like copper, lead, tin, zinc, and petroleum. In Chile, for example, U.S. direct investments soared from $15 million in 1913 to $423 million in 1929. U.S. companies in Chile mined the copper that went into the wiring for electrical lines and the new electric refrigerators, stoves, and washers. In Venezuela, U.S. oil giants, like Gulf Oil and Standard Oil of New Jersey, pushed aside the British-Dutch combine, the Royal-Dutch Shell Oil Company, and gained control of Venezuela's rich oil resources. The value of U.S. direct investments rose from $3 million in 1913 to $206 million in 1929. Prior to 1921, Venezuelan fields produced only a negligible amount of oil. By 1929, Venezuela produced 137 million barrels of oil and ranked as the third largest oil producer in the world, after the United States and the Soviet Union. In gaining a majority share of Venezuelan production, the U.S. oil companies received able assistance from the U.S. government. State Department officials informed President Juan Vicente Gómez that the United States opposed Royal-Dutch Shell having a monopoly of oil concessions. U.S. officials did not protest, however, when Standard Oil of New Jersey began to take control of Venezuelan oil. They also looked the other way when oilmen proffered lucrative bribes to President Gómez. The British resigned themselves to second-class status, recognizing what one diplomat lamented as "the power of the dollar."[23]

U.S. banking houses supplanted the European financial institutions as the chief holders of South American bonds. Prior to 1913, South American governments financed their capital investments, such as water and sewage systems, by selling bonds to European investors. In the postwar period, the South Americans wanted access to U.S. capital markets. But knowing that South Americans had often defaulted on their debts in the nineteenth century, the United States recommended that governments first put their financial households in order. In the 1920s, Dr. Edwin Walter Kemmerer arrived as an "unofficial" guest in the capital cities of Bolivia, Chile, Colombia, Ecuador, and Peru. Professor Kemmerer, who taught economics and finance at Princeton University, became known as the "Money Doctor of the Andes." Kemmerer made clear to South American officials that if they wanted access to capital they would need to create international confidence in the stability of their currencies. Kemmerer required governments to tie their currency to the gold standard, establish a central bank (*banco central*) that would control the currency, and maintain austere, balanced budgets each fiscal year. Kemmerer preached that governments could issue bonds to underwrite major projects that would generate revenue, like railroads, but not for non-self-supporting public works like schools. Once certified by Dr. Kemmerer, a South American government would receive the seal of approval from Washington and access to the money of a New York banking house like Dillon, Read. In the five Andean countries that Kemmerer advised, U.S. direct and portfolio investments increased by 1,241 percent from 1913 to 1929. By comparison, British investments in the five countries increased by only 13.6 percent in the same period. By adopting

Kemmerer's ideas, South American governments also became closely tied to the international capitalist system that the United States now dominated.[24]

GOOD NEIGHBOR POLICIES

The collapse of international capitalism, the onset of the Great Depression, and mounting bitterness over the repeated armed interventions in Latin America led to a reassessment of the U.S. approach to Latin America. The Nicaraguan patriot Augusto César Sandino had earned international sympathy for his fight against the occupying U.S. marines. At a tempestuous inter-American conference in Havana in 1928, Latin American delegates led by Argentina, Mexico, and El Salvador resolved that no state had the right to intervene in the internal affairs of another. The United States successfully tabled that resolution, but U.S. officials understood that the nation would have to alter tactics. Prior to his inauguration, Herbert Hoover (1929–33) made a good will tour of South America. The new administration also embraced the "Clark Memorandum," an analysis of the Monroe Doctrine prepared in late 1928 by State Department officer J. Reuben Clark. The memorandum repudiated the claim that the Monroe Doctrine sanctioned intervention. Nonetheless, Hoover declined to disavow publicly the right to intervene in Latin America.

The economic catastrophes of the early 1930s undermined Hoover's goodwill efforts. Between 1929 and 1933, the value of inter-American trade declined by 75 percent. The economic depression in the United States accounted for most of the decline, but Latin Americans blamed the high duties imposed by the Hawley–Smoot Tariff (1930) for their woes. Latin American nations fell into an economic abyss. Vitally dependent on international trade for their solvency, Latin Americans defaulted on the bank loans they had secured in the 1920s through the Kemmerer missions. Turmoil spread throughout the region, with governments collapsing. Latin Americans also began to question the principles of the international capitalist system.

The Franklin D. Roosevelt administration (1933–45) seemingly transformed inter-American relations with the Good Neighbor policy. President Roosevelt withdrew troops and financial advisors from the Caribbean region and relinquished treaty rights, like the Platt Amendment, that Latin Americans found obnoxious. The administration also publicly repudiated the Roosevelt Corollary. At a series of inter-American conferences, U.S. delegates voted with Latin Americans on resolutions outlawing military intervention. This process culminated in 1948, when the Harry S. Truman administration accepted the Charter of the Organization of American States (OAS), which prohibited any state from intervening "directly or indirectly, for any reason, whatever, in the internal or external affairs of another state."

The administration also revived inter-American trade, trying to help the Western Hemisphere emerge from the Great Depression. In 1929, trade with the twenty Latin American nations had accounted for approximately 20 percent of

U.S. international trade. Armed with the Reciprocal Trade Agreements Act (1934), which empowered the president to reduce tariffs by up to 50 percent in exchange for equivalent concessions, the administration negotiated in the 1930s trade agreements with eleven Latin American countries. By 1939, the value of U.S. trade with Latin America had nearly doubled from its 1933 low, although it was still below the 1929 peak. The administration also responded to economic nationalism in Latin America. It tacitly conceded that Latin Americans needed to diversify their economies when, in 1940, it granted Brazil a $45 million credit to construct a steel mill. The administration grudgingly accepted Mexico's expropriation of the holdings of U.S. oil companies, and it helped Venezuela write its oil law of 1943, a bill that required foreign oil companies to share with Venezuela at least 50 percent of their profits from the sale of Venezuelan oil.

The Good Neighbor approach helped forge a strong wartime alliance. By February 1942, eighteen Latin American nations had declared war or severed relations with the Axis powers. Chile joined the belligerency in 1943, leaving Argentina as the only neutral nation in the hemisphere. Sixteen nations permitted U.S. forces to use air and naval bases on their territory. Brazil sent an expeditionary force to Italy, and Mexico sent an air squadron to the Pacific theatre.

Latin America's major contribution to Allied victory came in the form of commodities and raw materials. Non-military agencies of the United States bought nearly $2.4 billion worth of commodities from Latin America out of an approximate total of $4.4 billion spent throughout the world. The United States relied on Latin America for such strategically vital raw materials as beryllium, copper, manganese, mica, quartz crystals, tantalum, tin, tungsten, and zinc. Venezuela supplied the United Kingdom with 80 percent of its oil imports. Even recalcitrant Argentina sold its beef and wheat to the Allies. During World War II, Latin America served as the arsenal for the United States and the United Nations.

Although President Roosevelt had measurably improved the tenor and tone of inter-American relations, the United States had not forfeited its regional power. In 1933–1934, the administration refused to recognize the new, nationalistic government of Ramón Grau San Martín and ringed Cuba with U.S. warships. With the blessing of the Roosevelt administration, Sergeant Fulgencio Batista became the dominant political figure in Cuba. The United States could no longer cite the Platt Amendment to sanction military intervention. Nonetheless, by controlling Cuba's access to the U.S. sugar market, through the new trade treaty of 1934, the United States continued to exercise leverage over the island's political and economic life. U.S. forces still patrolled the military and naval base at Guantánamo Bay. U.S. marines withdrew from Haiti in 1934, and U.S. financial experts stopped collecting, after 1941, the export/import taxes of the Dominican Republic and Haiti. But the Roosevelt administration required the Dominicans and Haitians to deposit their funds in New York banks and insisted that U.S. bankers oversee the repayment of international debts.[25] The administration also pointedly informed Chile in 1943 that it would be deprived of postwar economic aid if it did not declare war against the Axis powers. The administration further deployed diplomatic pressure, albeit unsuccessfully, to force Argentina into the Allied camp.[26]

U.S. power and influence in Latin America, especially in South America, grew during World War II. The effect of the war was to devastate Germany and weaken the United Kingdom, the two major competitors for trade and investment in the region. Exaggerating the threat of Axis subversion in the hemisphere, U.S. authorities eagerly assisted Latin Americans in confiscating German commercial holdings. Over 4,000 Germans were deported from countries such as Colombia and Ecuador to the United States to internment camps in Texas. Only eight of the 4,058 deported were allegedly involved in espionage. Latin American leaders, especially dictators, cooperated with the deportation program, seeing both an opportunity to curry favor with the United States and a chance to seize the property of the German nationals.[27] To enhance hemispheric solidarity and counter any Nazi propaganda, the Office of the Coordinator of Inter-American Affairs, led by Nelson Rockefeller, saturated Latin American newspapers, airwaves, and theaters with visions of the U.S. way of life. The War Department also expanded U.S. influence by disbursing $400 million in military equipment through the Lend-Lease program. U.S. military officers replaced Western Europeans as the principal advisors to South American military units.

The Franklin Roosevelt administration pursued traditional sphere-of-influence goals in Latin America. The administration wanted to exclude European influences, preserve U.S. leadership in the hemisphere, dominate the Caribbean basin, and maintain political stability. Armed interventions had proven costly, unpopular, and counterproductive—they had not produced peace and order, and they had jeopardized trade and investment. In any case, the tumultuous Caribbean and Central American nations achieved their own stability in the 1930s under dictators like Batista, Somoza, and Trujillo. These strongmen relied on their respective national guards to enforce order. Even as it waged war against dictatorship in Asia and Europe, the Roosevelt administration conducted cordial, even effusive, relations with these unsavory tyrants, because they bowed to U.S. leadership, professed to be anti-Nazi, and kept their countries quiet.

Although President Roosevelt may not have radically restructured Latin American policies, he nonetheless inspired many Latin Americans. The president was not a fervent racial egalitarian like his wife, Eleanor Roosevelt. But Roosevelt treated Latin Americans with dignity and respect. He dispatched ambassadors, like Josephus Daniels to Mexico and Dr. Frank Corrigan to Venezuela, who sympathized with Latin American efforts to build progressive societies. The president's policies and pronouncements—the New Deal, the Atlantic Charter, the Four Freedoms—motivated liberal groups like the American Popular Revolutionary Alliance or *Aprista* movement of Peru and *Acción Democrática* of Venezuela to believe that they could break the power of the military and the landed oligarchy and establish popular governments committed to social reform. Latin American democrats, like Juan José Arévalo of Guatemala, José Figueres of Costa Rica, and Eduardo Santos of Colombia, identified with Roosevelt and considered him a friend of Latin America.

The Franklin D. Roosevelt administration conducted cordial relations with Latin American tyrants like Fulgencio Batista of Cuba, Rafael Trujillo of the Dominican Republic, and Anastasio Somoza García of Nicaragua. Here President Roosevelt greets Nicaragua's Somoza in Washington in 1939. Roosevelt largely adhered to the non-intervention principles of the Good Neighbor policy. But the dictators of the Caribbean and Central America provided the security and stability that the United States had unsuccessfully sought during the era of armed U.S. intervention. U.S. support for Latin American dictators would become a major Cold War issue. (Corbis Images)

Moreover, the idealistic rhetoric of the war against fascism seemed to undermine the legitimacy of dictators at home. In Central America, dictators fell in Guatemala and El Salvador in 1944, and Somoza had to relax his hold on Nicaragua.[28] President Roosevelt had further managed to leave Latin Americans believing that the United States would be a partner in their economic growth. During the war, the United States pledged that, once the enemy was defeated, it would support the economic development and diversification of Latin America. Latin Americans dreamed of Pan American cooperation and substantial economic aid.

THE NEW INTERNATIONAL POLICE POWER

During the Roosevelt years, the United States and Latin America embraced the Western Hemisphere ideal—the idea that "the Americas constitute a group of nations separate from the 'Old World' of Europe."[29] The Western Hemisphere or

Pan American ideal assumed a compatibility of interests between the powerful United States and its southern neighbors. As President Santos of Colombia put it in a 1941 letter to Roosevelt, the two nations shared a common vision, cherishing "moral, religious, and political liberty."[30] The United States seemed to have put into practice the stirring language of the Monroe Doctrine. But the Good Neighbor policy had an inherent contradiction that would be exposed during the Cold War. The noted historian of the Good Neighbor policy, the late Bryce Wood, praised Roosevelt for adhering to the principles of nonintervention and noninterference. The Good Neighbor policy was "not simply rhetoric." The United States "not only renounced intervention and interference in domestic politics, but it actually did not intervene or interfere." The Good Neighbor, Wood opined, represented "a radical change from the 1920s, when intervention and interference were normal features of inter-American relations." Other historians have suggested that Wood exaggerated the extent of change that the Roosevelt administration brought forth in inter-American relations. In any case, Wood conceded in his studies of the Good Neighbor policy that the Roosevelt administration anticipated "reciprocity" from Latin American countries—"the expectation that that favorable responses would be forthcoming to initiatives from Washington on matters of mutual concern." The United States further expected that Latin American states would exercise restraint in the treatment of U.S. business enterprises.[31]

In practice, "reciprocity" signified that the United States expected Latin Americans to follow the U.S. lead in the international arena. During World War II, the United States demanded that Argentina and Chile declare war against the Axis powers. In 1943–1944, the United States withheld diplomatic recognition of the Bolivian government of Major Gualberto Villarroel, until he dismissed aides who the United States suspected of having fascist sympathies. During the Cold War, the United States would turn against Latin American nations who did not accept the U.S. perception of the external threat of the Soviet Union and the internal danger of Communist subversion. Without publicly acknowledging it, U.S. presidential administrations would return to the premises of the Roosevelt Corollary when they did not receive "favorable responses" from Latin American states on vital international issues. Cooperating with the Soviet Union or pursuing left-wing socioeconomic policies constituted the Cold War's version of "chronic wrongdoing." The United States would necessarily have to exercise again "international police power," albeit the new cops on the beat might be CIA agents instead of U.S. marines. The United States would also extend its reach in the Western Hemisphere. During the first third of the twentieth century, the United States overthrew governments— Cuba, Nicaragua, Venezuela—with some geographic proximity to the United States. In the postwar period, however, the United States fought a "global Cold War," destabilizing governments not just in nearby Guatemala and the Dominican Republic but also in Brazil and Chile and in former British possessions like British Guiana (Guyana) and Grenada. Because the confrontation with the Soviet Union was perceived as involving the very survival of Western civilization, U.S. officials also confidentially admitted to themselves that the United States could not abide

by treaty obligations not to intervene in Latin America. As did their predecessors from Grover Cleveland to Franklin Roosevelt, U.S. Cold War leaders held
that upholding international peace and security depended upon keeping the traditional U.S. sphere of influence intact and in line. When Latin Americans resisted
Cold War objectives, U.S. policymakers reacted with the same interventionist policies and superior attitudes that had characterized U.S. behavior in the first part of
the twentieth century.

CHAPTER 2

The Kennan Corollary

The Harry S. Truman administration constructed the framework of the Cold War policies that the United States would pursue against the Soviet Union. In 1947, the administration accepted the premises of "containment." The United States would prevent the expansion of the Soviet Union and the international Communist movement. In March 1947, President Truman announced his Truman Doctrine, vowing that the United States would provide economic and military assistance to nations threatened by communism. With the Marshall Plan, the United States promised to rebuild Western Europe as a bulwark against the Soviet empire in Eastern Europe. In 1949, the United States formed a military alliance, the North Atlantic Treaty Organization (NATO), with allies in Europe and North America. Finally, in mid-1950, President Truman confidentially approved a detailed blueprint for Cold War, National Security Council Memorandum No. 68/2 (NSC 68/2). The document warned that the Soviet Union and communism threatened the survival of Western civilization. The United States must respond, by developing awesome military power to combat and defeat the international Communist movement.

During the Truman years, the United States would perceive Latin America as a Cold War arena, albeit not yet as a central front in the struggle against the Soviet Union. U.S. officials would make decisions about Latin America based on their weighing of the international balance of power. In the postwar years, they viewed Latin America through a global rather than a regional prism. Latin Americans needed to be steady allies of the United States who followed the U.S. lead in the international arena and supplied primary products and raw materials to the United States and its allies. Latin Americans had to understand that the United States could no longer pay attention to the region. The United States had the staggering responsibility of protecting Europe and Asia from communism. The Cold War made Latin America globally insignificant. When Latin Americans protested these analyses, U.S. officials drew darker conclusions. Latin Americans were irresponsible, emotional, and immature. They were negligent, ignoring the threat of communism both abroad and at home. Truman administration officials told themselves that the United States could not abide by its non-intervention commitments when it came to communism in the Americas. They also ventured that authoritarian rulers, who kept Latin American societies secure and stable, might best serve the international goals of the United States.

GEORGE KENNAN GOES TO LATIN AMERICA

In an ironic and largely unknown way, a revered U.S. diplomat, who professed to know little about Latin America, reasoned out what would become the Cold War policy of the United States for the region. George F. Kennan was a veteran foreign-service officer who specialized in Russian/Soviet affairs. Kennan sent the famous eight-thousand-word "Long Telegram" from Moscow in 1946 and published an article, "The Sources of Soviet Conduct," in 1947 in the influential journal *Foreign Affairs*, under the pseudonym of "X." In these pieces, Kennan argued that ideology rather than national security concerns underlay the foreign policies of the Soviet Union under the brutal Joseph Stalin. The Soviet Union acted aggressively, constantly testing and probing the tenacity of democratic nations, because it was driven by the Marxist–Leninist imperative to destroy the international capitalist system. Stalin kept the world in a constant state of turmoil as a way of justifying and covering up his barbaric dictatorship. The United States could not peacefully coexist with such a nation and leader, because it was the implacable desire of Communists to destroy the United States and its allies. Kennan advised that the United States needed to be steadfast and patient and to "contain" the Soviet Union. Faced with resolute resistance from the West, the Soviet Union would eventually implode, succumbing to the internal contradictions inherent in the Communist system. In his commentaries, Kennan did not make clear where the United States should contain the Soviet Union and by what means. Kennan's words could be interpreted as urging global containment by military means. Kennan also drew no sharp distinction between the Soviet Union and the ideology of communism. National leaders, such as Vietnam's Ho Chi Minh, might adopt communism for their own purposes and not to supplement the power of the Soviet Union. Kennan would later claim that he had used imprecise language and did not intend to urge a global crusade against the international Communist movement. Nonetheless, his ideas informed such crucial initiatives as the Truman Doctrine. From 1947 to 1950, Kennan led the State Department's Policy Planning Staff, which developed plans for waging Cold War.

In February 1950, Kennan made what he called a "Cook's Tour" of Latin America to learn about the region. The official purpose of the trip was to attend a meeting of U.S. ambassadors to Latin America in Rio de Janeiro. Kennan traveled by train to Mexico City and then flew to Caracas, and thereafter to Rio, São Paulo, Montevideo, Buenos Aires, Lima, and Panama. If there ever was a case of the "ugly American" or *el gringo feo*, it was George Kennan in Latin America. Mexico City was noisy at night, disrupting Kennan's sleep. Kennan recorded in his diary that "the sounds of its nocturnal activity struck me as disturbed, sultry, and menacing." Caracas "appalled" Kennan with its "screaming, honking traffic jams," and "its feverish economy debauched by oil money." Rio was "repulsive" with its "unbelievable contrasts between luxury and poverty," and São Paulo "was still worse." Montevideo and Buenos Aires did not overly offend Kennan, although they "inflicted on me a curious sense of mingled apprehension and melancholy." But "in Lima, I was depressed by the reflection that it had not rained in the place for twenty-nine years and by the thought that some of the dirt had presumably been there, untouched, for all that time." It also "galled" Kennan that he had to call on heads of state in these bleak cities and act diplomatically. It was "all painful and slightly disreputable," he sighed.[1]

When he returned to Washington, Kennan wrote a ten-thousand-word report for the secretary of state on Latin America as a "problem" in U.S. foreign policy. Kennan did not dwell on his personal sufferings in Latin America but persisted in his xenophobia and ethnocentrism. As a general consideration, "it seems to me unlikely that there could be any region of the earth in which nature and human behavior could have combined to produce a more unhappy and hopeless background for the conduct of human life than in Latin America." Assuming the role of geographer, Kennan pronounced North America as blessed by topography and climate, whereas South America had been cursed. Into "this unfavorable geographical background" came the Spanish conquistadors with their "religious fanaticism, a burning frustrated energy, and addiction to the most merciless cruelty." The intermarriage of the Spanish with the indigenous population and with African slaves "produced other unfortunate results which seemed to have weighed scarcely less heavily on the chances for human progress." Kennan repeated the arguments of nineteenth-century North Americans, who alleged that Latin Americans were condemned to perpetual backwardness because of their Catholicism, their racial heritage, and their enervating lives in tropical climes. Kennan theorized that "Latin American society lives by and large by a species of make-believe," a "little word of pretense," because Latin Americans implicitly recognized the "bitter realities" of their deficient thought, society, and culture.

Known for his "realistic" approach to international affairs, Kennan had harsh recommendations for the conduct of U.S. policies toward Latin America in the Cold War. He ridiculed Pan-Americanism and multilateral organizations, such as the Organization of American States, as "a form of agreeable and easy escapism from the real problems of foreign policy." As he told U.S. ambassadors in Rio, U.S. policy should aim at preventing Latin America from being mobilized against the United States, either militarily or psychologically, and at protecting access to "our" raw materials. The United States should not hesitate to remind Latin Americans that the United States was a great power and "that we are by and large much less in need of them than they are in need of us." Whether Latin Americans liked or understood the United States mattered little. Kennan suggested telling Latin Americans: "We are really only concerned for your respect. You must recognize that we are a great and strong people; that we have our place in the world."

The major challenge for the United States would be to prevent the spread of communism in Latin America, which Kennan predicted would come not from external attack but through internal subversion. Reviewing the history of the Monroe Doctrine, Kennan believed the United States had the diplomatic tradition to demand the exclusion of Communists from the hemisphere. Not surprisingly, Kennan doubted whether Latin Americans had the societal resolve to resist the blandishments of the Communists. Kennan therefore concluded that "harsh governmental measures of repression may be the only answer; that these measures may have to proceed from regimes whose origins and methods would not stand the test of American concepts of democratic procedure; and that such regimes and such methods may be preferable alternatives, to further communist successes." To argue that tyranny and dictatorship in Latin America was vital to U.S. national security did not trouble Kennan. He cited Secretary of State John Quincy Adams who opined in 1821 that cultural, religious, and racial deficiencies would prevent the new South American republics from establishing "free or liberal institutions of government." As Adams saw it, "arbitrary power, military and ecclesiastical, is stamped upon their education, upon their habits, and upon all their institutions."[2]

Kennan's tome evoked no discussion within the Truman administration. Officials within the Latin American section of the State Department asked Secretary of State Dean Acheson not to distribute the report. Kennan believed that his musings about the cultural deficiencies of Latin Americans were judged "intolerable." He thought his report had been locked away, kept out of State Department files. In fact, the report gathered dust in the file cabinet for twenty-five years, until it was declassified in 1976 with other records from 1950.[3] Kennan left his position in Policy Planning in August 1950. In the preceding months, he, like other officials, focused on the outbreak of the Korean War.

Kennan's memorandum can be dismissed as the uncharacteristic ravings of an otherwise distinguished public servant. Kennan, forty-six, was perhaps in the midst of some mid-life or career crisis. Kennan, who lived to be 101, changed his views on the Cold War and Latin America. He supported giving the Panama Canal back to Panama and called for the diplomatic recognition of Fidel Castro's Cuba. He testified against the Vietnam War. He repudiated Ronald Reagan's strident behavior toward the Soviet Union. After the collapse of the Soviet Union, he observed that "the general effect of Cold War extremism was to delay rather than hasten the great change that overtook the Soviet Union."[4] He also warned citizens that the invasion of Iraq in 2003 would bring unforseen, unwanted consequences.

Although undebated and disowned, Kennan's report revealed the style and substance of Cold War policies for Latin America. Latin America had no significance of its own. It existed to serve U.S. Cold War interests. Latin American leaders were naïve about global affairs and unrealistic in expecting their powerful northern neighbor to assist Latin America's development. Latin Americans were not only naïve but also foolish and irresponsible. They lacked the cultural requisites

George F. Kennan, a foreign-policy expert, authored the famous article "The Sources of Soviet Conduct" that served as the basis for the containment strategy that the United States pursued against the Soviet Union during the Cold War. In 1950, Kennan also submitted a lengthy report on Latin America. Although Kennan's superiors in the U.S. State Department declined to circulate his report, Kennan's views became U.S. policy for Latin America. Winning the Cold War—preventing any hint of political radicalism in the Western Hemisphere—commanded a higher priority than promoting democracy and respect for human rights. (Corbis Images)

to create modernized, democratic societies with high-performance economies. Dictatorship might be the only answer for preventing communism and protecting U.S. vital interests. The United States had the power and glory and the historical tradition of the Monroe Doctrine to save Latin Americans from themselves. As Walter LaFeber noted, during the Cold War the United States reinstated the Roosevelt Corollary to the Monroe Doctrine. Another distinguished historian, Gaddis Smith, suggested that U.S. Cold War policies be labeled the "Kennan Corollary."[5]

POSTWAR VISIONS

As World War II concluded, bright hope rather than George Kennan's dark pessimism characterized inter-American relations. Both domestic and international developments had drawn the inter-American community closer together. In 1944 only four of the twenty Latin American republics—Chile, Colombia, Costa

Rica, and Uruguay—could be called representative democracies that respected civil liberties. By 1946, only five nations—the Dominican Republic, El Salvador, Honduras, Nicaragua, and Paraguay—remained authoritarian states. The other Latin American states could claim in some sense to be democratic. In Guatemala, for example, a mass popular uprising toppled the dictator, Jorge Ubico y Castañeda (1931–44). During the twentieth century, Latin American societies had become more complex, with lawyers, doctors, teachers, students, labor, and small businesses forming associations and unions. These "middle sector" groups demanded that the traditional arbiters of Latin American life—the landed oligarchy, the military, and the Roman Catholic Church—extend voting rights and share power. Middle-sector groups also called on the state to promote social welfare by improving health and education and passing laws to protect workers. Leaders like President Juan José Arévalo of Guatemala (1945–51) admired Franklin Roosevelt and wanted a New Deal for their countries.[6]

The idealism inherent in the war against European fascism and Japanese militarism also undermined tyrants and strengthened the cause of social progressives. Throughout the war, the Roosevelt administration had disseminated propaganda that the war was being fought to protect civil and human rights and to promote economic and social mobility. In Nicaragua, for example, laborers, protesting the regime of Anastasio Somoza García, carried banners declaring "Roosevelt Has Said That the Tyrants of the Earth Will Be Wiped Out." The Roosevelt administration also signaled that it preferred democratic leaders. In 1943, it denied a request of General Maximiliano Hernández Martínez of El Salvador (1931–44) for one thousand submachine guns through the Lend-Lease military aid program. As a State Department officer noted, "these lethal toys [are] more likely to be used for a very different purpose than they were intended."[7] The next year Salvadorans overthrew the despotic Hernández Martínez. The United States appreciated Brazil's decision to send an expeditionary force to Italy. Ambassador Adolf A. Berle, Jr., a friend of Roosevelt and fervent New Dealer, made it clear that the United States wanted to see a democratic evolution in Brazil. In 1945, he told the Brazilian press that he expected that dictator Getúlio Dornelles Vargas (1930–45) would permit a free election.[8] The Brazilian military forced Vargas out of office, and elections took place.

Latin American democrats believed that they would have the financial resources to transform their societies. Latin American economies had prospered during the war, as the region served as the arsenal for Allied victory. Latin Americans had accumulated credits of $3.4 billion, because the capital goods that they wanted to purchase in the United States were scarce because of wartime rationing. Colombia's foreign exchange reserves, for example, increased by 540 percent during the war.[9] Latin Americans felt confident not only that they would be able to cash in their reserves but also that the United States would provide new capital. President Roosevelt and his chief emissary to Latin America, Undersecretary of State Sumner Welles, had implied that the region could count on the United States in the postwar world for economic development assistance. Latin Americans also expected to wield diplomatic power. Fifty-one nations were charter members of the new United Nations. The United States and its Latin American friends held twenty-one of the votes in the General Assembly. Historians Leslie Bethell and Ian Roxborough perceive the period from 1944 to 1948 as "a critical conjuncture in the political and social history of Latin America."[10] Reform-minded democrats, who had the backing of the United States, dreamed of a socially just Latin America.

In form, Latin America accomplished much between 1945 and 1948. At the U.N. organizing conference held in San Francisco in 1945, the U.S. delegation, at the urging of the new assistant secretary of state for Latin American affairs, Nelson Rockefeller, agreed with Latin Americans that the United Nations should sanction regional security organizations. This agreement became Article 51 of the U.N. charter. All further agreed to let Argentina, which had remained neutral during the war, back into the inter-American community and the United Nations. Thereafter, in 1947, the administration signed a mutual defense pact with Latin America at Rio de Janeiro, and a year later, at Bogotá, it joined with Latin Americans in incorporating Pan-Americanism into the charter of the Organization of American States. The OAS charter explicitly prohibited intervention in the internal affairs of member states.

The Rio Treaty and the OAS reflected the spirit of the Good Neighbor policy and wartime solidarity. But they also reflected different perspectives on inter-American relations. Secretary of War Henry L. Stimson spoke for many U.S. officials, seeing Article 51 as a way to preserve the unilateral character of the Monroe Doctrine and a U.S. sphere of influence. As Stimson noted, "I think it is not asking too much to have our little region over here," if Russia "is going to take these steps...of building up friendly protectorates around her."[11] In accepting Article 51, President Truman was also affirming the views of President Roosevelt, who assured Latin Americans that the inter-American system would not be supplanted by a new international organization. At San Francisco, Latin Americans, led by Mexico and Colombia, lobbied for the inclusion of regional alliances into the U.N. charter. With the OAS, Latin Americans would have a forum to influence the United States, a treaty that codified the nonintervention principle, and a vehicle for transferring economic aid.

Although Latin Americans achieved their organizational goals, the substance of postwar inter-American relations dismayed them. The United States emerged from World War II as the world's dominant power with global ambitions and responsibilities; regional concerns would be subordinated to the larger task of rebuilding Europe and Japan and containing the Soviet Union. President Truman and his foreign-policy team also had no background or interest in Latin America. President Roosevelt considered Latin America significant, and he listened to powerful figures like Welles, Berle, and Rockefeller who gave priority to the inter-American community. Truman and his secretaries of state, James Byrnes, George Marshall, and Dean Acheson, evinced little interest in the region, did not speak Spanish or Portuguese, and did not appoint influential people to lead the Latin American Affairs division of the State Department. Truman and Acheson also displayed the same boorish attitudes toward Latin Americans that permeated George Kennan's infamous memorandum. Truman thought Latin Americans were like Jews and the Irish—"very emotional" and difficult to handle. Secretary Acheson wrote in his memoirs that "Hispano-Indian culture—or lack of it" had been "piling up its problems for centuries." For Acheson, Latin America meant "an explosive population, stagnant economy, archaic society, primitive politics, massive ignorance, illiteracy, and poverty."[12]

Neither Truman nor his secretaries of state thought they had an obligation to assist what they deemed a benighted region and culture. The Roosevelt administration had scheduled a special economic conference for 15 June 1945. Latin Americans wanted to talk about international commodity agreements, controls on foreign investment, linking the prices of raw materials to finished goods, and economic aid. For the next seven years, the Truman administration would come up with all manner of excuses of why it could not attend an inter-American economic conference. In 1946, for example, the administration delayed action as it engaged in a noisy debate with Argentina's Colonel Juan Perón (1946–55) about his alleged fascist sympathies. The administration feared that an economic conference would be a diplomatic fiasco, with the United States resisting demands for economic aid and commodity agreements. Brazil had already asked in early 1946 for a five-year $1 billion loan. U.S. officials responded that Latin America would prosper if it honored free trade and investment principles and prepared for the massive orders of raw materials that would surely come from a rebuilding Europe. By 1946, State Department officials wanted "to kill" the conference idea, but, fearing a stormy reaction from Latin Americans, chose only to postpone it. The United States had reneged on its wartime pledges of economic cooperation. As State Department officer Louis Halle bluntly put it, "the United States no longer desperately needs Latin America."[13]

The handling of wartime contracts further dismayed Latin Americans. The United States had promised not to terminate wartime contracts abruptly, to allocate capital goods fairly, and to remember that Latin America had sold its strategic commodities in a controlled market, with prices fixed. After the war, however, the United States abruptly lifted price controls, and prices rose rapidly; Latin America quickly exhausted its more than $3 billion in credits. Chile, for example, by selling its copper and nitrates at artificially low prices and buying goods for industrial development in a free market, may have lost $500 million. In effect, Latin America made a $3 billion non-interest-bearing loan to the United States and could not collect on the principal. The United States answered that it had repaid Latin Americans by sacrificing men and matériel in war, protecting the hemisphere from totalitarianism.[14]

Latin American hopes for economic aid revived after Secretary of State Marshall announced his plan to reconstruct Europe. If the United States was prepared to help former enemies, then a "Marshall Plan for Latin America" might follow. At the Rio Conference, delegates wanted to focus on economic cooperation, but Marshall persuaded them to wait until meeting in Bogotá. There, the secretary quashed all hopes of economic aid. In a speech that was greeted by stony silence, Marshall promised only to increase the lending authority of the Export-Import Bank by $500 million to facilitate trade. The European Recovery Program would aid Latin America by restoring markets for raw materials and tropical foods. Once Europe rebuilt its industrial plant, Latin America would have another source of supply for capital goods. Latin Americans interpreted such arguments to mean that their region would be confined to its traditional role of supplying the industrial world with raw materials. In any case, between 1945 and 1952, Belgium and tiny Luxembourg received more economic aid from the United States than did all of Latin America.

In lieu of economic assistance, the U.S. prescription for Latin America's health included self-help, technical cooperation, liberal trade practices, and, in particular, private enterprise and investment. The Truman administration repeatedly preached that Latin Americans could have stacks of money if they created a "suitable climate" for foreign investors. Latin Americans found such arguments wanting, knowing that Latin America already accounted for nearly 40 percent of U.S. direct investments globally and 30 percent of U.S. international trade. The United States misled Latin America during the war and now "neglected" the region. Debates about the efficacy of international capitalism aside, the Truman administration left Latin America as the one non-Communist area in the world not under a direct aid program, because it positioned its analyses of inter-American relations within the context of the Cold War. The Soviet Union did not threaten the region. As Ambassador Herschel Johnson explained to the Brazilian press, "the situation might be graphically represented as a case of smallpox in Europe competing with a common cold in Latin America."[15]

The dreams of Latin American democrats and reformers vanished. In 1948, military officers overthrew new, popular governments in Peru and Venezuela. Elsewhere reform and change slowed dramatically. The Truman administration bore some responsibility for the collapse of democratic reform. Latin American democrats had expected that the United States would help fund social reform. As the Mexican foreign minister put it, economic cooperation was "the one way to provide [the] only sound basis for hemisphere peace." The Truman administration, with its overwhelming focus on Cold War issues, also changed the discourse within the inter-American community. Talk and fear of international communism replaced the promotion of democratic values. Anticipating Kennan's critique of Latin American societies, U.S. diplomats lamented "the revolutionary and anti-democratic traditions embedded in the minds of Latin Americans."[16] In 1944, Nicaragua's Somoza had hesitated to push through a constitutional amendment that would perpetuate his power, fearing both domestic and U.S. reaction. In 1947, he overthrew Nicaragua's new president, who had been in office less than a month, and installed his latest puppet, because the new president tried to oust Somoza from command of the *Guardia Nacional*. The Truman administration initially withheld diplomatic recognition but ultimately relented, recognizing Somoza's anti-Communist credentials and faithful support at the United Nations.

Historians like Bethell, Roxborough, and Greg Grandin go too far, however, when they assign primary responsibility to the United States for the disintegration of democracy and social reform in the immediate postwar years.[17] As the noted scholar of Brazilian history, Thomas E. Skidmore, observed, U.S. historians have often "underestimated the power of conservative forces in Latin American societies."[18] Latin American elites fought tenaciously to retain power and privilege. In Guatemala, President Arévalo, who enacted land and labor reforms, survived twenty attempts to overthrow him between 1945 and 1951. In Venezuela, the democratic experiment, led by young leaders of the ruling Acción Democrática party or *adecos*, lasted only three years. Military officers, encouraged by aggrieved groups like wealthy landowners, overthrew President Rómulo Gallegos on 24 November 1948 in a bloodless coup, or *golpe frío*. The Truman administration had been supportive of the *adecos*, approving of their commitment to democracy and reform and their anti-Communist views. The administration lamented the November *golpe*. When it recognized the military junta in early 1949, it issued a statement deploring "the use of force as an instrument of political change."[19]

ANTICOMMUNISM AND INTERVENTIONISM

During the Truman years, U.S. policy evolved, with anticommunist fears overwhelming aspirations for democracy, social justice, and human rights. The administration initially did not worry that either the Soviet Union or the international Communist movement threatened the region. During the war, the United States assisted Latin American nations in establishing diplomatic relations with the Soviet Union, its wartime ally. In March 1945, for example, Undersecretary of State Joseph Grew permitted the Soviet ambassador to use his home in Washington so he could meet informally with Brazilian diplomats. As late as mid-1948, the State Department concluded in NSC 16 that "Communism in the Americas is a potential danger, but that, with a few possible exceptions, it is not seriously dangerous at the present time." The administration professed these views in the same year that it decided that the Soviet Union had a master plan. In NSC 7 of 30 March 1948, which anticipated NSC 68/2 of 1950, the administration warned that "the ultimate objective of Soviet-directed world communism is the domination of the world." NSC 7 called for a "world-wide counter-offensive."[20]

Through 1948, the Truman administration acknowledged that anti-Communist policies had the potential to encourage and sanction wholesale repression in the region. In 1947, the Dominican Republic of Rafael Trujillo had suggested the negotiation of an inter-American anti-Communist agreement. State Department officers knew that the Dominican dictator would use such an agreement to brand all opponents as "Communists" and outlaw, imprison, and murder them. As a policy paper put it, "there would be many cases in which such anti-Communist agreements would be directed against all political opposition, Communist or otherwise, by dictatorial governments, with the inevitable result of driving leftist elements into the hands of the Communist organization." Strong anti-Communist forces—the Church, the armed forces, large landowners—flourished in Latin America. "Unfortunately, they sometimes come close to the extreme of reaction which is very similar to Communism as concerns totalitarian police state methods." Through "extreme selfishness and lack of any sense of social responsibility," Latin American elites ignored widespread poverty and illiteracy, alienating "large segments of the population which otherwise would probably be anti-Communist." The United States needed to think hard about cooperating with reactionary forces "in light of our long-range national interests." Defeating international communism meant cultivating "anti-Communist labor, liberal, and Socialist elements."[21] The Truman administration had, of course, undercut that recommendation by denying Latin America economic development assistance.

In mid-1948, the State Department calculated that Communist party membership in the twenty Latin American republics totaled 360,000 people. Scholars have suggested a somewhat higher total membership of 500,000 Communists.[22] But Latin American Communists scarcely constituted a revolutionary vanguard. Moscow largely ignored its ideological brethren during the war and in the immediate postwar years. Mexican Communists led by the labor leader Vicente Lombardo Toledano were closely tied to Mexico's ruling party. Latin American Communists had a history of adhering to Communist theology. A revolutionary situation would not arise until Latin America entered the industrial phase of history. But only larger nations—Argentina, Brazil, Mexico—had partially industrialized. Latin American Communists proved cautious in taking up arms in the Cold War. Cuba's Communist Party did not join with Fidel Castro until after the Cuban revolutionary won power in 1959. Marxist-inspired, radical nationalists, not Communist Party members, would agitate Latin America from the 1960s on.

After 1949, the Truman administration stopped issuing nuanced analyses of Latin America's political culture and started professing deep concern about the region. Latin Americans did not suddenly embrace radical ideas. And Soviet dictator Joseph Stalin, in the last years of his rule, did not unexpectedly evince interest in Latin America. Anti-Communist fears, both abroad and at home, overwhelmed the good judgment of U.S. officials. The Soviet Union successfully tested an atomic weapon in 1949, Mao Zedong and his Communist forces established the People's Republic of China in 1949, North Korea, with tacit support from Joseph Stalin, invaded South Korea in 1950. The global balance of power seemed to be turning against the United States. At home, unscrupulous politicians, led by Senator Joseph McCarthy (R-WI) and Representative Richard M. Nixon (R-CA), alleged that traitorous Communists operated within the U.S. government. The United States dragged Latin America into the Cold War. The Kennan Corollary became U.S. policy.

The Truman administration began to criticize publicly attitudes and policies of Latin Americans. Secretary of State Acheson gave one major address on Latin America to the Pan American Union in September 1949. The speech was filled with platitudes, with Acheson conceding he had nothing new to say. The secretary did take time to remind Latin Americans that the United States would not assist the region's development with public funds. Acheson left Latin America to his young friend, Assistant Secretary Edward R. Miller, Jr. Miller, a graduate of Yale and Harvard Law School and a Wall Street lawyer, had grown up in Cuba and Puerto Rico. His father owned sugar plantations and mills in Cuba. Miller spoke excellent Spanish and Portuguese. As Miller saw it, Latin America was now a "problem of self-pity," because it wanted to ignore the Cold War and return to the 1930s, when "the Good Neighbor Policy was virtually our sole foreign policy." That experience, combined with a consequential high-level attention devoted to Latin America, "had fostered an exaggerated and extreme sense of self-importance on the part of individuals connected with Latin American governments." Miller kept such views confidential, but he authorized a subordinate, Louis Halle, to reveal them in a July 1950 article, "On a Certain Impatience with Latin America," in *Foreign Affairs.* Imitating George Kennan in the 1947 "X" article, Halle chose the pseudonym of "Y." Halle argued that the United States would have to follow the dictates of "noblesse oblige" toward Latin American nations, for they were like children, not yet ready to exercise for themselves the responsibility of adult nations.[23] Miller had requested that Acheson withdraw George Kennan's memorandum from circulation. In fact, both Acheson and Miller shared Kennan's condescending outlook toward Latin American civilization.

Assistant Secretary Miller also voiced the heightened fear and perception of international communism. Miller and his colleagues imagined threats rather than discovering them. In his 1949 speech, Acheson had noted there was no "direct threat against our independence." In 1950, in a comprehensive review of the region, the State Department concluded that the Communists had "lost ground." As late as 1951, Miller assured Congress that the Soviet Union's role in Latin America "at this time will not be great." Miller criticized the social and economic policies of Guatemala, but he reckoned that they could be blamed on President Arévalo, a "wooly-head."[24] U.S. officials also knew that by 1952 five countries had severed relations with the Soviet Union and outlawed Communist activities. For example, the Chilean legislature passed in 1948 the Law for the Permanent Defense of Democracy, which banned the Chilean Communist Party and removed all Communists from the voter rolls. The Soviets had diplomatic relations with only Argentina, Mexico, and Uruguay and only a minuscule amount of trade in the hemisphere.

The Truman administration lacked evidence of Communist subversion and it continued to realize that an inter-American, anti-Communist agreement would be used by authoritarians to "suppress all types of liberal opposition." Nonetheless, the administration decided to redefine the Monroe Doctrine and the OAS charter. In a speech in April 1950, two months before the outbreak of the Korean War, Assistant Secretary Miller reviewed the history of intervention. He condoned the decisions of presidents like Theodore Roosevelt and Woodrow Wilson, arguing that they had ordered troops into Caribbean nations to forestall European interference and perhaps colonialism—these decisions had been "necessary evils," or "protective interventions." Miller accepted the Good Neighbor policy, the juridical equality of states, but he warned that "if the circumstances that led to the protective interventions by the United States should rise again today, the organized community of American states would be faced with the responsibility that the United States had once to assume alone." The doctrine of non-intervention incorporated into the OAS charter was not absolute; if a member state were threatened by Communist political aggression, the OAS would have to act for the common welfare. This action would be "the alternative to intervention," the "corollary of non-intervention."[25]

Secretary Miller left much unsaid in his speech. He surely understood that Latin Americans considered the non-intervention pledge the core principle of the inter-American community. The thirty armed interventions in the first part of the twentieth century had outraged Latin Americans. Policy planners in the Dwight D. Eisenhower administration would confidentially concede that they would never be able to persuade Latin American states to approve intervention against internal Communist subversion. President Eisenhower approved a secret policy that the United States would take all actions "deemed appropriate" to defeat communism in the Western Hemisphere. Such actions would include covert interventions. Miller's speech represented the most explicit statement that the United States could not honor the non-intervention pledge in the Cold War, until President John F. Kennedy made similar points in his "Kennedy Doctrine" speech of 18 November 1963, his last speech on inter-American affairs. President Lyndon Johnson made the policy obvious when he invaded the Dominican Republic in 1965 and pronounced his "Johnson Doctrine." The "Miller Doctrine" was, of course, a restatement of the Roosevelt Corollary and the Kennan Corollary.[26]

The Truman administration coupled the Miller Doctrine with a decision to arm Latin America against communism. Defense planners wanted Latin America to be militarily dependent on the United States. Prior to 1941, South Americans had purchased arms and contracted military training missions from Europe, including Germany and Italy. Defense officials proposed an arms standardization for the hemisphere. The United States would provide arms if Latin America would cooperate in postwar hemispheric defense, make available its military bases to U.S. air and naval forces, and agree not to purchase equipment and training from foreign sources.

Although the Truman administration submitted to Congress in both 1946 and 1947 a military aid package for Latin America, it did not secure funding. Congressional critics managed to delay legislation, arguing that military aid was wasteful, would bolster authoritarian regimes, and would trigger a hemispheric arms race. State Department officials silently shared those concerns. In any case, the United States lacked arms to transfer, because programs such as Greek-Turkish aid, NATO, and support for Chinese national forces took priority over inter-American military cooperation.[27]

On 19 May 1950, President Truman authorized military aid for Latin America, approving NSC 56/2, "United States Policy Toward Inter-American Military Cooperation." NSC 56/2 fit into the thinking of NSC68/2, noting that "the

cold war is in fact a real war in which the survival of the free world is at stake."[28]
The document left vital issues unanalyzed. NSC 56/2 did not explain whether the
Soviet Union intended to invade Latin America or make clear how providing Latin
Americans with obsolete tanks would deter the Red Army. The document also did
not resolve the political and diplomatic questions raised by transferring arms to
poor, weak, undemocratic nations. What military aid guaranteed, however, was
access to high-ranking Latin American military officers, who traditionally favored
conservative, anti-Communist policies. For the Truman administration, such
questions seemed inconsequential after the outbreak of the Korean conflict. As it
did with NSC 68/2, the war helped "sell" NSC 56/2. In 1951 Congress authorized
$38 million for direct military assistance for Latin America, and in 1952 added
nearly $52 million to that sum.

Military aid did not inspire Latin Americans to rally to the U.S. cause. After
President Truman declared a national emergency following attacks on U.S. troops
in Korea by Chinese forces, Secretary of State Acheson hastily called an inter-
American conference of foreign ministers, which met in Washington between
March and April 1951. Six years of neglect and broken promises had taken their
toll on inter-American solidarity. For this war, Latin Americans were only willing to give "rhetorical" support to their northern neighbor. The conference's key
resolution, calling for increased production of strategic materials, was tied to a
statement citing Latin America's need for economic development. Only Colombia
responded to requests for troops, dispatching a battalion of troops and a frigate
to the Korean theatre. The United States was especially disappointed by Brazil's
refusal to join the war effort. In the previous month, Assistant Secretary Miller
had journeyed to Rio de Janeiro to request a division of troops for Korea. Latin
America's largest nation had sent an expeditionary force to Italy during World
War II. Miller received a chilly reception in Rio. As the Brazilian foreign minister observed, "Brazil's present position would be different and our cooperation
in the present emergency could be probably greater," if Washington "had elabo-
rated a recovery plan for Latin America similar to the Marshall Plan for Europe."[29]
Alarmed at the course of inter-American relations, Miller began to argue that the
United States would have to grant Latin America at least a small amount of assistance. But the administration was too harried and the economy too strained by the
Korean conflict for the United States to consider another economic aid program.

The decision by Latin American nations, save Colombia, to sit out the Korean
War signaled how far inter-American relations had deteriorated during the Truman
years. In both the United States and Latin America, the popular view had been that
hemispheric relations had been strong and cordial between 1933 and 1945. In the
1952 presidential campaign, the Republican Dwight D. Eisenhower, exploited the
issue. In a speech in New Orleans on 13 October 1952, Eisenhower charged that
Latin Americans had lost confidence in the United States. He recalled that during
World War II "we frantically wooed Latin America—but after the war the Truman
administration proceeded to forget these countries just as fast" and "terrible dis-
illusion set in throughout Latin America." The United States reneged on

promises to cooperate economically with its neighbors. The result was economic distress, "followed by popular unrest, skillfully exploited by Communist agents there." "Through drift and neglect," the Truman administration had turned a good neighbor policy into "a poor neighbor policy." Candidate Eisenhower promised change.[30]

President Eisenhower did not deliver on his campaign promise when it came to inter-American relations. Continuity, not change, would characterize the U.S. approach to Latin America. Just as it had with Europe and Asia, the Truman administration had developed Cold War policies for Latin America that would endure for four decades. The "Kennan Corollary" and the "Miller Doctrine" proved to be long-lasting features of U.S. foreign policies. Latin Americans needed to understand their place in the world. They lived in the U.S. sphere of influence. Their duty was to support the United States in the apocalyptic struggle with the international Communist movement. Any deviance by a Latin American nation from the U.S. vision of the proper world order threatened U.S. security and the global balance of power. Latin Americans often lacked the political maturity to understand how the world worked. The United States had the right and responsibility to correct the international misbehavior of Latin Americans. This meant overthrowing suspect governments and bolstering right-wing tyrants who aped U.S. foreign policies. Indeed, the Eisenhower administration took a momentous step that had far-reaching ramifications for Latin Americans and inter-American relations, when, in 1954, it destabilized a popularly elected government in Guatemala. The covert intervention was not, however, solely the initiative of President Eisenhower and the Central Intelligence Agency. True to the Kennan Corollary, the Truman administration had already begun to move against Guatemalan political and social democracy.

CHAPTER 3

Guatemala—The Mother
of Interventions

The U.S. decision in the early 1950s to destroy the constitutional government of Guatemala represented a momentous event in the history of inter-American relations. The attack on Guatemala signaled that the United States could no longer abide by the non-intervention principle—the heart of the Good Neighbor policy and the fundamental tenet of the Organization of American States. Guatemala served as a training ground for subsequent U.S. interventions in countries such as Cuba, Brazil, British Guiana, and Chile. In Guatemala, the Central Intelligence Agency would develop tactics—psychological warfare and the controlled penetration of military units, labor unions, religious organizations, student groups, and media outlets—that would be used throughout the Western Hemisphere during the Cold War. The overthrow of the Guatemalan government contributed to political polarization in the region. Latin Americans drew the lesson from the Guatemalan imbroglio that the United States would oppose fundamental change through constitutional processes. For some, violent, revolutionary upheaval became the only legitimate path to change and social justice. The intervention also had grave consequences for the people of Guatemala and the region. The intervention triggered rounds of political terror that would last four decades and leave up to two hundred thousand Guatemalans dead. Taking an approving note of the repression in Guatemala, conservative elites and their military minions in countries such as Argentina, Brazil, Chile, and El Salvador unleashed wholesale violence against their political opponents. Latin America would become the "killing zone" of the Cold War.

THE DRESS REHEARSAL

The destabilization of Guatemala is traditionally associated with the presidential administration of Dwight D. Eisenhower. Early in his administration, President Eisenhower authorized two covert interventions, Iran (1953) and Guatemala (1954), that had momentous international ramifications. The overthrow of the government of Mohammad Mossadeq (1951–53) continues to bedevil U.S. relations with Iran in the twenty-first century. In the case of Guatemala, the Eisenhower administration restarted a campaign that had been initiated by the Harry S. Truman administration. Although the Truman administration felt under siege between 1950 and 1952, both by unfavorable international developments in Asia and Europe and mounting domestic criticism, it still found time to wage Cold War in Latin America. It began to follow the dictates of the "Kennan Corollary." During its last years in office, the administration plotted against the popularly elected Guatemalan governments of President Juan José Arévalo and his successor, Jacobo Arbenz Guzmán (1951–54). The administration favored democracy and reform for Latin America. But it insisted that reform stay within U.S.-defined limits. In the context of the hysteria that permeated the early Cold War, the United States opposed any change that hinted of radicalism.

President Arévalo, a self-professed admirer of Franklin Roosevelt and the New Deal, faced as daunting challenges as did the U.S. president during the Great Depression. Arbenz assumed power in 1945, in the aftermath of his country's middle-sector uprising in October 1944 against dictator Jorge Ubico. Arévalo credited the New Deal and the idealism of Roosevelt's "Four Freedoms" as the inspiration for the October Revolution. Guatemala had problems that characterized other poor Latin America nations. A landed elite, the military, and the Roman Catholic Church had long wielded power and privilege in the Central American nation. These groups opposed change and social justice, repeatedly trying to overthrow President Arévalo and block his reform agenda. Like its neighbors, Guatemala had a fragile, agricultural economy, depending on the sale abroad of primary products, like coffee and tropical fruit, for its solvency. Any downturn in the global economy reverberated through Guatemalan society. Guatemala also had unique issues. It was a racially polarized society. About half of the population was indigenous, descendants of the ancient Mayans. They lived in the central highlands and spoke native languages. They had long suffered economic and racial discrimination at the hands of westernized, Spanish-speaking groups (Europeans and *mestizos*) known as *ladinos*. Beginning in the late nineteenth century, Guatemalan elites used their control of government machinery to steal land in the highlands area, create vast coffee plantations or *fincas*, and force indigenous people to labor on them. Terms like "serfdom," "debt peonage," even "slavery" accurately characterized the socioeconomic conditions of Guatemala's indigenous people. With their unchecked power, landowners subjected plantation workers to appalling indignities. As historian Greg Grandin noted, "plantation life rested as much on rape and sex as it did on forced labor."[1]

Guatemala's statistical profile reflected the nation's deep inequalities. Over 70 percent of the population was illiterate—the highest in Latin America. Among indigenous people, illiteracy was 90 percent. When they were paid, agricultural workers earned between five and twenty-five cents a day. The nation's per capita income was less than $200, with the landless poor earning about $70 a year. Life expectancy was less than forty years, with infant mortality rates reaching

50 percent. Despite these grim statistics, Guatemala's population was growing. International health organizations had made impressive gains controlling the historic scourges of humankind, like smallpox and malaria. Guatemala's population grew from 2.4 million in 1945 to 3 million by 1954.[2]

Change in Guatemala would inevitably have an international dimension. The United Fruit Company of Boston dominated Guatemala. The banana company had been prominent in Guatemalan life since the early twentieth century. It acquired vast tracts of land, eventually amounting to 550,000 acres, on Guatemala's Atlantic and Pacific coasts. It also controlled railroads and telephone and electrical systems. United Fruit was locally known as the "octopus" or *el pulpo*, with its tentacles reaching everywhere in Guatemalan life. The company also reinforced Guatemala's racial divisions. It initially imported Afro-Caribbean people to work the banana plantations and then instituted "Jim Crow" racial segregation on the plantations. Company executives also discriminated in pay and housing against native Guatemalans. They took care, however, to cultivate Guatemala's traditional power holders.[3] United Fruit and Guatemalan elites became predictable allies in their opposition to President Arévalo's progressive agenda. The company, landowners, the military, and the Church hierarchy could also count on the support of the region's dictators when they resisted change. Rafael Trujillo of the Dominican Republic, the Somoza family in Nicaragua, and, after 1950, Colonel Marcos Pérez Jiménez of Venezuela, all feared that democracy and social progress in Guatemala would, by example, encourage their domestic opponents and threaten their respective oligarchies. The dictators organized conspiracies against the Guatemalan government.

Freedom of association, free speech, the rights of labor, and land tenure issues became the central focus of agitation and debate in Guatemala. In the new democratic Guatemala, political life flourished, with political parties forming, including a Communist organization, Partido Guatemalteco del Trabajo (PGT). In 1952, it had five hundred members, with less than two hundred actively involved in politics. No member of the PGT had a significant position in either the Arévalo or Arbenz governments. President Arbenz was a friend, however, of José Manuel Fortuny, the leader of the PGT, and looked sympathetically on Marxist doctrines. Beginning in the late 1940s, the CIA began to monitor the travel of Guatemalan Communists and look for signs of ties with Moscow. The CIA would never find any meaningful international Communist influence in Guatemala. Nonetheless, the agency, led by Colonel J. C. King of the Western Hemisphere Division, repeatedly issued dark warnings about Communist influence in Guatemala. In the agency's view, President Arbenz's toleration for known Communists made him at best a "fellow traveler," and at worst a Communist himself. In January 1952, headquarters asked its CIA agents in Guatemala City to compile a list of "top flight Communists whom new government would desire to eliminate immediately in event of successful anti-Communist coup."[4] The anti-Communist madness known as "McCarthyism" that gripped domestic life in the United States also permeated analyses of international politics.

Guatemala's enactment in 1947 of a law that established basic labor rights and granted workers and peasants the right to organize unions proved a critical turning point in the country's relations with United Fruit and the United States. The legislation gave Guatemala's workers some of the basic rights that U.S. workers achieved during the Progressive era and the New Deal. Guatemalans began to strike on United Fruit's plantations, demanding better wages and more humane working and living conditions. Long accustomed to dictating to workers, United Fruit executives complained loud and long to the embassy in Guatemala City and the State Department. They pleaded that the company had been singled out for discriminatory legislation. In fact, the law also permitted peasants to organize on large coffee *fincas*. Company lobbyists also predictably labeled the new labor laws as "communistic." Both the embassy and the State Department reacted to United Fruit's whining. Washington pressured Guatemala by delaying Guatemala's applications for international loans and reducing the already modest economic aid program. Aid for projects in education, health, and sanitation, which amounted to $483,000 in 1948, fell to $50,000 by 1953. U.S. Ambassador Richard C. Patterson, Jr. (1948–50) embraced United Fruit's interpretation of Guatemala's reforms. In 1950 in a speech to the Rotary Club, Patterson implicitly labeled Guatemala a Communist country by pronouncing his famous "duck test." A duck wore no label identifying it as a "duck." But, Patterson observed, if the bird quacked and swam like a duck, it was probably a duck.[5] Within the framework of Cold War ethos that informed Ambassador Patterson's thinking, Guatemala passed the "duck test." Guatemala was a stooge of the Soviet Union.

The promulgation of an agrarian reform law, Decree 900, on 17 June 1952, intensified the Truman administration's hostility toward Guatemala. The nation's census of 1950 underscored the pressing need for a reform of land tenure patterns. Two percent of landowners controlled 72 percent of Guatemala's land. By contrast, 88 percent of farmers owned only 14 percent of the land. Decree 900 expropriated idle land on government and private estates and redistributed it in plots of 8 to 33 acres to peasants who would pay the government 3 to 5 percent of the assessed value annually. The government pledged to compensate the previous owners with 3 percent bonds maturing in twenty-five years. The law was an intricate and rational response to Guatemalan conditions: it left untouched, for example, estates of up to 670 acres, if at least two-thirds of the land was cultivated; moreover, as appropriate for a mountainous nation, it exempted lands that had a slope of more than thirty degrees. Decree 900 also fit squarely into past and recent international efforts to create independent farmers operating with a democratic, capitalist framework. The law, like the nineteenth-century Homestead Act of the United States, was designed to create a nation of individual landowners; the allocated land went mainly to individual families rather than to cooperatives. General Douglas MacArthur and the occupying U.S. forces in postwar Japan also encouraged land reform, believing that land-owning farmers provided a basis for a democratic society.[6]

United Fruit shrieked that Decree 900 was aimed at dismantling the company's operations in Guatemala. Because eighty-five percent of the company's land was uncultivated, the company anticipated losing four hundred thousand acres. United Fruit claimed that it needed vast reserves for crop rotation and soil conservation and as insurance against disastrous hurricanes. United Fruit further argued that the uncultivated land was worth at least $75 an acre. But, for taxable purposes, the company had declared the value of the land at only $3 an acre. The Arbenz government planned to compensate United Fruit based on what the company had been paying in property taxes. Although United Fruit, as Guatemala's largest landowner, would lose the most land under Decree 900, the law was not aimed solely at it. Government officials were also assessing the nature of the internal struggle for the future of Guatemala. Under Decree 900, Guatemala would redistribute 1.5 million acres to one hundred thousand families. The government wanted to break the hold of the landed elite on the indigenous population. Land reform would facilitate vital changes in health, education, and social welfare. Wealthy Guatemalans, military officers, and prelates of the Roman Catholic Church predictably reacted with fear and loathing to the idea of the dark-skinned, rural poor exercising power. Decree 900 even reached into the presidential palace. President Arbenz and his wealthy wife, María Vilanova Arbenz, saw the state expropriate 1,700 acres of their fallow land.[7]

For U.S. officials, the promulgation of Decree 900 did not stir memories of Thomas Jefferson's faith in the value of the independent yeoman farmer or Abraham Lincoln's commitment to the slogan of "free soil, free labor, free men." Land reform had become associated with Joseph Stalin's forced collectivization of Russian peasants or *kulaks* in the 1920s and what the "Red Chinese" were carrying out in rural China. As one CIA officer noted, Decree 900 "makes land available to all Guatemalans in the Communist pattern." Agrarian reform would weaken the landowning class, strengthening the "Communist tendencies of the present Guatemalan Government."[8] The CIA drew up a contingency plan, code-named PBFORTUNE, to overthrow President Arbenz. The CIA's instrument was Colonel Carlos Castillo Armas, former *Commandante* of Guatemala's *Escuela Militar* (Military Academy). Castillo Armas had studied military issues in the United States at Ft. Leavenworth, Kansas, and was judged "definitely pro-American" by U.S. military officers. Castillo Armas had led an unsuccessful military assault against the Guatemalan government in November 1950. The diminutive Colonel, who was 5'5" tall and weighed 135 lbs., carried the pseudonym of John H. Calligeris and the CIA's code-name of "RUFUS."[9]

RUFUS planned to lead 650 men with sufficient strength to initiate an armed revolt in Guatemala. CIA planners discussed providing Castillo Armas with $50,000 worth of arms—500 automatic rifles, 180 machine guns, 500 hand grenades, and 600,000 rounds of ammunition. Castillo Armas operated out of Managua, Nicaragua. President Anastasio Somoza García and his son, Anastasio Somoza Debayle, known as "Tachito," coordinated the operation. The Somozas pledged military and logistical support to the Guatemalan conspiracy. Rafael

Trujillo of the Dominican Republic also promised to aid Castillo Armas "with arms, aircraft, men, and money." In turn, the murderous Trujillo requested that Castillo Armas kill four anti-Trujillo Dominicans residing in Guatemala City. Castillo Armas stated that he would "be glad to carry out the executive action," pointing out "that his own plans included similar action and that special squads were being designated."[10]

Within the U.S. government, the CIA took the lead in planning and coordinating the covert operation with Castillo Armas, the Somozas, and Trujillo. The agency, which had been created by the National Security Act (1947), had seen its capacity to take action rise. Its staff of three hundred in 1949 had increased to six thousand by 1952. Allen Dulles, the deputy director of the CIA, Frank Wisner, the deputy director for plans, and Colonel King oversaw PBFORTUNE. These men would be involved in directing other covert operations in Latin America over the next decade. Beyond supplying Castillo Armas with money and advice, the CIA planned to ship contraband arms, labeled "farm machinery," from New Orleans to Nicaragua. President Truman, although not directly involved in the planning, approved of the operation. In early July 1952, he received a briefing from Colonel Cornelius J. Mara, a military aid. "Neil" Mara had discussed the operation with President Somoza. Somoza had previously boasted to Truman, during a state visit to Washington in the spring of 1952, that he could "knock off" President Arbenz, "with six hundred pieces of hardware." Mara's report convinced Truman, who immediately authorized CIA action without informing the Department of State.[11]

The CIA failed, however, to persuade everyone within the government that U.S. security required an attack against an OAS member. The Truman administration did not display the unity of purpose that characterized subsequent presidential administrations' campaigns to destabilize and overthrow targeted Latin American governments. In July 1952, Allen Dulles led a CIA delegation to the State Department, where they met with Assistant Secretary Edward Miller and Thomas Mann, the deputy assistant secretary of state. Dulles asked Miller and Mann whether they wanted a new government in Guatemala and whether they wished the "CIA to take steps to bring about a change of government." The State Department officers replied that they wanted a new government and that their office would not oppose a Guatemalan government established by force. They did not respond clearly, however, to the question of whether they wanted the CIA to participate in the overthrow of President Arbenz, although CIA officers believed that "by implication" they received a positive answer.[12] Indeed, Assistant Secretary Miller seemed determined to remove President Arbenz and save the United Fruit Company. CIA officers recalled that Miller said "that a large American company must be protected almost as strongly as the United States Government because South Americans do not make any distinction between the two in their political thinking." Two years previously, Miller had justified a policy of intervention by pronouncing his "Miller Doctrine." Nonetheless, General Walter Bedell Smith, the director of the CIA, was dissatisfied with the lack of a direct answer from Miller on the CIA's role. Director Smith called Undersecretary of State David K. E. Bruce and received a satisfactory answer on whether the State Department supported a covert intervention.[13]

Support for the intervention within the State Department waned, however, as the Truman presidency neared its end. Officers like Miller and Mann worried about the diplomatic repercussions of violating the OAS Charter. They realized that the U.S. hand could not be kept hidden. The CIA discovered that the Guatemalan government was intercepting correspondence between Castillo Armas and his agents. Moreover, the Nicaraguan and Dominican ambassadors had approached Mann to discuss the conspiracy, and "Tachito" Somoza had asked Miller about shipments of arms. These indiscretions led Colonel King of the CIA to conclude that "this confirmed our general belief that no Latin American can be trusted to keep his mouth shut." By October 1952, Miller wanted the CIA to limit itself to supplying money to Castillo Armas but not to ship arms to him. Perhaps Assistant Secretary Miller did not want to be publicly identified with undermining the basic premise of the Good Neighbor policy—the non-intervention pledge—as he left office. In any case, a CIA document of 8 October 1952 notes that "State stops the show."[14]

Robert L. Beisner, the distinguished biographer of Dean Acheson, believes that the powerful secretary of state deserves full credit for killing the 1952 conspiracy against President Arbenz. Acheson cared little about Latin America and disdained Latin American culture. Busy tending to crises and issues in other parts of the world, Acheson seems not to have been kept apprised on the ongoing conspiracy. By the fall of 1952, he had learned of Miller and Mann's apprehensions and of plans to ship arms from the United States to Castillo Armas. Beisner persuasively argues that Acheson either telephoned Truman or met with him during the first half of October 1952. No memorandum of the conversation exists. Beisner believes that Acheson probably emphasized to the president that indiscreet Latin Americans had blown the cover of the plot. But Acheson, who believed in the tenets of international law, considered the agency's plans to overthrow governments in Guatemala and Iran both illegal and "asinine." Acheson judged Europe, especially Germany, to be the central front of the Cold War. He characteristically took a hard line toward the Soviet Union over Europe, advising President John F. Kennedy to consider using nuclear weapons during the Berlin crisis of 1961. Acheson offered only withering criticism, however, of the president's decision to invade Cuba at the Bay of Pigs. Acheson thought no development in Latin America merited risking the international standing of the United States.[15] Secretary Acheson's calculation of the international balance of power combined with his dismissal of all things Latin American combined to give President Arbenz and Guatemala a reprieve from the power of the United States.

Secretary Acheson had not, however, put a permanent stop to the U.S. campaign to undermine the Guatemalan Revolution. On 10 October 1952, Colonel King informed RUFUS through an intermediary that the United States would not ship arms to him, because of the indiscrete actions of the Nicaraguans and Dominicans. But the CIA had not abandoned either Castillo Armas or its hostility toward President Arbenz. CIA Director Smith authorized $15,000 in support for Castillo Armas through 1952. The CIA station in Guatemala City continued propaganda and psychological warfare efforts, and CIA agents continued to plot with the Guatemalan military. CIA agents also organized commando groups to carry out sabotage and "to kill all political and military leaders." In a 1 December 1952 report, an agent boasted that "I have in my home a city map showing the location of the homes and offices of all targets."[16] The implementation of this violence would have to await the inauguration of a new presidential administration in Washington.

OPERATION PBSUCCESS

The Eisenhower administration would wage a foreign policy of relentless anti-communism in Guatemala and throughout the region during the 1950s. During the 1952 presidential campaign, Republicans denounced the Truman administration for losing Eastern Europe and China to communism and pledged to roll back Communist advances, liberate captive peoples, and win the Cold War. Turning rhetoric into reality presented, however, complex, dangerous problems. Confronting the Soviet Union over its empire in Eastern Europe could precipitate World War III and the destruction of Eastern Europe in a nuclear exchange. Clashes with troops from the People's Republic of China in Korea had led to major U.S. casualties. Indeed, General Eisenhower had suggested during the campaign that he would find a solution to the military stalemate in Korea. But rolling back communism in Latin America posed little risk of global conflict and would help the administration make good on its claim that it was fulfilling its campaign pledge to wage vigorous Cold War.

Less than two months into office, the Eisenhower administration had its basic approach to Latin America outlined, adopting NSC 144/1. NSC 144/1 interpreted inter-American affairs solely within the context of the global struggle with the Soviet Union. The document had little to say about political and social democracy or human rights in Latin America. What the United States wanted was for Latin America to support the U.S. position at the United Nations, eliminate the "menace of internal Communist or other anti-U.S. subversion," produce strategic raw materials, and cooperate in defending the hemisphere. President Eisenhower approved NSC 144/1, after having previously heard an alarming briefing from his new director of the CIA, Allen Dulles. Dulles warned that the political and economic situation was deteriorating in Latin America and that "the Kremlin was exploiting the situation." In particular, Dulles warned that "Communist infection" in Guatemala was "such to mark an approaching crisis."[17]

The National Security Council staff study that served as the basis for NSC 144/1 took the same haughty attitude toward Latin America that informed George Kennan's 1950 report. The study claimed that the region was filled with social democrats, "immature and impractical idealists," who "not only are inadequately trained to conduct government business efficiently but also lack the disposition to combat extremists within their ranks, including communists." Latin American reformers weakened respect for property rights, a pillar of capitalism and anticommunism, by advocating the expropriation of haciendas and plantations without adequate compensation. Latin American leaders also ignored their international responsibilities, failing to grasp the aggressive, expansionist nature of the Soviet Union. The staff study predicted that the majority of Latin American nations would oppose a multilateral intervention to rescue a Latin American nation from communism. It therefore concluded that "overriding security interests" required the United States to consider acting unilaterally, recognizing that "this would be a violation of our treaty commitments, would endanger the Organization of American States...and would probably intensify anti-U.S. attitudes."[18]

The adoption of NSC 144/1 signaled that the CIA could resume its campaign to overthrow President Arbenz of Guatemala. On 8 March 1953, CIA Director Dulles informed colleagues "we now expect to be in a position to proceed with our phase of the project if desired."[19] The transition had been seamless. Allen Dulles's brother, John Foster Dulles, was now secretary of state. His former boss at the CIA, Walter Bedell Smith, was undersecretary of state. Smith agreed that the conspirators would not repeat the mistake of the past by seeking the approval of State Department officers. The CIA would confine its consultations to Secretary Dulles and Undersecretary Smith. Indeed, Louis Halle of the State Department's Latin American Division would prepare a lengthy memorandum in 1954 challenging the premise that communism and the Soviet Union underlay Guatemala's October 1944 revolution and President Arbenz's land reform policies. As a State Department study had earlier noted, the overthrow of President Arbenz would represent "a Czechoslovakia in reverse."[20] The United States would be acting like an imperial power, much as the Soviet Union did in Eastern Europe in the immediate postwar years.

On 12 August 1953, Eisenhower's NSC authorized the overthrow of President Arbenz. The CIA was given principal responsibility for the intervention, under the supervisory direction of Colonel King. PBFORTUNE was renamed PBSUCCESS and granted an initial budget of $3 million. Overthrowing Arbenz was "now the number one priority in the Agency." The administration sent a new ambassador, John E. Peurifoy, to Guatemala City to coordinate with the CIA. Allen Dulles thought the incumbent ambassador, Rudolf E. Schoenfeld, "timid" and insufficiently forceful in defending U.S. interests. Dulles recommended a "two-fisted guy" for the country. Peurifoy, who was an admirer of Senator Joseph McCarthy, fit the bill. He had served from 1950 to 1953 as U.S. ambassador in Greece and organized an anti-Communist government that included the Greek royal family. On 1 September 1953 Frank Wisner of the CIA briefed Peurifoy that "this Agency has now been authorized to take strong action against the government of President Arbenz in the hope of facilitating a change to a more democratically oriented regime." Peurifoy pledged to support the program, requesting only that the CIA send to Guatemala City a "Chief" who was fluent in Spanish.[21]

Analysts have pointed to the ties that the Dulles brothers and other administration officials had to United Fruit to explain the launching of PBSUCCESS.

John Foster Dulles, for example, was an international lawyer whose law firm, Sullivan and Cromwell, represented United Fruit.[22] But U.S. concerns about Guatemala transcended United Fruit's objections over the labor law of 1947 and Decree 900. In the context of the Cold War, the United States persuaded itself that such reforms constituted a Communist menace. One study noted that land reform would break the power of the conservative, anti-Arbenz landowners and would "furnish a basis for the strengthening of political and Communist control over the rural population." Secretary Dulles spoke truthfully from his perspective when he told journalists that "if the United Fruit matter were settled, if they gave a gold piece for every banana, the problem would remain just as it is today as far as the presence of Communist infiltration in Guatemala is concerned." At an NSC meeting, Dulles urged the Justice Department to file a long-pending antitrust suit against United Fruit, because "many of the Central American countries were convinced that the sole objective of United States foreign policy was to protect the fruit company."[23]

Finding hard evidence to sustain U.S. fears about communism in Guatemala continued to prove problematic. A State Department intelligence study reported on 1 January 1953 that the Guatemalan Communist Party, the PGT, had between 500 and 1,000 members. But the study could find no Guatemalan connections with the Soviet Union, other than to raise the "guilt by association" charge, noting that Guatemalans toured Soviet bloc countries and attended international meetings that Communists attended. The Soviet Union did not have diplomatic representation in Guatemala. As late as 21 April 1954, less than two months before the covert intervention, the CIA, in a paper prepared at PBSUCCESS headquarters in Florida, could not cite any direct contact between Guatemalan Communists and Moscow. The paper offered ideology, not facts, when it reasoned that "all Communist Parties, acting under the direction of the Soviet Union, follow the same general pattern in seeking to capture free social institutions and democratic governments."[24] After the overthrow of President Arbenz, the CIA initiated Operation PBHISTORY to find "the mass of documentation which undoubtedly exists in Guatemala attesting to activities and workings [of] international communism there." The PBHISTORY team subsequently reviewed 500,000 documents in the Foreign Ministry and the PGT archives and "masses of Communist propaganda, books, leaflets, and magazines." The history team conceded in a summary report of 28 September 1954 that it found "very few" documents that could be characterized as "Communist damaging." The best the team apparently could do was to find invoices totaling $22.95 that revealed the PGT had purchased books from a Moscow bookstore.[25]

Ambassador Peurifoy arrived in Guatemala City in October 1953 and had a "frank" six-hour discussion with President Arbenz on 17 December 1953 at Arbenz's home. Arbenz and his wife, María Christina, entertained the ambassador and his wife at dinner. Peurifoy pressed the president about Communist influence in the government. Arbenz freely and happily admitted his friendship with prominent Communists, like José Manuel Fortuny and Víctor Manuel Gutiérrez. In Arbenz's judgment the two Communist leaders were "honest" and followed Guatemalan, not Soviet, interests. Arbenz even contradicted his wife who denied that party members participated in government organizations. Arbenz emphasized that Communists in the government were "local." Ambassador Peurifoy rejected the president's effort to depict Guatemalan Communists as nationalists. Reprising Ambassador Patterson's "duck test" of 1950, the ambassador informed Washington that "I came away definitely convinced that if President is not a Communist he will certainly do until one comes along, and that normal approaches will not work in Guatemala."[26]

Scholars have debated what beliefs informed President Arbenz's public policies. The president, who was in his late 30s, was a striking, athletic, career military officer who came from a middle-class background. His father had been a pharmacist. A graduate of Guatemala's military academy, Arbenz participated in the overthrow of Ubico and served as minister of defense under President Arévalo. In the 1950 presidential campaign, Arbenz garnered 60 percent of the vote, defeating two conservative candidates. Arbenz's wife, María Christina Vilanova, was the daughter of a wealthy plantation owner from El Salvador. Appalled at the treatment of the rural poor in El Salvador, María Christina resigned her role as a member of high society and committed herself to social activism. In her beauty, concern for the poor, and influence with her husband, she reminded many of Eva Perón of Argentina.

Three decades after Arbenz's overthrow, Piero Gleijeses, a superb scholar, interviewed María Christina and Guatemalan Communists such as Fortuny. They alleged that President Arbenz read widely in the history of Marxism and the Soviet Union and accepted Marxist views on the sweep of history. In María Christina's words, "Jacobo was convinced that the triumph of communism in the world was inevitable and desirable. The march of history was toward communism. Capitalism was doomed."[27] After his overthrow, Arbenz joined the PGT in 1957 and spent time in Fidel Castro's Cuba in the 1960s. Arbenz disliked life in Communist Cuba. The distraught Arbenz, who spent the rest of his life in exile, drowned in his bathtub in Mexico in early 1971. President Arbenz never wrote a memoir or gave extensive interviews outlining his political views.

Whatever the merits of the claim that President Arbenz had secretly converted to communism, Decree 900 was not intended to collectivize agriculture in Guatemala. Arbenz's relatives and colleagues pointed out to Gleijeses that Guatemala was still in a feudal stage of development, and, under Marxist theories, that Guatemala would have to pass through a capitalist phase. Agrarian reform in Guatemala indeed followed the models favored by Jefferson and Lincoln and advocated by President John F. Kennedy in the 1960s with his Alliance for Progress program for Latin America. By redistributing land, the Arbenz administration also sought to break the hold of the oligarchy on Guatemala's dispossessed, rural poor. President Arbenz's colleagues further affirmed that the president spoke forthrightly when he assured Ambassador Peurifoy that Guatemalans thought and acted "local" and did not consult with Moscow.

The Eisenhower administration believed that they found hard evidence and that they had reaped a propaganda bonanza, when, on 15 May 1954, a Swedish freighter, the *Alfhem*, docked at Puerto Barrios, Guatemala, with a shipment of arms from Czechoslovakia. The CIA learned that the Bank of Guatemala had transferred $4.8 million to a Czech firm. But the purchase hardly proved that Guatemala had joined the Communist camp. The Soviet client state had not granted arms to Guatemala; it had sold them on a "cash and carry" basis. Moreover, the Eisenhower administration had reports of Guatemalan officials trying to purchase arms in Western Europe.[28] The arms purchase reflected the Arbenz administration's accurate assessment that the country would soon be invaded. The United States had also imposed an arms embargo on Guatemala. In the end U.S. officials had to fall back on ideological convictions to justify the intervention in Guatemala. In May 1954, Secretary of State Dulles admitted to a Brazilian official that it would be "impossible to produce evidence clearly tying the Guatemalan Government to Moscow; that the decision must be a political one and based on our deep conviction that such a tie must exist."[29]

THE INVASION

The CIA's plan to overthrow President Arbenz consisted of three major components: a psychological warfare operation; an invasion of the country led by Colonel Castillo Armas; and a campaign to coerce Guatemalan military officers into striking against their president. In Guatemala, the CIA developed the techniques of "controlled penetration," infiltrating student, labor, church, women's, business, and media groups and inciting them to oppose the regime through strikes and demonstrations. Controlled penetration would be repeatedly used to destabilize regimes throughout Latin America over the next three decades. For example, CIA agent E. Howard Hunt worked with Archbishop Mariano Rossell Arellano of Guatemala City. The archbishop issued a vitriolic anti-Arbenz pastoral letter, and CIA pilots dropped thousands of copies of the letter throughout the countryside. In doing so, Archbishop Rossell and Hunt ignored the advice of the papal nuncio in Guatemala, representing the Pope Pius XII in Rome. The papacy did not think that Decree 900 threatened the Roman Catholic Church.[30]

The CIA's unsparing effort to vilify the Arbenz government and generate panic in Guatemala often took on ludicrous tones. The agency distributed thirty thousand anti-Communist comic books. It used the famous broadcast, *The War of the Worlds* (1938) by Orson Welles as a model for spreading propaganda via the radio. U.S. citizens who listened to the broadcast wondered whether the Martians were invading the homeland. In Guatemala's case, the leader of the Martians was Colonel Castillo Armas. The CIA station, *La Voz de la Liberación*, told Guatemalans that Castillo Armas led a massive army of crack troops. CIA broadcasters also disseminated "black propaganda," informing military officers that Arbenz had concluded a secret pact with the Soviet Union that would lead to "the bolshevization of army," complete with political commissars and a Red Army indoctrination team. All boys and girls of sixteen years of age allegedly would be sent to special camps for one year of labor duty and political training so as to break the influence of the church and family on young people. When, in January 1954, the Arbenz government exposed key elements of PBSUCCESS, operational headquarters recommended responding by fabricating a "big human interest story, like flying saucers, birth of sextuplets in remote area to take play away."[31]

A sense of irony and self-awareness did not characterize CIA officials and operatives. CIA officers justified destroying a popularly elected government by reasoning that democracy was an "unrealistic" alternative for Guatemala. One case officer opined that "premature extension of democratic privileges and responsibilities to a people still accustomed to patriarchal methods can only be harmful." When Arbenz exposed parts of the conspiracy, a CIA officer rallied agents in the field by reminding them that "the morale of the Nazis in the winter of 1932, just before the seizure of power in Spring 1933, was at all time low ebb."[32] The CIA not only thoughtlessly compared themselves to Nazis but also replicated tactics employed by the Nazis in the 1930s. Before invading Poland in 1939, Nazi Germany created a pretext for the invasion by putting German prisoners in uniform, murdering them, dumping the bodies along the Polish border, and blaming Poland for the crime. In "Operation Washtub," the CIA planted arms along the Nicaragua's Pacific coast and charged Guatemala with aggression against its neighbor. The always cooperative President Somoza also reported that a Soviet submarine surfaced off Nicaragua's coast.[33] Fabricating evidence, especially planting arms, would be a regular tactic used by the CIA in Latin America during the Cold War.

The CIA had great difficulties organizing an army to invade Guatemala and spark a popular rebellion. Castillo Armas organized his forces in Nicaragua and "invaded" Guatemala from Honduras on 18 June 1954. The Guatemalan colonel led a ragtag army of 480 men, divided into four groups. The diminutive Castillo Armas crossed the border dressed in a leather jacket and checked shirt and driving a battered station wagon. He was photographed with a pistol stuck in the middle of his waistband, pointing downward. In the preceding months, the CIA had grown frustrated with the Guatemalan colonel. It inquired about what happened to some of the money it had passed to him. The CIA considered intelligence and propaganda to be its purview and accused Castillo Arms of violating previous agreements. It also alleged that the colonel breached secrecy by not confining his communications to secure channels. Operational headquarters in Florida actually suggested that Castillo Armas be administered a polygraph or "lie-detector" test or in CIA lingo an "LCFLUTTER." In mid-May, a month before the invasion, a CIA analyst offered a devastating assessment of "Calligeris." The Colonel lacked military aptitude, was stubborn, and judged colleagues by their loyalty to him rather than on their military skills. Castillo Armas also had no military support within the country.[34] These critiques proved accurate. Castillo Armas's "shock troops" were no match for Guatemala's six-thousand-strong regular army. By 21 June, Guatemalan forces had soundly defeated the rebel forces in two encounters. Three days after it started, the invasion was effectively over. *La Voz de la Liberación* continued to

Colonel Carlos Castillo Armas (in middle) waves to his followers during the "invasion" of Guatemala in June 1954. The army of Castillo Armas did little actual fighting in the movement to overthrow the government. The CIA managed to create an atmosphere of crisis within the country and persuaded senior Guatemalan military officers to strike against President Jacobo Arbenz. CIA officers privately questioned the political skills, military abilities, and honesty of Castillo Armas. The position of the presumably loaded pistol in Castillo Armas's belt would lend credence to the doubts that CIA officers held about the colonel's competence. (Corbis Images)

announce rebel victories. Nonetheless, a sense of despair, even panic, permeated CIA headquarters and the U.S. embassy in Guatemala City.

The CIA and Ambassador Peurifoy had correctly estimated, however, that the key to victory was not in relying on Castillo Armas's fighting spirit but in undermining the loyalty of military officers to President Arbenz. The initial CIA plan of September 1953 for destabilizing Guatemala observed "that the army is the only organized element in Guatemala capable of rapidly and decisively altering the political situation." It lamented that the army high command remained loyal to the president and the constitution. In late December 1953, Peurifoy agreed that the United States needed to "select the Guatemalan Armed Forces as the primary area in which any effort to stimulate anti-government action is most likely to be fruitful."[35] The Eisenhower administration accordingly applied all manners of pressure on Guatemalan officers. It cut off U.S. arms shipments to Guatemala and rewarded neighboring Central American nations with new military assistance pacts. U.S. diplomatic and military officials and the CIA intensified daily contacts with Guatemalan officers and worked on passing "on to them selected statements and observations best calculated to weaken the morale and the shake the faith of the Guatemalan armed forces in the present Guatemalan regime." The CIA's disinformation or "black propaganda" campaign included warning officers that their personal and professional lives would be jeopardized by President Arbenz's drive to transform the nation "into the beachhead of international communism in the Western Hemisphere." By late April 1954, the CIA had identified key military leaders who it believed would turn against Arbenz, including Minister of Defense José Angel Sánchez and Chief of the Armed Forces Colonel Carlos Enrique Díaz.[36]

The Guatemalan military overthrew President Arbenz on 27 June 1954. Military officers apparently concluded that the United States would not permit them to destroy the army of Castillo Armas and that U.S. marines would soon be on the shores of Guatemala. This fear had been reinforced by President Eisenhower's decision to permit the CIA to have U.S. pilots stationed in Nicaragua drop bombs on Guatemala City. The CIA took care, however, not to bomb Guatemalan forces or installations, fearing that would turn the military against Castillo Armas. Beyond fearing a U.S. invasion, Guatemalan officers may have also acted out of ideological concerns. Military officers were *ladinos* and had traditionally sided with landowners and the church. Many resented the growing empowerment of Mayan Indians and the pace and direction of change in the Guatemalan countryside. Raw ambition and greed also informed the high command's decision to undermine the constitution. CIA analysts had counted on military officers being "opportunistic." One CIA agent had $10,000 a month in bribes to proffer and bought the loyalty of Colonel Elfego Monzón, a minister without portfolio.[37]

The Guatemalan military did not initially embrace the CIA's man, "RUFUS," as the savior of Guatemala. Colonel Díaz seized power on the evening of 27 June in the name of the October 1944 Revolution. His action reflected the widespread disdain that military officers had for Castillo Armas. The CIA station chief explained to Díaz, "Colonel, you are not convenient for American foreign policy." Authorized by Secretary of State Dulles to "crack some heads together," Ambassador Peurifoy faced down five Guatemalan military juntas.[38] On 1 September 1954, the ambassador announced a settlement with officers that left Castillo Armas the president of a military junta. Castillo Armas ruled Guatemala until 26 July 1957, when he was assassinated by a palace guard. The guard was found dead a short time later.

THE LESSONS OF GUATEMALA

The CIA intervention in Guatemala taught different historical lessons. President Eisenhower was immensely pleased that his bold policy had triumphed. The Truman administration had "lost" Eastern Europe and China. The president could now claim that with the successful covert interventions in Iran and Guatemala he was rolling back the Communist tide. Eisenhower pointed to Guatemala with pride during the 1956 presidential campaign. The president had a grand reception in the White House for CIA agents. He joshed with them, wondering why they had let Arbenz escape. And he shook everyone's hand, ending with CIA Director Dulles and said, "Thanks Allen, and thanks to all of you. You've averted a Soviet beachhead in our hemisphere."[39]

The overthrow of Arbenz reinforced the administration's inclination to ignore the non-intervention principle, disdain Latin American reformers, and bolster anti-Communist dictators. In subsequent NSC policy statements on Latin America, the administration included the statement that the United States would take all actions "deemed appropriate" to sever ties between any Latin American nation and the Communist bloc. The administration maintained warm relations with the dictators of the Caribbean basin—the Somoza family, Rafael Trujillo, and Fulgencio Batista of Cuba. In 1955, in a toast to Batista in Havana, Vice President Richard M. Nixon compared the Cuban dictator to Abraham Lincoln. After Nixon returned to the United States, he reported that "Latinos had shown a preference for a dictatorial form of government rather than a democracy." President Eisenhower awarded the Legion of Merit, the nation's highest award for foreign personages, to Manuel Odría (1948–56), the military dictator of Peru, and Colonel Marcos Pérez Jiménez (1952–58), the strongman of Venezuela. Both tyrants earned Washington's gratitude by dutifully following the anti-Communist line. Both President Eisenhower and Secretary of State Dulles told subordinates they preferred Latin American democrats, but their policies belied their words. As John Dreier, the U.S. ambassador to the OAS, observed, Secretary Dulles "was inclined to feel that governments which contributed to a stability in the area were preferable to those which introduced instability and social upheaval, which would lead to Communist penetration." Dulles, therefore, was "very tolerant" of dictatorships "as long as they took a firm stand against communism."[40]

The CIA emerged from PBSUCCESS brimming with confidence. The overthrow of Arbenz seemed to validate the tactics of covert intervention. In the thrill of victory, CIA officials would forget, however, that part of their plan—the "invasion" of Guatemala by Castillo Armas—had failed miserably. The disastrous Bay of Pigs invasion of Cuba in April 1961 would be patterned on the Guatemalan intervention. Nonetheless, the tactics of "controlled penetration" and psychological warfare worked effectively in subsequent destabilization campaigns in Brazil, British Guiana, and Chile. In the aftermath of the successful interventions in Iran and Guatemala, President Eisenhower commissioned his friend, General Jimmy Doolittle, to oversee a commission that assessed the CIA's capabilities of covert intervention. In October 1954, the Doolittle Commission reported to Eisenhower that winning the Cold War demanded that the United States have "an aggressive covert psychological, political, and paramilitary organization more effective, more unique, and, if necessary, more ruthless than that employed by the enemy." Revisiting the language of NSC 68/2, the Doolittle Commission warned that the United States faced "an implacable enemy whose avowed objective is world domination by whatever means and by whatever cost." "No rules" applied in this struggle. "Hitherto acceptable norms of human conduct do not apply." In order to survive, the United States would have to reconsider "long-standing American concepts of 'fair play.'"[41] This philosophy would permeate CIA activities—assassination, terrorism, and sabotage—in Latin America throughout the Cold War.

The CIA intervention in Guatemala also had a dramatic impact on the thinking of Latin Americans. The dictatorships predictably acquiesced in the *golpe de estado*. But Latin American intellectuals and politicians immediately understood that the United States had discarded the non-intervention principle. Legislators in Argentina, Chile, and Uruguay passed resolutions either supporting President Arbenz or condemning U.S. "aggression" in Guatemala. Student and labor groups in countries such as Bolivia, Cuba, Ecuador, and Mexico demonstrated against the intervention and issued statements of protest. In the urbane, placid city of Santiago, Chile, students, dressed in coats and ties, burned the U.S. flag in Plaza de Armas, the central plaza. Chilean protestors also burned President Eisenhower in effigy. The poet and future Nobel Laureate, Pablo Neruda, and Eduardo Frei Montalva, the future president of Chile, led a mass march on 24 June 1954 through the streets of Santiago in support of President Arbenz.[42]

Latin American leftists drew bitter, hard lessons from the U.S. intervention. Among the leaders of the march in Santiago was Salvador Allende Gossens, the Chilean socialist. Allende had spoken favorably about how President Roosevelt had transformed U.S. foreign policy, and in the early 1950s, U.S. diplomatic officials had welcomed Allende's entry into Chilean electoral politics. U.S. diplomats judged Allende to be an effective counter to authoritarian Chilean politicians. But the CIA intervention soured Allende on the United States. His prominent defense of President Arbenz helped make Allende a national leader. He thereafter took a trip to the Soviet Union and published an article in *Pravda*, the Soviet newspaper, noting that Chileans had "learned the methods of reactionary forces from the experience of Guatemala." U.S. officials thereafter considered Allende a foe of the United States. Allende nearly won the Chilean presidency in 1958, losing by only thirty thousand votes. At a campaign rally of over sixty-five thousand supporters, Allende declared that the U.S. State Department pursued policies that were "odious and anti-popular."[43]

Ernesto "Che" Guevara, the young Argentine medical doctor, witnessed the CIA intervention. During his years as a medical student, Guevara had engaged in a life-changing experience in 1951–1952, touring South American on a motorcycle with a friend. His journey was immortalized in the posthumously published travelogue, *The Motorcycle Diaries* (1993) and subsequent feature film (2004) of the same title. Guevara, who grew up in comfort in Buenos Aires, encountered poverty and injustice, working in a leper colony in Peru and meeting impoverished Chilean copper workers. After passing his medical examinations in 1953, Guevara left Buenos Aires, announcing to relatives that his destiny was to be "a soldier of the Americas." Guevara eventually made it to revolutionary Guatemala, where he studied Marxism intensively with other young Latin American intellectuals and avant-garde artists who had congregated in Guatemala City. Guevara met Cuban rebels who, with Fidel Castro, had tried to overthrow Fulgencio Batista in 1953.

He also studied and fell in love with the Peruvian economist, Hilda Gadea, who became his first wife. Guevara criticized President Arbenz for not destroying his rightist opposition and not arming his supporters. After the *golpe*, Guevara fled to the Argentine embassy and escaped Guatemala. Guevara took three lessons from the overthrow of President Arbenz. In order to defend a socioeconomic change, revolutionaries had to destroy the old army and build a new people's army loyal to the revolution. A government should give peasants and workers the means to defend a revolution by arming them. Finally, Latin American revolutionaries should anticipate the United States sponsoring a counterrevolution.[44] Guevara would apply these lessons in combating domestic and international opposition to the Cuban Revolution.

GUATEMALA IN BLOOD

Whereas U.S. officials and Latin American leaders debated the meaning of the CIA intervention, Guatemalans suffered the consequences of the *golpe*. Greg Grandin, a historian of the rural savagery in Guatemala, estimates that the military, police, and vigilante groups murdered between three thousand and five thousand supporters of Arbenz in the immediate months after the overthrow.[45] Throughout its planning, the CIA discussed assassination with Castillo Armas and compiled a list, labeled a "disposal list," of Guatemalans to be executed. One agent waxed literary about assassination, noting on 1 June 1954 that "no real analysis has been made to date to determine who is 'to be' or 'not to be.'" A CIA research paper, "A Study in Assassination," discussed the advantages and disadvantages of killing tools and methods, including employing firearms, explosives, blunt and edged weapons, and manual techniques. Much of the killing took place in the countryside, where the landed oligarchs took their vengeance on peasants who had gained land and power from Decree 900. On a United Fruit plantation, more than one thousand rural organizers were taken into custody and murdered. In the banana town of Morales, a United Fruit foreman, Rosendo Pérez, fired his machine gun into the face of an Afro-Guatemalan union organizer and then executed more than twenty other captured union organizers.[46]

"Communist" became a term loosely applied in post-Arbenz Guatemala under a new law, "the Preventive and Penal Law against Communism." The CIA helped the Castillo Armas's regime compile a register of those who allegedly participated in Communist activities. By November 1954, the list included over seventy-two thousand names. In essence, Guatemalans who had publicly identified with the October Revolution were dubbed criminals. Castillo Armas appointed José Bernabé Linares to be the new director of the *Guardia Judicial*, the same post Linares held under dictator Jorge Ubico. Linares had established a reputation for torturing those in custody with electric-shock baths and head-shrinking steel skullcaps. A Guatemalan official boasted to a U.S. embassy officer that with the new anti-Communist law, which suspended the writ of *habeas corpus*, "we can pick up practically anybody we want and hold them as long as we want."[47]

Vice President Richard M. Nixon poses in 1955 with Colonel Carlos Castillo Armas of Guatemala in this attempt to justify the overthrow of the constitutional government of President Jacobo Arbenz. After the ouster of Arbenz in 1954, the Dwight Eisenhower administration dispatched a team of investigators to Guatemala City to try to discover evidence of ties between Guatemala and the Soviet Union. The best that investigators could find was some literature that was allegedly "Communist." (Corbis Images)

Beyond suppressing political dissent, Castillo Armas focused his counter-revolution on crushing peasants and workers, the beneficiaries of the October Revolution. The franchise was again limited to literate Guatemalans, effectively disenfranchising the indigenous population. Decree 900 had benefited one hundred thousand families or about five hundred thousand people. Castillo Armas dispossessed the *campesinos*, returning the land to United Fruit and the rural oligarchy. Castillo Armas instituted a U.S.-designed land resettlement program, but it assisted only about twenty-five thousand Guatemalans. By 1956, the U.S. trade union, the American Federation of Labor (AFL), which had supported the overthrow of Arbenz, was reporting that agricultural workers were "in conditions of servitude if not actual slavery," working eighty-four hours a week and earning fifty cents a day. The AFL was further appalled by the regime's labor policies. It repealed the 1947 labor law, abolished collective bargaining rights, and predictably labeled trade union activity as "communism."[48]

The Eisenhower administration pledged to foster a democratic, modern Guatemala. As Secretary of States Dulles observed, "it was important that an example be given to the free world of the success of a people in recovering after Communist rule." The administration dedicated over $100 million in economic assistance, accounting for 15 percent of U.S. grant aid to Latin America in the 1950s. U.S. political officers, economic technicians, military advisors, and trade union officials trooped to Guatemala, proffering advice and money. As an historian of the counterrevolution noted, the United States nearly established a "parallel government" in Guatemala from 1954 to 1961.[49] But the parallel government did not produce a peaceful, prosperous, or socially just nation. Castillo Armas and his successor, the archconservative General Miguel Ydígoras Fuentes (1958–63), restored the traditional arbiters of Guatemalan life—upper-class *ladinos*, landed interests, the Church hierarchy, and the military—to their accustomed positions of privilege and power. Guatemalan leaders understood that U.S. officials would overlook financial corruption and political repression as long as they trumpeted anti-Communist views and respected U.S. investments. President Ydígoras permitted the CIA to train Cubans on Guatemalan soil in 1960–1961 in preparation for the Bay of Pigs invasion. The renewed injustice in Guatemala troubled even CIA agents. David Phillips, who directed *La Voz de la Liberación*, condemned Castillo Armas as "a bad president, tolerating corruption throughout his government and kowtowing to United Fruit Company more than to his own people."[50]

By the mid-1960s, Guatemala had descended into a hell of violence, torture, and death that lasted three decades. By the 1990s, perhaps two hundred thousand Guatemalans had perished; more than 90 percent of these deaths came at the hands of the military or their grisly allies, paramilitary groups and right-wing death squads with names like *Mano Blanca* ("White Hand") and *Ojo por Ojo* ("Eye for an Eye"). Perhaps another two hundred thousand Guatemalans fled the terror, running away first to Mexico and then sometimes to the United States. The CIA intervention in 1954 had effectively removed Guatemala's non-violent, political center. Within the context of both Latin American and U.S. history, the labor and land reforms pursued by Presidents Arévalo and Arbenz were moderate and aimed at redressing Guatemala's centuries of socioeconomic injustice. After 1954, Guatemalans demonized one another, confronting their political opponents with horrifying aggression. Richard H. Immerman, one of the first chroniclers of the CIA intervention, concluded in 1982 that "the CIA's 1954 coup made moderation impossible." In 1999, Guatemala's "Truth Commission," The Commission for Historical Clarification (Comisión para el Esclarecimiento Histórico), seconded Immerman's conclusion in its twelve-volume study of Guatemala's agony from 1954 to 1996. The commission, which was sponsored by the United Nations, observed that "after the overthrow of Colonel Jacobo Arbenz in 1954, there was a rapid reduction of the opportunity for political expressions." Thereafter, "fundamentalist anti-communism" led to the outlawing of "the extensive and diverse social movement and consolidated the restrictive and exclusionary nature of the political system."[51]

After the initial bloodletting in the months after Arbenz's overthrow, the Castillo Armas and Ydígoras regimes suppressed strikes and demonstrations against the loss of land and labor rights with selective brutality. Guatemalan governments resorted to wholesale, indiscriminate violence, after the political left resorted to guerrilla warfare. On 13 November 1960, young, nationalistic military officers, in the MR-13 Rebellion, rose in a rebellion against Ydígoras. The officers protested both the government's corruption and the CIA's use of Guatemala as a training base for Cuban exiles. Deciding immediately that Fidel Castro was behind the rebellion, President Eisenhower authorized the CIA's B-26 bombers already stationed in Guatemala to bomb and strafe the rebels. Eisenhower repeated the same mistake of 1954—wrongly assuming that international Communists had infiltrated Guatemala. Within a few days, the government broke the military rebellion. But some young officers continued the fight, deciding that they would have to enlist workers and peasants to their cause if they wanted to restore Guatemala's sovereignty and end its debasement.[52] Guatemalan Communists who had survived the *golpe* of 1954 and others who believed in the ideals of the October Revolution also decided to take up arms, proclaiming that peaceful and legal forms of political struggle were not possible in Guatemala. Young radicals, who were inspired by the Cuban Revolution, also joined the fight, forming the *Fuerzas Armadas Rebeldes* (Armed Rebel Forces). By the mid-1960s, several hundred guerrillas operated in Guatemala.

The John F. Kennedy and Lyndon Johnson administration intensified Guatemala's agony. The United States wanted democracy and peaceful evolutionary progress but raised the alarm when Ydígoras announced that he would permit an open presidential election in 1963. Former President Arévalo vowed to return to Guatemala and compete in the election. Arévalo had denounced the 1954 intervention in his scathing allegory, *The Shark and the Sardines* (1956). He had a good chance of winning in a multi-candidate election, because he represented the progressive hopes of the past. The Kennedy administration flatly opposed Arévalo's return to office. In a meeting, President Kennedy warned Ydígoras that Arévalo "would undoubtedly campaign as an anti-Communist moderate, but he would be dangerous if he won [the] election." Colonel King of the CIA also called on Ydígoras. In a meeting with the Guatemalan foreign minister, Secretary of State Dean Rusk referred to the "Arévalo menace." When the Guatemalan president inexplicably resisted U.S. pressure, the Kennedy administration encouraged a military *golpe*. On 31 March 1963, Colonel Enrique Peralta Azurdia (1963–66) seized power. The U.S. ambassador in Guatemala City reported that Colonel Peralta and his men acted "from an honest conviction that such action was required to protect the country from a succession of events which would once again lead it into Communist control."[53] In 1966, the Guatemalan military scheduled a free election, and a non-Communist liberal, Julio César Méndez Montenegro (1966–70), won. Méndez Montenegro, who was Guatemala's last civilian president for sixteen years, was allowed to take office by the military only after he signed a statement relinquishing civilian oversight of the military and giving it *carte blanche* in internal security matters.

Beyond encouraging military domination of Guatemala, the Kennedy and Johnson administrations bolstered the nation's coercive forces. In September 1961, President Kennedy approved military assistance for Guatemala, accepting a finding that it was among the "prime targets" for Communist subversion. Between 1961 and 1963, the administration sent $4.3 million in military aid, as compared to the $950,000 in military aid that the Eisenhower administration delivered between 1956 and 1960. The Defense Department assured President Kennedy that the new aid would help Colonel Peralta maintain order. U.S. Army Special Forces and Air Commando teams visited Guatemala, and Guatemalan officers received counterinsurgency training in a center established in their country. Seven hundred twenty officers a year also took basic police courses and studied riot control techniques under U.S. auspices. The Kennedy and Johnson administrations would ultimately supply the 6,500 Guatemalan police officers and men with all their handguns, 50 percent of their shoulder weapons, and over 6,000 tear gas grenades. As Guatemala's Truth Commission noted, U.S. military assistance "was directed towards reinforcing the national intelligence apparatus and for training the officer corps in counterinsurgency techniques, key factors which had significant bearing on human rights violations during the armed confrontation." U.S. military aid and the concomitant anti-Communist policies culminated "in criminal counterinsurgency."[54]

The Guatemalan army and police made ferocious use of their new hardware and training. Under the rubric of *Operación Limpieza* ("Operation Cleanup"), Guatemalan forces, advised by U.S. police trainers, carried out eighty roundups and multiple assassinations in early 1966. In March 1966, they captured about thirty insurgents, including Víctor Manuel Gutiérrez, a leader of the PGT and former ally of President Arbenz. Security forces interrogated, tortured, and executed the prisoners. Judicial police subjected Gutiérrez to a torture known as *la capucha*, covering his head with a cowl and shocking him with electrical currents. Gutiérrez apparently succumbed to a heart attack during the torture. Security forces placed the bodies of Gutiérrez and the other insurgents in burlap bags and dumped them in the Pacific Ocean.[55] By denying access to the corpses, security forces intensified the grief of the victims' friends and relatives. Guatemalan security forces had also established a new, terrifying precedent in Latin America. In the 1970s, the military and death squads in Argentina and Chile would similarly dispose of the bodies of their victims, dropping them in the ocean or burying them in the desert. The concept of the "disappeared" or *desaparaecido* would become a terrifying reality in Latin America. People would vanish and security forces would deny any knowledge of what happened. Parents throughout Latin America, like the mothers of the Plaza de Mayo in Buenos Aires, would spend decades vainly trying to discover the fate of their children. Beyond "disappearing" people, Guatemalan security forces initiated the practice of "scorched earth" tactics, destroying villages in order to undermine popular support for insurgents. In October 1966, security forces murdered eight thousand rural folk, setting the stage for far worse atrocities against the indigenous population in the 1980s. The political right's brutality knew no bounds. In 1968, security forces murdered Rogelia Cruz Martínez, an architecture student, leftist, and former "Miss Guatemala." In this case, the butchers publicly displayed Cruz's mutilated and raped, naked corpse.

The forces of the left acted violently, blowing up electrical towers, attacking military installations, murdering government officials, robbing banks, and kidnapping wealthy Guatemalans for ransom. They also attacked the U.S. presence, killing U.S. military advisors and, in August 1968, assassinating Ambassador John Gordon Mein. But nothing in the history of Western law, philosophy, or statecraft justified the wholesale, wanton murder that the Guatemalan military perpetrated on the population. The response to armed insurgents transcended issues of defending the state or fighting the good Cold War fight against Soviet- or Cuban-inspired Marxism. The military, supported by elites, landed oligarchs, and the Church hierarchy, was determined to preserve the pre-1944 status quo. John Longan, a U.S. security trainer, organized *Operación Limpieza*. As he considered the course and conduct of the operation, Longan conceded that Guatemalan security forces "will be continued to be used, as in the past, not so much as protectors of the nation against Communist enslavement, but as the oligarchy's oppressors of legitimate social change."[56]

In the words of historian Piero Gleijeses, the U.S. covert intervention in Guatemala in 1954 was the "original sin."[57] It condemned Guatemala to a life of horror. For the United States, however, it would be a sin worth committing again in the Cold War.

CHAPTER 4

War Against Cuba

For five decades, the United States has pursued hostile policies toward Cuba under the leadership of Fidel Castro (1959–2008) and his brother, Raúl Castro (2008–). As of 2010, the United States has not conducted diplomatic relations with Cuba since 1961, and it has maintained the trade embargo it imposed on the Caribbean island in 1962. Five years after overthrowing an alleged Communist government in Guatemala, the United States encountered a new, threatening presence in its traditional sphere of influence. Fidel Castro and his 26th of July Movement seized power in early 1959 and rapidly transformed Cuba into a radical state allied with the Soviet Union. Castro, an authoritarian populist, converted to communism and proclaimed his duty to make revolution throughout the world. The United States reacted to the Castro challenge with fury and force. Beyond isolating Cuba, diplomatically and economically, U.S. officials waged war against the island, sponsoring an invasion and authorizing sabotage and terrorism. The United States also conspired to assassinate Cuban leaders. During the first ten years of life with Fidel Castro, the United States did not succeed in toppling the Castro regime, although it managed to contain the Cuban Revolution. Nonetheless, the United States remained obsessed with Castro's Cuba. The basic thrust of U.S. policy toward the rest of Latin America would be to prevent a "second Cuba" in the region.

THE CUBAN REVOLUTION

Fidel Castro and his band of bearded guerrillas, *los barbudos*, rode on tanks into Havana in January 1959. Their triumphant entry into the capital city, which was greeted with wild, delirious crowds, marked the culmination of Castro's six-year struggle against dictator Fulgencio Batista. Batista had used his control of the Cuban army to dominate the island's political life since the 1930s and had occupied the presidency between 1940 and 1944. In 1952, Batista again seized presidential power. With his army and police in disarray, the venal and vicious Batista hustled his relatives onto an airplane as the New Year dawned and flew to the safety of the Dominican Republic, the home of dictator Rafael Trujillo.

Fidel Castro (1926–), the son of a prosperous sugar planter who had emigrated from Spain, had led a privileged life. He was a good athlete and an excellent student, attending a preparatory school administered by Jesuit priests and then earning a law degree from the University of Havana. Castro participated in student politics at the university. Castro first came to international attention on 26 July 1953 when he led a group of 135 young rebels, students, urban workers, and peasants in a disastrous storming of the army barracks at Moncada, located in the Cuban city of Santiago. He received a fifteen-year sentence for his rebellion but was freed from prison in 1955 by the confident Batista. Castro and his brother Raúl fled to Mexico to plan another assault on the Batista regime. In 1956, Fidel Castro and eighty-one other men struggled ashore after their leaky ship, *Granma*, beached on Cuba's eastern shore. Within a few days, Batista forces killed most of the insurgents. The sixteen survivors, who included the Castro brothers and Argentine revolutionary Ernesto "Che" Guevara, retreated into the Sierra Maestra, the mountains of southeastern Cuba. Castro steadily rebuilt his forces to over 1,000 men and launched hit-and-run attacks against Bastista's forces. The turn to guerrilla warfare was out of necessity rather than choice. Castro had counted on a mass uprising following the landing of the *Granma*. Che Guevara especially designed the guerrilla warfare tactics. The determination and courage of the guerrillas inspired other Cubans, and by 1958 the insurgency had spread from rural areas into the cities. Batista's power and legitimacy was as much undermined by demonstrations and strikes conducted by professional, union, and student organizations as by Castro's forces. By the end of the year, support for Batista had evaporated. Castro, an authoritarian, proved effective at quickly gathering power in his own hands and overwhelming the other anti-Batista groups.[1]

What Castro and the 26th of July Movement intended for Cuba was initially unclear. The manifesto of the movement was Castro's long, rambling, "History Will Absolve Me" speech, which he gave at his trial and subsequently rewrote in prison. Castro promised agrarian and industrial reform, administrative honesty, and a liberal and progressive constitution for Cuba. During the two years he spent in the Sierra Maestra, Castro released letters and issued declarations that his movement was libertarian and democratic, but also reformist and perhaps socialistic. Those thoughts had been especially conveyed in a dramatic interview Castro gave to *New York Times* correspondent Herbert Matthews, who was spirited to Castro's mountain hideaway in February 1957. Although his statements were vague and ambiguous, scholars do not believe that Castro was trying to deceive Cubans or the international community. Prior to 1959, Castro lacked a clear vision for a post-Batista Cuba, and he had not committed himself to an ideological doctrine. Castro was almost certainly not a Marxist-Leninist, an ally of the Soviet Union, or an agent of the international Communist movement. The Cuban Communist Party, which was one of Latin America's largest Communist parties

Fidel Castro, his brother, Raúl Castro (kneeling in front of Fidel), and other members of Castro's revolutionary staff appear in southeastern Cuba in June 1957. Castro and his followers had been fighting and organizing against the regime of Fulgencio Batista since landing in Cuba on the *Granma* in December 1956. Castro and his guerrilla fighters would claim credit for toppling Batista and would subsequently seize control of Cuba in January 1959. In fact, the uprising against Batista was widespread, with many urban insurgents. (Corbis Images)

with seventeen thousand members, provided no substantial aid to the 26th of July Movement. Cuban Communists had a long history of cooperating with Batista. As exemplified in analyses published in the Soviet Union's official newspaper, *Pravda*, international Communists judged Castro a well-intentioned but naïve, romantic revolutionary.[2]

Like other educated Cubans, Castro held ambivalent views about the United States. He appreciated the wealth and technological prowess of the United States and wished the same for Cuba. He also enjoyed U.S. popular culture, playing baseball and following major league teams. But Cubans resented the role that the United States had played in Cuba's history. After assisting Cuba's struggle for independence in 1898, the United States attached the Platt Amendment (1901–33) to the Cuban constitution, giving the United States the right to intervene militarily and oversee Cuba's internal affairs. The United States also created a permanent military base, Guantánamo Bay, in Cuba. U.S. troops repeatedly landed in independent Cuba, and U.S. warships plied the waters in sight of Havana's harbor. The U.S. ambassador was usually considered the second most powerful figure in Cuba, after the Cuban president. With their money guaranteed by the bayonets of U.S. marines, U.S. investors came to dominate Cuba's economic life. With approximately

$900 million invested in Cuba in 1959, U.S. investors accounted for 40 percent of the country's sugar production. U.S. companies also controlled public utilities, oil refineries, mines, railroads, and the tourist industry. Cubans took further offense that U.S. tourists considered Havana their playground for gambling, narcotics, and prostitution. The U.S. criminal underworld, "the Mafia," operated freely in Batista's Cuba. Castro took note of the popular feeling that the United States had stolen Cuba's independence in issuing his first statement after Batista's army capitulated. In a radio broadcast on 1 January 1959, Castro pledged: "This time, fortunately for Cuba, the revolution will truly achieve power. It won't be as in 1895, when the Americans came at the last hour and took over the country."[3]

Reforming Cuban society inevitably meant altering both Cuba's peculiar socio-economic structure and the overwhelming U.S. presence in Cuba. Casual observers might judge Cuba a relatively prosperous country in the 1950s. In international rankings, Cuba stood 31st in the world in per capita income—an income roughly similar to Latin American countries like Argentina, Uruguay, and Venezuela. Havana was a glittering metropolis, the Malecón was a stunning walkway along Havana's northern shore, and tourists loved the island's gorgeous beaches. But there were grave structural imbalances in the Cuban economy. About one-third of Cuba's labor force was employed in sugar production. Sugar production required, however, a sizeable labor force only during the harvest period, or *zafra*; most of the year, during the *tiempo muerto* or "dead time," rural workers were unemployed. Sugar work, combined with some government-funded road maintenance work, provided six hundred thousand rural workers only four to five months of gainful employment a year. In the impoverished countryside, where over 40 percent of Cubans lived, access to schools and health care facilities was limited. Over 40 percent of rural folk could not read or write. Afro-Cubans, who especially predominated among the rural proletariat, suffered the further indignity of experiencing racial discrimination and even segregation. Population pressures compounded Cuba's problems. Increasing at 2.5 percent a year, the population had grown from five million in 1945 to seven million in 1960. The Cuban economy could not accommodate the fifty thousand young people who were entering the work force each year. Perhaps one-third of Cubans were unemployed or underemployed.[4]

Cubans, including Castro, blamed the United States for Cuba's poverty and backwardness. Cubans held that the constant U.S. meddling in Cuban life had fostered a political system that had produced only corrupt tyrants like Batista or weak, inept rulers like Carlos Prío Socarrás (1948–52). Whereas they denounced U.S. interference, Cubans felt compelled to compare their lot to the lifestyles of their rich and famous northern neighbors. Cubans, who lived as close as 90 miles to Florida, interpreted their socioeconomic status within the context of the United States, not the Dominican Republic or Nicaragua. What mattered to Cubans was that Cuba was significantly poorer than Mississippi, the poorest U.S. state. Frustrated Cubans further held that their nation lacked the economic independence that would give them the opportunity to build a prosperous society. Throughout the twentieth century, the United States controlled Cuba's trade. Under the Sugar Act (1948), the United States reserved 55 percent of sugar consumption for domestic producers and 45 percent to foreign sources. Cuba was assigned a generous 70 percent of the foreign quota. The sugar trade represented about 80 percent of the value of Cuba's exports. In turn, 80 percent of Cuba's imports came from the United States. The bilateral trade arrangement gave Cuban's access to U.S. consumer goods, albeit not a U.S. standard of living. Cubans further understood that the Sugar Act gave the United States enormous power over Cuban society. By altering or repealing the Sugar Act, the United States could generate chaos in Cuba. This sense of dependence and helplessness fueled Cuban demands for change.[5]

Castro's agrarian reform law of April 1959 set the tone for U.S.-Cuban relations. The law expropriated farmlands over one thousand acres, with compensation to be paid in Cuban bonds and based on the land's declared value for taxes in 1958. The revolutionary government vowed to create a life of equality and justice for the rural poor. Sugar barons, both foreign and domestic, had predictably undervalued their land in Batista's Cuba. Howls of protest from Washington, U.S. investors, and propertied Cubans seemed only to encourage the Castro government to limit further the prerogatives of the wealthy in Cuba. Tens of thousands of Cubans fled the island, landing in Miami, Florida. Cuban revolutionaries also drove the criminal underworld out of Cuba, closing down the narcotics rings, brothels, and gambling dens. By the end of 1961, Castro had expropriated U.S. investments in Cuba.

Between 1959 and 1961, the Cuban Revolution took on the tone and shape of a Communist revolution. On 1 December 1961, Castro publicly declared: "I am a Marxist-Leninist, and I will continue to be a Marxist-Leninist until the last days of my life." In moving toward communism, Fidel Castro joined his brother Raúl and Che Guevara, both committed radicals. Castro probably concluded that communism provided solutions to Cuba's unique and pressing socioeconomic problems. The Soviet Union, given its impressive economic growth rate since 1917 and scientific triumphs in outer space in the 1950s, seemed a viable model for poor countries. As he faced domestic opposition, Castro also welcomed and embraced Cuban Communists. Communism may have also suited Castro's authoritarian personality. The Communist concept of the "dictatorship of the proletariat" would enhance Castro's drive for personal domination of Cuba. Historians of Latin American history have often noted that Castro was a Latin-American type—a *caudillo* or strongman in the tradition of Juan Manuel de Rosas (1832–35) of Argentina. But Castro was a *caudillo* with political ideas.[6]

As his growing radicalism reaped mounting hostility from the United States, Castro turned to the Soviet Union for help. In the 1950s, Soviet Premier Nikita Khrushchev had widened Soviet contacts with Asian and African nations emerging from colonialism. But the Soviets gave short shrift to Latin America, conceding the overwhelming U.S. influence in the region. In 1959, Soviet leaders began to sense the radical nature of the Cuban Revolution. In April 1959, the Soviets approved Raúl Castro's request to send Spanish-speaking military officers to Cuba to help reorganize the Cuban military. Remembering what happened to President Jacobo Arbenz Guzmán of Guatemala, Cubans wanted an army loyal to the revolution. In October 1959, the Soviets sent Alexsandr Alekseev as an unofficial envoy to discuss establishing diplomatic relations. Alekseev, who was fluent in Spanish, served as the Soviet ambassador in Havana from 1962 to 1968. In February 1960, at Castro's request, the Soviets held a trade fair in Cuba and signed a commercial agreement with the Cubans, which included purchasing Cuban sugar. At least initially, the Soviet Union was overjoyed to join the Castro-led revolution. Anastas Mikoyan (1895–1978), the first deputy premier of the Soviet Union, attended the trade fair in Cuba. As Mikoyan recounted to Secretary of State Dean Rusk, "You Americans must realize what Cuba means to us old Bolsheviks. We have been waiting all of our lives for a country to go communist without the Red Army. It has happened in Cuba, and it makes us feel like boys again."[7] As the 1960s progressed, the Soviets would learn to temper their boyish enthusiasm for the Cuban Revolution.

THE CUBAN THREAT

Fidel Castro's rapid elimination of the historic U.S. economic influence in Cuba threatened by example the approximately $8 billion in U.S. direct investments in the rest of Latin America. U.S. companies had massive investments in strategically vital resources such as Chilean copper and Venezuelan oil. As United Fruit Company officials had done in the early 1950s in regard to Guatemala, U.S. capitalists—cattle barons and sugar executives—bombarded presidential administrations with livid complaints about Cuban perfidy. But in responding to the Castro threat, U.S. officials in the Dwight Eisenhower, John Kennedy, and Lyndon Johnson administrations did not regularly use the language of property rights or refer to the tenets of international capitalism in their public pronouncements and private deliberations about Cuba. They perceived Castro's Cuba as a direct threat to U.S. national security in the Cold War. Destroying U.S. economic influence in Latin America was part of the threat, but not the core of the challenge that the Cuban Revolution presented. U.S. leaders vowed to destroy the Castro regime, because they feared that revolutionary Cuba would spread international communism throughout the hemisphere. On his last day in office, 19 January 1961, President Eisenhower told President-elect Kennedy that "in the long-run the United States cannot allow the Castro government to continue to exist in Cuba."[8] President Kennedy accepted his predecessor's judgment. As his administration often put it, communism in the Western Hemisphere imperiled the United States, impeded the U.S. ability to act in other areas of the world, and threatened to become a divisive domestic political issue. U.S. presidential administrations exaggerated, however, the dangers that Cuba presented to the United States, and took actions that intensified the U.S. conflict with Cuba.

In early 1962, Fidel Castro, in his Second Declaration of Havana, asserted that "the duty of every revolutionary is to make revolution." In October 1965, Castro read aloud on television Che Guevara's farewell letter to the Cuban leader. Guevara, who was popularly identified with guerrilla warfare, vowed "to fight against imperialism wherever it may be." In January 1966, Cuba hosted the Tricontinental

Conference, attended by five hundred delegates from the "tricontinent" of Asia, Africa, and Latin America. The conference created a new organization, with headquarters in Havana, to support armed revolutionary activity throughout the world. In Castro's words, "the battle will take on the most violent terms." In April 1967, the Tricontinental organization received a message from Guevara "somewhere in the world." Che Guevara was putting into practice his commitment to armed revolutionary struggle, leading a small band of guerrillas in southeastern Bolivia. Beyond the rhetoric and resolutions and Guevara's exploits, Cuba served as the "Liberation Department" or "guerrilla central" for Latin American radicals. Perhaps fifteen hundred to two thousand Latin Americans, by CIA estimates, received political indoctrination and military training in revolutionary Cuba in the early 1960s.[9]

In analyzing and assessing Cuba's commitment to spread revolution in Latin America, a variety of issues must be highlighted. In the 1960s, Cuba covertly assisted radicals in Colombia, Guatemala, Peru, and, most notably, in Venezuela. In Venezuela, radicals attacked the popularly elected government of Rómulo Betancourt (1959–64) and tried to intimidate Venezuelans into not participating in the December 1963 presidential elections that led to the victory of Raúl Leoni (1964–69). Although Venezuela's Communist party for a time perpetrated violence, the chief agitators and terrorists were young members of *Movimiento de Izquiereda Revolucionaria* (Movement of the Revolutionary Left) or MIR. Venezuela's guerrilla fighters, who numbered between one thousand and two thousand, created havoc and committed unspeakable crimes in the country. The Venezuelan government reported that more than four hundred people died in revolts in mid-1962. But blame for death and destruction in Venezuela could not be mainly ascribed to Fidel Castro. A CIA study concluded that MIR members "ran their own shows," were a home-grown revolutionary organization," and could be described as "an extreme-nationalist, revolutionary nationalist movement." Venezuelan Communists, who entered the fray in late 1962 and quit by 1965, rejected Castro's criticism of their actions, deploring "the role of revolutionary 'pope' which Fidel Castro arrogates to himself." Cuba's intervention in Venezuela also did not occur in a political vacuum. President Betancourt was Castro's chief adversary in Latin America. He permitted anti-Castro Cubans to operate from Venezuela. The Venezuelan president supported U.S. efforts to overthrow Castro, even informing U.S. officials that he favored the assassination of Castro, would finance it, and help find someone to do the job.[10]

President Betancourt and the Venezuelan military and police gradually suppressed the leftist rebellion. Betancourt's success was repeated throughout Latin America in the 1960s. Radicals failed throughout the region, as highlighted by the Bolivian military's capture of Che Guevara's pathetic band of warriors in 1967. The memory of Guevara's ill-fated mission creates an impression that Cubans were engaged in guerrilla warfare through the hemisphere in the 1960s. In fact, scholars have estimated that only about forty Cubans fought in Latin America during the 1960s. Cuban volunteers, soldiers, and doctors joined anti-colonial movements in the 1960s, but in Africa, not Latin America. Between 1962 and 1964, perhaps two thousand Cubans operated in Algeria, Zaire (Congo), and Guinea-Bissau. This preceded the massive Cuban military intervention in Angola in 1975–1976. U.S. intelligence analysts were unaware, for example, that Guevara led a column of Cuban fighters in Zaire in 1965. Cubans yearned for the heroic life and the mystique of guerrilla warfare. Castro further theorized that Cuba, a racially mixed, impoverished, colonized nation, shared a special empathy for African liberation movements. But the Cuban interventions also involved *realpolitik*. The United States waged war against Cuba. Cubans feared a U.S. invasion of the island. Castro and his advisors concluded that the United States would live with the Cuban Revolution only when confronted with revolutionary movements throughout the world. As one Cuban put it, by challenging "the Yankees along all the paths of the world," Cuba would divide their forces, "so that they wouldn't be able to descend on us (or any other country) with all their might." In Che Guevara's words, Cuba's survival depended on nurturing "two, three, many Vietnams."[11]

Castro and Guevara rarely bothered to inform the Soviet Union about their African adventures. U.S. officials assumed that Castro served as a surrogate for the Soviet Union and that Cuba would do Soviets' bidding, spreading the Communist manifesto throughout Latin America. But Cuban-Soviet relations were filled with tensions and inconsistencies. Between 1959 and 1962, the partnership intensified, culminating in the Cuban agreement to allow the Soviet Union to install nuclear-tipped, ballistic missiles on the island. The Soviets also became the underwriters of the Cuban Revolution, providing economic aid and vital resources like oil. But between October 1962 and 1968, bilateral relations deteriorated. The Cubans believed that the Soviets had sacrificed Cuban security in negotiating an end to the Cuban missile crisis. They considered the non-invasion pledge that the United States gave to the Soviets to be worthless, for the United States continued to wage a covert war against Cuba from 1963 to 1965. In Guevara's words, the resolution of the missile crisis represented "sad and luminous days" for the Cubans. Cuban revolutionaries had learned the shocking, awful truth that the Soviets were not prepared to die for either Cuba or the cause. The Soviets wanted national security, economic growth, and better relations or a détente with the United States. From November 1962 through 1979, Soviet-American relations steadily improved, with gaudy summit meetings, nuclear-arms control agreements, cultural exchanges, and trade treaties. From the Cuban perspective, the pursuit of détente by the Soviets exposed them as cowardly imperialists.[12]

The Soviets drew different lessons from the missile crisis. They saw the Cubans as emotional and irresponsible, recalling that in the midst of the crisis Castro had sent a letter to Khrushchev recommending a preemptive nuclear strike against the United States. This could have led to general war and the destruction of human civilization. The Cubans had to learn to follow the Soviets' lead and remember that within the world socialist movement Soviet security had the highest priority. In terms of Latin America, this meant not challenging the United States in its traditional sphere of influence. The Soviets also wanted to maintain control over Latin America's Communist parties, which ranged in number from 150 members in Panama to more than sixty thousand in Argentina. Moscow judged Latin America's revolutionary potential as dismal and advised local Communists to organize and to eschew violence and subversion. U.S. intelligence analysts ironically agreed with Moscow, rating the Argentine Communist party, the largest in the Western Hemisphere, as "not an influential political force." When Castro visited the Soviet Union in May 1963, Premier Khrushchev informed the Cuban that the Soviet Union would not support armed insurrection in Latin America and that Castro should not attempt to dictate the policies of Latin American Communists. The Cuban foreign minister would later say that Castro believed that Khrushchev wanted nothing to do with Latin America and "would never send a single revolver to the region." The Soviets took a dim view of the Tricontinental Conference and Castro's sarcastic characterization of Latin American Communists as more eager to pass resolutions than to foment revolution. The new Soviet leader, Leonid Brezhnev (1964–82), erupted when he found out in 1966 that Che Guevara was in Bolivia. Brezhnev's colleague, Alexsei Kosygin, delivered a stern rebuke to Castro in Havana in mid-1967, demanding that Cuba cease its meddling in Latin America. Remarkably, Kosygin had just concluded a summit with President Johnson in Glassboro, New Jersey, and implied to the president that he would deliver just such a message to Castro. The Cold War between Cuba and the Soviet Union continued until mid-1968. Castro declined to attend the fiftieth anniversary celebration in Moscow of the Bolshevik Revolution of November 1917. Brezhnev cut Cuba's oil supplies. Castro ordered the arrest of Cuba's pro-Soviet Communist Party leader, Aníbal Escalante. Escalante would receive a fifteen-year sentence for treason.[13]

Ideological blinders prevented U.S. officials from always grasping the essence of the Cuban–Soviet split or assessing the shortcomings of the efficacy of international communism in Latin America. To be sure, the Cuban Revolution had profound influence in Latin America. But Cuba's dramatic role in the region's history did not arise from Cuban support for armed rebellion. Latin Americans—the young, the poor, intellectuals—admired the Cuban Revolution because of what it accomplished within Cuba. The most important influence that Cuba exercised in the hemisphere was the power of its example. Like Communist societies throughout the world and history, the Cuban economy flopped, both in the 1960s and thereafter. The country became relatively poorer and stayed dependent on the sugar trade for its economic solvency. Cuba traded one patron—the United States—for another—the Soviet Union. But as one historian put it, Cuba was an "austere success." Cuban Communists created an egalitarian society, raising the wages of the rural poor and delivering to them services in health, education, and welfare. As measured in indices such as life expectancy, infant mortality rates, and literacy, Cuba developed a society that measured well against Western industrial democracies. Cuban teachers, dispatched to the countryside, reduced illiteracy from 24 to 4 percent in the 1960s. Cuba also did an excellent job controlling its explosive population growth, whereas its impoverished Caribbean and Central

American neighbors continued to see their populations double every twenty years. Afro-Cubans, traditionally the poorest of Cubans, especially benefited from this redistribution of resources.[14] Admiring these accomplishments, Latin America's masses closed their eyes to the lack of political rights in Cuba. The island nation remained a repressive political dictatorship under Castro.

The Cuban Revolution also excited the imagination of Latin Americans, because of what it accomplished outside of Cuba. Cuba became an internationally significant nation, culturally and politically. Cuba funded artists and filmmakers who played major roles in the cultural arena. *Memorias del subdesarrollo* (*Memories of Underdevelopment*), the 1968 film directed by Tomás Gutiérrez Alea, garnered international awards. Film historians consider it a seminal work. The film explores how an aspiring writer, who led a privileged life, responds to the vast social changes sweeping revolutionary Cuba. The writer's parents had fled to Miami. Alea would later direct Cuban films that would merit Oscar nominations from Hollywood. Cuban athletes also starred, winning gold, silver, and bronze at the Olympics. The great Alberto Juantorena, "el caballo" (the horse), dominated the track and field events at the 1976 summer games in Montreal. Latin Americans took further satisfaction in Cuba's prominent role at international conferences of "Third World" nations. Fidel Castro was an international celebrity. Che Guevara became a mythic figure. Latin American leaders normally did not enjoy such status. Latin Americans also applauded Cuba's escape from U.S. domination. Latin American intellectuals had not forgotten what had happened to Guatemala in 1954.

TO PLAYA GIRÓN (THE BAY OF PIGS)

U.S. leaders conceded the appeal that the Cuban Revolution had for tens of millions of frustrated, impoverished Latin Americans. They designed the Social Progress Trust Fund and the Alliance for Progress economic aid programs in the 1960s as a response to demands for revolutionary change (Chapter 5). Although understanding that Latin Americans yearned for their place in the sun, Eisenhower, Kennedy, and Johnson administration officials gave the highest priority to destroying the Cuban Revolution and murdering its leaders. Using a term that became widespread in the twenty-first century, the United States waged "state-supported terrorism" against Cuba in the 1960s.

The Eisenhower administration initially reacted in a confused and uncertain fashion to Fidel Castro and the 26th of July Movement. Like most international observers, the administration wondered what Castro believed and whether he had the power and support to take control of Cuba. State Department analysts labeled Castro as "immature" and "irresponsible." The administration did not perceive the Castro movement as Communist. On 23 December 1958, Christian Herter, the future secretary of state, informed President Eisenhower that, although Communists were utilizing the movement "to some extent," "there is insufficient evidence on which to base a charge that the rebels are Communist dominated."

In early 1959, CIA Director Allan Dulles testified to U.S. legislators that Castro was not a Communist agent. These assessments were accurate. Nonetheless, the Eisenhower administration opposed Castro taking power. In March 1958, the administration cut off arms shipment to its long-term client, Fulgencio Batista, after his U.S.-supplied air force inflicted heavy civilian casualties while bombing rebel positions. In late December, it encouraged Batista to abdicate his throne. The administration ineffectually looked for a credible, anti-Castro third force to take control of Cuba. But the administration could not temper the revolutionary fever that swept over Cuba.[15]

Less than a year after Castro's triumphal entry into Havana, the United States decided it could not abide the Cuban. On 5 November 1959, Secretary Herter recommended to Eisenhower that the United States generate opposition "to the extremist, anti-American course of the Castro regime." In December, Colonel J. C. King of the CIA's Western Hemisphere Division recommended to his boss that "thorough consideration be given to the elimination of Fidel Castro." King used the same language that CIA officers had used in compiling assassination targets of Guatemalans. Sensing that Cuba would become a domestic political issue in the upcoming presidential campaign, Vice President Richard Nixon, in late December, urged the president to focus on Cuba. The vice president had met Castro for three hours in Washington in April 1959. At that time, Nixon believed that Castro could be saved. He considered the Cuban's ideas on economic development to be naïve and simplistic, but came away impressed with Castro the person. Castro had those "indefinable qualities that make him a leader of men." Nixon further predicted that Castro "was going to be a great factor in the development of Cuba and very possibly in Latin American affairs generally." Taking the patronizing tone toward Castro that had characterized the U.S. approach to Cuba for sixty years, Nixon called for the United States to try "to orient him in the right direction." The Cuban Revolution's attack on both the realities and symbols of U.S. power in Cuba undermined Nixon's hopes. Cuba's growing flirtation with the Soviet Union hardened administration attitudes. By January 1960, President Eisenhower was calling Castro a "mad man." In February, Eisenhower told a senator he had received plans for clandestine action against Castro "approximating gangsterism."[16]

On 17 March 1960, President Eisenhower put the United States on a course to overthrow Castro. Eisenhower authorized "A Program of Covert Operation Against the Castro Regime." The program, initially budgeted at $4.4 million, included launching a propaganda offensive, organizing anti-Castro forces within Cuba, and training a paramilitary force outside Cuba for future action.[17] Eisenhower's plan had the earmarks of PBSUCCESS. The administration hoped to replay its success in destroying the Arbenz government of Guatemala. Over the rest of the year, the administration attacked Cuba. The CIA broadcast anti-Castro tirades from a radio station on Swan Island, a dot of land off the coast of Honduras. The administration tried to strangle the Cuban economy, cutting off sugar imports and banning exports to the island. The CIA began to train Cuban exiles in Guatemala with the mission of carrying out an amphibious invasion of Cuba. The exile army would grow from 300 men to over 700 by the end of the year and eventually to 1,400 men in April 1961.

The CIA also took up Colonel King's proposal to "eliminate" Fidel Castro. The agency, with the approval of Director Dulles, contacted criminal figures interested in carrying out "gangster action" against Castro. CIA operatives presumably calculated that the Mafia wanted Castro dead so that it could resume its nefarious activities in Cuba. At the gangsters' request, CIA technicians developed poison pills to place in Castro's food and drink. The CIA worked with Sam Giancana, who was on the attorney general's list of the "ten most wanted men" in America. Giancana, a successor to Al Capone of Chicago, was the "Cosa Nostra" boss of the mob's Cuban operations.[18] Finally, on 3 January 1961, President Eisenhower broke diplomatic relations with Cuba.

President-elect John F. Kennedy's attitude toward Cuba evolved rapidly. As a senator, he denounced the Eisenhower administration for supporting the Batista regime through the 1950s. Like many U.S. citizens, Senator Kennedy welcomed the overthrow of Batista and hoped that Castro was a moderate democratic reformer. But in 1960, Kennedy seized on the mounting tension with Castro and turned it into a major campaign issue. The radicalization of the Cuban Revolution and growing relationship between Cuba and the Soviet Union corroborated his basic campaign issue—the United States was losing the Cold War. The president-elect received a briefing from Allen Dulles on the covert campaign against Castro. In two meetings with Kennedy, on December 6 and January 19, President Eisenhower emphasized the need to oust Castro, telling the president-elect that the United States was helping the exile army "to the utmost" and the their training should be "continued and accelerated."[19] Kennedy accepted Eisenhower's judgment that the Cuban Revolution posed a mortal danger to U.S. vital interests.

President Kennedy carried out Eisenhower's policy. The U.S.-backed invasion of Cuba took place at the Bay of Pigs on the island's southwestern shores on between 17 and 19 April 1961, less than three months after Kennedy took office. Castro's forces quickly routed the 1,400-man invasion force known as "Brigade 2506." His soldiers killed 114 and captured another 1,179 of the exiles. Castro's doctors estimated his fighters suffered 3,650 casualties, including more than 1,600 dead. Castro took personal command of the Cuban military, directed the counterattack, and won domestic and international prestige for having defeated the United States. Castro seemed a hero to many Latin Americans.

President Kennedy received pressure to authorize the invasion. If he had cancelled the invasion, he would have been rejecting the plans of the nation's most trusted military leader, General Dwight Eisenhower. He would also have what Director Dulles called a "disposal" problem. The Cuban exiles training in Guatemala would return to the United States and loudly complain to journalists and politicians that President Kennedy feared Castro and that he lacked the fortitude to wage Cold War. But aborting the invasion would have averted a disaster. Although not debated within the administration between January and April 1961, there was a politically expedient way for Kennedy to relieve the pressure. Newspapers and journals reported about the Cuban exiles training in Guatemala. Cuban exiles in

Miami openly discussed the invasion plans. The president privately grumbled that Castro did not need intelligence agents in the United States, for "all he has to do is read our papers."[20] Kennedy could have conceivably lamented this exposure and terminated the training. Instead, he asked editors to suppress the news.

President Kennedy also received misleading advice about the invasion from key advisors, especially Richard Bissell, the CIA's deputy director of plans. Bissell met frequently with Kennedy and sent him numerous memorandums. Bissell structured his arguments in a way to compel the president to authorize the invasion. Bissell assured the president that the invasion had a good chance of overthrowing Castro or sparking a damaging civil war in Cuba. If the invasion did not go forth, however, Bissell warned that Latin Americans would lose faith in the United States and that "David will again have defeated Goliath." Moreover, the failure to overthrow Castro in the near future would lead "to the elimination of all internal and external Cuban opposition of any effective nature." When Kennedy repeatedly demanded that the U.S. role be limited in the operation, Bissell always assured the president that the invasion would succeed without overt U.S. support. Kennedy assumed that the exiles would be able to retreat into Cuban mountains if they could not hold and expand their beachhead at the Bay of Pigs. Bissell failed to make clear that the nearest mountains were far away and the area around the Bay of Pigs was filled with swamps.[21]

The counsel that President Kennedy received was not, however, one-sided; he received strong advice to cancel Eisenhower's plan. Congressional leaders like Senator J. William Fulbright, the chair of the Senate Foreign Relations Committee, and State Department officers raised philosophical, diplomatic, and practical objections to the unprovoked invasion of a sovereign country. Former Secretary of State Dean Acheson, an inveterate Cold Warrior, told the president that one did not have to be a certified public accountant "to discover that 1,500 Cubans were not as good as 25,000 Cubans" [the size of Castro's army]. Presidential aide Arthur Schlesinger dismissed the idea that the U.S. hand could be kept hidden in the invasion. Given the long U.S. history of military intervention in Caribbean countries, global observers would immediately assume that the United States controlled the Cuban exiles. The U.S. standing in the world would be harmed. As Schlesinger warned, "Cuba will become our Hungary," referring to the ugly Soviet invasion of Hungary in 1956.[22]

In the end, President Kennedy authorized the Bay of Pigs invasion because he wanted Castro overthrown and because he thought the exile army could accomplish that goal with a minimal cost to the United States. In early April 1961, the president dispatched Colonel Jack Hawkins to Guatemala to assess the fighting abilities of the brigade. Colonel Hawkins impressed the president with his report, noting that "these officers are young, vigorous, intelligent, and motivated with a fanatical urge to begin battle." The exiles assured Hawkins that once the battle began all they wanted was supplies and would not need direct U.S. military support.[23]

More than dubious reports, however, led Kennedy to give the signal to invade Cuba. He embraced the mass delusion that had existed in the United States since 1959 about political life in Castro's Cuba. Cubans allegedly suffered under Castro and prayed for their deliverance. The invasion supposedly would produce a "shock" in Cuba, triggering a mass uprising. Those who planned the Bay of Pigs always understood that the exile brigade could not conquer Cuba. As the planners noted, "the primary objective of the force will be to survive and maintain its integrity on Cuban soil." Brigade 2506 leaders predicted that thereafter thirty thousand Cubans would rush to the side of their liberators, and Cuban soldiers would desert Castro. CIA analysts tossed around wildly inflated numbers, ranging from one thousand to seven thousand, of resistance fighters already in Cuba. But enemies of the Cuban Revolution were more likely to reside in Miami than in Havana. Another CIA report cited a private survey that "less than 30 percent of the population was still with Fidel" and "in this 30 percent of the population are included the negroes, who have always followed the strong man in Cuba, but will not fight."[24] Beyond being racist, the survey was historically inaccurate, for Afro-Cubans had fought for the island's independence in the 1890s. In a postmortem report on the Bay of Pigs, the Inspector General of the CIA wrote that "we can confidently assert that the CIA had no intelligence evidence that Cubans in significant numbers could or would join the invaders or that there was any kind of effective and cohesive resistance movement under anybody's control."[25]

Historical discourse about the Bay of Pigs invasion has focused on President Kennedy's decision not to authorize U.S. air and naval support on the day of the invasion. Such a U.S.-centered approach inevitably leads scholars to ignore important facts. The Guatemalan intervention had taught Latin Americans, including the Castro brothers and Che Guevara, unforgettable lessons. Castro and his forces prepared for an invasion. Fidel and Raúl Castro built an army of twenty-five thousand and a loyal, self-defense force of over two hundred thousand Cubans, who were armed with weapons from the Soviet bloc. In April 1961, one battalion of troops patrolled every beach in Cuba. Castro's intelligence agents anticipated an invasion, because, just like President Kennedy, they could read in U.S. publications about the training base in Guatemala. Cuban spies presumably had also penetrated the exile community of Miami. Prior to the invasion, Cuban security forces also arrested citizens on the island suspected of disloyalty. Finally, in Fidel Castro, the Cubans had an experienced military commander who had fought for three hard years in the Cuban mountains. Before and during the invasion, Castro acted decisively. A pre-invasion air strike by the exiles on April 15 had destroyed Cuban airplanes. To forestall further losses, Castro ordered pilots to be prepared to take off at a moment's notice. The pilots actually slept underneath their planes. If President Kennedy had authorized additional air strikes, the bombers would have likely hit empty airfields. The Bay of Pigs should be counted as a Cuban victory.

OPERATION MONGOOSE

President Kennedy did not waver from the goal of destroying the Cuban Revolution and insuring that Castro's victory at the Bay of Pigs was short-lived. On 5 May 1961, he presided over a meeting of the NSC and ruled that U.S. policy would continue "to aim at the downfall of Castro." The United States would not invade Cuba now, but neither would it foreclose the possibility of a future military invasion. The president designated his brother to be his point man on Cuba. Robert Kennedy roughly informed U.S. military and intelligence officials that "the Cuban problem" was the top priority of the government and that "no time, money, efforts, or manpower is to be spared." The attorney general often berated senior CIA officers about their lack of success in Cuba. Richard Bissell recounted being "chewed out" by the Kennedy brothers at the White House "for sitting on his ass and doing nothing about Cuba." Richard Helms, Bissell's successor at the CIA, was told in early 1962 by Robert Kennedy, speaking for his brother, that "the final chapter on Cuba has not been written."[26]

President Kennedy judged Castro's Cuba a dire threat to vital U.S. national interests. But his administration's assessment of the Cuban threat did not sustain those fears. In preparation for the NSC meeting of May 5, Paul Nitze of the Defense Department coordinated a lengthy evaluation of "Cuba's threat to the national interests." The report depicted Cuba as more of a psychological than a real threat to the traditional U.S. domination of the Western Hemisphere. The Cuban Revolution inspired radicals and militants throughout the region. Cuba assisted these potential revolutionaries through propaganda and perhaps the supply of funds. But the administration had "no hard evidence of an actual supply of arms or armed men going from Cuba to other countries to assist indigenous revolutionary movements." In any case, poverty and economic discontent, not Castro, generated social ferment throughout Latin America. The report also considered it "a remote possibility" that the Soviet Union would transform Cuba into a military base for a strategic attack on the United States. Castro's real crime was that "he had provided a working example of a communist state in the Americas, successfully defying the United States."[27]

While awaiting a new campaign for undermining Castro, President Kennedy brushed aside a Cuban peace offer. On 17 August 1961, Che Guevara spoke late into the night with presidential aide Richard Goodwin. Both men were attending an inter-American conference in Uruguay. Guevara had previously sent Goodwin a fancy box filled with the finest Cuban cigars. Guevara suggested that by discussing issues like the U.S. expropriated properties, trade, and Cuba's role in Latin America that the two countries could reach a *modus vivendi*—a way of living together. Goodwin informed his president of the conversation. Nothing developed from the Goodwin–Guevara exchange. President Kennedy's only tangible gesture was to smoke one of Guevara's cigars.[28]

In November 1961, the president launched a new war against Castro, "Operation Mongoose," under the direction of General Edward G. Lansdale. Lansdale was a flamboyant Air Force officer who claimed expertise in counterinsurgency and guerrilla warfare based on his experience in the Philippines and Vietnam in the 1950s. Armed with a $50 million budget, Lansdale assembled a team of over four hundred CIA employees and thousands of Cuban exiles who operated from headquarters near the University of Miami campus. The mission of the exiles was to make their way from Florida to Cuba in speedboats, infiltrate the island, collect intelligence, organize resistance fighters, and carry out sabotage on the island. A Cuban official later cited "5,700 acts of terrorism, sabotage, and murder" in 1962 alone. Lansdale's plan was predicated on sparking a massive popular rebellion in Cuba that would prompt demands for a rescue mission. The U.S. military would then have the international legitimacy to invade the island and dispose of Castro. Like the Bay of Pigs planners, Lansdale denied Castro's political strength. In November 1961, a chastened CIA had conceded that "the great bulk of the population still accepts the regime and a substantial number still support it with enthusiasm." Lansdale constantly pressured CIA analysts to modify their conclusions, as if changing things on paper in Washington would alter political loyalties in Cuba.[29]

The Kennedy administration applied other pressures to Cuba. It imposed a near total trade embargo on Cuba. It demanded that Latin Americans drive Cuba out of the inter-American community, the Organization of American States. The Defense Department drew up extensive plans to attack Cuba with air strikes, parachute drops, and an amphibious assault. In the spring of 1962, U.S. Marines trained for an amphibious assault by invading Vieques Island, Puerto Rico. The military exercise carried the codename "ORTSAC," or "Castro" spelled backwards. Attorney General Kennedy proposed staging a violent incident at the U.S. military base at Guantánamo Bay, thus providing a rationale for an attack on Cuba. Under pressure from the administration the Joint Chiefs developed "Operation Northwoods" as a complement to Operation Mongoose. Among the schemes military planners suggested was sinking a boatload of Cuban refugees sailing for Florida or shooting Cuban refugees in the United States. Castro would be then blamed for the violence.[30]

The CIA's assassination efforts against Castro, which began under President Eisenhower, continued throughout the Kennedy presidency. The proposed schemes included killing Castro with poisoned pills, pens, darts, or cigars, shooting him with a telescopic rifle, or taking advantage of Castro's love for the sea by either giving him a diving suit with a deadly contaminant or rigging an exotic-looking seashell with explosives near Castro's favorite snorkeling area. The CIA also hoped the Mafia would carry out a gangland-style "rubout" of Castro. Historian Howard Jones has argued that assassination was the "lynchpin" of the Bay of Pigs invasion scenario. CIA planners expected that a leaderless Cuba would be in chaos, when Brigade 2506 hit the Cuban beaches.[31]

What precise knowledge President Kennedy had of these conspiracies cannot be determined. Shortly after taking office, NCS advisor McGeorge Bundy received a briefing on the CIA's assassination capabilities. In May 1962, Attorney General Kennedy received a thorough briefing about the CIA's contacts with gambling syndicate figures John Roselli and Sam Giancana. No document has yet appeared proving that either Bundy or Robert Kennedy told the president about the assassination plots. According to aides, President Kennedy asked for military intervention plans for the day when Castro might be removed from the Cuban scene. He also broached the subject of assassination with his good friend, Senator George Smathers (D-FL), and with a journalist. Both men later said that the president expressed distaste for the idea. Biographers like Arthur Schlesinger have also claimed that a Roman Catholic like Kennedy could not countenance assassination. On the other hand, Richard Helms, who commanded the CIA's clandestine service, answered a journalist's question about whether President Kennedy wanted Castro dead. Helms replied that "there is nothing on paper, of course." Helms added that "there is certainly no question in my mind that he did."[32] No document exists that shows that the president ordered the end of assassination efforts against Castro.

Scholars and journalists have speculated about what led the Kennedy administration to engage in this bizarre, extreme behavior. Secretary of Defense Robert McNamara would later lament that the administration was "hysterical" about Castro. Investigative journalist Seymour Hersh, who interviewed former CIA operatives, has charged that the Kennedy brothers had a personal vendetta against Castro, taking a blood oath to make Castro and his Communist friends pay for the staining of the family's honor at the Bay of Pigs.[33] Although personal animus may have informed the administration's policies, no document or taped conversation has appeared in which the Kennedy brothers vowed revenge against Castro. Concerns about national security, the global balance of power, and domestic politics informed their discussions about Cuba.

MISSILE CRISIS

President Kennedy's national security fears came true on 16 October 1962, when he learned that the Soviets were developing sites in Cuba for medium- and inter-mediate-range ballistic missiles equipped to carry nuclear weapons. U.S. intelligence analysts had not anticipated this development. Soviet Chairman Nikita Khrushchev and Fidel Castro bear significant responsibility for the crisis. President Kennedy had publicly warned that "the gravest issues would arise" if the Soviets sent "ground to ground missiles" to Cuba. Soviet and Cuban officials repeatedly assured the United States that the Soviet Union would not base offensive weapon systems in Cuba. But the Kennedy administration also caused the confrontation. The administration had committed acts of war against Castro's Cuba. The president did not think about the consequences of his anti-Cuban policies. In fact, at the beginning of the crisis, Kennedy confessed that he did not understand the motives behind missiles in Cuba, blurting out that "it's a goddamn mystery to me." From the Soviet and Cuban perspective, all evidence—assassination plots, the rejection of Che Guevara's peace offering, Operation Mongoose, the trade embargo, military training exercises in the Caribbean—pointed to the conclusion that the United States wanted to invade Cuba and murder its leader. Secretary of Defense McNamara has conceded that "with hindsight, if I had been a Cuban leader, I think I might have expected a U.S. invasion."[34]

The course and conduct of the Cuban Missile Crisis are familiar.[35] After extensive discussions in Moscow in mid-1962 with Cuban leaders, the Soviets received permission from the Cubans in early September 1962 to install nuclear weapons in Cuba. The Soviets planned to send thirty-six medium-range missiles, twenty-four intermediate-range missiles, forty-eight light IL-28 bombers, and tactical nuclear weapons. The Soviets could hit cities in the United States with the missiles and bombers. The approximately one hundred tactical nuclear weapons could be used to repel an invasion of the island. After the discovery, President Kennedy met secretly with advisors for almost a week. The president immediately vowed that "we're going to take out those missiles." Initial discussions focused on a military response, perhaps an air strike on the missile sites. The president decided, however, to postpone the military solution advocated strenuously by the Joint Chiefs of Staff and to impose a naval blockade, or "quarantine," around Cuba. On October 22, in a televised address, President Kennedy informed the nation of the crisis, announced the quarantine, and demanded that the Soviets remove the missiles. Over the next week, tensions mounted between the two superpowers. But on October 28, the president and Soviet Chairman Khrushchev struck a deal. The Soviets would remove the missiles, and, in turn, the United States would pledge not to invade Cuba. The United States also confidentially promised to dismantle Jupiter missile sites in Turkey. By November 20, Kennedy announced the end of the crisis, with the Soviets having withdrawn the missiles and bombers from Cuba. U.S.–Soviet relations thereafter improved, with nuclear arms control treaties in the 1960s and an era of détente in the 1970s.

Cuban–Soviet relations soured in the aftermath of the missile crisis. Chairman Khrushchev had been unnerved by a letter he received from Castro during the crisis. Warning that an attack on the island was imminent, Castro urged Khrushchev not to "allow the circumstances in which the imperialists could launch the first nuclear strike." Troubled by Castro's rash talk about nuclear war, Khrushchev unilaterally decided to withdraw the tactical nuclear weapons from Cuba. The United States had not discovered these nuclear weapons. Castro further angered Khrushchev when he refused to allow an international inspection team on the islands. The furious Cubans alleged that the Soviets had sacrificed Cuban security and socialist solidarity for the removal of the Turkish missiles and a better relationship with the United States. Subsequent developments also seemed to confirm the Cuban belief that the "no-invasion pledge" was meaningless.[36]

RENEWED WAR

The denouement of the missile crisis did not lead to a détente between the United States and Cuba. The Kennedy administration continued to pursue an aggressive, belligerent policy toward Cuba. In his 27 October letter to Chairman Khrushchev, Kennedy offered a non-invasion pledge for the removal of missiles from Cuba. But after October 27, the administration conditioned its non-invasion pledge with the provisos that Cuba must cease being a source of Communist aggression, that the United States reserved the right to halt subversion from Cuba, and that the United States intended for the Cuban people to gain their freedom one day. Because it judged that Castro's Cuba would never conform to U.S. standards, the administration considered itself free to attack Cuba, foreswearing only an unprovoked military invasion of the island.

Between December 1962 and November 1963, the administration renewed its war against Castro on all fronts. The Agriculture and State Departments investigated whether the United States could hurt the Cuban economy by manipulating the price of sugar on world markets. The State Department pressured U.S. allies to curtail trade with Cuba. The administration also began the process of ejecting Cuba from the International Monetary Fund. The president coupled economic warfare with new military preparations. In April 1963, he urged his national security team to prepare for an invasion of Cuba, asking, "Are we keeping our Cuban contingency plans up to date?" Kennedy wanted to send troops to Cuba quickly in case of a general uprising.[37]

The administration's fury against Castro mounted when the Cuban spent the entire month of May 1963 in the Soviet Union. Khrushchev soothed Castro's hurt feelings over the missile crisis with a package of economic and military aid for Cuba. In April, Kennedy had approved the sabotage of cargoes on Cuban ships and the crippling of ships. He also authorized inciting Cubans to harass, attack, and sabotage Soviet military personnel in Cuba "provided every precaution is taken to prevent attribution." After Castro's trip, the president demanded and received an integrated program of propaganda, economic denial, and sabotage against Cuba. On June 19, Kennedy, dubbed "Higher Authority" in CIA parlance, approved a sabotage program against Cuba, expressing "a particular interest" in external sabotage operations. The CIA was subsequently authorized to carry out thirteen major sabotage operations in Cuba, including attacks on an electric power plant, an oil refinery, and a sugar mill. On November 12, Higher Authority conducted a major review of his anti-Castro program and received an upbeat assessment from the CIA. The president was also informed that the CIA would launch new attacks, including the underwater demolition of docks and ships. The memorandums of record state that "Higher Authority" rather than President Kennedy attended these meetings. This was to give the president, again in CIA language, the option of "plausible denial." U.S. officials wanted the president of the United States to be able to deny that he had authorized terrorism and sabotage.[38]

Khrushchev protested these attacks on Cuba, averring that the United States had reneged on the agreement that ended the missile crisis. President Kennedy deflected the complaints, charging that the Cubans were fomenting revolution throughout the Western Hemisphere. Lacking evidence to sustain those claims, the United States perhaps fabricated evidence, as it previously had in 1954, when, with "Operation Washtub," the CIA planted arms in Nicaragua and blamed Guatemala. In early November 1963, Venezuela announced that it had discovered a cache of Cuban arms on a Venezuelan beach, allegedly left for leftist radicals determined to disrupt upcoming elections. This detection of the purported Cuban intervention raised many questions. Former CIA agents have subsequently written that they believed that their colleagues planted the arms in Venezuela. In May 1963, the

CIA sent an anti-Cuba plan to the NSC that included the idea of placing caches of arms from Communist countries in selected regions of Latin America, "ostensibly proving the arms were smuggled from Cuba."[39]

Assassination plots against Castro also continued after the missile crisis. On 22 November 1963, the day of the president's death in Dallas, CIA agents rendezvoused in Paris with a Cuban official, Rolando Cubela Secades, code-named AM/LASH. The agents passed to Cubela a ballpoint pen rigged with a poisonous hypodermic needle intended to produce Castro's instant death. In the previous month, the CIA had assured Cubela that it operated with the approval of Attorney General Kennedy. Former CIA operatives have also alleged that the president signaled encouragement to AM/LASH. On November 18 in Miami, in what turned out to be his last speech on inter-American affairs, Kennedy referred to Castro as a "barrier" to be removed.[40]

Some scholars have suggested that Kennedy showed interest, during his last months in office, in improving relations with Castro. Intermediaries were authorized to speak with Cuban officials. The Kennedy administration attached, however, stringent conditions to these preliminary discussions, insisting that Cuba would have to break ties with the Soviet Union, expel Soviet troops from the island, and end subversion in Latin America. The United States also wanted Castro to renounce his faith in communism. In short, President Kennedy was prepared only to accept Castro's surrender.[41] His administration never renounced its policy of either overthrowing Castro or plotting his death.

LYNDON JOHNSON AND CUBA

President Lyndon B. Johnson maintained the U.S. policy of hostility toward Castro's government. The Johnson administration refused to negotiate with Castro's Cuba, and it intensified the economic pressure on the island. In mid-1964, it persuaded two-thirds of the members of the Organization of American States (OAS) to support a resolution calling on member states to sever all political and economic ties with Cuba. Defenders of the resolution included anti-Communist, dictatorial regimes like Brazil and Nicaragua. This resolution was in retaliation for Cuba's alleged intervention in Venezuela. Democratic states, like Chile and Uruguay, who had opposed the resolution eventually complied with the OAS mandate. Only Mexico resisted U.S. pressure and maintained its ties with Castro's Cuba.

The Johnson administration also cajoled European allies to join the economic embargo of Cuba. In Johnson's characteristic salty language, he wanted "to pinch their [Cuban] nuts."[42] After the OAS meeting, Secretary of State Dean Rusk met with the ambassadors of allies like Spain, Belgium, the Netherlands, and West Germany to press the U.S. case against Cuba. Belgium, for example, succumbed to the U.S. pressure and cancelled a sale of locomotives to Cuba. The administration especially wanted its closest ally, the United Kingdom, to sever relations Cuba. President Johnson made a personal appeal to Prime Minister Sir Alec Douglas-Home in a meeting at the White House in 1964. The U.S. position was that "economic sanctions against Cuba was the only weapon short of an act of war that could make the support of Castro's Cuba more costly to the Soviet Union." The United States further believed that an embargo of trade could create "conditions of economic stringency that might ultimately bring about the elimination of the Communist regime." The British rejected, however, the U.S. arguments and continued to trade with Cuba. The United Kingdom depended on trade for its economic vitality.[43]

The Johnson administration, like the Eisenhower and Kennedy administrations, refused to accept the legitimacy of the Cuban Revolution. The administration also had a confrontation with Cuba in 1964. A dispute over a Cuban fishing boat led Fidel Castro to cut the water supply to the military base at Guantánamo Bay. President Johnson responded by transforming the base into a sealed enclave with little Cuban contact. The United States created its own water supply, constructing a desalinization plant. But President Johnson made one significant change in his predecessor's policy. He gradually shut down the campaign of assassination, sabotage, and terrorism directed at Castro's Cuba. Johnson, who had not been actively involved as vice president in the covert war against Castro, received his first comprehensive briefing on CIA activities on 19 December 1963. CIA officials reviewed the various sabotage and terrorism attacks that President Kennedy had personally approved in June and November of 1963. At the briefing, President Johnson asked the pointed question "whether there is any significant insurgency within Cuba." Desmond Fitzgerald, the CIA official who directed the covert campaign, admitted that "there is no national movement on which we can build." Thereafter, at the briefing, President Johnson ruled that the CIA's next attack on a major target—the Matanzas power plant—would be cancelled.[44]

Over the next eighteen months, President Johnson shut down the covert war against Fidel Castro. The United States stopped sponsoring raids on Cuban targets, it terminated the funding of Cuban exile groups who planned to attack Cuba, and it severed its contacts with potential assassins. By June 1965, the United States no longer waged covert, violent war against Cuba. Johnson overruled powerful bureaucracies like the CIA and the Joint Chiefs of Staff of the U.S. military who wanted to continue to attack Cuba. His decision was supported by influential administration figures like Secretary Rusk, Secretary of Defense McNamara, and the new Assistant Secretary of State for Latin America, Thomas Mann.

President Johnson probably had several reasons for reversing the Eisenhower–Kennedy policy of attacking Cuba. The new president disliked Attorney General Kennedy, the person most identified with the anti-Castro campaign. He wanted to improve relations with the Soviet Union and did not want another Soviet–American confrontation over Cuba. Johnson wanted to be perceived as a steady, reliable man of peace during the 1964 presidential campaign. In any case, Johnson already had his share of foreign policy challenges, especially in Vietnam. His decision to invade the Dominican Republic in late March 1965 in order to forestall an alleged Communist takeover only compounded his international problems. President Johnson also seems to have been repelled by the nature of some

U.S. actions, such as assassination plots, against Castro's Cuba. Shortly after taking office, he told CIA Director John McCone that he no longer wanted his CIA chief to have the image of a "cloak and dagger role." After he left office, Johnson revealed in an interview that "we were running a damned Murder Incorporated in the Caribbean."[45]

Perhaps the key reason for Johnson's decision to halt the war against Castro was that he concluded that the CIA's war against Castro would not work. Attacks on Cuba's economic infrastructure and maritime raids on coastal targets were designed to spark a mass uprising in Cuba against Castro. However grudgingly, Johnson and his advisors conceded that Fidel Castro enjoyed widespread popular support. President Johnson wanted to "get rid of" Castro. But as Assistant Secretary Mann explained about Castro, "as long as that army is loyal to him, he is going to be there until he dies." Mann further observed in a memorandum to Secretary of State Rusk that Cuban political figures in exile in Miami, Florida, had little support within Cuba.[46]

After mid-1965 and for the rest of the Johnson presidency, the United States pursued "containment" policies against Fidel Castro. In essence, it adapted the policies it practiced against the Soviet Union. The administration authorized the CIA to disseminate propaganda, covertly collect intelligence and counterintelligence, and wage economic warfare against Cuba. The United States would make life hard for Cubans, hoping either that the Communist system would collapse in Cuba or that Castro would die.

CHE GUEVARA IN BOLIVIA

Castro would not die in the twentieth century. But his *compañero*, Ernesto "Che" Guevara, would be executed in the village of La Higuera, in southeastern Bolivia, by a Bolivian soldier on 9 October 1967. The president of Bolivia, General René Barrientos Otuña (1964–69), issued the order to execute the prisoner. Che Guevara's capture and execution in a remote part of Bolivia exposed the complicated realities of promoting revolution in Latin America. Guevara's demise and the defeat of his guerrilla army in Bolivia further demonstrated that the United States held exaggerated fears about Cuba's revolutionary role in the hemisphere.

Guevara's decision in 1966 to organize a guerrilla movement in Bolivia reflected his political philosophy, Cuba's geopolitical challenges, and his yearning for glory. Guevara rejected Nikita Khrushchev and Leonid Brezhnev's call for "peaceful coexistence" with the United States and the Western capitalist nations. He also abhorred Latin American Communist parties who participated in peaceful, political activities and spurned armed revolution. Guevara preached the "the tricontinental strategy" of promoting revolution in Asia, Africa, and Latin America and defeating imperialism. The Vietnamese Communists had shown the way by defending national liberation and socialism and sinking the United States into the quagmire of endless war. Guevara's contribution to revolutionary thinking was his "*foco* theory." A small band of guerrillas could spark a mass revolutionary movement. The guerrillas could count on the forces of imperialism, including the United States, responding to the *foco* threat in a heavy-handed way, alienating the local population and turning them into guerrilla supporters. The insurgency would spread throughout the country. With the United States militarily tied down in Asia, Africa, and Latin America, socialist countries like Cuba would be free. The United States would no longer be able to focus on attacking Cuba and murdering its leaders. Guevara's patron, Fidel Castro, subscribed to Guevara's worldview, but always had to be conscious of the Soviet Union's disapproval of armed rebellion in Latin America. Cuba depended on the Soviet Union for economic and military aid. Guevara's strategy also fit his sense of heroic destiny. He once told reporters: "I am convinced that I have a mission to fulfill in this world, and on the altar of this mission I have to sacrifice my home, I have to sacrifice all the pleasures of daily life, I have to sacrifice my personal security, and I might even have to sacrifice my life."[47]

Guevara's experience in Bolivia made obvious the errors in his thinking. He presumed a universal code of revolution. Whereas Guevara, an Argentine, was an international revolutionary, not all who wanted change and social justice were. Cuba was not the world or even Latin America. Impoverished, oppressed Latin Americans dreamed of a better life, but they also had loyalties to their nation, their region or state, their ethnic and racial heritage, and their Roman Catholic religion. The *campesinos* of southeastern Bolivia proved not to be the sea in which guerrillas could swim. Neither Guevara nor his men could speak the local indigenous language, Guaraní. Bolivian country folk did not join the guerrilla movement, declined to supply the guerrillas, asked Guevara to leave the region, and reported Guevara's movements to the Bolivian army. Guevara and his men had to resort to stealing food and supplies from villages in order to survive. Bolivian Communists, adhering to the dictates of Moscow, also refused to enlist in Guevara's movement. Bolivian Communist leader Mario Monje warned: "When the people learn that this guerrilla movement is led by a foreigner, they will turn their backs and refuse to support it." Monje added: "You will die very heroically, but you have no prospects of victory." Guevara's vanity and recklessness also contributed to the Bolivian disaster. He insisted on sole control of the guerrilla movement, declaring in Bolivia that "here I am adviser to no one." Guevara failed to heed the advice he once received from Gamal Abdel Nasser, the nationalist leader of Egypt. The Egyptian wondered why Guevara talked of accepting "the challenge of death." Nasser noted: "You are a young man. If necessary we should die for the revolution, but it would be much better if we could live for the revolution."[48]

Guevara slipped into Bolivia in November 1966. He would be joined by sixteen Cubans, Bolivians, and a few other Latin Americans, eventually creating a force of forty-seven combatants. These numbers easily superseded the numbers of men who retreated into the Cuban mountains in 1956. But the Castro brothers and Guevara had glorified their guerrilla movement, forgetting that they had a vital network of urban support in Cuba in the late 1950s. Only a handful of urban

Bolivians supported the guerrillas, and their organization was penetrated by the CIA and Bolivian police. The Bolivian army, numbering about a thousand men, chased the guerrillas for seven months in 1967, eventually trapping them in a canyon. Bolivian soldiers found Guevara in a pathetic state. Guevara, who turned thirty-nine in 1967, realized that he no longer had the physical agility that he had in Cuba in the 1950s. A life-long asthmatic, the former doctor could not find the medicine in rural Bolivia that he needed. He appeared emaciated and dirty. His hair was long, straggly, and matted, his clothes were torn, and he had rough leather sheaths, not boots, on his feet. Before being captured on 7 October 1967, Guevara had been wounded in the calf. After executing Guevara, the Bolivian military flew the body to the town of Vallegrande, where the corpse was photographed. Guevara achieved mythic status in death. To some, Guevara in death resembled Jesus Christ. The reality, however, was that Guevara failed as a revolutionary everywhere, except for Cuba.

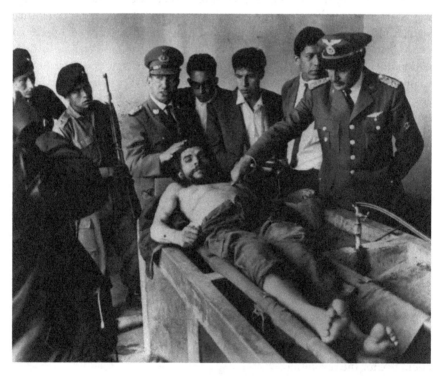

The body of Ernesto "Che" Guevara is surrounded by Bolivian soldiers in this photograph taken in Vallegrande, Bolivia, in October 1967. By the time the Bolivians captured him, Guevara was in poor physical shape, looking emaciated and bedraggled. Although the Bolivians displayed Guevara like a hunting trophy, the international impact of the photograph was not as they perhaps intended. The photograph added to Guevara's mythic status. To some, Guevara looked as they imagined Jesus Christ might have looked in death after his crucifixion. (Corbis Images)

The United States played a role in the defeat of Guevara. In response to the Cuban revolution, the Kennedy administration had transformed military aid policies for Latin America from hemispheric defense to counterinsurgency—developing tactics to defeat guerrilla movements. The Kennedy administration increased military aid to Latin America to $77 million a year, a 50 percent increase over the average of the Eisenhower years. In fiscal 1962, the peak year, the United States trained nine thousand Latin American officers and enlisted personnel. Overall, during the 1960s, an average of 3,500 Latin American officers and men annually attended military schools such as the U.S. Army Caribbean School in the Canal Zone, renamed the "School of the Americas." Select Latin Americans trained at the Special Warfare School at Fort Bragg, North Carolina, the home of the famed "Green Berets." Latin Americans studied topics taught in Spanish on the essentials of counterinsurgency—clandestine operations, communism and democracy, defoliation, the use of informants, interrogation of prisoners and suspects, handling mass rallies and meetings, intelligence photography, and polygraphs.[49]

At the request of President Barrientos, the Johnson administration dispatched a highly decorated combat veteran and trainer, Major Ralph "Pappy" Shelton of the Green Berets, to Bolivia in April 1967. He trained a Bolivian ranger battalion that joined the hunt for Guevara and captured him. U.S. advisors did not join the Bolivians in the field. A CIA operative, Felix Rodríguez, helped organize an intelligence network in the rural areas and briefly interrogated the captured Guevara. The United States did not request the execution of Guevara. Johnson administration officials thought the Bolivians had acted unwisely in killing the renowned Argentine revolutionary. Walt W. Rostow, President Johnson's national security advisor, called the execution "stupid," perhaps believing that the Bolivians had created a martyr for the Communist cause.[50]

The death of Guevara symbolized what had been apparent for some years—the collapse of revolutionary movements throughout Latin America. As a State Department official happily summarized in 1967, "The confident predictions of sweeping Communist victories which have often emanated from Havana have not been borne out." In March 1968, the U.S. intelligence community reiterated the State Department's optimism, noting in a "National Intelligence Estimate" (NIE) on "The Potential for Revolution for Latin America" that "in no case do insurgencies pose a serious short-run threat to take over a government." In truth, the Cubans had talked more about revolution in Latin America than in actually fomenting it. Their only sustained efforts had been in Venezuela and Bolivia. Both efforts had failed miserably. Throughout the 1960s, Latin American Communists obeyed Moscow and abjured armed conflict. Moscow informed Latin American nations that it did not support resolutions, such as at the Tricontinental Conference, calling for revolution in Latin America. Except for gaining a difficult ally in Cuba, the Soviet Union did not appreciably increase its influence in the region in the 1960s. During the Cold War, only three nations—Argentina, Mexico, and Uruguay—continuously maintained ties with the Soviet Union, and only Mexico always kept its embassy open in Havana. The Soviet Union allocated only about 6 percent of its foreign aid to the non-Communist world to Latin America. Excluding Cuba, its trade with Latin America was minuscule. The balance of trade always favored the Latin Americans. For example, the hungry Soviets needed to purchase Argentine wheat, because of perennial shortcomings in the Soviet agricultural sector.[51]

By mid-1968, Fidel Castro accepted the major objectives of Soviet foreign policy, which included peaceful coexistence with the West. Castro waited for news of victory from Bolivia. But the Cuban leader lacked the logistical resources to aid Guevara and his guerrilla band. Guevara's defeat and Brezhnev and Kosygin's fury over Guevara's mission forced Castro back into the Soviet camp. Castro shocked idealistic supporters and admirers of the Cuban Revolution around the world when, in August 1968, he publicly defended the appalling Soviet invasion of Czechoslovakia. Soviet tanks had entered Prague to crush the liberal reforms of the "Prague Spring" pursued by Alexander Dubček. Castro now appeared to be little more than a Communist stooge, for he conceded that the Soviet Union had illegally violated Czechoslovakia's sovereignty. Castro could only offer that the socialist camp had the right to prevent a socialist country from breaking away. Both Soviet and U.S. officials habitually characterized Castro as emotional, immature, and irresponsible. In fact, Castro was shrewd, calculating, and realistic. He stayed in power for five decades because he had a pragmatic side to his governing philosophy. The Cuban Revolution's survival depended on Soviet economic and military assistance, for the United States had succeeded in isolating the island. Fidel Castro could not follow the path of ideological purity; he could not "be like Che."[52]

The United States had not achieved total victory in its war against Fidel Castro's Cuba. A Communist state survived in the traditional U.S. sphere of influence. And the Kennedy brothers had not succeeded in "eliminating" the Castro brothers. The policy of sponsoring assassination, sabotage, and terrorism had fallen short of its goals. But the United States had contained the Cuban Revolution. By the end of the 1960s, Cuba no longer posed a revolutionary threat to the region. U.S. political and economic pressure had also hobbled the island. The containment of Cuba involved more than just attacking Castro and his revolution. The United States tried to undercut the appeal of the Cuban Revolution by building a better life for Latin Americans through the Alliance for Progress economic development program. The Kennedy and Johnson administrations also attacked and undermined Latin American leaders deemed soft on Castro and communism.

CHAPTER 5

No More Cubas—The Kennedy and Johnson Doctrines

The United States waged war against Fidel Castro and the Cuban Revolution on many fronts in the 1960s. The United States sponsored an invasion of the island by Cuban exiles and conducted a campaign of assassination, sabotage, and terrorism against Cuban leaders and their revolutionary supporters. By the mid-1960s, U.S. officials concluded that they could not destroy the Cuban Revolution through violence. They resorted to containing the Cuban Revolution, keeping the island diplomatically and economically isolated. U.S. officials believed, however, that they needed to counter the Cuban Revolution with more than force. They recognized that Latin Americans had legitimate aspirations for economic progress and social justice. The John F. Kennedy administration designed a grand program—the Alliance for Progress—to transform and modernize Latin America. President Kennedy pledged to transfer U.S. wealth to uplift the conditions of Latin America's poor. The U.S response to Cuban communism would be representative democracy and socioeconomic progress. The United States had revivified Western Europe with the Marshall Plan. The Kennedy and Lyndon Johnson administrations believed that they could repeat the historic achievements of the Marshall Plan by building, in the 1960s, sturdy, stable Latin American nations that would resist the false promises of communism and remain closely allied to the United States.

High ideals and nobility of purpose did not, however, always characterize the U.S. approach to Latin America in the 1960s. The Kennedy and Johnson administrations wanted democracy and development for the region, but they held exaggerated fears about Communist expansion in the Western Hemisphere. Both Presidents Kennedy and Johnson were racial egalitarians who enjoyed the company and friendship of Latin Americans. But the two presidents and their advisors did not trust Latin American leaders when it came to the menace of communism. From the U.S. perspective, preventing a "second Cuba" in the region remained the highest foreign-policy goal for both international and domestic reasons. National security fears triumphed over U.S. dreams for the good life for Latin Americans. The Kennedy and Johnson administrations intervened throughout Latin America, invading counties, destabilizing popularly elected governments, penetrating Latin American associations and institutions, and manipulating elections. The two administrations helped created the political and ideological climate in Latin America in which mass murder and gross violations of human rights characterized political life during the 1970s and 1980s.

ALLIANCE FOR PROGRESS

President Kennedy unveiled his reform program for Latin America in an impressive White House ceremony on the evening of 13 March 1961, just a month before the Bay of Pigs invasion. After hosting an elegant reception for 250 people, including the diplomatic corps of the Latin American republics and congressional leaders, the president and his wife, Jacqueline Bouvier Kennedy, directed guests to move to the East Room. They seated themselves on gilt-edged chairs arranged in semi-circles on both sides of the rostrum. President Kennedy's speech was simultaneously broadcast by the Voice of America in English, Spanish, French, and Portuguese, the languages of the Western Hemisphere. Kennedy thrilled his attentive audience, telling Latin Americans what they had been waiting nearly two decades to hear. The United States would underwrite the region's social and economic transformation. The United States would join in a "vast cooperative effort, unparalleled in magnitude and nobility of purpose, to satisfy the basic needs of Latin American people for homes, work and land, health and schools—*techo, trabajo y tierra, salud y escuela*." Dubbed the Alliance for Progress—*Alianza para el Progreso*—the new program would be Latin America's "Marshall Plan."[1]

Kennedy delivered over $600 million in emergency economic aid to Latin America in early 1961. His administration gave, however, real substance to his splendid rhetoric at an inter-American economic conference held in August 1961 at the Uruguayan seaside resort of Punta del Este. Secretary of the Treasury C. Douglas Dillon informed Latin American delegates that they could count on receiving $20 billion in public and private capital over the next ten years, "the decade of development." In early twenty-first-century terms, this would be the equivalent to the impressive sum of over $100 billion. With this influx of foreign money combined with an additional $80 billion that Latin Americans could reasonably expect to generate in internal savings, Latin American nations would achieve a real economic growth rate of 2.5 percent a year. Administration officials chose to be publicly cautious; they actually expected that growth might reach 5 percent a year. Marvelous changes would flow from foreign aid and economic growth. The Charter of the Punta del Este Conference enumerated more than ninety lofty goals. Latin Americans would witness a five-year increase in life expectancy, a halving of the infant mortality rate, the elimination of adult illiteracy, and the provision of six years of primary education to every school-age child.[2]

The Alliance for Progress meant more than improvements in health, education, and welfare. This would be a revolution that would surpass the Cuban Revolution. Political freedom and social reform would go hand in hand with material progress. Archaic tax and land-tenure structures would be dismantled and self-serving tyrants cast aside. President Kennedy vowed that North and South Americans would "demonstrate to the entire world that man's unsatisfied aspiration for economic progress and social justice can best be achieved by free men working within a framework of democratic institutions."[3]

The Kennedy administration decided to embark on a campaign to underwrite change and social development in Latin America because it perceived that the region was vulnerable to radical social revolution. President Kennedy characterized the region as "the most dangerous area in the world."[4] If poverty and injustice were preconditions for upheaval, Latin America was indeed ripe for revolution. In several countries—Bolivia, the Dominican Republic, El Salvador, Guatemala, and Haiti—malnutrition was widespread, with a grossly inadequate daily per capita consumption of 2,000 calories or less and a daily intake of fifteen grams of animal protein. In eight other countries, daily per capita consumption only approached 2,400 calories, the bare minimum necessary to sustain people who toiled in fields and factories. By comparison, in 1961, U.S. adults consumed every day over 3,000 calories and sixty-six grams of animal protein. Hungry people had predictably poor health records. Guatemalans had a life expectancy of less than fifty years, twenty years less than for a U.S. citizen. In the Andean nations of Ecuador and Peru, approximately 10 percent of newborns died during their first year of life. The poor of Latin America also lacked education and skills. Adult illiteracy rates ranged from 35 to 40 percent in relatively prosperous nations like Brazil and Venezuela. This misery was concentrated in the countryside, with *campesinos* working tiny plots of land and a rural oligarchy operating vast estates or *latifundia*. In Colombia 1.3 percent of landowners controlled over 50 percent of the land, and in Chile 7 percent owned 80 percent of the land. Desperate rural people were fleeing to urban areas, moving into squalid shantytowns that surrounded cities like Bogotá, Caracas, and Rio de Janeiro.[5]

Although it had never been especially troubled by poverty and desperation in Latin America, the Dwight Eisenhower administration poured the foundation for the Alliance for Progress. The administration knew that Latin Americans protested that they had been "neglected" in the postwar period. Between mid-1953 and mid-1958, the United States had provided $12.8 billion in foreign aid. But only $783 million, less than 7 percent, had been directed toward Latin America. Latin American democrats further resented that the administration had lavished medals and military support on right-wing dictators because they professed to be anti-Communist. Latin Americans visibly expressed their anger with U.S. policies in May 1958, when Vice President Richard M. Nixon toured South America. Protestors hounded Nixon in Argentina, Peru, and Uruguay, and, in Caracas, Venezuela, a howling mob tried to assault the vice president. In the aftermath of the Nixon trip, Eisenhower and his advisors began to listen to Latin Americans, like President Juscelino Kubitschek of Brazil (1956–61), who spoke of inter-American economic cooperation, an "Operation Pan America." President Kubitschek had won international acclaim for launching the creation of a fantastic capital city,

Brasília, in the heart of the country. The Eisenhower administration responded by funding an Inter-American Development Bank. In the aftermath of the Cuban Revolution, the administration went further, putting $500 million into a Social Progress Trust Fund (1960) to underwrite health, education, housing, and land reform projects.

Beyond the sense of crisis that informed U.S. perspectives about Latin America, U.S. officials judged it a propitious time to foster progressive reform in Latin America. In a series of popular upheavals dubbed the "twilight of the tyrants," ten Latin American military dictators fell from power between 1956 and 1960. Middle-class reformers, like Rómulo Betancourt of Venezuela, replaced the military men. They vowed to rule democratically and to reform the region's archaic social structures. Betancourt and influential political leaders like Arturo Frondizi of Argentina and José Figueres of Costa Rica joined with Kubitschek in pleading for U.S. help. They unabashedly played on the U.S. fear of communism. Latin America's poverty and injustice, they warned, was a fertile breeding ground for the Communist contagion to fester and spread. A second, third, and fourth "Cuba" might be on the horizon. Indeed, Che Guevara attended the conference at Punta del Este and debated Secretary of the Treasury Dillon. Guevara boasted that Latin America's "new age" would be under "the star of Cuba," not the Alliance for Progress.[6]

President Kennedy perceived the Cuban Revolution as part and parcel of Soviet Premier Nikita Khrushchev's "wars of national liberation strategy." In a lengthy address given in Moscow on 6 January 1961, Khrushchev briefly raised the issue. Scholars have questioned whether Khrushchev intended to provoke the president-elect; they have suggested that the Soviet leader was addressing doctrinal issues with the Communist camp.[7] Nonetheless, Ambassador to Brazil Lincoln Gordon, who helped design the Alliance for Progress, decided that Khrushchev had signaled his intention to use Cuba as "a base for military and intelligence activities against the United States and for further opportunistic conquests in Latin America."[8] President Kennedy drew similar conclusions from his one, unpleasant meeting with Khrushchev in Vienna in June 1961. Upon returning home, the president soberly reported to the nation that his Soviet adversary predicted that in the developing countries "the revolution of rising peoples would eventually be a Communist revolution, and that the so-called wars of liberation, supported by the Kremlin, would replace the old methods of direct aggression and invasion." Kennedy added that it was "the Communist theory" that "a small group of disciplined Communists could exploit discontent and misery in a country where the average income may be $60 or $70 a year, and seize control, therefore, of an entire country without Communist troops ever crossing any international border." Secretary of State Dean Rusk followed the president's public warning with a confidential alert to U.S. diplomats in Latin America. Khrushchev was targeting Latin America.[9]

Not to oppose the alleged Communist master plan for Latin America would imperil the national security of the United States. The United States would be surrounded if Communists came to power in Central and South American nations. U.S. officials also believed that they had to maintain U.S. credibility "in our own backyard." The U.S. ability to act on the global stage would be impeded if it could not maintain order and stability in Latin America, the traditional U.S. sphere of influence. Secretary Rusk once noted to Argentine diplomats that the Communist adversaries measured the resolve of the United States in the Western Hemisphere. "A lack of determination on our part," Rusk warned, might encourage Soviet aggression in the divided city of Berlin.[10]

Not only national security anxieties but also domestic political calculations informed President Kennedy's approach to the region. The president was loath to face in his 1964 reelection campaign the same charge—losing a Latin American country (Cuba) to communism—that he had thrown at the Eisenhower/Nixon team in 1960. Throughout his tenure, Kennedy predicted disaster in Latin America. In January 1961, he told an aide "the whole place could blow up on us." In November 1962, he cautioned Argentina's General Pedro Eugenio Aramburu to be alert, observing "that the next twelve months would be critical in Latin America with respect to renewed Communist attempts at penetration." In October 1963, a month before his death, he warned that Latin America posed "the greatest danger to us." A few months earlier, in a meeting with Prime Minister Harold Macmillan, Kennedy demanded that the United Kingdom postpone the independence of its South American colony, British Guiana. Kennedy alleged that British Guiana might become a Communist state. British Guiana would then join Cuba as a major campaign issue and jeopardize the president's reelection.[11] As presidential advisor and biographer Arthur Schlesinger put it, it was his boss's "absolute determination" to prevent a second Communist outpost in the Western Hemisphere.[12]

Although motivated by Cold War imperatives, the president and his team approached the task of building a prosperous, democratic, anti-Communist Latin America with supreme confidence. They thought they knew how to "modernize" Latin America. They fashioned the Alliance for Progress on contemporary social science theories, espoused by intellectuals, which included Ambassador Gordon and presidential assistant Walt W. Rostow. In the postwar period, social scientists had enunciated formal theories on political and economic development. They posited a universal, quantitatively measurable movement of all societies from a "traditional" situation toward a single ideal form or "modern" organization. Traditional societies, as they presumably existed in Latin America, had authoritarian political structures, rural, backward economies, and a lack of faith in scientific progress and the entrepreneurial spirit. A modern society, which would look remarkably like the United States, would be characterized by a competitive political system, a commercialized and technologically sophisticated economic system, mass consumption, high literacy rates, and a geographically and socially mobile population.[13] The assumption that "modern" Latin Americans wanted to replicate superior U.S.-style institutions and inculcate Anglo-American values in their societies belied the concept of an "alliance."

The mission of the United States was to accelerate the modernization process, before the Communists could subvert it. The United States would identify and support urban, middle-class leaders in Latin America who favored democracy, universal education, and state policies that promoted economic development and social welfare. The United States would assist these leaders with substantial amounts of economic aid until these Latin American societies could generate enough internal capital to underwrite their own economic development. At that point, presumably within ten years, Latin American nations would have reached the "take-off stage," as outlined in Rostow's famous treatise, *The Stages of Economic Growth: A Non-Communist Manifesto* (1960). The modernization theory further held that democratic structures would flourish in nations that could sustain their own economic growth.

The lessons of history affirmed the administration's faith in the modernization process. U.S. leaders were proud that the past Democratic administration of Harry S. Truman had rebuilt war-torn Western Europe and Japan. The Alliance for Progress would be the "Marshall Plan for Latin America." The United States would pursue a policy of "enlightened anti-Communism."[14] The United States would win the Cold War in Latin America by performing righteous works. The United States would build sturdy, progressive societies that uplifted the poor and dispossessed. These modernized societies would naturally align themselves with the United States and reject the false promises of Khrushchev, Castro, and their fellow Communist travelers.

President Kennedy displayed the enthusiasm, confidence, and empathy inherent in the Alliance for Progress. During his abbreviated presidency, he toured Colombia, Venezuela, Mexico, and Costa Rica and received tumultuous welcomes. He participated, for example, in a land redistribution ceremony in Venezuela. Kennedy also opened the Oval Office to Latin American presidents, former presidents, foreign, finance, and labor ministers, ambassadors, generals, trade unionists, and economists. A telling example of the president's commitment occurred during his visit to Costa Rica. He noticed an unoccupied hospital and told aides to find funds to staff it. The U.S. Agency for International Development subsequently granted $130,000 for a children's hospital in San José.[15] Bedeviled by his quagmire of a war in Vietnam, President Johnson spent less time with Latin Americans. He made only one major trip to Latin America, meeting leaders at Punta del Este in 1967 to review the Alliance. Johnson enjoyed, however, reading reports about schools and hospitals being built in Latin America with Alliance funds.

THE DECADE OF DEVELOPMENT

The enthusiasm, energy, and optimism that infused the Alliance for Progress did not result in meaningful political and social change in Latin America. The Alliance proved to be a notable policy failure of the Cold War. During the 1960s, sixteen extra constitutional changes of government shook Latin America. Latin American economies hardly reached the "take-off stage," registering an unimpressive annual growth rate of about 2 percent. Most of the growth took place at the very end of the 1960s. The Alliance failed to reach any of its ninety-four numerical goals in health, education, and welfare. The number of unemployed Latin Americans rose from eighteen million to twenty-five million during the decade.

U.S. officials misled themselves trying to apply dubious social science theories and misleading historical analogies like the "Marshall Plan for Latin America." Latin America was not Europe. Western European countries had been devastated by war, but they had financial and technical expertise, familiarity with industrial forms of organization, institutionalized political parties, strong national identities, and, except for Germany, a robust democratic tradition. The Truman administration had helped "rebuild" countries whose social fabrics, political traditions, and economic institutions were notably similar to those of the United States. On the other hand, the Spanish/Portuguese (Iberian) and Amerindian political heritages emphasized planned economies, strong central governments, and the organization of society into corporate groups. Latin Americans traditionally gave greater significance to group achievement than to individual success. Latin Americans further believed that national progress came from a unified government rather than one slowed by a mixed form of power sharing with checks and balances. In his last address on inter-American affairs, President Kennedy conceded that the Alliance for Progress should not be compared to the Marshall Plan, for "then we helped rebuild a shattered economy whose human and social foundation remained. Today we are trying to create a basic new foundation, capable of reshaping the centuries-old societies and economies of half of a hemisphere." Yet Kennedy assured his audience that idealism, energy, and optimism would bridge the vast cultural gap and bring about the "modernization" of Latin America.[16] Although recognizing the challenges ahead, Kennedy was still assuming that Latin Americans wanted their modernized societies to replicate the social structures of the United States.

The United States also lacked the power to reform Latin America. In the postwar years, the United States militarily occupied both Germany and Japan, reordering their societies. General Douglas MacArthur, for example, directed the writing of the Japanese constitution, requiring the redistribution of land and limitations on military expenditures. In the 1960s, the Kennedy and Johnson administrations repeatedly meddled and intervened in Latin America. But the United States could hardly claim the right to invade a Latin American country because the government wasted resources, abused *campesinos*, or discriminated against citizens of African or indigenous heritages. Neither Kennedy nor Johnson could act in Latin America, as they did when they dispatched federal marshals to protect the civil rights of African-Americans in the U.S. South.[17] In any case, the history of U.S. rule in Latin America taught sobering lessons. During the first third of the twentieth century, the United States had militarily occupied countries like Cuba, the Dominican Republic, and Nicaragua in the name of democracy and progress. But the United States had not successfully exported its values. Dictators like Fulgencio Batista, Rafael Trujillo, and Anastasio Somoza García, not democrats, had emerged in the aftermath of those occupations.

The Alliance for Progress also proved far less generous than the Marshall Plan. President Kennedy regretfully had to inform Latin American leaders in private that the United States "could not give aid to Latin American countries in the same way that it helped to rebuild Europe with the Marshall Plan." Through his eloquence and spectacularly successful trips to Latin America, he had galvanized public and congressional support for the Alliance. But with Kennedy's rapid expansion of military spending on nuclear weapons, and Johnson's war in Vietnam, the United States took on heavy financial burdens in the international arena. Legislators, worried about government spending, cut both Kennedy's and Johnson's budget requests for foreign aid, sometimes by as much as 25 percent. Most Marshall Plan aid was in the form of grants, whereas the Alliance offered loans, which had to be eventually repaid. In the 1960s, the region received about $15 billion of the promised $20 billion. Even then, with Latin American nations being required to repay principal and interest on pre-1961 and Alliance loans, this meant that the actual net capital flow to Latin America during the 1960s averaged about $920 million a year. This was the equivalent of about $4 per Latin American per year. By comparison Marshall Plan money, which did not have to be repaid, amounted to $109 a year in assistance for every person in the Netherlands.[18]

The Alliance money that Latin America received did have salubrious effects. Both Presidents Kennedy and Johnson could read upbeat reports about schools and hospitals being built and more people gaining access to potable water. Democratic leaders in countries such as Costa Rica, Chile, and Venezuela performed within the spirit of the Alliance for Progress. During the early 1960s, Venezuela, for example, received over $200 million in loans and grants from the United States to finance public housing and public works projects. The United States further backed Venezuela's requests for an additional $200 million in loans from international agencies like the Inter-American Development Bank and World Bank. President Rómulo Betancourt and his successor, Raúl Leoni, toiled diligently for the poor, resettling approximately 160,000 families on their own farms, allocating budgetary expenditures to health and education, and cutting unemployment. But Venezuela never hit the Alliance's target of 2.5 percent annual growth, and 75 percent of Venezuelan youth still did not complete the sixth grade. Economic growth stagnated, because Venezuela depended on the export of oil, and oil prices declined precipitously in the 1960s, falling from $2.65 a barrel in 1957 to $1.81 in 1969.[19]

Population growth eroded many gains. With a 2.9 percent annual rate of increase, Latin America experienced the most rapid population increase in the world in the 1960s. Colombia saw its population increase from 15.6 million to 21 million, and Brazil added 25 million people, from 70 to 95 million. Alliance programs helped cut the percentage of Latin American children not attending school from 52 to 43 percent, but, because of this population growth, the actual number of children not attending school increased during the 1960s. Latin America added 151,670 hospital beds in the 1960s and ended up with fewer hospital beds per thousand people in 1969 than in 1960.[20]

President John F. Kennedy participates in a land redistribution ceremony in La Morita, Venezuela, on 16 December 1961. Also present is President Rómulo Betancourt (dark glasses) of Venezuela. Land reform was an essential part of the Alliance for Progress's plan to transform the socioeconomic structure of Latin America. Venezuela was one of the few Latin American counties to achieve in the 1960s some of the Alliance's goals. (Cecil Stoughton/John F. Kennedy Library)

The Alliance for Progress did not place population control on its agenda. President Kennedy took no interest in population control, apparently believing it to be politically and medically impractical and morally dubious. He once disputed what proved to be the accurate prediction that the world's population of 3 billion in 1960 would double to 6 billion in 2000. In truth, no Latin American leader raised population issues with Presidents Kennedy and Johnson. Nicaragua took the position that it was underpopulated. Oral contraceptives, an effective method of birth control, became commercially available in the United States in 1960. Bolivian nationalists reacted furiously when they discovered that Peace Corps volunteers dispensed oral contraceptives to the rural poor. The family planning program was small, non-aggressive, and voluntary and initially approved by Bolivian authorities. Nonetheless, some Bolivians perceived birth control as part of conspiracy to reduce Bolivia's geopolitical power, and the government responded by expelling the approximately one hundred Peace Corps volunteers in 1971.[21] Latin America's most populous nations, Mexico and Brazil, would eventually take effective steps to encourage family planning and population control in the 1970s and 1980s.

Latin American leaders also bore responsibility for the Alliance's failures. Their governments often proved incapable of designing the long-range plans required for putting their countries on the path of sustainable economic growth. By January 1962, only Colombia had submitted a development plan. Governments wasted U.S. money on short-term, politically expedient projects or directed the spending at enhancing the living standards of middle-income groups, rather than the poor. Latin American leaders, other than in Chile and Venezuela, also hesitated to attack traditional land tenure patterns, with 5 to 10 percent of the population, the landed oligarchy, owning 70 to 90 percent of the land. The rural regions were the locus of Latin America's poverty, underdevelopment, and population explosion. Ecuadorian agricultural laborers, for example, earned fifteen cents a day. Mexico continued to sustain its post-1940 economic growth in the countryside. In the aftermath of the Mexican Revolution (1910–20), successive Mexican governments had redistributed over one hundred million acres of land, often in the form of communal holdings or *ejidos*. The Alliance for Progress played, however, a minimal role in Mexico.

In their defense, Latin American leaders pointed to the declining terms of trade as the cause for the region's economic stagnation. In order to generate the $80 billion on domestic savings mandated by the Alliance, Latin America needed to sell on the global markets their primary products—coffee, sugar, bananas, copper, tin, lead, zinc, and oil. But the prices of these tropical foods and raw materials declined in the 1960s even as the prices of imported industrial machinery and finished goods, the very things needed for economic development, rose. The price of coffee, Latin America's chief export, fell from ninety cents a pound in the 1950s to thirty-six cents a pound in the early 1960s.[22] In May 1969, at an inter-American conclave, delegates produced the "Consensus of Viña del Mar," calling on the United States to open its markets to Latin American exports and to work for fair terms of trade. Recognizing the failure of the Alliance for Progress, Latin Americans now wanted trade, as much as aid, from the United States.

DEVELOPMENT VERSUS ANTICOMMUNISM

The failure of the Alliance for Progress cannot be explained solely by faulty social science theories, misread lessons of history, or structural problems. If so, historians could limit their analyses to noting that President Kennedy virtuously but unsuccessfully tried to end poverty and injustice in the hemisphere with a bold, imaginative program. Scholars could then add that the Alliance, like the Great Society domestic reform program, became a casualty of President Johnson's tragic venture in Vietnam. They would further point to President Kennedy's untimely death in November 1963. Kennedy had repeatedly told aides that he had not given up on his cherished program. Kennedy presumably would not also have blundered, by dispatching five hundred thousand U.S. troops to Vietnam. More money would have been available for Latin American development. Indeed, U.S. economic aid to Latin America dropped during the Johnson years, although Latin American economies did better in the late 1960s than during the Kennedy years.

A fair assessment of Kennedy and Latin America reveals that the president's Cold War initiatives undermined the Alliance for Progress. Kennedy judged regional governments on whether they affirmed the U.S. faith that Fidel Castro's Cuba represented the focus of evil. He demanded that Latin American nations break diplomatic relations with Cuba and enlist in the U.S. campaign to strangle Cuba's economy. He further required Latin American leaders to outlaw domestic Communists and to forswear from establishing relations with the Soviet Union or the Communist bloc. Constitutional heads of state, like Arturo Frondizi of Argentina, João Goulart of Brazil, and Cheddi Jagan of British Guiana, and Juan José Arévalo, the former president of Guatemala, failed Kennedy's Cold War test. These leaders respected constitutional processes and praised the Alliance for Progress, but they believed that the administration was obsessed with Castro. They also discounted the threat of Cuban communism to their counties and the hemisphere. The Kennedy administration would not, however, trust any

Cheddi Jagan, the prime minister of British Guiana, meets with President John F. Kennedy in the White House on 25 October 1961. Jagan thought the meeting went well and that the president would look sympathetically on the British colony's request for economic assistance. Kennedy decided, however, that Jagan was untrustworthy in the context of the Cold War and that he could not accept an independent Guyana under the leadership of Jagan. The president authorized the CIA to undermine Prime Minister Jagan and pressured the United Kingdom to find an alternative to Jagan. (Abbie Rowe/John F. Kennedy Library)

progressive leader or group deemed suspect on the issues of Castro and communism. The Kennedy administration authorized 163 major covert operations in less than three years, many of them in Latin America. It launched campaigns to undermine the authority of Frondizi, Goulart, and Jagan and to prevent Arévalo from returning to electoral office in Guatemala. These destabilization campaigns produced ironic results. The authoritarian, anti-Communist leaders who seized power in Argentina, Brazil, Guatemala, and British Guiana opposed free elections and disdained the idea of social reform, the essence of the Alliance for Progress.

President Johnson also waged ruthless Cold War in Latin America. He fulfilled President Kennedy's goals of driving President Goulart out of power in Brazil and Prime Minister Jagan out of British Guiana (Guyana).[23] He authorized the military invasion of the Dominican Republic, depriving the supporters of constitutionalism from restoring the legitimate president to power. U.S. military and civilian advisors became intimately involved in the Guatemalan government's and military's slaughter of political opponents and Mayan Indians. Under President Johnson, the CIA also became adept a manipulating elections in countries such as Bolivia and Chile. In the Dominican Republic and Guyana, the CIA went beyond pouring funds into the campaign coffers of favorite candidates and worked to rig elections to ensure the victory of strident anti-Communists. As exemplified in U.S. policies toward the small nation of the Dominican Republic and Latin America's largest and most populous nation, Brazil, fervent anticommunism permeated the U.S. approach to Latin America in the 1960s.

DOMINICAN REPUBLIC

During the 1960s, U.S. officials devoted almost as much time to the Dominican Republic as they did to its Caribbean neighbor, Cuba. A month after the Bay of Pigs invasion, the United States confronted another Caribbean crisis when Dominican dissidents assassinated the nation's long-time dictator, Rafael Trujillo, on 30 May 1961. The assassins caught Trujillo driving on a lonely stretch of road. The aged dictator was on his way to see his twenty-year-old mistress. The assassins riddled Trujillo's body with twenty-seven rounds of ammunition. Both the Eisenhower and Kennedy administrations had authorized the CIA to make contact with Trujillo's enemies. The assassins carried pistols and carbines with them supplied by the CIA. The weapons had arrived via diplomatic pouch and were passed to the assassins by the U.S. consul in Ciudad Trujillo (Santo Domingo) through an intermediary. For the assassins, the weapons served as a tangible sign that the United States approved of their plans.

For the United States to turn against the Dominican dictator, who had slavishly backed U.S. foreign policy for three decades, was a remarkable historical development. In the aftermath of the Nixon trip to South America, the collapse of dictators throughout the region, and the Cuban Revolution, U.S. officials and informed citizens concluded that the traditional U.S. support of anti-Communist dictators had been shortsighted. Officials worried that desperate Dominicans would turn to political extremism and communism if not released from Trujillo's tyranny. They foresaw history repeating itself, reasoning that Cubans had turned to Fidel Castro when they saw no end to the dictatorship of the U.S. ally, Fulgencio Batista. Both the Eisenhower and Kennedy administrations pressured Trujillo to leave the country, suggesting a comfortable exile on a sunny beach. When the defiant Trujillo rejected U.S. demands, the Eisenhower administration broke diplomatic relations, imposed economic sanctions on the island country, and contacted men prepared to eliminate Trujillo. President Kennedy continued that policy.[24] When he delivered his Alliance for Progress speech in March 1961, Kennedy conspicuously paired Cuba and the Dominican Republic, affirming that the United States rejected dictatorships of the left and right.

Terror and repression gripped the Dominican Republic after Trujillo's death. The dictator's son, known as "Ramfis," seized power, capturing and torturing his father's enemies. Ramfis was aided by his father's two brothers, known locally as "the wicked uncles." The Trujillos had not only oppressed Dominicans for thirty years; they had also stolen from them, turning the country into the Trujillo family hacienda. The restoration of the family tyranny posed a dilemma for the new Kennedy administration, still reeling from the Bay of Pigs debacle. According to presidential aide Arthur Schlesinger, President Kennedy speculated what policy he should now pursue. Kennedy said: "There are three possibilities in descending order of preference: a decent, democratic regime, a continuation of the Trujillo regime, or a Castro regime. We ought to aim at the first, but we really can't renounce the second until we are sure that we can avoid the third."[25] Kennedy's memorable remark about the descending order of possibilities on the post-Trujillo era proved to be a reliable guide to what choices his and other Cold War presidential administrations would make in the Dominican Republic and throughout the hemisphere.

In the case of the Dominican Republic, the administration used extreme pressure, which included shows of U.S. naval and air force, to force the Trujillo family out of the country in late 1961. Ramfis Trujillo slipped away on his yacht, bringing along his father's refrigerated body and bags full of money. The United States had again intervened in a Latin American country in a Cold War context. But this time it attacked a right-wing dictatorship in the name of creating "a decent, democratic regime." The Kennedy administration thereafter arranged for a transition government and supervised a fair presidential election in late 1962, which saw the election of Juan Bosch, an intellectual and poet and a man renowned for his honesty, dedication, and frugality. The Kennedy administration provided the new government with $40 million in U.S. loans and grants to help underwrite public construction projects. President Bosch lasted, however, only nine months in office, before being overthrown by a right-wing, reactionary coalition in September 1963. Bosch had shepherded through the Dominican assembly a modern constitution that created a secular state and protected the rights of workers. He also maintained public order, preserved individual liberty, and preached fiscal responsibility. These reforms predictably earned Bosch the enmity of traditionally privileged sectors of Dominican society. The hierarchy of the Catholic Church, for example, denounced President Bosch, because the new constitution permitted divorce.

Whereas the Kennedy administration did not encourage this *golpe de estado*, it did little to save President Bosch and ultimately decided to recognize the Dominican junta. It lost faith in Bosch, because he had not outlawed the Communist party and imprisoned Dominican radicals. President Bosch had reasoned that after three decades of tyranny, freedom of expression and association should be respected. He allowed exiled political leftists to come home and participate in political activities. He also repealed the U.S.-sponsored Emergency Law of 1962, which controlled the entrance of subversives and permitted their deportation. Bosch's supporters considered the Emergency Law a Trujillo-like measure. President Kennedy's major priority for the Dominican Republic was not, however, safeguarding civil liberties. He repeatedly told aides that "we don't want to have another Cuba to come out of the Dominican Republic." The State Department informed the president that the new Dominican junta seemed amenable to enacting "a Dominican Republic version of our Smith Act." By November 1963, U.S. policy toward the Dominican Republic had come full circle, or back to President Kennedy's second choice in the descending order of possibilities—"a continuation of the Trujillo regime."[26] U.S. officials prepared to deal with men such as Colonel Elías Wessin y Wessin, who trained under Trujillo, pilfered public funds, and indiscriminately condemned all opponents as "Communists."

In disdaining Bosch, U.S. officials also revisited the patronizing attitude toward Latin Americans contained in George Kennan's infamous 1950 report. President Bosch did not meet U.S. expectations of a Cold Warrior. Secretary of State Dean Rusk and Undersecretary of State George Ball judged Bosch an impractical dreamer, lacking administrative skills. Ball labeled Bosch as "unrealistic, arrogant, and erratic" and "incapable of even running a small social club, much less a country in turmoil." The U.S. ambassador, the undiplomatic John Barlow Martin, reported to Washington that Bosch was "a lousy president." To be sure, Bosch did not always act like a modern North American chief executive. He declined to delegate responsibility, and he spent countless hours listening to the problems of poor Dominicans. But in the aftermath of the Trujillo tyranny, few Dominicans had administrative or governmental experience. And the new president, who worked sixteen-hour days, spent time with people who had been subjected to unspeakable crimes for decades. The Johnson administration also denigrated the exiled president. National Security Advisor McGeorge Bundy characterized the Dominican Republic as "a crooked, foggy, and irresponsible island." Thomas Mann, President Johnson's chief advisor on Latin America, belittled Bosch to the president, noting that "Bosch writes books." Mann added: "He's the most impractical fellow in the world. Sort of an idealist. We don't think that he is a Communist [but we] don't think that [he] understands that the Communists are dangerous." Abe Fortas, President Johnson's loyal friend, complained that "this fellow Bosch is a complete Latin poet-hero type and he's completely devoted to this damn constitution."[27] Fortas's denigrating comments about a politician's faith in constitutional procedures seemed ironic coming from a man who would take a seat on the U.S. Supreme Court.

INVASION

Johnson administration officials were negotiating with former President Bosch because the United States had invaded Bosch's country. In April/May 1965, President Johnson ordered twenty-two thousand U.S. troops into the Dominican Republic. Civil war erupted in the streets of Santo Domingo, because humble Dominicans wanted their honest and humane president back in office. On 24 April 1965, segments of the Dominican Armed Forces led by Colonel Francisco Caamaño Deñó rose in rebellion against the conservative government headed by Donald Reid Cabral. Citizens joined the insurrection, demanding the return of President Bosch, who was in exile in Puerto Rico. Military officers, led by Colonel Wessin y Wessin, seized power and began attacking the insurgents, strafing and bombing them with jet aircraft. The insurgents, who suffered heavy casualties, showed remarkable resiliency, however, and gained control over large sectors of Santo Domingo.

President Johnson initially responded to the Dominican civil war by dispatching a contingent of U.S. marines on April 28 to facilitate the evacuation of foreign residents and tourists in the island. Several thousand foreign nationals from forty-six countries were evacuated without a serious incident. But Johnson and his advisors in Washington and Santo Domingo saw larger stakes in the Dominican civil war than protecting foreign bystanders. As they sensed a political crisis looming in early 1965, Ambassador W. Tapley Bennett, Jr., Thomas Mann, and State Department and CIA officers discussed how they would keep Juan Bosch out of the Dominican Republic. Ten days before the beginning of the civil war, U.S. officials spoke of encouraging Colonel Wessin y Wessin, pushing the unpopular Reid Cabral out of power, and then arranging for election of the arch-conservative Joaquín Balaguer to the presidency.[28] Once violence broke out in the island nation, the Johnson administration placed the civil war within the context of U.S. national security interests. The embassy in Santo Domingo and CIA officials began to speak of "pro-Castro" elements among the insurgents. There may have been pro-Bosch Dominicans who once traveled to Cuba and even trained there. But the United States had flimsy evidence to sustain fears of connections to international communism. On April 30, presidential advisor Bill Moyers told Johnson that "the CIA man in Cuba tells me Havana is still taken off balance by this." Secretary of Defense Robert McNamara added in a telephone conversation with the president that the CIA had not "shown any evidence that I have seen that Castro has been directing this or has had any control over those people once they got back there."[29] Castro was again receiving credit for a revolution that was not his.

Despite these admonitions, Johnson decided to order combat-ready troops into the Dominican Republic. The 1965 intervention represented the first overt

U.S. intervention in Latin America in over thirty years. In a televised address to the nation, on 2 May 1965, the president pronounced his Johnson Doctrine— "the American nations cannot, must not, and will not permit the establishment of another Communist government in the Western Hemisphere." The United States had to act immediately, because "what began as popular democratic revolution, committed to democracy and social justice, very shortly moved and was taken over and really seized and placed into the hands of a band of Communist conspirators."[30] The containment and defeat of the international Communist movement mattered more than adhering to the legal niceties of hemispheric affairs. Although Johnson emphasized the multilateral nature of the concern about communism in the Dominican Republic, the invasion was a unilateral action. The United States justified its action to the OAS after military action had begun. The intervention violated the non-intervention principle of the OAS charter. The invasion also violated the nonintervention pledge that had been the fundamental nature of Franklin Roosevelt's Good Neighbor policy and seemingly shattered the sense of hemispheric partnership inherent in the Alliance for Progress.

Johnson's dramatic decision reflected both his ideas and the view of Latin America held by U.S. officials throughout the Cold War. Johnson took responsibility for the disastrous intervention. In a telephone conversation on 23 May 1965 with Fortas, Johnson lamented his decision, crying out that "the man that misled me was Lyndon Johnson, nobody else! I did that! I can't blame a damn human." Johnson had indeed become obsessed with the Dominican civil war. In the first nine days of the crisis, he met with major advisors on the Dominican civil war 180 times. Between April and June 1965, he spent more time on the Dominican Republic than on civil rights legislation or the war in Vietnam. During this period, Johnson lost all perspective, producing lists in McCarthy-like fashion of alleged Communists in the Dominican Republic. Journalists deflated Johnson's lists, noting some were double-listed, in jail, or not in the region. As criticism mounted, Johnson exaggerated even more, claiming "some 1,500 people were murdered and shot, and their heads cut off."[31] The pro-Bosch forces had not, however caused most casualties. The military's bombing of poor neighborhoods in Santo Domingo took a heavy toll of Dominican citizens.

When he was not dwelling on the horrors of beheaded Dominicans, Johnson offered familiar explanations for a U.S. intervention in Latin America. Johnson wanted to be perceived as a tough anti-Communist to immunize himself from right-wing criticism of his domestic agenda, the Great Society and civil rights legislation. He vowed that he would not suffer the same loss of political standing that Truman had for "losing" China and that Dwight Eisenhower and Richard Nixon had for not preventing the Cuban Revolution. Although he claimed, "I am not an intervener," Johnson apparently judged that pursuing progressive policies for U.S. citizens justified trampling on the rights of Latin Americans. Like other Cold War presidents, Johnson also imbibed in "backyard" credibility thinking, holding that regional strength translated into global vitality. In March 1965,

Johnson had taken the momentous step of changing the U.S. military mission in Vietnam from advising South Vietnamese forces to U.S. forces taking the fight to the Communist enemy. As he asked, "what can we do in Vietnam, if we can't clean up the Dominican Republic?" Johnson also saw a global Communist conspiracy, telling National Security Advisor Bundy on 1 May that "I see a pattern and I just cannot be silent," for "what they are doing in Vietnam and the Dominican Republic is not totally unrelated."[32] In pronouncing his Johnson Doctrine, Johnson was, of course, reiterating the confidential views of George Kennan, Edward Miller, and Eisenhower's national security council on the need to take all measures "deemed appropriate" to keep communism out of the hemisphere. In his 2 May 1965 address to the nation, Johnson repeated President Kennedy's public pledge of "no more Cubas." In his last address on inter-American affairs, on 18 November 1963, Kennedy pronounced his "Kennedy Doctrine," making it a matter of "international responsibility" to come "to the aid of any government requesting aid to prevent a takeover aligned to the policies of foreign communism."[33]

Like previous U.S. officials, President Johnson questioned the abilities of Latin American democrats to be Cold Warriors. The United States organized an OAS peacekeeping mission of 1,769 troops to supplement the U.S. occupation force in the Dominican Republic. But five of the six nations contributing troops were led by dictators. The military dictators of Brazil sent 1,152 troops, the largest contingent. In 1964, the United States had helped the Brazilian military overthrow a civilian government. Juan Bosch did not qualify as Johnson's definition of an alpha male. In Johnson's words, "this Bosch is no good." Johnson had been unimpressed with the Dominican leader, when, in January 1963, he attended Bosch's presidential inauguration. The president agreed with Thomas Mann that Bosch lacked the strength and intelligence to defeat Communists.[34] As recorded by presidential aide Jack Valenti, Johnson predicted, in a meeting in the White House Cabinet Room on 30 April, that in the Dominican Republic "We will have one of 3 dictators: 1) U.S., 2) Moderate dictator, 3) Castro dictator."[35] The United States would find its "moderate dictator" in Joaquín Balaguer.

ELECTING BALAGUER

The overwhelming U.S. military presence in the Dominican Republic helped forestall a lengthy, bloody civil war. Although ostensibly neutral in the political struggle, U.S. civilian and military leaders deployed the troops in a way that aided the anti-Bosch forces and forced the Bosch legions to accept a political compromise. During the occupation, U.S. forces chose and then rejected seven different leaders, finally settling in September 1965 on Héctor García Godoy as a provisional president. García Godoy, who served as Bosch's foreign minister, would serve until national elections could be held in mid-1966. Bosch returned to the Dominican Republic in late September 1965. The United States wanted Bosch to run for president so as to provide legitimacy to the upcoming elections.

Some scholars hold that the turn of events in the Dominican Republic from September 1965 through the elections of June 1966 demonstrate that President Johnson tried to salvage a decent outcome from the intervention that now embarrassed him. One scholar coined the fatuous term "gunboat democracy" to justify Johnson's intervention. Analytical historians have described a "largely fair presidential contest" in 1966 that saw Balaguer achieve a smashing electoral victory over Bosch and a third candidate. These historians uphold General Bruce Palmer's account of his mission to the island nation. Palmer, who commanded the occupying forces, claimed that U.S. military and international observers oversaw a "truly honest election."[36] When Cold War issues were at risk, the United States was no more willing to allow a free and open election in Latin America than were Kremlin authorities inclined to permit Poles, Hungarians, or Czechs to choose their own destinies.

Prior to the outbreak of civil war, U.S officials had identified Joaquín Balaguer as the U.S. man for the Dominican Republic. On 26 April 1965, barely two days into the crisis, President Johnson accepted Thomas Mann's recommendation that Balaguer would give the United States the government that it wanted in the island nation.[37] Balaguer, a prolific poet, novelist, and essayist, was a sycophant of Rafael Trujillo, having served the dictator in figure-head capacities. He penned *El pensamiento vivo de Trujillo* (1955) (*The Living Thought of Trujillo*). The expression "God and Trujillo" appeared in his works. Balaguer, a person of European heritage, criticized racial intermarriage in his writings. The Dominican Republic was a diverse, multi-racial society. A life-long bachelor (1906–2002), Balaguer lived with his six sisters.

According to the announced results of the 1 June 1966 elections, Balaguer won 57 percent of the votes, whereas Bosch garnered only 39 percent. In 1962 Bosch had won 60 percent of the vote in the presidential election. Historians have tried to explain Bosch's poor showing. Fearful of his personal safety, Bosch did not campaign effectively in 1966. Some Dominican voters may have also yearned for stability, after the five tumultuous years that followed the assassination of Trujillo. Dominicans knew that the United States wanted Balaguer to win and anticipated that substantial U.S. aid would follow. During the 1960s, the Dominican Republic received over $400 million in Alliance for Progress funds, the fourth highest amount in Latin America. This was remarkable generosity to a small country with a population of 3.5 million.[38] Most of this money arrived in the post-1965 period. President Balaguer used U.S. aid for job-creating public works projects.

The Johnson administration's campaign for Balaguer went beyond foreign aid. President Johnson would have nothing of democracy in the Dominican Republic. Richard Helms, the acting director of the CIA, informed colleagues that the president repeatedly told him and CIA Director John McCone that the candidate favored by the United States would win the Dominican election. Helms added: "The President's statements were unequivocal. He wants to win the election, and he expects for the Agency to arrange for this to happen." The U.S. embassy in Santo Domingo coordinated with the committee in Washington that oversaw covert interventions, the "303 Committee," spending "substantial" sums of money on the Balaguer campaign, constantly polling the electorate, and increasing the covert electoral aid whenever Bosch appeared to be gaining popular support.[39] Washington also brazenly ordered its embassies to assure skeptical Latin Americans that "there is no basis for suspicion [that the] election may be rigged."[40]

Despite its plea of innocence, the United States probably engaged in wholesale vote rigging in the Dominican Republic. As late as 28 April 1966, a National Intelligence Estimate on the Dominican Republic noted that "we believe the election will be close" and "we cannot predict the outcome with any confidence."[41] Eric Thomas Chester, a political activist and author, has identified dubious electoral practices and decisions that favored Balaguer. The voter turnout for the 1966 election was remarkably 30 percent higher than in the 1962 presidential election. Almost 1.4 million Dominicans allegedly voted in 1966, 80 percent of the eligible electorate. Chester confessed that he could not find the proverbial "smoking gun" to prove that the United States stuffed ballot boxes.[42]

Chester could have strengthened his case about the Dominican Republic by observing that the United States was in the business of vote rigging in other parts of the Western Hemisphere during the 1960s. In British Guiana (Guyana), for example, the United States took extraordinary steps to insure that its candidate, Forbes Burnham, the leader of Afro-Guyanese, won elections and kept Cheddi Jagan and his Indo-Guyanese supporters from power. Like Presidents Jacobo Arbenz and Juan Bosch, Jagan fell under the rubric of being either a Communist, soft on communism, or oblivious to the Communist menace. In 1968, the U.S. ambassador in Georgetown worked with the 303 Committee and Prime Minister Burnham in drawing up fictitious lists of absentee voters in Guyana and showing great imagination in creating voter lists of Guyanese allegedly living abroad in the United Kingdom, Canada, and the United States. Two horses grazing on a vacant lot in Manchester, England, became Guyanese citizens and supporters of Prime Minister Burnham in the 1968 election.[43]

President Balaguer dominated Dominican political life for three decades, holding the presidency for twenty-two years (1966–78, 1986–96). He fulfilled President Johnson's wish for a "moderate dictator" who kept his country quiet and who reliably backed U.S. foreign-policy initiatives. Although not as savage as Rafael Trujillo, Balaguer was a ruthless caudillo who used carrots and sticks to stay in power. With U.S. economic assistance, access to the U.S. sugar market, and by opening the country's sugar interests and tourist industry to the U.S. conglomerate Gulf and Western, Balaguer generated enough new income from 1966 to 1978 to give his nation economic growth although not economic development or social justice. In September 1969, a National Intelligence Estimate noted that "maldistribution of the country's wealth and limited opportunities for personal advancement," combined with unchecked population growth, led to high rates of unemployment and underemployment, expanding city slums, and large numbers of landless peasants.[44] Balaguer ruled on behalf of the traditional oligarchy, the military, and light-skinned Dominicans. From 1966 to 1978, Balaguer sanctioned political murders by the military and terrorist groups. An especially notorious death squad, *La Banda* ("The Gang") had ties to the military and police. Perhaps three thousand political leftists were assassinated.[45] From the U.S perspective, the imperatives of the Cold War demanded hard choices. As President Kennedy framed the issue, better a Trujillo than a Castro.

BRAZIL

U.S. policies toward the Dominican Republic highlighted the core concerns of the United States in Latin America during the Cold War. But developments in the small, impoverished island nation did not reverberate throughout Latin America. Brazil, however, wielded significant influence in the region. In the name of anti-communism, the Kennedy and Johnson administrations encouraged the Brazilian military to seize power from a constitutional government. Generals ruled Brazil from 1964 to 1985, giving their nation impressive, albeit uneven, economic growth, with industrialization and economic diversification. The generals and admirals also directed harsh political repression and gross violations of basic human rights. Military men throughout South America admired the "Brazilian miracle." By the mid-1970s, generals dominated South America. They claimed they could give their nations the political stability and technological sophistication that would allow their economies to grow and flourish. These military rulers also conducted savage wars against political leftists and those who defended the rule of law.

Both the Kennedy and Johnson administrations considered a healthy relationship with Brazil to be essential to winning the Cold War in Latin America and maintaining the U.S. sphere of influence in the region. Brazil had experienced tumultuous economic times from 1956 to 1961 under President Kubitschek. Beyond building Brasília, Kubitschek had fostered industrialization, creating a motor vehicle industry, increasing electrical generation, and expanding the nation's highways. "Fifty years of progress in five" had been his motto. But Kubitschek had fostered economic growth by borrowing international capital and through deficit financing. Price inflation had ensued, with prices rising by 35 percent a year. The Brazilian also had not solved the country's regional economic disparity. Growth took place in the South and Central parts of the country. Brazilians were migrating from impoverished hinterlands to the great cities of Rio de Janeiro and São Paulo. The Northeast, where one-third of the population resided, had languished. Some of the poorest people in Latin America lived in states such as Bahia and Pernambuco. Both Brazilian elites and U.S. officials feared growing radicalism in the Northeast. In promoting the Alliance for Progress, Kubitschek hoped that Brazil would receive the money it needed to continue development.

At the beginning of the 1960s, U.S. officials accepted Kubitschek's sense of urgency. As State Department planners noted, "If U.S. policy fails in Brazil, it will become extremely difficult to achieve success elsewhere in Latin America."

President Kennedy agreed, adding that "Latin America is critical to [the] West," and "Brazil is [the] key country in Latin America." Thomas Mann informed President Johnson that "Brazil is the keystone of our interests on the continent of South America."[46] The U.S. dilemma was that it did not trust Kubitschek's presidential successors, Jânio Quadros (1961) and João Goulart (1961–64). Both Brazilian presidents supported the Alliance for Progress. But the Kennedy administration condemned these constitutional leaders, because Brazil refused to break diplomatic relations with Cuba and because it established commercial ties with the Soviet Union. Presidents Quadros and Goulart also tolerated domestic leftists.

In the early 1960s, the democratic leaders of the southern cone countries—Argentina, Brazil, Chile, and Uruguay—rejected the U.S. threat assessment of "Castro/communism." Castro ruled a small island country of impoverished sugar workers thousands of miles away from the glittering metropolises of Buenos Aires, Montevideo, Rio de Janeiro, and Santiago. Southern cone leaders stood firmly on the principle of non-intervention and argued that sanctions against Cuba "would only serve to push it irrevocably into [the] hands of the Sino-Soviet bloc." These leaders further worried that a Cold War confrontation with Cuba would exacerbate political tensions in their countries, exciting extremists on both sides of the political spectrum. As President Goulart once put it, Castro had become a "dramatic symbol of revolutionary aspirations of underprivileged masses throughout Latin America." If the United States was patient, the Castro regime would "deteriorate under its own weight." But the United States would do a great disservice by agitating the Cuban problem, because "Latin American masses are instinctive[ly] on [the] side of tiny Cuba whenever it [is] menaced by [the] colossus of the North."[47]

The Kennedy administration dismissed such analyses, believing that South Americans were naïve about the Communist threat. The administration also discounted other Brazilian facts. Brazil supported the United States during the Cuban missile crisis, and President Goulart proposed solutions to the crisis. Brazilians pointed out that there had been no known case of a Brazilian training in Cuba for subversive activities. To be sure, Brazil established relations with the Soviet Union in 1961, permitted the Soviets to stage a trade fair in Rio de Janeiro in 1962, and signed a commercial agreement in April 1963. Brazilian leaders defended these new ties by citing public opinion polls, which showed strong popular support for an independent foreign policy. Brazilians had long dreamed that their country, given its size and great natural resources, should play a leading role on the international stage. Brazilians did not think that an expanded international role would come at the expense of the traditional friendship it enjoyed with the United States. In any case, Brazil had hardly become tied to the Soviet bloc. Soviet-Brazilian trade grew from 5 million to 66 million rubles between 1959 and 1963. But that commerce represented only 3 percent of Brazil's trade. The balance of trade favored Brazil, because the Soviets offered goods of poor quality.

The Kennedy administration first tried to modify Brazil's international behavior by offering bright carrots. In March 1961, it proffered the new Quadros administration a $100 million gift to help it import capital goods and then asked for Brazilian support for the impending Bay of Pigs invasion. As outgoing ambassador to Brazil John Moors Cabot recalled: "It was obvious it was just a bribe. I mean that's what it amounted to. And Quadros, with increasing irritation, said no."[48] In May 1961, President Kennedy made his pitch. Meeting with the Brazilian Finance Minister, Kennedy observed that the United States had just agreed with the International Monetary Fund to give Brazil $335 million in credits. The president then lectured the Brazilian. In negotiating the loan, the United States "had completely avoided mention of political factors," but the Brazilians had to understand that "the United States was interested in the Castro regime because it is a weapon used by international communism in an effort to take over additional Latin American countries." Kennedy lamented that it would be impossible to drive Cuba out of the OAS unless the major Latin American nations agreed "on the basic analysis of the situation."[49] Quadros again refused to change Brazil's independent foreign policy, and he further irritated the United States by hosting Che Guevara and awarding him Brazil's Order of the Southern Cross.

On 25 August 1961, Quadros unexpectedly resigned and his vice president, João Goulart, eventually succeeded to the presidency. A career politician, Goulart had served as vice president to President Kubitschek and as a minister of labor. A fiery speaker and populist, Goulart identified himself with the nation's powerless. He had various ties to leftist groups, including the Brazilian Communist Party. Brazilian conservatives, including military officers, distrusted Goulart and initially tried to block his ascension to power. Goulart took office on 2 September 1961, after the Brazilian Congress passed a constitutional amendment curbing the powers of the presidency. He regained full presidential powers in January 1963, however, as the result of a plebiscite.

The Kennedy administration shared the Brazilian military's suspicion of President Goulart, interpreting his political maneuvers through a Cold War prism. Goulart sustained that suspicion by maintaining President Quadros's independent foreign policy and refusing to break relations with Cuba. He exasperated U.S. officials with his fickle and inconstant fiscal and monetary policies that swallowed up the substantial U.S. aid, which amounted to over $700 million between 1961 and 1963. Inflation spun out of control, with prices rising over 90 percent in 1964. Other sins included expropriating the U.S. telecommunications giant, International Telephone and Telegraph, arousing labor and student groups with inflammatory speeches, and appointing cabinet ministers with politically radical sentiments. He also called for higher prices for primary products, implicitly suggesting that better terms of trade, not the Alliance for Progress, would generate the economic growth that Latin America needed. In short, an irresponsible President Goulart seemingly opposed all U.S. objectives in Latin America and, at best, was indifferent to the international Communist conspiracy. The new U.S. ambassador in Brasília, Lincoln Gordon, predicted that Goulart intended to stay in power beyond his term and "take Brazil into the Communist camp."[50]

Kennedy administration officials had available to them other analyses of President Goulart's intentions. Juscelino Kubitschek twice met with President Kennedy, assuring him that Goulart was not a Marxist, that he supported the Alliance for Progress, and that Goulart had a "genuine liking" for Kennedy. Goulart himself tried to reassure Kennedy when he visited the White House in April 1962. Goulart considered his audience with Kennedy to be the crowning moment of his presidency. CIA analysts also presented nuanced views of Goulart. They discounted the view that Goulart had a radical agenda for Brazil. The CIA essentially saw Goulart as an "opportunist," who was intent on preserving political power. Other administration officials argued that Goulart had to ally with political leftists, because he accurately feared that conservatives, including military generals, plotted against him. These discerning interpretations of Brazilian politics failed to persuade the administration to abandon its Cold War verities. As President Kennedy remarked, the situation in Brazil "worried him more than that in Cuba."[51]

THE QUIET INTERVENTION

Scholars have detailed how the United States destabilized the Goulart government. One scholar dubbed the covert campaign "the quiet intervention." In December 1962, President Kennedy dispatched his brother, the attorney general, to Brazil to confront Goulart over his "putting those leftists and Communists in positions of power." Although the three-hour meeting ended inconclusively, Robert Kennedy decided that the United States could not trust the Brazilian president. Beyond reprimanding Goulart, the administration manipulated the Brazilian political scene. In 1962 the CIA spent $5 million funding the campaigns of candidates for fifteen federal Senate seats, eight state governorships, two hundred fifty federal deputy seats, and some six hundred seats for state legislatures. The CIA, working through U.S. labor unions, also covertly funded Brazilian trade union groups, encouraging them to organize strikes and demonstrations against Goulart. The U.S. unions coordinated their intervention with the U.S. embassy and the Brazilian military. The CIA had first developed the tactic of "controlled penetration" of associations like labor groups in Guatemala in 1954 and was simultaneously using the tactic in British Guiana to destabilize Prime Minister Cheddi Jagan's government. The Kennedy administration's anti-Goulart campaign included undermining the cherished Alliance for Progress. The administration funneled Alliance funds to conservative state governors, like Carlos Lacerda of Guanabara (encompassing Rio de Janeiro), who were friendly to the United States and hostile to Goulart. These governors had records of ignoring the needs of the Brazilian poor. In contrast, the United States limited economic aid to the state of Pernambuco and its desperately poor city of Recife, because the governor of Pernambuco was a political ally of President Goulart.[52]

The Kennedy administration also tasked two study groups with exploring ways to strengthen U.S. ties with the Brazilian military to prepare for a "more friendly alternative regime." The administration reached out directly to Brazilian generals when, in 1962, it dispatched Colonel Vernon Walters to Brazil as a military attaché in the U.S. embassy. Walters, who was fluent in Portuguese, had served with Brazilian officers during World War II, when Brazil sent an expeditionary force to fight in Italy. As Walters later recalled, somebody "high in the administration" briefed him that President Kennedy would not be averse to seeing Goulart overthrown and replaced by an anti-Communist who supported U.S. international policies. Walters's circumspect language belied the extent of his activities in Brazil. He developed a social relationship with General Humberto de Alencar Castello Branco, who would lead the military conspiracy against Goulart. Walters was told of the military's plans in minute detail and passed the intelligence on to Ambassador Gordon and then on to the White House. Walters also relayed the Brazilian military's request for logistical support from the United States. After receiving the requests, Walters would tell his Brazilian friends that he "had no authority to discuss such matters."[53] The play acting of Walters allowed Ambassador Gordon and officials in Washington to offer "plausible denials" that they had encouraged the Brazilian military to strike.

On 2 April 1964, Brazilian generals and admirals disposed of Goulart. The new Johnson administration had prepositioned war matériel and readied a U.S. naval task force for duty of the coast of Brazil, in case the military men encountered resistance to the destruction of the Brazilian democracy. As President Johnson noted to aides, "I think we ought to do everything that we need to do." In an apparent reference to Goulart, President Johnson added that "we just can't take this one."[54] The administration granted diplomatic recognition to the new interim government eighteen hours after its installation. Whereas the overthrow of Goulart came about early in the Johnson presidency, it was the fulfillment of President Kennedy's policy. The Johnson administration continued the policy of funneling Alliance money to conservatives. Immediately after the overthrow of Goulart, it granted Brazil an emergency $50 million loan. Overall, the Brazilian generals secured $1.2 billion in Alliance funds from 1964 to 1969, despite ignoring Alliance objectives of democracy and social justice. The new U.S. ambassador, John W. Tuthill, reported in June 1967 that the generals "have failed so far to comply with important [Alliance for Progress] goals." Tuthill found it "inexcusable" that the generals had not developed an economic program.[55]

Brazil's international behavior assuaged concerns about its abandonment of the Alliance for Progress. General Castello Branco severed relations with Cuba and provided President Johnson with diplomatic cover by sending Brazilian soldiers in 1965 to serve in an OAS peacekeeping force in the Dominican Republic. The generals continued to pursue, however, the nationalistic goal of an independent foreign policy. They rejected U.S. requests to send troops to Vietnam. Brazil also continued to trade with the Soviet Union.

THE BRAZILIAN "MIRACLE"

Scholars have emphasized that, whereas the United States urged the Brazilian military to strike against President Goulart, the generals and admirals pursued their own agendas. The Brazilian military had traditionally exercised a "moderating" role in Brazilian constitutional history. They had intervened to resolve clashes between civilian politicians, held power briefly, and then returned to the barracks. But Brazilian officers increasingly disdained the political class, became alarmed about inflation, and shared the view that Brazil had a great but unfulfilled destiny. They also judged themselves as superior Brazilians, because they had attended professional military academies and studied in war colleges abroad, especially in the United States. They believed that their patriotism and scientific training gave them the honesty and ability to choose and oversee politically neutral social scientists and engineers who would transform the Brazilian economy. With the help of ample U.S. financial assistance, the military governments first attacked inflation through stringent budgetary and fiscal measures. Once inflation rates fell to a manageable 20 to 25 percent in the late 1960s, the military rulers and the technocrats launched massive public works projects—a hydroelectric dam near the Paraguayan border, a trans-Amazonian highway, and nuclear power projects. They also assisted wealthy landowners to diversify into crops such as soybeans and oranges, breaking the nation's dependence on exports of coffee and sugar. Between 1968 and 1974, the Brazilian economy, "the Brazilian miracle," grew at an impressive annual rate of 11 percent. The benefits of this growth went primarily to upper-middle and upper-income groups. Brazil also became dependent on international borrowing.

Although military officers thought themselves above politics, they were arch-conservatives, resisting changes in Brazil's hierarchical social structure and denouncing cultural pluralism. Change equated with "communism." President Goulart's proposal to enfranchise illiterate people threatened social stability. The military rulers and their minions shaved the heads, imprisoned for months, and then forced into exile the great, innovative recording artists Caetano Veloso and Gilberto Gil, because they loathed their new musical movement, *Tropicalismo*, which fused Brazilian pop with rock and roll and *avant garde* music. Fernando Enrique Cardoso, who challenged classical economic theory with his "dependency" or *dependencia* school of economic interpretation, lost his teaching position at the Universidade de São Paulo. Professor Cardoso would later become president of Brazil (1995–2003). The generals found women's rights, feminism, even birth control and oral contraceptives politically and sexually deviant. Female activists, who were denounced as *putas communistas* ("Communist whores"), were subjected to appalling abuses—torture and rape—at the hands of the Brazilian military and police. The torturers reveled while delivering electrical shocks to the sexual organs of female university students.[56]

In the name of order, progress, and anticommunism, the generals and admirals gave Brazilians two decades of savage rule. In December 1968, General Arturo da Costa e Silva, who succeeded General Castello Branco, issued Institutional Act (No. 5), which abolished Congress and transformed Brazil into a military dictatorship. Criticism of the government became a national security issue subject to military justice. The dismantling of the Brazilian constitution polarized politics in the

country. Strikes, demonstrations, bombings, terrorism, and urban guerrilla warfare broke out. The generals responded brutally, murdering and torturing opponents. Between 1964 and 1971, perhaps three thousand Brazilians were murdered
by the military and police. In one notorious incident, in March 1968, the military
violently broke up a demonstration by university students in Rio de Janeiro protesting the poor quality of food in student cafeterias. Some fifty thousand people
took part in the funeral procession for the student of humble origin that the military killed in the raid. The military commander of the city responded that the army
must treat the student protestors like "an enemy attacking the fatherland's territory
and threatening the nation's basic institutions."[57] Student complaints about cafete-
ria food had become a national security issue for the Brazilian regime.

Scholars have argued that the radical left, inspired by the Cuban Revolution,
provoked military repression in Brazil and throughout the southern cone countries of Argentina, Chile, and Uruguay by resorting to violence. Those who make
such points have their historical chronology out of order.[58] Brazil did not have an
armed insurrectionary movement before 1969. The Brazilian Communist party
thought violence a suicidal option. Resistance and violence came in response to
the military regime's crushing of the labor unions and its raiding of universities.
The number of Brazilian combatants was small, probably less than five hundred,
and by 1974 the regime had liquidated its armed enemy.[59] Neither Castro's Cuba
nor the Soviet Union bears responsibility for the mass murders that characterized
the national histories of the southern cone countries in the late 1960s and 1970s.

Brazilian generals, not Fidel Castro, can take credit and blame for the horrors
that gripped South America in the 1970s. The Brazilian military's seizure of power
helped create an ironic "domino effect" in South America. By the mid-1970s,
generals ruled throughout the continent. The Brazilian alliance between the military and technocrats seemed an appealing model to Latin American conservatives. Generals in Argentina, Chile, Uruguay, and elsewhere adopted the Brazilian
brand, abolishing democracy, smashing "Communists," and promising economic growth. As early as 1966, U.S. diplomats in Buenos Aires reported that the
Argentine military identified with Brazilian military regime, believing that they
shared "the identical spirit of renovation, of anti-communism, anti-corruption,
anti-inefficiency and of unreserved support for pro-Western foreign policy." The
Argentine generals also took note that the United States continued to lavish financial assistance on the Brazil's military rulers.[60] The Brazilians did more than lead
by example. Brazilian military, police, and death squad leaders worked with the
Uruguayan police, teaching them anti-terrorist tactics. Brazil's neighbors would
take the violence to a new level. By the mid-1970s, Uruguay had the most political
prisoners per capita of any nation in the world.[61] In Argentina, the generals and
their minions may have murdered as many as thirty thousand Argentines in what
was labeled "the dirty war" (la guerra sucia).

As these gross violations of basic human rights unfolded, U.S. officials reacted
with disappointment. Within a month after the attack on Goulart, Ambassador
Gordon confessed "to considerable dismay" to learn that the generals he embraced

displayed reactionary colors. One of their first acts had been to cancel for ten years the political rights of President Kubitschek. In 1965, Robert Kennedy, now a senator from New York, complained about U.S. friendship with Brazil. The year before, Attorney General Kennedy had expressed satisfaction with the overthrow of Goulart, noting that "Brazil would have gone Communist." As the repression mounted, Washington comforted itself with the fantasy that Brazilians could not be expected to conform to the standards of Western civilization. Under the signature of Secretary of State Dean Rusk, one State Department officer told the embassy in Brasília that "we realize that Brazil's needs and performance cannot be measured against North American or northwest European standards of constitutional democracy, nor even easily expressed in Anglo-Saxon terms." Such a grotesque assessment represented a complete repudiation of the promise of the Alliance for Progress.[62]

U.S. officials engaged in self-delusion when they expressed shock and horror over Brazil's political evolution. The United States had participated in the military's seizure of power and provided $1.2 billion in economic assistance thereafter. The United States also trained the forces of repression. Between 1962 and 1974, the United States operated the Office of Public Safety (OPS), a police training program. The OPS provided $337 million in training, equipment, and advisors to Third World police. In Brazil, the OPS spent $10 million and trained one hundred thousand police. U.S. legislators disbanded OPS in 1974 in response to public outrage that followed revelations that the agency had assisted police units that tortured and murdered. President Kennedy had authorized the program, arguing that Latin America needed internal security to achieve the economic development goals enumerated in the Alliance for Progress. Police training was linked to the U.S. effort to orient the Latin American military away from hemispheric defense and toward counterinsurgency. The program's public goal was to reduce crime in Latin America by teaching police how to act in a legal, rational professional manner.

Analysts of OPS argue that the program contributed to authoritarianism, violence, and militarism in Latin America. The OPS "internationalized" U.S. national security concerns, turning the U.S. fear of international communism into the obsession of Latin American security forces. OPS trainers also encouraged the bureaucratic innovation of placing military men in charge of police units, thereby, in one scholar's words, "militarizing the police and inculcating a war model of social control." Brazilian police officers took courses, many of them at the International Police Academy in Washington, on subjects such as "prisons as schools for terrorists" and "subversive manipulation and domestic intelligence." The OPS also offered a course in a border town in Texas for Latin American police on manufacturing and using explosives. Brazilian authorities contemplated blowing up gas lines in Rio de Janeiro, which would have caused mass casualties, and then blaming the tragedy on political leftists. U.S. officials always denied that they encouraged Latin American police to torture and murder. But one OPS advisor, Dan Mitrione, helped Brazilians organize a militarized police "shock unit" of men over six feet tall who patrolled at night in Rio's poor neighborhoods or *favelas* and practiced a "shoot-to-kill" policy. (Mitrione would subsequently work for the OPS in Uruguay and be murdered by leftists. Mitrione became the subject of the famous film *State of Siege* [1972] by Costa-Gavras). OPS officers in Brazil reported favorably about Operacão Bandeirantes (OBAN), a joint military-police operation established in 1969 in São Paulo that perpetrated murder and torture. Critics compared OBAN, both in structure and in purpose, to the Phoenix Program, the U.S. assassination program in South Vietnam which eliminated over twenty-six thousand suspected Viet Cong. Theodore Brown headed the Phoenix Program immediately after concluding his tenure as director of the OPS program in Brazil.[63]

The United States did not need to teach Brazilians torture tactics. Brazilian police had long tortured criminal suspects, using a technique known as "the parrot's perch." The victim was suspended naked on a horizontal pole and subjected to beatings and electrical shocks. Minions of the military regime developed the *geladeira* or refrigerator, a five-foot-square windowless cubicle equipped with loudspeakers, strobe lights, and heating and cooling units. Inside the *geladeira*, political prisoners were subjected to high-technology attacks on their senses.[64] Brazilian security forces also proved adept at spreading fear and terror throughout society. Cardinal Paulo Evaristo Arns, the Archbishop of São Paulo, regularly received in the archdiocesan office twenty to fifty people every week, all trying to discover the whereabouts of their apprehended relatives. In one case, a young woman informed Cardinal Arns that she found her husband's wedding ring left on her doorstep. She was uncertain whether this meant he was dead or whether she should continue searching for him. Cardinal Arns had no answer for her. He understood that the pain was unimaginable for those who saw their loved ones disappear behind prison bars, without being able to guess what happened to them. As he wrote, for the young wife "deep darkness covers the earth, as it did when Jesus died."[65] U.S. officials, and OPS and CIA officers associated with security forces who tortured individuals and terrorized Brazilian society. They did not ask hard questions about the "deep darkness" and frequently denied in public testimony that security forces violated basic human rights. The United States had succeeded in exporting its Cold War concerns to Brazil and elsewhere in Latin America, with appalling consequences.

From a Cold War perspective, the Kennedy and Johnson administrations waged a successful foreign policy with Latin America. At the beginning of the 1960s, President Kennedy had dubbed Latin America the "the most dangerous area in the world." But by the end of the decade, the region was secure, stable, and remained within the U. S. sphere of influence. Fidel Castro's Cuba had been contained, Che Guevara was dead, there were no "second or third Cubas," and the Soviet Union continued to have minimal influence in the Western Hemisphere. The Kennedy and Johnson Doctrines had triumphed. Both Democratic presidents had talked, however, about winning the Cold War by building democratic, progressive societies in Latin America through the Alliance for Progress. Instead, the

Democratic administrations invaded countries, destabilized constitutional governments, and rigged elections. The two administrations sacrificed noble visions of a prosperous, free, and socially just hemisphere for the short-term security that anti-Communist, right-wing dictators could provide. Their successors, the duo of Richard Nixon and his close advisor, Henry Kissinger, would extend and expand that dubious legacy.

CHAPTER 6

Military Dictators—
Cold War Allies

The decade of the 1970s turned into a gruesome time for civic-minded Latin Americans, especially in the southern cone countries of Argentina, Brazil, Chile, and Uruguay. Military dictators conducted a vicious war against political leftists and anyone else who stood for democracy and respect for basic human rights. In the name of anticommunism and social order, uniformed military units and their colleagues in death squads butchered tens of thousands of South Americans. So appalling was the political repression in South America that international observers compared it to life in Nazi Germany in the 1930s. The United States aided and abetted the criminal behavior of Latin America's military rulers. President Richard M. Nixon and his faithful aide, Henry A. Kissinger, believed that military dictatorship was in the best interest of Latin Americans. Military dictators could also be counted on to respect the Cold War concerns of the United States. Nixon and Kissinger cultivated the Latin American military, providing diplomatic and material support to the military authoritarians and rationalizing and excusing their murderous behavior. The U.S. leaders also took credit for destroying the constitutional regime of Salvador Allende in Chile. In the Nixon–Kissinger view of the world, creating a stable relationship with the Soviet Union and a global balance of power entailed keeping Latin Americans in their place—under military rule.

THE LOW PROFILE

Richard M. Nixon, the man and the president, poses conceptual difficulties for both scholars and U.S. citizens. In the period from 1946 to 1952, as a congressman and senator, Nixon had been a reckless anti-Communist, closely tied to the extremist wing of the Republican Party associated with Senator Joseph McCarthy. Nixon presumably matured as vice president, learned from his electoral defeats in 1960 and 1962, and from years of study, travel, and consulting in international affairs. By the late 1960s, political pundits spoke of the "new Nixon," poised, confident, a world statesman. In the 1968 presidential race, he ran a gentle campaign, pledging to bring U.S. citizens "together again." He had a plan for peace in Vietnam. As president, he had significant, even momentous, accomplishments in the international arena. He wound down Lyndon Johnson's war in Vietnam, withdrawing the last U.S. troops in 1973. He also struck big deals with the two Communist superpowers. Traveling to Beijing in early 1972, he established U.S. contacts with the People's Republic of China. He journeyed to Moscow, signed a major nuclear arms treaty, and preached the virtues of détente with the Soviet Union. The president spoke of working for "a generation of peace." Nixon further anticipated the changing nature of international relations, calling attention to the onset of globalization. In 1971, in a speech to news media executives, he foresaw the end of a bipolar world revolving around the Soviet–American confrontation and the emergence of a multi-polar world led by the United States, the Soviet Union, China, Japan, and Western Europe. As Nixon prophesied, "these are the five that will determine the economic future and, because economic power will be the key to other kinds of power, the future of the world in other ways in the last third of the twentieth century."[1]

Although appreciating Nixon's perception of the patterns of international history, U.S. citizens were dismayed to learn that their president still retained the duplicitous, spiteful tendencies that had characterized the "old Nixon." In the domestic sphere, Nixon and his aides preached the virtues of "positive polarization," turning regions and citizens against one another, especially on the issue of racial relations. Nixon ended the war in Vietnam, but it took him five wasteful years, causing needless Asian and U.S. casualties. He also secretly expanded the war into Cambodia, causing irreparable harm to that poor, helpless nation. True to their "realist" conception of international relations and the balance of power, Nixon and Kissinger "tilted" toward Pakistan during the Indo-Pakistani War (1971). They perceived the government in Islamabad as a traditional U.S. ally and a check on the power of the Soviet Union. International analysts strongly disagreed, judging that India deserved praise for intervening to rescue the people of East Pakistan (Bangladesh) from the genocidal policies perpetrated by the Pakistani government. Nixon would resign the presidency in disgrace in 1974, when it became apparent that he had committed "high crimes and misdemeanors" in the "Watergate" scandal. Nixon was condemned by his own voice, for he had taped many conversations in the Oval Office. Nixon had ordered the taping, believing they would provide a historical record of great deeds for future generations to admire. The "Nixon tapes" revealed, however, a man who used scurrilous language and indulged in shocking ethnic and racial slurs. In 1971 in a discussion with Ambassador to Iran Douglas MacArthur II, for example, Nixon made the despicable assertion that "those Africans, you know, are only 50 to 75 years from out of the trees, some of them."[2] On the tapes, Nixon proved himself to be petty, mean, and vindictive—the same man who had been tagged "tricky Dick" in his 1950 senatorial campaign.

In his attitude and policies toward Latin America, Nixon displayed the same contradictory, paradoxical behavior that epitomized his career in other areas of domestic and international life. By the time he took office in January 1969, Nixon had visited most Latin American countries. As vice president, he had toured Central America and the Caribbean in 1955 and South America in 1958. He had embraced and toasted Fulgencio Batista in Havana and nearly lost his life when a mob in Caracas attacked his limousine in May 1958. Nixon seemed to take a philosophical attitude toward his frightening experience in Venezuela. Dispatching presidential aide Robert Finch on a good-will trip to South America in 1971, Nixon joked "what I had in mind is to make it sort of like my '58 trip, except without the rocks."[3] In 1967, preparing for his presidential run, Nixon visited Peru, Chile, Argentina, Brazil, and Mexico. In Argentina, he praised the military government and declared that "United States-style democracy won't work here. I wish it would."[4]

As president, Nixon pledged a new approach toward Latin America. The Alliance for Progress had failed, leaving Latin Americans embittered. Latin Americans further denounced the economic relationship between Latin America and the developed world. In May 1969, in the "Consensus of Viña del Mar," Latin American nations called "for a fairer international division of labor that will favor the rapid economic and social development of the developing countries, instead of impeding it as has been the case hitherto." Latin Americans demanded changes in the lending and trading practices of the United States. Two weeks after taking office, Nixon ordered that "a broad study be prepared reviewing our overall policy toward Latin America."[5] Henry Kissinger, the new head of the NSC, was ordered to lead the review. Nixon also sent Governor Nelson Rockefeller of New York on a fact-finding tour of the region.[6] Rockefeller had worked in the State Department on Latin American affairs during World War II.

Kissinger, who admitted he knew little about Latin America, conducted the NSC review like a professor in a graduate seminar, asking big, probing questions about the nature of the "special relationship" between the United States and Latin America. He admitted that "the principals were more concerned with other areas of the world" but that the president wanted "specific answers concerning our goals in Latin America." The discussants admitted the United States had acted in a "paternalistic" fashion toward the region; the Alliance for Progress had not been an alliance. The National Security Study Memorandum (NSSM) No. 15 of July 1969 took seriously Latin American concerns about aid and trade. The United States should loosen restrictions on how foreign aid could be spent and give special preferences to imports from developing regions like Latin America. Governor Rockefeller's report, which was submitted in August 1969, gave similar recommendations. Both the NSC study and the Rockefeller Report focused on foreign economic policy rather than on security issues. Intelligence analysts testified that neither the Soviet Union nor Cuba had launched any new initiatives in the region. The apocalyptic language that had characterized policy papers on inter-American relations during the Kennedy–Johnson years was missing. Henry Kissinger thought the United States should concentrate on encouraging long-term economic development and "foster a Latin American system of independent, self-reliant states." Kissinger told President Nixon that he rejected the option of focusing on cultivating anti-Communist friends. To be sure, the study continued to see Latin America as part of the U.S. sphere of influence, asserting that "we would feel, as a nation, that our power had been greatly diminished in the world were Latin America to slip out of our orbit—and so would other nations."[7] Nonetheless, one veteran State Department officer noted that "we constructed and articulated a conceptual framework for Latin American policy which was (I believe) realistic and reasonable—even historic."[8] The officer, Viron P. Vaky, had a reputation for being critical of U.S. policies, having denounced the U.S. role in human rights abuses in Guatemala in the mid-1960s.

President Nixon incorporated ideas from NSSM 15 and the Rockefeller Report in his one major address on Latin America given to the Inter-American Press Club on 31 October 1969. Nixon had told the NSC that "the U.S. government should avoid doing too much in Latin America, and must recognize it could not control the region, but could influence it." In his speech, Nixon chided John Kennedy and his cherished Alliance for Progress, observing that the United States had "pursued the illusion that we alone could remake continents" and that "we have sometimes imagined that we knew what was best for everyone else." At times, he said, the United States had been guilty of "overweening confidence in the rightness of our own prescriptions." Nixon pleased Latin Americans by stating that his adminis- tration would seek "a more mature partnership in which all voices are heard and none is predominant." Nixon promised to consider the aid and trade issues that rose at the conference at Viña del Mar and assured the audience that the United States would now permit Latin Americans to spend U.S. foreign aid throughout the region, not just in the United States. In line with his tone of restraint, Nixon pledged not to interfere in the internal politics of Latin American nations. The United States preferred democracy, but "we must deal realistically with govern- ments in the inter-American system as they are."[9]

President Nixon and Henry Kissinger's rhetorical promises of coopera- tion and mutual respect toward Latin America were belied by their public acts and private thoughts. The Nixon administration made little effort to persuade Congress to fulfill Nixon's promises to continue aid, "untie" foreign aid, and reduce tariff and non-tariff barriers against Latin American exports to the United States. The United States sharply reduced economic assistance to the region; aid to Latin America in 1971, for example, was $463 million, 50 percent less than a typical year in the 1960s. Conditions were still tied to development assistance. Aid recipients were not permitted to spend their grants in Western Europe or Japan, even though those areas might sell the desired capital goods and sophisticated equipment at a favorable price. Washington also imposed new tariff restrictions, such as a 10 percent surcharge on all imports in late 1971. Viron Vaky lamented to Kissinger that the United States was reneging on its promises of a "mature partnership," because "most of our government does not believe or accept it, or does not understand it." Vaky added that "most people have an unconscious perception of Latin Americans as 'lesser breeds'; as long as that is our visceral reflex we cannot have a satisfactory relationship in this day and age."[10] Presidential counselor Finch returned in early 1972 from his tour of South America and wrote to Nixon that the United States lacked a "coherent plan" for Latin America. The "lower profile" had left the United States nearly invisible in the region.[11]

The dearth of progress in inter-American relations in the 1970s flowed directly from the attitudes of two U.S. foreign-policy principals—Kissinger and Nixon. Kissinger's unfamiliarity with Latin American thought, society, and culture arose from his judgment that the region weighed little in his treasured balance of power theory of international relations. But Kissinger's lack of expertise also arose from his contempt for Latin Americans. He rejected the offer, of a childhood friend who became an official at the Inter-American Development Bank, to provide information on Latin America with the snide response: "If I need any information on Latin America, I'll look it up in the Almanac." In July 1969, he lectured the Chilean foreign minister, Gabriel Valdés, on Latin America's role in history. Since 1964, the United States had worked closely with Minister Valdés's ruling Christian Democratic government. As Kissinger interpreted history, "nothing important can come from the South. History has never been produced in the South. The axis of history starts in Moscow, goes to Bonn, crosses over to Washington, and then goes to Tokyo. What happens in the South is of no importance." Kissinger dreaded listening to speeches by Latin Americans, deriding Latin American officials as "a bunch of gassers."[12]

Kissinger's arrogant comments about Latin Americans were restrained compared to those of his boss. When alone with his enablers, like presidential aides H. R. Haldeman, General Alexander Haig, Attorney General John Mitchell, Secretary of the Treasury John Connally, and Kissinger, Nixon voiced contempt about all things Latin American. Like Kissinger, he dismissed the region's geopolitical importance. "Latin America doesn't matter," he exclaimed in 1971. "People don't give a damn about Latin America." Nixon added: "The only thing that matters is Japan, China, Russia, and Europe."[13] Kissinger informed the NSC in August 1971 that Nixon was uninterested in attending a discussion about U.S. policy toward Latin America. The president disliked giving economic aid to Latin America's needy, labeling Alliance for Progress programs to build homes as "welfare handouts." Nixon also could not be bothered to pay a presidential visit to the region. He further considered it "too goddamn dangerous" for him to travel there. Instead, he dispatched Rockefeller, Finch, and Connally to Latin America to engage in "hand-holding." Connally also was instructed to dwell on the president's accomplishments with China and the Soviet Union in 1972. As Nixon observed, consulting with Latin American heads of state was salutary, for "it builds them up to let them feel that we are interested in their views."[14]

In President Richard Nixon's worldview, international order, and stability required Latin Americans staying in their place. When he read reports of Roman Catholic priests organizing the poor in Latin America, he ordered the CIA to study the issue. The Church, influenced by the teachings of the beloved Pope John XXIII (1958–63), the liturgical reforms of Vatican II (1962–65), and the conference of Latin American bishops in Medellín (1968) had become active in social and economic issues. The Church in Latin America expressed "a preferential option for the poor" and taught that hunger and poverty were not God's will. Nixon, who called himself "the strongest pro-Catholic who is not Catholic," labeled these developments as "the deterioration of the attitude of the Catholic Church." He calculated that one-third of Latin American Catholics were now "Marxists." Military governments were best for Latin Americans; they could not "afford the luxury of democracy." All "Latin" countries—Spain, Italy, and Latin American nations—needed "strong leadership."[15] President Nixon instructed Robert Finch to call on military governments in Argentina and Brazil and "don't worry about whether they're dictators or not, because, there, the only friends we've got are the dictators."[16] Nixon ordered the government to sell advanced U.S. weapon systems, like jet fighters, to military governments. The president reacted negatively when he heard that Assistant Secretary of State Charles Meyer advised Anastasio Somoza Debayle (1967–79) that he needed to liberalize his regime in Nicaragua in order to avoid the fate of his father, who had been assassinated in 1956. The Somoza family had operated Nicaragua like a family hacienda since 1936 and had permitted the CIA to use Nicaragua as a training ground during the Cold War. Nixon responded to Meyer's injunction: "Well, then frankly, I don't want him to liberalize his regime; I hope he keeps it like it is." Nixon's buddy, Secretary of the Treasury Connally, backed his boss, noting "My God, I would hope so. He's the only friend we've got down there." The Secretary of the Treasury had become a confidant of Nixon on Latin America, because Connally, in Nixon's words, "believes that, as far as American public opinion is concerned, the American people are just aching for us to kick somebody in the ass, and that he wants us to do it."[17]

Compared to other U.S. presidents during the Cold War, Richard Nixon's embrace of military dictators was unabashed. Dwight Eisenhower, John Kennedy, and Lyndon Johnson had destabilized constitutional governments in Latin America and seen them replaced with military rulers. But Nixon's predecessors had never gone so far as to insist that Latin Americans were incapable of functioning in democratic societies. In 1955, President Eisenhower rejected Secretary of the Treasury George Humphrey's argument that the United States "should back strong men in Latin American governments," because "whenever a dictator is replaced, Communists gained." Eisenhower pointed out to subordinates that he "firmly believe[d] that if power lies with the people, then there will be no aggressive war." "In the long run," therefore, "the United States must back democracies."[18] President Kennedy always listed a "decent, democratic regime" as his vision for Latin American nations. President Johnson admitted to himself that he had acted unwisely in ordering the invasion of the Dominican Republic. Nixon, however, was not troubled by self-doubts when it came to dictatorship in Latin America. As he observed to the NSC, he would not repeat the mistake he felt certain that the United States had made when it abandoned Fulgencio Batista, the dictator of Cuba.[19] In his scorn for Latin American civilization, President

Nixon was reiterating the condescending, patronizing views expressed by officials such as George Kennan, Dean Acheson, George Humphrey, Thomas Mann, John Connally, and Henry Kissinger.

BONDING WITH BRAZIL

President Nixon discovered one group of Latin Americans he admired—the military rulers of Brazil. At the end of 1968, as he prepared to take control of the NSC, Henry Kissinger had received a forceful memorandum from General Vernon Walters on Brazil. Walters, who had served as the U.S. liaison with the Brazilian military conspirators in 1964, was now a senior defense attaché in France. Walters called on the incoming administration to favor Brazil, because of its potential to be a major power. Walters dismissed concerns about Institutional Act No. 5, the abolition of the Brazilian congress and the imposition of a military dictatorship, asserting that "there is no harsh repression in Brazil and the President [General Artur da Costa e Silva] has stated that he neither desires nor will he tolerate a dictatorship." Walters's friends in the Brazilian army assured him that they did not want to govern the country. But Walters did not believe that Brazil was ready for a civilian, democratic government. The military government was "friendly and cooperative," whereas the regime's opponents "are largely hostile to the United States." Walters concluded his memorandum with an apocalyptic Cold War warning: "If Brazil were to be lost it would not be another Cuba. It would be another China."[20]

The new Nixon administration took Walters's memorandum seriously, because it reinforced its own views on Latin America and because of the General's unique standing among Cold Warriors. An arch-conservative Roman Catholic who was fluent in many languages, Walters was on friendly terms with Richard Nixon. Walters was with Vice President Nixon when he was attacked in Caracas in 1958. He translated for Nixon, as well as for Presidents Truman and Eisenhower. While on duty in Paris, Walters helped arrange secret meetings between Henry Kissinger and North Vietnamese representatives to discuss the war in Vietnam. Nixon rewarded Walters by appointing him the deputy director of the CIA (1972–76). According to Director of the CIA Richard Helms, "Nixon thought of General Walters as his man in CIA and the only man who could be trusted to carry out his orders."[21] Walters had no doubts about waging Cold War in Latin America. On 3 November 1970, shortly after Salvador Allende assumed the Chilean presidency, he wrote to the White House that "we are engaged in a mortal struggle to determine the shape of the future of the world. There is no acceptable alternative to holding Latin America. We simply cannot afford to lose it." President Nixon wrote on the margins of Walters's memorandum, expressing agreement with the general's judgment.[22]

In 1969, President Nixon directed the NSC to undertake a broad-ranging review of U.S. policy toward Brazil. He approved arms sales, technical assistance, food aid, and program loans for the Brazilian regime, rejecting worries in the NSC and State Department that "close identification with the Médici regime will alienate other sectors of Brazilian society which in the longer term may be more important to [the] achievement of a constructive U.S.-Brazilian relationship."²³ After Allende came to power, Nixon intensified contacts with President Emílio Garrastazú Médici (1969–74), the most repressive of Brazil's ruling generals. Nixon instructed William Rountree, the U.S. ambassador to Brazil, "to assure that the Brazilian Government and the Brazilian military do not get the impression that we are looking down our noses at them because of their form of government."²⁴ In December 1971, Nixon hosted Médici in Washington and held two lengthy meetings. General Walters translated the conversations and joined the discussions. President Nixon did not raise issues of torture, press censorship, and gross violations of human rights in Brazil with his guest. He did inquire about President Médici's popularity. General Walters assured President Nixon that Médici's appearance at public events like soccer games evoked enthusiasm among spectators. Médici called General Walters "a living witness" to the "1964 Brazilian Revolution."²⁵ Nixon and the Brazilian leader enjoyed each other's company. Henry Kissinger reported that his boss had been "extremely pleased" with the discussions. General Walters reported that Nixon instructed him to tell President Médici that "with only very few chiefs of state had he developed so quickly a close relationship."²⁶

Presidents Nixon and Médici agreed on two fundamental points—that countries needed "stability" for economic growth and that there should be a relentless war against communism in the hemisphere. Nixon assured the Brazilian that the U.S. initiatives with China and the Soviet Union did not imply any change in U.S. hostility toward Fidel Castro. Nixon and Médici discussed Brazil's overt and covert aid to Bolivian dictator Hugo Banzer Suárez (1971–78) and Uruguay's strongman, Juan María Bordaberry Arocena (1972–76). Brazil had covertly aided Bordaberry's election in 1971. Nixon knew of the intervention in Uruguay but was unaware but "very happy" to hear of Brazil's role in Bolivia. Nixon further observed that "there were many things that Brazil as a South American country could do that the U.S. could not." Nixon subsequently boasted to Prime Minister Edward Heath of the United Kingdom that "the Brazilians helped rig the Uruguayan election." He remarked to Secretary of State William Rogers that he wished Médici "was running the whole continent." So pleased was Nixon with Brazil's anti-Communist policies that he and Médici agreed to communicate outside of normal diplomatic channels. Henry Kissinger would speak for Nixon, and Médici would rely on Foreign Minister Gibson Barbosa and on Colonel Manso Netto for "extremely private and delicate matters."²⁷

"Private and delicate matters" included attacking Salvador Allende's Chile. Responding to Nixon's questions, President Médici assured Nixon that Allende would suffer the fate of President João Goulart and that the Chilean military was capable of overthrowing Allende. The Brazilians were exchanging officers with the Chileans to work toward that end. Nixon told Médici that the United States could not take direction from the Brazilians but that it was "very important" that Brazil and the United States worked together on Chile. Nixon promised that "if money were required or other discreet aid, we might be able to make it available," although "this should be held in the greatest confidence." The two presidents agreed, in Nixon's words, that "we must try and prevent new Allendes and Castros and try where possible to reverse these trends." Nixon ended the discussion by pointedly informing President Médici that he would recall General Walters from Paris and appoint him to be the deputy director of the CIA. Médici observed that Walters "would help the President on many of his problems, especially those in Latin America."[28]

CHILE

As highlighted in the Nixon–Médici colloquy, President Nixon and his advisors became consumed by what they perceived as a mortal threat to U.S. interests in Latin America and to the international balance of power—the election of a self-proclaimed Marxist, Salvador Allende Gossens, to the Chilean presidency in November 1970. The Nixon administration first tried to prevent Allende from assuming office. The administration thereafter worked to undermine the Chilean economy and create the preconditions for a military *golpe de estado*. Richard Nixon and Henry Kissinger's death wish for the Allende government came true on 11 September 1973, when the Chilean military, led by General Augusto Pinochet Ugarte, attacked the constitutional government and overthrew it. President Allende died that day. General Pinochet (1973–90) subjected Chileans to seventeen years of ferocious military rule. The U.S. intervention in Chile during the Nixon years was not, however, an isolated event but part of a longer and larger process of discouraging Chileans and other Latin Americans from voting for political leftists.

Chileans considered themselves citizens of a unique Latin American country. The country is peculiar geographically, stretching 2,630 miles along the Pacific Coast but averaging only 100 miles in width. Chile is an isolated, confined country, with frozen wastelands and Tierra del Fuego in the south, the awesome Atacama Desert in the north, the ocean to the west and the imposing Andes mountain chain, the *cordillera*, to the east. Most Chileans, 9.3 million in 1970, lived in the center of the country in an area stretching less than three hundred miles. Chileans celebrated their history. Chileans had maintained, except for brief interruptions, a constitutional system since 1833, with the gradual enfranchisement of all adults. Chileans perceived themselves as living in an urbane, literate society that took art, literature, and political philosophy seriously. Chileans also took pride in noting that they had generally avoided the violent confrontations that had marred their neighbors' histories. Like the advanced European societies, Chile developed a twentieth-century social welfare state, especially under the leadership of President Arturo Alessandri Palma (1920–25).

The present and the future did not seem as fortuitous to Chileans, for the country had grave social and economic problems. Chile saw its population double between 1930 and 1960, and it added an additional 1.6 million people in the 1960s.

Food production did not keep up with population growth, and Chile became a net importer of food. Inefficiencies and injustices in the agricultural sector of the economy accounted for this poor performance. Seven percent of landowners controlled 80 percent of the land and often did not put their land to productive use. Most of Chile's four hundred thousand rural families were landless. The rural poor migrated to the outskirts of urban centers such as Santiago, dwelling in shanty-towns, known locally as *callampas* or "mushrooms." Perhaps 25 percent of Chile's burgeoning population lived in absolute poverty.

Global economic developments compounded Chile's problems. The country depended on the sale of copper for 60 percent its foreign earnings. Copper prices had generally fallen in the post–World War II period, although prices spiked up briefly in the mid-1960s because of U.S. demand for copper engendered by the war in Vietnam. U.S. companies, Anaconda and Kennecott, produced Chilean copper for the world market. The U.S. companies processed the copper in the United States, depriving Chile of the added value. Although copper extraction represented 11 percent of the economy, the copper industry generated only seventeen thousand jobs for Chileans. With the economy barely growing from the 1950s on, Chilean authorities responded with monetary expansion, foreign borrowing, and deficit financing. Annual inflation rates of 30 to 40 percent flowed from those decisions. Then, in 1960, Chile suffered a destructive earthquake in the Puerto Montt region that created over $200 million in damages.

Economic instability had the effect of dividing the Chilean polity roughly into thirds. Wealthier Chileans voted for traditional political parties like the Conservatives, Liberals, and Radicals. Chilean conservatives trusted in the solutions of the past, relying on foreign investment and trade to generate the funds for the social welfare system. In the middle stood a new party, the Christian Democrats, who emulated the Christian Democratic movement in West Germany and Italy. The Christian Democrats believed in evolutionary change, emphasizing land, tax, and educational reforms within a Christian framework. Communists and socialists, led by Allende in the *Frente de Acción Popular* (Popular Action Front) or FRAP, offered Marxist solutions for Chilean problems. Allende favored the nationalization of the copper industry and the redistribution of land. After 1959, the FRAP would cheer for the Cuban Revolution. In the presidential election of 1958, Allende nearly won, finishing only 3 percent, or about thirty-four thousand votes, behind the conservative choice, Jorge Alessandri Rodríguez, the son of the former president. Eduardo Frei Montalva, the leader of the Christian Democrats, finished third. Alessandri won only 31.6 percent of the vote but became president, because the Chilean legislature customarily ratified the election of the presidential candidate who secured a plurality of votes.

The Kennedy administration hoped to make Chile a "showcase" for the Alliance for Progress. During the 1960s, Chile received $743 million in Alliance money, the third highest amount in Latin America. Chile also had access to an annual line of credit of $200 to $300 million from U.S. commercial banks. But Kennedy and his advisors grew frustrated with the conservative Alessandri, calling Chileans the "poorest performers" in the region.[29] Alessandri declined to take significant steps to curb Chile's inflationary pressures, and he failed to develop a comprehensive plan for socioeconomic reform. By 1962–1963, the Kennedy administration had decided to cast its lot with Eduardo Frei and the Christian Democrats in the presidential elections scheduled for September 1964. Frei pledged to carry out the type of land and social reform envisioned in the Charter of Punta del Este. The Kennedy administration accepted Frei's proposed "Chileanization" of the copper industry. Chile would purchase part ownership of the companies; the companies, in turn, would be expected to use the proceeds of the sale to increase production and establish processing and fabricating facilities in Chile. Chile would thereby increase export earnings, and workers would find new employment opportunities. President Kennedy hoped to visit Chile in 1964, because he wanted to have "maximum possible impact" on the presidential election.[30]

The United States directly intervened in the Chilean election. Between 1962 and 1964, the CIA spent $4 million on polling, posters, and on radio and television advertisements for the Christian Democrats. The money was also used to organize student, labor, and women's groups and peasants and dwellers in the *callampas*. On a per capita basis, the CIA spent more money on the 2.4 million registered Chilean voters than did Lyndon Johnson and his opponent, Senator Barry Goldwater (R-AZ), in the 1964 U.S. presidential election. In the 1960s, the CIA became practiced at campaigning, helping run covert campaigns in Brazil, Bolivia, British Guiana, and the Dominican Republic. U.S. spending on public projects in Chile exceeded the covert campaign. The U.S. embassy in Santiago approved "impact projects" for electorally significant areas. The embassy distributed small loans and grants, usually less than $500,000, to purchase and equip a mobile health unit in a poor area or to repair a school building. Total spending on these impact projects amounted to $30 million in 1963 alone. U.S. officials in Chile also carried out a propaganda campaign—flags, lapel pins, films, photo exhibits, comic books—to insure that Chileans understood that the Alliance for Progress aided poor Chileans.[31] U.S. officials identified the Christian Democrats with the Alliance. Frei and his party welcomed the covert and overt role of the United States. In May 1964, Frei joshed with embassy officials about the money, "expressing 'unusual optimism' concerning his electoral prospects—although he 'jokingly observed that his selfish interests should lead him paint a bleaker picture to US authorities for obvious reasons.'"[32]

The United States not only wanted to boost Eduardo Frei, the Christian Democrats, and the Alliance for Progress but also it aimed to derail the campaign of Allende and the FRAP. The Kennedy and Johnson administrations accepted the judgment of Ambassador Charles Cole that FRAP would end democratic government in Chile and "would be so dangerous for U.S. interests in Chile and in all Latin America that U.S. policy should be to strive to prevent it."[33] Cold War verities overcame qualms about the irony of defending democracy by manipulating democracy through secret funding. In July 1964, the executive secretary of the 303 Committee, the group that oversaw covert operations, summarized thinking: "We can't afford to lose this one, so I don't think there should be economy shaving in this instance. We assume the Commies are pouring in dough, we have no proofs. They must assume we are pouring in dough, they have no proofs. Let's pour it on and in."[34] Like other Communist parties in the region, the Chilean Communists received an annual subsidy, $275,000 in 1965, from Moscow. Salvador Allende also accepted cash from Soviet agents. These amounts were minuscule compared to the U.S. effort in Chile.[35]

The CIA weakened the democratic process in Chile by urging citizens to view political opponents as mortal enemies. The agency launched a "Scare Campaign," depicting via films, leaflets, and wall painting images of Soviet tanks and Cuban firing squads. It also disseminated "disinformation" and "black propaganda," planting false stories in an attempt to turn Chilean socialists and Communists against one another. The CIA proved especially effective in warning female voters that Chilean leftists wanted to destroy the traditional family and deprive women of their roles as mothers and wives. In analyzing the electoral returns of 1958, agents had noticed that Allende had run poorly among women, winning only 22 percent of the women's vote. The "gendered propaganda" of the Scare Campaign warned that, if Allende won, women would be forced into heavy labor. The Communists, as alleged in radio broadcasts by Juana Castro, the estranged sister of the Cuban dictator, would also send children to communal camps in Eastern European countries. So intent were U.S. officials at insuring that Chilean women voted that the U.S. embassy recommended establishing "baby-sitting pools" on election day. The U.S. effort produced solid results. The women's vote rose from the previous high of 35 percent to 46.5 percent of the total vote. Candidate Frei garnered the support of 62.8 percent of women voters.[36]

The embassy and the CIA celebrated the Christian Democrat's landslide victory in September 1964. Frei took 56 percent of the vote, whereas Allende won 39 percent, and Julio Durán of the Radical Party earned only 5 percent. The CIA had constantly polled the electorate, and their last polls predicted the final result.[37] Frei had been aided by the decision of conservative Chileans to vote for him and not Durán. Though badly defeated, Allende and the FRAP could take some solace from the election in which they had been badly outspent by the Christian Democrats, the U.S. embassy, and the CIA. Allende had increased his share of the electorate from 5 percent in 1952 to 28 percent in 1958 to 39 percent in 1964.

The United States had made a good bet in placing its money on the Christian Democrats. President Frei (1964–70) kept his promise to work for the Chilean poor, building four hundred thousand low-cost homes and resettling twenty-seven thousand families on their own farms. He also had some success taming Chile's inflationary fires, lowering the annual inflation rate from 80 percent in 1964 to 17 percent in 1966. But Frei did not reach all goals. He had hoped to resettle one hundred thousand families on farms. His "Chileanization" scheme did not produce as much copper or as many new jobs as planned. Between 1966 and 1970, the economy grew only at a 1.3 percent annual rate, well below the 2.5 percent target rate of the Alliance for Progress. Frei's relations with the United States also grew strained, although the Christian Democrats received an additional $525,000 in covert funding from the CIA. President Frei irritated the Johnson administration by denouncing the U.S. invasion of the Dominican Republic and by establishing diplomatic and trade relations with the Soviet Union. He also grew frustrated by the often unwelcome fiscal and monetary advice that he received from Washington and the U.S. embassy.[38] He published a stinging critique, "The Alliance That Lost Its Way" (1967) in the establishment journal *Foreign Affairs*. Like other Latin American leaders, Frei came to believe that better terms of trade were essential for the region's economic development.

THE 1970 ELECTION

Under the Chilean constitution, President Frei was barred from immediate reelection. Chile had become a politically polarized society, with signs of political aggression. In October 1969 General Roberto Viaux Marambio led a small military insurrection against the Frei government. General Viaux demanded the resignation of the Chilean commander-in-chief and a pay raise for the army. The insurrection ended when the government agreed to study the general's demands. A violent leftist group, the *Movimiento Izquierida Revolucionaria* (MIR), carried out kidnappings, bank robberies, and land seizures in the name of immediate revolution. The MIR counted three thousand Chileans as members, with about two hundred of them engaged in violence. The economy continued to stagnate with inflation at 35 percent and the country having a staggering public external debt of $2 billion. Nonetheless, Chileans, true to their traditions and self-perceptions, voted peacefully on 4 September 1970 for their next president.

The 1970 election was a reprise of the 1958 election, with three major candidates. Former President Alessandri ran again, appealing to conservative Chileans who disliked the reforms pursued by the Christian Democrats. Radomiro Tomic Romero led the Christian Democrats. Tomic pushed the Christian Democrats to the political left, promising the nationalization of the copper industry and extensive land and labor reforms. Salvador Allende led a new coalition of the Socialists, Communists, and four smaller parties in the *Unidad Popular* (Popular Unity). Allende also promised to nationalize major industries and to create a socialist society in Chile through the parliamentary process. The election evoked interest in the country, with 2.9 million Chileans voting, 83 percent of registered voters. In this election, Allende won a narrow plurality, with 36.6 percent of the vote. Alessandri finished second with 35.3, and Tomic trailed with 28 percent. With no candidate securing a majority, the Chilean congress would have the constitutional duty to choose the president on 24 October 1970. Salvador Allende would presumably assume the presidency on November 4, because Tomic and Christian Democratic legislators were expected to vote for Allende. Chile remained calm during the weeks between the popular and legislative vote. CIA officers in Washington lamented that Chile was a "placid lake" and that there was "very little mass feeling within Chile that the election of Allende was necessarily an evil."[39] Allende became president when 153 of the 200 eligible legislators voted for him on 24 October. The other forty-seven voted for Alessandri, abstained, or were absent.

The electoral results of September 4 sent President Richard Nixon into frenzy. Henry Kissinger would later recount that Nixon "was beside himself" and desperate to do "something, *anything* that would reverse the previous neglect." Ambassador to Chile Edward Korry remembered being startled, upon entering the Oval Office on October 13. Nixon was striking his fist against his open palm and swearing "that son of a bitch, that son of a bitch." Nixon noticed Korry's perplexed expression and explained: "Not you, Mr. Ambassador. It's that son of a bitch Allende. We are going to smash him."[40] The United States had acted ineffectually during the 1970 Chilean presidential campaign but thereafter, between 5 September 1970 and 11 September 1973, President Nixon and Henry Kissinger worked relentlessly to fulfill Nixon's oath to "smash" Salvador Allende. Scholars have an excellent understanding of the U.S. intervention in Chile. In 1975, the U.S. Congress, led by Senator Frank Church (D-ID) released two major studies, *Covert Action in Chile, 1963–1973* and *Alleged Assassination Plots Involving Foreign Leaders*. In the post-Vietnam and post-Watergate era, Senator Church and his colleagues responded to public alarm about the U.S. complicity with the repressive regime of General Augusto Pinochet. The continuing concern about U.S. ties to General Pinochet prompted the Bill Clinton administration to release twenty-four thousand documents in the "Chile Declassification Project" in 1999–2000.[41] Although many documents remain classified, and some documents are heavily censored or "redacted," the course and conduct of U.S. policy toward Chile, like the U.S. intervention in Guatemala in 1954, is readily evident.

Both the U.S. embassy in Santiago and the 40 Committee, the newly renamed committee that oversaw covert operations, found Chile's 1970 electoral choices unpalatable. Ambassador Korry wished President Frei could continue in office. Tomic of the Christian Democrats seemed too far to the political left, and Alessandri had been a lackluster president between 1958 and 1964. The embassy initially assumed that Alessandri would win the election by a small margin. The 40 Committee authorized $425,000 in covert spending, one-tenth of the 1964 expenditure, to be used in a "spoiling" campaign against the Allende coalition. As the election approached, U.S. officials in Santiago and Washington realized they had misjudged Chile's political milieu. By June 1970, Ambassador Korry asked the 40 Committee to allocate $250,000 to a contingency slush fund to bribe Chilean congressmen not to certify an Allende victory. The 40 Committee also authorized CIA contacts with the Chilean legislators and military officers to discuss extra-constitutional measures they would support, if Allende received a plurality of the vote. These preliminary discussions provided the basis for the CIA's plan of action between September 4 and October 24, dubbed Track I and Track II under the codename Project FUBELT.[42]

On 15 September 1970, President Nixon launched his war against Allende, when he raged at Richard Helms, the director of the CIA. Helm's famous handwritten notes read:

- 1 in 10 chance perhaps, but save Chile!
- worth spending
- not concerned risks involved
- no involvement of embassy
- $10,000,000 available, more if necessary
- full-time job—best men we have
- game plan
- make economy scream
- 48 hours for plan of action

Helms would later testify that "if I ever carried a marshal's baton in my knapsack out of the Oval Office, it was that day."[43] The next day, Helms appointed Thomas Karamessines, the deputy director of planning, to assume responsibility for FUBELT. David Atlee Phillips would be chief of the task force in Washington. In 1954, Phillips had directed the CIA's "Voice of Liberation" in Guatemala.

Although President Nixon had placed the government in a crisis mode, not everyone in the U.S. government feared that an Allende presidency threatened the national security of the United States. In 1969–1970, intelligence assessments of an Allende victory did not point to international peril. National Security Study Memorandum (NSSM) 97, for example, found that the United States had no vital interests in Chile and that the global balance of power would not be significantly altered by an Allende victory. The Soviet Union had again subsidized the Chilean Communist Party but had stayed publicly neutral during the presidential campaign. Chile was also about as far away from the Soviet Union as it could possibly be. Allende and his coalition would be unable to run roughshod over Chileans, for Chile was a pluralistic society with independent centers of power—the security forces, the Christian Democrats, elements of organized labor, the Chilean Congress, and the Catholic Church. As one State Department officer noted, "to equate an Allende victory with 'a Castro-type dictatorship' assigns insufficient weight to Chile's profound differences from Cuba." Ambassador Korry added in January 1970, Chile "is one of the calmer and more decent places on the face of the earth; its democracy like our own, has an extraordinary resilience."[44]

The principal foreign-policy makers rejected arguments that Chile or the United States could survive an Allende presidency. At a 40 Committee meeting on 8 September 1970, Henry Kissinger and Attorney General Mitchell seconded CIA Director Helms's "personal observation" that a President Allende would destroy Chile's pluralistic system and "quickly neutralize the military and police after which there will be no effective rallying point for opposition against him." Kissinger would often declare that "there'll never be another free election in Chile."[45] A Marxist Chile might also ally itself with the Soviet Union and join Cuba in sponsoring subversion in Latin America. But President Nixon and Kissinger interpreted Allende's election principally within symbolic terms, for as Kissinger once jibed: "Chile was a dagger pointed at the heart of Antarctica." Allende's election threatened the credibility of the United States in the region and throughout the world. Kissinger warned senior advisers that "we risk giving the appearance of weakness or of indifference to the establishment of a Marxist government in the Hemisphere." A new version of the domino theory would develop if political radicals were permitted to grasp power via democratic means. Allende's election would encourage Communists in France or Italy to believe that there was a peaceful road to power. Kissinger warned that "the imitative spread of similar phenomena [Allende's election] elsewhere would in turn significantly affect the world balance and our own position in it."[46] President Nixon drew similar conclusions. In 1971, he ordered CIA Director Helms to develop "a tough program, ask for plenty of money to do the job" to influence elections in Italy. As Nixon saw it, "Italy is a Latin country." The president further warned Helms: "I don't want to let this get screwed up like Chile."[47]

Nixon and Kissinger found that the Chilean constitutional system could not be readily undermined. Track I was a convoluted scheme to prevent the Chilean congress from certifying Allende's election. It involved bribing Chilean legislators and enlisting President Frei, former President Alessandri, and the Chilean military in a bewildering series of political and constitutional gambits. Chilean politicians refused, however, to buy into the scheme. Track II aimed at a *golpe de estado*, with the Chilean military seizing power. Between 5 and 20 October 1970, the CIA made twenty-one contacts with Chilean military and police officers. The agency provided gas grenades, machine guns, and $50,000 to conspirators. CIA agents also worked to create "a coup climate," a sense of political crisis and confrontation, by spreading propaganda, waging "psychological warfare," and encouraging U.S. businesses to stop spending in Chile. The administration also tried to destabilize the Chilean economy by deferring international loans and asking commercial banks to deny credit.[48] Track II collapsed, however, with the shooting on 22 October 1970 and subsequent death of General René Schneider, the commander-in-chief of the Chilean army. Military conspirators attacked General Schneider, who defended the Chilean constitution and refused to support a *golpe*. It was Chile's first political assassination in 130 years. General Schneider's shooting outraged Chileans. Two days after the shooting, Allende received over 75 percent of the congressional vote.

Nixon and Kissinger denied responsibility for General Schneider's assassination. On 15 October, Kissinger had ordered the CIA to cancel contacts with General Roberto Viaux, the principal conspirator, because he questioned the general's ability to carry out a *golpe*. But in his 15 October order, Kissinger told General Viaux to preserve his assets for future operations and ordered the CIA to continue "working clandestinely and secretly to maintain the capability for Agency operations against Allende in the future." Two days previously, Nixon told Karamessines, the director of FUBELT, that "it was absolutely essential that the election of Mr. Allende to the presidency be thwarted." Between 15 October and 22 October, CIA agents in

Chile continued contact with military conspirators. After the shooting of General Schneider, the CIA's chief of station in Santiago ventured that the military now had an opportunity to carry out a *golpe*. In Washington, David Phillips responded by congratulating CIA agents in Chile "of guiding Chileans to [a] point today where a military solution is at least an option for them."[49] The question of U.S. responsibility for General Schneider's death can be related to a previous presidential entanglement with assassination. President John Kennedy did not order the murder on 1 November 1963 of President Ngo Dinh Diem of South Vietnam. But Kennedy accepted responsibility for initiating a course of events in August 1963 that led to Diem's assassination. By comparison, Nixon sent a perverse letter to President Frei, calling the attack on General Schneider "a repugnant event" and "a stain on the pages of contemporary history."[50]

PRESIDENT SALVADOR ALLENDE

Dr. Salvador Allende Gossens (1908–73) had been active in Chilean parliamentary politics since the 1930s, having served in both houses of the Chilean legislature and as Minister of Health from 1938 to 1942. In the late 1960s, he was also president of the Chilean Senate. A medical doctor by training, Allende came from a privileged background. His father was doctor and social reformer. His son adopted both his father's profession and his interest in social change, co-founding Chile's Socialist Party in 1933. The 1970 presidential campaign represented Allende's fourth run for the presidency. Allende implicitly accepted the concept of Chilean exceptionalism or "la vía Chilena" ("the Chilean way"). For almost four decades, Allende, an energetic, tireless politician, made the case that Chile could construct a socialist paradise through constitutional processes and legislative enactments. Chile did need to follow the revolutionary path of the Soviet Union, China, or Cuba. As a Marxist, Allende blamed international capitalism for leaving Chile a poor, dependent society and nation. Allende also denounced "imperialism," by which he meant the domination of the international system by European colonialists and the United States over the past centuries. Allende was a friend of Fidel Castro and spoke warmly about Cuba's progress in health, education, and social welfare. The Chilean denounced the U.S. intervention in Guatemala, the Bay of Pigs invasion, the invasion of the Dominican Republic, and the war in Vietnam. But, unlike Castro, he also found fault with the foreign policies of Socialist countries. He denounced Soviet atrocities in Budapest in 1956 and the invasion of Prague in 1968. Allende argued that Chile should pursue an independent, non-aligned foreign policy. He supported President Frei's opening to the Soviet Union, and, as president, Allende established relations with Cuba and China. He also called for proper relations with the United States. On 4 November 1970, he passed a note to a State Department official attending his inauguration. President Allende pledged that Chile would never allow its soil to be used by a power hostile to the United States.[51]

Allende's electoral mandate and political strength could be interpreted in various ways. Counting the votes for Tomic of the Christian Democrats, over 60 percent of Chileans had voted for significant socioeconomic change. By 1970, Chileans agreed that control of copper production by U.S. mining companies should end. On the other hand, Tomic advocated more change than most Christian Democrats supported. Allende also did not have mastery of his own coalition. Many Socialists considered Allende too moderate and too wedded to parliamentary principles. The MIR interpreted the 1970 election as a mandate for revolution and accelerated the process of encouraging land seizures among rural folk. The Chilean Communists, the conservative members of the coalition, preferred an incremental approach to change. This faith in gradualism reflected the traditional approach of Communist parties in Latin America and the views of Moscow. Although political life in Chile became confrontational in Allende's Chile, conflict did not erode *Unidad Popular's* electoral base. In 1971, the coalition garnered 49 percent of the vote in local elections and 43 percent of the vote in March 1973 in congressional elections, adding two Senate seats and six seats in the Chamber of Deputies. *Unidad Popular* did not, however, win enough seats to control the legislature. After the March elections, it held twenty of the fifty seats in the Senate and 63 of 150 seats in the lower house.

During his three years in office, President Allende transformed the Chilean economy via constitutional means. He froze prices, raised minimum wages, and subsidized the prices of staples like milk, giving a quick boost to the living standards of the urban working classes. Fulfilling the national consensus, he nationalized the copper industry. His government also nationalized the coal and steel industries, the majority of banks, and other firms and businesses. The nearly $1 billion in U.S. direct investment in Chile disappeared. Supporters on the political left often forced the government's hand by occupying management offices until expropriation was announced. The government directed additional resources to health, education, and welfare, and saw the continued decline in infant mortality rates and the increase in the number of young people attending school that had begun during President Frei's years in office. Huge, boisterous crowds often assembled in support of Allende's march to socialism.

Strikes and furious demonstrations also arose in opposition to Allende's agenda. Propertied and conservative Chileans feared that Allende's ultimate goal was to turn Chile into a Communist country based on either the Soviet or Cuban model. Chileans would lose their freedom of speech, the right of assembly, and their Catholic religion. Women and mothers were certain that *Unidad Popular* planned to destroy the Chilean family. A regular feature of Chilean life became theatrical demonstrations led by women banging pots and pans with metal spoons in protest of government policies. These fears of oppression were highly exaggerated, for everyone in Chile, from the extreme right to the extreme left on the political spectrum, was free to speak, shout, or write their hysterical version of events from 1970 to 1973.

Predictions that Allende would align Chile with the Communist camp also proved inaccurate. Chile conducted normal diplomatic relations with Cuba and China. Castro came and stayed in Chile for a month in late 1971. In late 1972, President Allende traveled to Moscow, seeking economic aid. But these gestures hardly signified that Chile had allied with the Communists. Allende did not allow Cubans to use Chile as a base for revolution, and he ignored Castro's unsolicited advice to ignore constitutional procedures and arm workers. Moscow pursued détente with the United States. It was not interested in challenging the United States in its sphere of influence, for it wanted recognition of its suzerainty over Eastern Europe. The big prize would come with the Helsinki Accords (1975), with the West tacitly conceding both the Soviet domination of Eastern Europe and the permanent division of Germany. Soviet leaders disappointed Allende, declining to rescue Chile from its economic morass with a substantial foreign aid package.[52]

White-collar and skilled workers, the constituency of the Christian Democrats, had, however, legitimate anxieties over *Unidad Popular's* mismanagement of the Chilean economy. The government expanded consumption, without a matching increase in production. Goods became scarce; hoarding ensued. Investment in Chilean enterprises dried up. Chile scared off international investors with their nationalization policies. Chile refused to compensate the U.S-owned copper companies, alleging that they had earned excess profits over the century. Fearing the future loss of their holdings, Chilean entrepreneurs and landowners stopped innovating and investing. Agricultural production fell 22 percent in 1972–1973.

During his presidency, Salvador Allende visited with Fidel Castro, and Castro spent a month in Chile. Allende admired Castro and the Cuban Revolution. But Allende kept his pledge to the United States that he would not permit Chile to be a base for revolution or Soviet weaponry. President Allende also ignored Castro's unsolicited advice to arm Chilean workers. (Corbis Images)

Government bureaucrats proved inept at managing the new nationalized industries. The government spent wildly, albeit with the good intention of aiding the poor, and then printed money to cover the excessive spending. Price inflation predictably ensued, with inflation hitting perhaps 500 percent in 1973. The Chilean currency, the *escudo*, became nearly worthless. Officially, the *escudo* was pegged to the dollar at a ratio of 46 to 1. On the black market, the dollar was worth 280 to 300 *escudos*. Chile did not have the money to service its international debts and in November 1971 suspended payments, including payments on the $1.4 billion it owed to U.S. creditors. Strikes by merchants, shopkeepers, and truckers further disrupted economic activity. A strike by truckers in August 1973 paralyzed the Chilean economy.[53]

NIXON AGAINST ALLENDE

Chileans on their own created the preconditions for a political confrontation or what the CIA called a "coup climate." But between 4 November 1970 and 11 September 1973, the Richard Nixon administration employed the covert schemes, tricks, and deceptions that had been previously used in Guatemala, Cuba, Brazil, British Guiana, and the Dominican Republic to generate political warfare and economic chaos in Chile. The failure of Operation FUBELT and the tragic death of General Schneider had not chastened the administration. Richard Nixon and Henry Kissinger celebrated the death of Salvador Allende even as the Nixon presidency collapsed under the weight of the high crimes and misdemeanors known as "Watergate."

Within a few days after Allende's inauguration, the president and his national security adviser set both U.S. public and covert policy toward Chile. Nixon had his loathing of Allende reinforced by the stern memorandum about Chile's threat to Western interests he received from his friend, General Vernon Walters. After a lengthy NSC meeting on Chile, the president issued National Security Decision Memorandum (NSDM) 93 on 9 November 1970. The United States would take a "correct but cool" policy toward Allende. Public hostility toward Allende would provide the Chilean leader with an opportunity to rally domestic and international support. Although being diplomatic in speech, the administration vowed "to maximize pressures on the Allende government to prevent its consolidation and limit its ability to implement policies contrary to U.S. and hemispheric interests." The directive also called on the United States to cultivate "friendly military leaders" in the hemisphere, especially those in Argentina and Brazil. The directive was informed by the harsh talk at the NSC Meeting. Both Secretary of States William P. Rogers and Secretary of Defense Melvin Laird agreed that "we have to do everything we can to hurt him [Allende] and bring him down." The president indulged himself in one of his typical outbursts, emphasizing that "no impression should be permitted in Latin America that they can get away with this, that it is safe to go this way. All over the world it is too much the fashion to kick us around." Nixon said he was unconcerned about how democratic countries in Latin

America would react to U.S. policies. The "game" was to keep the military leaders of Argentina and Brazil closely aligned to the United States.[54] Prior to the NSC meeting, Kissinger had prepared Nixon, warning that Allende's election "poses for us one of the most serious challenges ever faced in this hemisphere" and that "your decision as to what to do about it may be the most historic and difficult foreign affairs decision you will have to make this year." With his characteristic disdain for Latin Americans, Kissinger rationalized Nixon's war against Allende with the view that "I don't see why we have to let a country go Marxist just because its people are irresponsible."[55]

As called for in NSDM 93, the United States conducted economic warfare against Chile. U.S. economic aid, which had been $260 million in 1967, amounted to only $7.4 million in 1972. Chileans could not obtain spare parts for their U.S.-made autos, trucks, and machinery because the Export-Import Bank denied commercial loans and credits to Chile. The United States also used its influence at the Inter-American Development Bank, the International Monetary Fund, and the World Bank to deny loans to Chile. The Inter-American Development Bank provided Chile with $46 million in loans in 1970 but only $2 million during the Allende presidency.[56] The United States defended its policies by pointing out that Chile expropriated foreign properties without compensation and that it suspended payments on international loans. But the policy was the fulfillment of Nixon's injunction to CIA Director Helms to make the Chilean economy "scream."

The CIA admitted to spending $7 million in Chile between 1970 and 1973, although the agency probably funneled additional funds into the country through third parties. President Nixon personally approved support, which amounted to over $1 million, to the conservative newspaper, *El Mercurio*. Nixon was a friend of the Chilean publisher and media mogul Agustín Edwards. The newspaper and Edwards's radio and television stations crusaded against Allende and, by 1972–1973, increasingly suggested that the Chilean military overthrow the government. As it did during the 1960s, the CIA also funded opposition parties, both conservative parties and the Christian Democrats. The Nixon administration justified the spending, because it told itself that Allende would destroy democratic freedoms in Chile. In April 1971, in the president's hideaway office in the Executive Office Building, Henry Kissinger opined to Nixon that Allende would follow the "German strategy" of Adolf Hitler of gradually eliminating dissent in order to create a "fascist" state. Two months later, speaking in the Oval Office of the White House, Kissinger and Nixon took turns denouncing Allende, with the president demanding a "harder line" on Chile. Kissinger agreed, claiming that the Chilean president was gaining control over the press and police and isolating the military. He predicted that there would "never be another free election in Chile."[57] In fact, elections took place in 1971 and 1973, Allende remained true to his parliamentary convictions, and Chileans published and shouted their opinions.

CIA money went to business groups and trade associations and to a right-wing paramilitary group, *Paz y Libertad* (Peace and Liberty), that perpetrated terrorism. The CIA probably did not directly organize and fund major confrontations, like the trucker's strike, but funded groups that supported the strikers. As a congressional investigative committee found, the CIA understood that "the interconnections among the CIA-supported political parties, the various militant trade associations (*gremios*) and paramilitary groups prone to terrorism and violent disruption were many." The American Institute for Free Labor Development (AIFLD) operated in Chile and brought anti-Allende union officials to Washington for training. The AIFLD was an arm of the major U.S. trade union, the AFL-CIO, and received substantial funding from CIA front organizations. The AIFLD played a major role in fomenting strikes and violent demonstrations against Prime Minister Cheddi Jagan in British Guiana between 1962 and 1964.[58] As in British Guiana, the CIA worked to create a "coup climate," in Chile or, in Melvin Laird's words, "to bring him [Allende] down."

The Chilean congressional elections of March 1973, which increased the political strength of *Unidad Popular*, prompted new thinking and plotting both in Chile and in Washington. Allende's political opponents had planned to impeach Allende and remove him from office if they gained control of two-thirds of the legislative seats. They now questioned whether they could defeat *Unidad Popular* in the 1976 presidential elections. Nixon administration officials were also disappointed by the results of Chile's congressional elections. The Latin American section of the State Department and the new ambassador to Santiago, Nathaniel Davis, hoped for a Track I-style political solution, defeating *Unidad Popular* in 1976, perhaps with a repeat of the 1964 covert intervention in the electoral process. Nixon, Kissinger, and the CIA had never, however, given up on Track II—a military overthrow of the government. Although it eliminated economic assistance to Chile, the administration maintained military aid and military equipment sales, providing over $33 million between 1971 and 1973, a more than 40 percent increase over the previous three years. Over six hundred junior officers and non-commissioned officers attended the U.S. Army's "School of the Americas" in Panama. The CIA funded an anti-Allende newsletter for military officers. It also kept in close contact with high-ranking Chilean officers, reporting, for example, in August 1971 that General Augusto Pinochet had kept his political thoughts to himself at a dinner party. In September 1972, a CIA source within the Pinochet camp reported that the general now believed that "Allende must be forced to step down or be eliminated." While in the Panama Canal Zone to negotiate the purchase of U.S. tanks, General Pinochet was told by U.S. military officers that "U.S. will support coup against Allende 'with whatever means necessary' when time comes."[59]

The details of the U.S. involvement in the Chilean military's attack on President Allende remain unclear. Under General Pinochet's command, the Chilean military seized the government on 11 September 1973. Warplanes bombed and strafed the presidential palace, *La Moneda*, pinpointing Allende's offices. After making a dramatic radio broadcast and reaffirming his faith in the Chilean people, President Allende committed suicide. The Nixon administration produced records demonstrating that the embassy and CIA officers were ordered during the summer of 1973 not to discuss a *golpe* with Chilean officers. The CIA, however, monitored the plotting and knew the date of the attack. In their memoirs, both Nixon and Kissinger claimed that the overthrow of Allende was a Chilean affair. Citing unidentified sources, one British scholar, Jonathan Haslam, has suggested officials in Washington used Pentagon facilities and secure communication lines in the naval port of Valparaiso to communicate with plotters. Halsam's sources also informed him that General Walters, now deputy director of the CIA, set up shop in offices behind the Hotel Carrera and near *La Moneda* in the days before the golpe.[60]

A telephone conversation between Nixon and Kissinger on 16 September 1973, five days after President Allende's death, casts doubt on their respective claims of innocence. Henry Kissinger had sought to block the release of that conversation and others for more than thirty years. After first discussing his plan to attend a Washington Redskins football game, Kissinger celebrated the end of the Allende government, complaining that the media did not share his joy over what

Chile's presidential palace, *La Moneda*, burns on 11 September 1973 after being bombed and strafed by the Chilean warplanes on the orders of General Augusto Pinochet. President Salvador Allende committed suicide that day in the palace. In his farewell address to the Chilean people, Allende asserted: "I have faith in Chile and its destiny." An impressive statue of Allende, with his famous words inscribed on the base, now stands near *La Moneda*.
(Corbis Images)

had happened in Chile. Perhaps thinking about the covert interventions in Iran and Guatemala, Kissinger added, "in the Eisenhower period we would be heroes." Nixon responded: "Well we didn't, as you know—our hand doesn't show on this one though." "We didn't do it," Kissinger declared, "I mean we helped them—created the conditions as great as possible." Nixon agreed: "That is right. And that is the way it is going to be played."[61]

Whether Allende's policies alone would have ultimately led to his ouster can be debated but cannot be answered. The United States had contributed to political polarization in Chile in the 1960s and helped foment political violence and economic chaos in the Allende years. Whether the murderous Pinochet regime could have lasted from 1973 to 1990, without the initial backing of the Nixon and Gerald R. Ford administrations, is also an issue of critical historical importance.[62]

PINOCHET AND HIS FRIENDS

The Nixon administration wasted little time in signaling its support for the end of constitutional rule in Chile. On September 13, in a cable from the White House Situation Room, the embassy in Santiago was instructed "to make clear its desire to cooperate with the military junta and to assist in any appropriate way." On the next day, the administration advised the Chileans to dispatch a delegation to the United Nations to defend the *golpe* from mounting international criticism. A few days later, the United States responded favorably to a Chilean request for one thousand flares and one thousand steel helmets for soldiers to be used in combat operations against the military regime's domestic opponents. On September 24, the United States extended diplomatic recognition to the Pinochet regime. The administration waited two weeks to resume relations, because Kissinger believed the United States had made a public relations mistake in 1964, when it immediately recognized the military government in Brazil. As the September 13 cable noted, "it is best initially to avoid too much public identification between us."[63]

Once relations were restored, the administration shipped the economic largesse to Chile that had been denied to the Allende government. In October and November 1973, it granted Chile $48 million in commodity credits to purchase wheat and corn. Between 1974 and 1976, Chile received $132 million in Food for Peace (P.L. 480) grants. Kissinger proudly informed the Chilean foreign minister that his nation received over two-thirds of the total food assistance for Latin America. Chile accounted for only 3 percent of the region's population. Chile also received $30 million in U.S. economic assistance for housing. President Nixon had once labeled housing assistance as "welfare." The rest of Latin America received only $4 million in housing aid. Loans and credits also flowed from international lending agencies. During its first three years, the military government received $238 million in loans from the Inter-American Development Bank, whereas the Allende government had received only $11.6 million. The Chilean military went on a buying spree, ordering $100 million in new equipment and spare parts. Chile emerged as the fifth largest customer in the world for U.S. military hardware. In

1974–1975, nearly nine hundred Chileans trained at the School of the Americas in Panama.[64]

The United States embraced Pinochet's Chile even as the military dictator plunged the nation into a netherworld. In the immediate aftermath of the *golpe*, the regime arrested fifty thousand Chileans. Thousands were impounded in the National Stadium, where soldiers carried out summary executions. Another favorite killing zone was the warship *Esmeralda* anchored at Valparaíso. High government officials, like Foreign Minister Orlando Letelier, were carted off to Dawson Island in the extreme south of the country in the frigid, windy Straits of Magellan. The political prisoners lived in squalor and were forced into hard labor. A worse fate awaited the perhaps five thousand Chileans who entered the Villa Grimaldi detention center, a walled estate on the outskirts of Santiago. One detainee, Gladys Díaz, a radio broadcaster and member of MIR, survived Villa Grimaldi and later recounted her ordeal. She and her husband were forced to watch each other being tortured. Her husband was later taken away and "disappeared." She was subjected to electrical shocks, drugs, and her head was plunged into toilet water in a technique known as "the submarine." A karate expert beat her up and broke her hip. Díaz was also made to witness two murders—one a beating by chains, the other by shooting. One notorious torturer defended allegations he was also a rapist by observing that he found his female victims, covered with dirt and urine and with blood running down their legs, as unappealing. In fact, female detainees testified to being subjected to "gang rapes" by Chilean security forces. The future president of Chile, Michelle Bachelet, and her mother also suffered abuse at Villa Grimaldi. Bachelet's father, Air Force General Alberto Bachelet, a constitutionalist and supporter of Allende, had previously died in detention after torture.[65] Chilean fact-finding commissions would later charge the regime with 3,197 recorded murders. Some thirty-six thousand Chileans testified to their torture or the torture of a family member. Over two hundred thousand Chileans, 2 percent of the population, went into exile in over one hundred countries. Chileans spread out, because they knew the regime would try to hunt them down and kill them. Scholars judge that the official findings are too conservative. Credible political detention estimates are one hundred fifty thousand to two hundred thousand people, with over one hundred thousand Chileans suffering torture while in the custody of state agents.[66]

General Pinochet and his minions claimed they were fighting World War III, saving Western Civilization and Christianity from Marxist barbarians. At first, the military junta had assured Chileans that there would be neither victims nor vanquished, and the military's mission was to "salvage" the country. The Christian Democrats, for example, initially supported the *golpe*. But by October 1973, General Pinochet portrayed himself as Chile's messiah. The attack on Allende had been God's work, and Pinochet committed himself to the "heroic struggle" to carry out a "moral cleansing" in order "to extirpate the root of evil from Chile." In March 1974, the regime issued an official rationale, a "Declaration of Principles," which proclaimed that Chile was an anti-Marxist country. The armed forces would stay in power indefinitely, until Chile's military leaders had redefined the Chilean mentality. Marxism and the doctrine of class struggle had to be replaced in the Chilean mind with fealty to conservative Catholicism, class harmony, and Chilean nationalism. The regime abolished all political institutions other than the courts. So profound was the regime's contempt for the trappings of liberal democracy— freedom of speech, freedom of association, elections—that it prohibited private groups, including professional associations, mothers' centers, and sports clubs, from holding elections for officers.[67]

Rejecting *la vía chilena* model, Pinochet adopted the violent methods of change that Josef Stalin imposed in the 1930s in his ghastly efforts to construct a "New Soviet Man." After seizing power, the regime, in a process labeled the "Caravan of Death," dispatched military death squads to provincial towns and executed local officials whose crime had been that they held office during the Allende years. The regime wanted to spread the anti-Marxist fervor, sow terror among the country folk, and find out which local military commanders were willing to obey Santiago's orders and commit atrocities. Pinochet's economic philosophy was to return Chile to nineteenth-century *laissez-faire* capitalism with limited government expenditures. Knowing that the living standards of the poor would fall, the regime periodically ordered soldiers to surround *callampas*, conduct searches of homes for weapons and subversive literature, and arrest males. The release of male prisoners would depend on the proper deportment of families and neighbors. The regime also permitted landowners to repossess their land and seek vengeance against *campesinos* who had received land titles from previous governments. In commanding the restructuring of Chilean thought, society, and culture, General Pinochet presented himself as a selfless servant of the people who was concerned only about the advancement of the nation. In fact, along with being a tyrant and a murderer, he was a thief. Investigations would subsequently reveal that he had hidden $28 million in foreign bank accounts.[68]

General Pinochet also directed state-sponsored international terrorism. He appointed Colonel Manuel Contreras to head a new secret police organization known by the acronym DINA. Colonel Contreras and his DINA brutes carried out the torture and murder of Chileans in places like Villa Grimaldi. Contreras reported directly to General Pinochet. Pinochet publicly denied that government agents tortured, but he reportedly confessed to two religious leaders that "you have to torture them, because without it they don't sing. Torture is necessary to extirpate communism."[69] Contreras and DINA also extended the terror to other countries. In September 1974, DINA agents assassinated General Carlos Prats and his wife with a car bomb attack. Prats was thrown out of the car and died instantly. The general's wife was trapped in the burning car and was carbonized. General Prats, who was living quietly in exile in Buenos Aires, had been the commander-in-chief of Chile's armed forces. Like General Schneider, General Prats had been loyal to the Chilean constitution and refused to participate in the overthrow of President Allende. General Pinochet and military supporters had forced General Prats to resign in the months before the 11 September 1973 attack on *La Moneda*.

Colonel Contreras extended his campaign of international terror, when, in November 1975, he met in Santiago with security chiefs from military governments in Argentina, Uruguay, Bolivia, and Paraguay to exchange information on Marxists and to collaborate in assassinating them. Many Chilean leftists, for example, had initially sought refuge in Argentina. The project earned the codename of "Operation Condor," named after the national bird of Chile. Brazil joined the terrorist network the next year. Operation Condor claimed prominent victims. DINA worked with Argentines to capture and secret back to Chile MIR leaders for torture and execution. Bernardo Leighton, a Christian Democratic leader, was shot in the back of the head in Rome. Leighton's wife was left paralyzed by a bullet that hit her in the spine.[70] Subjected to international criticism, Chile had released prominent political prisoners from Dawson Island. One, Orlando Letelier, fled to Washington and lobbied U.S. legislators to oppose Pinochet. In September 1976, DINA agents triggered a remote-control bomb that killed Letelier and his assistant, Ronni Moffitt, and wounded her husband. Letelier's legs were blown off. Ronni Moffitt had her carotid artery and windpipe severed by shrapnel. She drowned in her own blood. Minister Letelier and the Moffitts were traveling by car in an area known in Washington as "Embassy Row."[71]

Presidents Richard Nixon and Gerald Ford and their secretary of state, Henry Kissinger, accepted the Pinochet regime's barbaric behavior with equanimity. Cold War imperatives triumphed over a defense of human rights. On 1 October 1973, at a staff meeting, Kissinger ruled: "I think we should understand our policy—that however unpleasant they act, this government is better for us than Allende was." When confronted by CIA and State Department analyses of atrocities perpetrated by the Pinochet regime, Kissinger denied the reports, informing U.S. legislators that he doubted whether Chile was a country that engaged in a consistent pattern of gross violations of human rights. Kissinger challenged aides, like Assistant Secretary of State for Inter-American Affairs William D. Rogers, asking: "Is this government worse than the Allende government? Is human rights more severely threatened by this government than Allende?" Rogers, a good friend of Kissinger's, answered "yes" to both questions, adding that Allende had not closed down opposition parties or destroyed opposition newspapers. Kissinger ridiculed colleagues who raised human rights issues, explaining to the Chilean foreign minister that "the State Department is made up of people who have a vocation in the ministry. Because there are not enough churches for them, they went into the Department of State." Secretary of State Kissinger further belittled Senator Edward M. Kennedy (D-MA) for proposing legislation to cut off economic and military aid to Chile.[72] In 2008, President Michelle Bachelet would confer on Senator Kennedy the Order to the Merit of Chile Award, Chile's highest civilian award, for his efforts to restore democracy and respect for human rights.

The mounting criticism of his love affair with Pinochet's Chile seemingly persuaded Kissinger to defend human rights principles. He delivered an impressive exposition of human rights at an OAS meeting in Santiago in June 1976. Kissinger highlighted this speech in his memoirs and also observed that he raised human rights issues in his 8 June 1976 meeting with General Pinochet in his presidential office. The declassified memorandum of the conversation does not sustain Kissinger's memory of his meeting with Pinochet. The speech was intended to pacify critics in the United States. Kissinger assured Pinochet that "the speech is not aimed at Chile." He commiserated with the general, noting "my evaluation is that you are a victim of all left-wing groups around the world and that your greatest sin was that you overthrew a government which was going Communist." He asked Pinochet to make a gesture in the human rights field but qualified that request with the assurance that "none of this is said with the hope of undermining your government. I want you to succeed and I want to retain the possibility of aid." Pinochet claimed that Chile had reduced the political prisoner population to four hundred inmates. But he also denounced the criticism he received from Christian Democrats and Orlando Letelier's access to the U.S. Congress. Kissinger responded that he not spoken with any Christian Democrat in years.[73] Three months later, DINA agents assassinated Letelier.

A smiling Secretary of State Henry Kissinger shakes hands with General Augusto Pinochet in June 1976 in Santiago, Chile. Kissinger would later claim that he raised human rights issues with the Chilean dictator. The declassified memorandum of conversation reveals, however, that the secretary of state focused on congratulating Pinochet on overthrowing "a government which was going Communist." The Richard Nixon and Gerald Ford administrations provided critical help to General Pinochet in the immediate years after the overthrow of Salvador Allende. (Corbis Images)

Hypocrisy also characterized covert dealings with Chile. The Nixon administration cut off funding for the Christian Democrats after giving them a severance payment of $50,000 in June 1974. For twelve years, the United States had covertly funded the Christian Democrats on the premise that the United States needed to preserve competitive political discourse in Chile. Pinochet's military regime outlawed political parties. The administration also gave *El Mercurio* and the media empire of Augustín Edwards a final payment of $176,000. *El Mercurio* went from being an anti-Allende organ to serving as the regime's mouthpiece, publishing lies and disinformation on the assassinations of political figures. Chilean officials claimed that political leftists killed one another in internecine warfare.[74]

Nixon and Kissinger had alleged that Salvador Allende would turn Chile into a base for international subversion. With Operation Condor, General Pinochet and Colonel Contreras conspired to make Chile and the Southern Cone a home for international terrorists. In 1976, U.S. officials learned that Operation Condor had an assassination component. The CIA had good sources in the region. CIA Deputy Director Walters also had often conferred with Colonel Contreras in Santiago and Washington. After lengthy internal debate within the State Department, on 23 August 1976 Secretary Kissinger authorized U.S. ambassadors to approach heads of state in the Condor countries and register the U.S. view that assassination "would create a most serious moral and political problem." Ambassador to Chile David Popper responded that General Pinochet would be insulted if Popper implied that Pinochet had been connected with assassination plots. Popper asked for further guidance. The ambassador did not receive new instructions until after Letelier's assassination. State Department officials decided that the "Condor scheme" had not been activated. In October, Ambassador Popper had an aide approach Colonel Contreras, who predictably denied Chilean involvement in the Letelier assassination.[75] Latin American Communists had not attacked the United States. Instead, Cold War allies, the military dictators of the southern cone, had perpetrated the worst case of international terrorism on U.S. soil prior to the dreadful attacks on the World Trade Center and the Pentagon on 11 September 2001.

ANOTHER MILITARY DOMINO

The U.S. approach to the Chilean military regime would be replicated with Argentina, where generals who had run the country from 1966 to 1973 seized power again in March 1976. For ten years Argentina had been torn by violence, with military repression, urban guerrillas, a leftist revolutionary movement, and Peronists demanding the return to power of the old caudillo, Juan Perón, who had been overthrown and exiled by the military in 1955. The restoration of Perón and his wife Isabel Martínez de Perón (1973–76) to power only contributed to political violence and economic chaos. Between 1969 and 1973, the Nixon administration had helped the Argentine military rulers, offering economic advice and aid and developing back-channel communications with them. President Nixon believed, of course, that Latin America's future lay with Argentina and Brazil under military rule.[76] Kissinger enthusiastically welcomed the Argentine military's return to power, under the leadership of General Jorge Rafael Videla (1976–81). While in Santiago, Kissinger met with Argentine Foreign Minister César Augusto Guzzetti on 10 June 1976, two days after conferring with Pinochet in his presidential office. Kissinger told the Argentine that the United States sympathized with Argentina's fight against internal subversion and terrorism. Kissinger further observed: "We are aware you are in a difficult period. It is a curious time, when political, criminal, and terrorist activities tend to merge without any clear separation. We understand you must establish authority." The secretary of state sanctioned state terrorism, noting "if there are things that have to be done, you should do them quickly. But you should quickly get back to normal procedures." Kissinger met with Guzzetti a second time in Washington in October 1976. The foreign minister returned to Buenos Aires "euphoric," for he inferred that the Ford administration's "overriding concern was not human rights but rather that the Government of Argentina 'get it over quickly.'" "Getting it over quickly" signified the wholesale slaughter of Argentines. The U.S. ambassador in Buenos Aires, Robert C. Hill, protested these atrocities and provided Washington with explicit accounts of what was happening in Argentina. For his humanity, Ambassador Hill merited a rebuke for contesting, in Kissinger's words, "my policy."[77]

Employing the same perverted reasoning of Brazil's Médici and Chile's Pinochet, General Videla vowed to save Western civilization and Christianity by cleansing Argentine society of subversives and their sympathizers. An Argentine court would sentence General Videla to life imprisonment in 1985 for his abuses of human rights. Argentine military leaders spoke of killing fifty thousand people. They managed to murder perhaps thirty thousand in *la guerra sucia*. A disproportionate number of those arrested, tortured, and murdered were Argentine Jews.[78] The regime's anti-Semitism did not seem to register with Secretary Kissinger, whose family had fled Nazi Germany in the 1930s.

Fighting the Cold War and maintaining the balance of power commanded a higher value than promoting respect for human rights. Between 1969 and 1976, the U.S. presidential administrations also ridiculed the idea that Latin Americans could build orderly societies based on democratic values. The United States had successfully waged Cold War in the region. The United States maintained its sphere of influence, and the region's anti-Communist military leaders aligned themselves with the United States. Latin American citizens had paid, however, a brutal price for a winning U.S. policy.

CHAPTER 7

Cold War Horrors—
Central America

The last ten years of the Cold War, from 1979 to 1989, proved a dreadful time for Latin Americans, especially for citizens in the Central American countries of El Salvador, Guatemala, and Nicaragua. In the name of anticommunism, military units allied with right-wing death squads imitated the tactics of their ideological brethren in the Southern Cone, slaughtering perhaps three hundred thousand Central Americans. The ghastly violence prompted Gabriel García Márquez to direct his Nobel Prize speech in December 1982 to the "sorrow and beauty" of Latin America. The renowned novelist from Colombia, author of *Cien años de soledad* (1967) (*One Hundred Years of Solitude*), spoke of the agony of his region. Hundreds of thousands of Chileans and Uruguayans had fled their once peaceful countries. Imprisoned Argentine women gave birth and then had their babies stolen from them by security forces. The "diabolic dictator" of Guatemala was attacking indigenous Mayans, "carrying out, in God's name, the first Latin American ethnocide of our time." Because they had tried to change Latin America's poverty and injustice, "nearly two hundred thousand men and women have died throughout the continent, and over one hundred thousand have lost their lives in three small and ill-fated countries of Central America: Nicaragua, El Salvador and Guatemala." It would be, García Márquez reminded, as if the United States had lost 1.6 million people in four years.

In his remarkable address in Stockholm, Sweden, García Márquez did not charge other nations with responsibility for Latin America's suffering. He rejected, however, the idea that "violence and pain" was the natural condition of the region. Latin Americans were not the children of Cain. The Colombian asked, "Why think that the social justice sought by progressive Europeans for their own countries cannot also be a goal for Latin America, with different methods for dissimilar conditions?"[1] Unfortunately for Latin Americans, yearnings for social justice became enveloped by Cold War fears. In the 1980s, during the presidency of Ronald Reagan, the United States aided and abetted the violence that García Márquez deplored. The United States signaled support for Efraín Ríos Montt, the "diabolical dictator" of Guatemala, poured a billion dollars of military aid into El Salvador, and underwrote a civil war in Nicaragua. The death and destruction that García Márquez deplored in 1982 multiplied and spread during the 1980s. Unspeakable atrocities became commonplace in Central America.

JIMMY CARTER AND HUMAN RIGHTS

The year 1979 marked a turning point in the history of Central America. The domestic political warfare that had waxed and waned in Guatemala since 1954 entered a new, extraordinarily violent phase. In tiny El Salvador, a military dictator fell, but government repression accelerated with a thousand Salvadorans being murdered each month. In Nicaragua, the last member of the Somoza dynasty, Anastasio Somoza Debayle (1967–79), fled the country after years of civil war. Somoza's flight did not, however, usher in a period of peace and prosperity for Nicaragua. Opponents of the new revolutionary regime in Nicaragua would launch a brutal counterrevolution. That Central America would become the last major battleground of the Cold War in Latin America during the presidency of Jimmy Carter seemed ironic and tragic. Carter had taken office in January 1977 pledging a new approach toward Latin America that was not based on Cold War policies.

By the mid-1970s, the consensus that had informed U.S. public opinion about the Cold War had broken down. U.S. citizens began to challenge the premises of the Truman Doctrine and NSC 68/2. The key Cold War documents of the late 1940s had posited that the Soviet Union was bent on world domination through the subversive methods of the international Communist movement. The U.S. debacle in Vietnam had posed the question of whether the United States could or should defeat every manifestation of communism. Citizens began to argue that there were limits to U.S. power. The U.S. experience in Vietnam also raised questions about the "domino theory" of Communist expansionism. The presidential lying associated with the war in Vietnam and the Watergate scandal also caused citizens to wonder whether they could trust their government. Richard Nixon's opening to the People's Republic of China and his policy of détente with the Soviet Union further suggested that the leading Communist nations were great powers, not revolutionary powers. China and the Soviet Union presumably wanted to maximize their power within the existing international system rather than overthrow the international order.

In regard to Latin America, debate about Cold War policies had been muted for three decades. Most U.S. citizens were unaware of covert interventions in countries such as Brazil, British Guiana, and Guatemala. After 1960, Fidel Castro evoked little sympathy in the United States. And the burgeoning Cuban exile community in Florida and New Jersey opposed any dialogue with Castro's Cuba. To be sure, Senator J. William Fulbright (D-AK), the chair of the Senate Foreign Relations Committee, denounced President Lyndon Johnson's decision to invade the Dominican Republic in 1965. But Fulbright's condemnation of the "arrogance of power" was perceived within the senator's critique of Johnson's military buildup in Vietnam. The overthrow of Salvador Allende and the subsequent repression in Chile evoked, however, dismay within the United States. U.S. citizens who were conversant with international affairs understood that General Augusto Pinochet had subjected a model country to "violence and pain." Emboldened by the loss of presidential credibility brought about by Vietnam and Watergate, congressional committees revealed that the United States had covertly intervened in Chile and hatched assassination plots in Latin America. Senator Edward M. Kennedy and Representative Donald M. Fraser (D-MN) led congressional efforts to restrict economic and military aid to Latin American countries that abused their citizens. In 1974, Congress abolished the Office of Public Safety (OPS), the police training program established during the John F. Kennedy presidency. In the new post-Vietnam and Watergate atmosphere, citizens learned that U.S. police trainers had advised Brazilian and Uruguayan police and security forces who had tortured and murdered.[2] Legislators also called on the State Department to appoint foreign-service officers who would focus on human rights issues.

Perhaps the key reason for the rise of critical inquiry in the mid-1970s about Cold War polices in Latin America was the growing realization that foes of the United States posed no threats to U.S. national security. The Soviet Union had never expressed much interest in the region, and, after 1962, it flatly opposed Cuban adventures. The Soviets had received recognition of their sphere of influence in Eastern Europe in the Helsinki Accords (1975) and tacitly conceded the U.S. sphere in Latin America. Fidel Castro talked about rather than fomented revolution in Latin America. Castro focused on aiding liberation movements in Africa. Che Guevara had been dead for years. Right-wing military tyrants, not political leftists, dominated the region. Within the context of international developments in the 1970s, U.S. support for blood-thirsty military regimes in South America struck many U.S. citizens as both short-sighted and immoral. Secretary of State Henry Kissinger's argument that the ruling generals in Argentina, Chile, Brazil, and Uruguay deserved U.S. sympathy and support appalled citizens.

Jimmy Carter, the former governor of Georgia, became the champion of those who called for a human rights dimension to U.S. foreign policy. Carter, who took his Christian faith seriously, understood that he could gain political advantage by lambasting U.S. support for dictators. In the second presidential debate with President Gerald R. Ford, Carter referred to Chile eight different times. Carter asserted in the presidential campaign that "our commitment to human rights must be absolute." In his inaugural address, President Carter declared, "Because we are free, we can never be indifferent to the fate of freedom elsewhere. Our moral sense dictates a clear-cut preference for those societies which share with us an abiding respect for individual human rights." Commemorating the thirtieth anniversary of the Universal Declaration of Human Rights (1948) by the United Nations, Carter asserted that "human rights is the soul of our foreign policy."[3] Carter put substance into his words by appointing Patricia Derian to head the State Department's new Bureau of Human Rights and Human Affairs. Derian, a person of conviction and courage, was a Democrat and civil rights activist from Mississippi who had successfully desegregated her party's political delegations.

The Carter administration focused on human rights abuses in the countries of the southern cone, especially Argentina. Thousands of Argentines had been executed or had disappeared becoming *los desaparecidos* (the disappeared) in the six months before Carter's inauguration. General Jorge Videla and his military colleagues seemed to have taken to heart Secretary of State Kissinger's advice that "if there are things that have to be done, you should do them quickly." The atrocities committed by Argentine security forces reached new levels of human degradation. Headless and handless torsos washed up on Argentine beaches. A mother received the body of her daughter with a rat sewn up inside her vagina. In 1976, Ambassador Robert C. Hill, a conservative career foreign-service officer, had lodged over thirty protests about human rights violations with the Argentine government. Military thugs, traveling in their ubiquitous, unmarked Ford Falcons, were even snatching U.S. citizens, including Elida Messina, a member of the Fulbright Commission in Buenos Aires. Ambassador Hill was undercut, however, by his boss, Henry Kissinger.[4]

Even before receiving her senatorial confirmation, Derian journeyed to Buenos Aires to confront Argentina's military rulers. The administration also authorized a foreign-service officer, F. Allan "Tex" Harris, to meet with relatives of *los desaparecidos* and compile files on their cases. In 1977, the Mothers of the Plaza de Mayo began to march silently in front of the presidential palace, the Casa Rosada, to bear witness to their missing children. In Montevideo, the new U.S. ambassador, Lawrence Pezzullo, evoked "enormous hostility" from the Uruguayan military for pushing a human rights and democratic agenda. Pezzullo's predecessor, Ambassador Ernest Siracusa, as described by Derian, was "great pals with leading people in the dictatorship." As a sign of disapproval, the Carter administration also cut economic and military aid to the Southern Cone countries, and, in one high-profile decision in 1978, the administration opposed a $270 million Export-Import Bank loan to Argentina to construct turbines for a hydroelectric plant.[5]

Scholars who have examined the efficacy of Carter's human rights policy believe it had a significant impact in southern South America. U.S. pressure did not topple any of the military regimes. But measured in quantitative terms, violations of human rights declined. In Uruguay, the number of political prisoners dropped from as many as 5,000 in 1977 to fewer than 2,500 in 1979. General Pinochet' regime murdered or "disappeared" fewer Chileans between 1977 and 1980 than in any other four-year period between 1973 and 1990. Both murders and disappearances declined somewhat in Argentina's *la guerra sucia*. Prominent Argentines, like newspaper publisher Jacobo Timerman, credited President Carter and Patricia Derian for saving their lives. Military regimes undoubtedly pursued their own agendas during the Carter presidency. But U.S. pressure may have strengthened the hands of officers within military circles who favored the reduction of violence and the return to civic life.[6] Latin American democrats appreciated U.S. officials who defended democracy and human rights. In 1983, Argentina restored democracy, and President Carter and Derian were guests of honor at the inauguration of President Raúl Alfonsín (1983–89). Derian would later testify in Argentina at the trial of a military officer accused of human rights abuses. In 2006, Argentina awarded Derian with its highest award for foreign personages. In 2008, Senator Kennedy would receive a similar award from President Michelle Bachelet of Chile.

Although it could point to progress, the Carter administration applied its human rights policies inconsistently in Latin America, especially after 1979. The policy met resistance from powerful institutions and people. Some career foreign-service officers questioned whether traditional friends like Argentina should be judged harshly. Allan Harris reaped criticism from his superiors and almost lost his job for his vigorous work with the relatives of the missing. (Much later, the American Foreign Service Organization, a union of foreign-service officers, named a special award after Harris for officers who engaged in creative dissent.) Patricia Derian encountered difficulties scheduling meetings to discuss human rights issues with her superiors in the State Department. Political conservatives ridiculed the policy of criticizing anti-Communist dictators. Henry Kissinger conspicuously sat with General Videla at a World Cup *fútbol* match in Argentina in 1978 and thereafter held a news conference and criticized the Carter administration for not understanding that human rights had to be sacrificed in a war against terrorism. U.S. businessmen complained that sanctions hurt trade and investment in Argentina. President Carter also found that relations with Argentina and Chile were complex. The president hosted Generals Videla and Pinochet in Washington in 1977, because he wanted united Latin American support for the Panama Canal treaties, which returned the Canal Zone to Panama. In a response to a journalist's question, Carter repudiated his own campaign charges. As president, he had discovered the lack of "any evidence that the U.S. was involved in the overthrow of the Allende government in Chile."[7]

As they had repeatedly throughout the Cold War, international developments outside of Latin America shaped U.S. policies toward the region. President Carter had significant international accomplishments—the Panama Canal Treaties (1977–78) and the Camp David Accords (1978), leading to peace between Israel and Egypt. In his post-presidential years, Carter worked tirelessly for peace and human rights and was awarded the Nobel Peace Prize in 2002. But during the last two years of his presidency, 1979–80, Carter lost control of events and his presidency. Political instability in the Persian Gulf region disrupted oil supplies, leading to an over-300-percent increase in gasoline prices in the United States. Price inflation and an economic recession followed. The long-time U.S. client in Iran, Mohammad Rezā Shāh Pahlavi (1941–79), fled the country in the face of a popular uprising led by Muslim religious fundamentalists. Angry over past U.S. support for the repressive Shāh, Iranian activists stormed the U.S. embassy in Teheran in November 1979 and made hostages of embassy personnel. A U.S. military rescue effort in 1980 failed miserably, feeding popular perceptions that the nation and President Carter were weak and impotent. A month after the Iranian hostage crisis began, the Soviet Union invaded Afghanistan. Soviet leaders had made a disastrous decision that would undermine the Soviet Union and the Communist system both at home and abroad. But in the context of other developments, the Soviet invasion of Afghanistan reverberated throughout the U.S. political system. The era of détente between the United States and the Soviet Union was over. Many U.S. citizens now believed that they had overreacted to the lessons of Vietnam and Watergate. The United States had to pursue a bold, aggressive foreign policy, because the Soviet Union was still bent on world domination. Backing anti-Communist regimes and dictators was a safer choice than promoting democracy and human rights. The world of NSC 68/2 and the Kennan Corollary would return with the defeat of Carter and the election of Ronald Reagan in November 1980.

CENTRAL AMERICAN EARTHQUAKES

Developments in Central America in the late 1970s fueled the renewed Cold War hysteria in the United States. Pre-Columbian people in Middle America called themselves "the sons of the shaking earth," referring to the natural disasters—earthquakes, volcanoes, and tropical storms—that often beset the region. Indeed, devastating earthquakes struck Managua, the capital of Nicaragua, in 1972; the outskirts of Guatemala City, Guatemala, in 1976; and San Salvador, the capital of El Salvador, in 1982 and again in 1986. But earthquakes were not merely geological phenomena for Central Americans in the 1970s and 1980s. The political and social systems of El Salvador, Guatemala, and Nicaragua erupted as revolution, civil war, and barbarity rocked the region.

Central America's Cold War upheavals grew out of poverty, social inequalities, and political repression. Meanness, injustice, and dictatorship had long characterized life in the small countries of Central America. Central Americans had periodically risen in rebellion against their lot—the nationalist movement of Augusto Sandino (1927–33), the peasant uprising in El Salvador in 1932, the Guatemalan Revolution of 1944. But life seemed to become intolerable in the 1970s for many Central Americans. Measured by growth in gross national products, Central American nations had done well in the period from 1961 to 1975. Alliance for Progress economic aid had spurred economic growth. Nicaragua, for example, had been a success story of the Alliance, with a 4 percent annual growth rate in the 1960s. Economic growth helped diversify societies, creating a small professional class of lawyers, doctors, and teachers, small business people, and urban industrial workers. As planners for the Alliance for Progress hoped, these middle-sector people, like José Napoleón Duarte, the mayor of San Salvador, would ultimately demand popular political participation. But the advancement of middle-sector groups had to be measured against the growing agony of Central America's *campesinos*, the majority of the population. The region's powerbrokers, such as the Somoza family of Nicaragua and the few hundred intermarried families that dominated El Salvador, popularly known as *Los Catorce* (the Fourteen), seized on economic opportunities to transform Central American agriculture. They challenged the land titles of *campesinos*, consolidated landholdings, and developed export products such as cotton and cattle. A few thousand Salvadorans owned 60 percent of the farmland. Landlessness increased and production of food for domestic consumption declined. In 1960, 12 percent of Salvador families were landless; by 1971, the number of landless had risen to 41 percent of families. *Los Catorce* also controlled the banking system and manufacturing in El Salvador. Fifty percent of Nicaragua's population survived on a per capita income of less than $100. On the other hand, the Somoza family amassed a wealth of over $300 million. A family member, Luis Manuel Debayle, known popularly as *Tío Luz* ("Uncle Light") directed the national power and light company that sold electricity to the burgeoning cattle ranches and cotton plantations.[8] By the early 1970s, 1.4 percent of landowners controlled 41 percent of the land in Nicaragua.

Population growth intensified the region's problems. With an annual growth rate of 3 percent, the region's population doubled every twenty to twenty-five years. The six Central American nations—Costa Rica, El Salvador, Guatemala, Honduras, Nicaragua, and Panama—had a combined population of 9.2 million people in 1950. Fifty years later, Central America's population has increased by 400 percent to 37.2 million people. Minuscule El Salvador saw its population rise from 1.9 million in 1950 to 5.2 million in 1990. This increase occurred even as seventy-five thousand Salvadorans perished during the political violence of the 1980s, and another five hundred thousand fled the country. In the midst of earthquakes, revolution, and civil war, Nicaragua's population increased from 3 million in 1975 to 5.1 million in 1990. Increases in life expectancy accounted for most population growth, as international bodies, like the World Health Organization, conquered diseases that had historically ravaged humankind. The triumph of science and medicine compounded the problems of Central America's poor who lived in unfair and unjust societies like El Salvador, Guatemala, and Nicaragua. These nations were filled with young people who found neither work nor hope.

External actors and influences exacerbated tensions within Central America. The communications revolution—film, transistor radios, television—helped create among Central Americans a desire for a better life. President John F. Kennedy and the Alliance for Progress had fed those aspirations by encouraging Central Americans to believe that poverty and despair were not their preordained lot in life. But, because the Kennedy and Johnson administrations worked with Central America's elites, the Alliance ended up frustrating Central Americans who yearned for social justice. The president's counterinsurgency programs further strengthened the region's repressive forces. President Somoza was a graduate of the U.S. Military Academy at West Point. Somoza, whose base of power was control over the National Guard, sent over one hundred of his high-ranking officers to take counterinsurgency courses, like "Counter-Resistance" and "Irregular Warfare," at the School of the Americas in the Canal Zone between 1961 and 1978. Somoza also ordered cadets enrolled in Nicaragua's military academy to spend their final year of officer training at the School of Americas.⁹ Nicaraguan and other Central American officers trained against the threat of Cuban-inspired communism. The Cuban Revolution continued to be a potent symbol to Central America's poor, because it had measurably improved the health, education, and welfare of the Cuban population. By the 1970s, Cuba could boast of life expectancy, infant mortality, and literacy rates that approached those of wealthy nations. Fidel Castro provided advice and guidance to Central Americans who wanted to emulate Cuba's successes.

The Roman Catholic Church played a unique role in Central America and throughout Latin America during its time of upheaval. The clergy embraced the ideas and reforms inherent in the ideas of Pope John XXIII, Vatican II, and the 1968 conference of Latin American bishops in Medellín. The Medellín conference had denounced both capitalism and communism as equal affronts to human dignity and placed blame for hunger and misery on the rich and powerful. Cardinal Paulo Evarista Arns, the archbishop of São Paulo, for example, resisted military tyranny in Brazil and upheld the philosophy of a "preferential option for the poor." Not all Latin American clergy had transformed themselves, however, into the servants of the poor and oppressed. In Argentina, priests ministered to and consoled military authorities who tortured and murdered during *la guerra sucia*. Cardinal Juan Carlos Aramburu, the archbishop of Buenos Aires, publicly denied that there were disappeared people in Argentina.¹⁰ In Central America, however, priests actively organized the rural poor to demand social justice. The archbishop of San Salvador, Oscar Arnulfo Romero, was largely apolitical, but he became outspoken in condemning government violence and vigilantism. Rightwing extremists assassinated the saintly Archbishop Romero in his cathedral in 1980. In the sermon he delivered moments before his death, the archbishop called for the end of official oppression, noting that "no soldier is obliged to obey an order contrary to the law of God." Other priests identified with revolution. The renowned poet and Jesuit priest, Ernesto Cardenal, served as minister of culture in Nicaragua from 1979 to 1988. Miguel d'Escoto Brockmann served as foreign affairs minister in Nicaragua's revolutionary government. Father d'Escoto had been ordained in the Maryknoll missionary congregation in the United States. Foreign missionaries, including U.S. clergy, encouraged the poor to be politically active in Central America. In one notorious incident, in December 1980, a Salvadoran death squad tortured, raped, and murdered four female missionaries from the United States. U.S. missionaries received active support from Catholics back home who organized in the 1980s in opposition to U.S. support for rightist groups in Central America.¹¹

REVOLUTION IN NICARAGUA

Nicaragua's revolution preoccupied the United States during the last decade of the Cold War. Anastasio "Tachito" Somoza Debayle proved the greediest and most brutal of the Somoza clan who had controlled Nicaraguan life since the 1930s. Somoza assumed power on 1 May 1967, shortly before the death of his elder brother Luis. During their four-decade-long domination of the country, the Somoza family occasionally paid lip service to constitutional procedures, permitting puppets to occupy the presidential office. But they secured their power by commanding the National Guard. The Somozas also kept their nation bound to the United States by trumpeting their anticommunism. They permitted the CIA to use the country as a staging ground for attacks on Guatemala and Cuba and dutifully supported U.S. positions at international fora like the United Nations. Tachito Somoza's reign of tyranny left domestic and international observers gasping. The family controlled a plasma bank that exported the blood of poor Nicaraguans who gave their blood in return for money. The Somozas literally sold the blood of their own people! Pedro Joaquín Chamorro, the publisher of the Nicaraguan newspaper, *La Prensa*, the only significant opposition paper in Nicaragua, exposed this appalling state of affairs. In January 1978, Somoza's henchmen assassinated Chamorro, riddling his body with shotgun blasts.

It took Nicaraguans almost seven years to overthrow Somoza. The beginning of the end started with an earthquake that destroyed the capital city Managua on 23 December 1972, leaving perhaps ten thousand dead. The international community and private groups rushed aid to Nicaragua. Schoolchildren in the United States donated their money. The great Latino baseball player, Roberto Clemente of the Pittsburgh Pirates, died helping Nicaraguans. Clemente's overloaded plane, carrying emergency relief supplies, crashed off the coast of Puerto Rico. Clemente had boarded the flight because he had learned that the supplies he had sent on three previous flights had not reached the earthquake survivors. Somoza and his sycophants had stolen the supplies. Nicaragua received $32 million in emergency aid; the Somoza clan stole half of the aid. Instead of providing public safety to the devastated Managua, National Guard soldiers looted the city.

Public disgust with Somoza's response to the natural disaster accrued among groups working to overthrow him. Since the early 1960s, insurgents had fought, with little success, against the Somozas. The National Guard, equipped and trained by the United States, had easily routed them. The principal insurgent organization was the *Frente Sandinista de Liberación Nacional* or Sandinista National Liberation Front. The Sandinistas admired the Cuban Revolution and took advice and arms from Cuba. In the 1970s, other insurgent groups consolidated with the Sandinistas. Civilian opponents of Somoza, including Violeta Barrios de Chamorro, the widow of the slain newspaper publisher, joined the Sandinista movement. The Sandinistas gained international fame by conducting a series of kidnappings of government officials and then releasing them. But the key to their growing strength was the utter depravity of the Somoza regime. International audiences witnessed in living color the execution of a newsman from the U.S. television network, ABC. A Nicaraguan soldier forced the correspondent to the ground and put an M-16 rifle to his head and shot him. Somoza and his National Guard waged war against Nicaragua, destroying villages and bombarding cities. Between 1977 and 1979, forty thousand to fifty thousand Nicaraguans, out of a population of 2.9 million, had died, virtually all at the hands of the National Guard. Somoza left his impoverished country in total ruins. Managua was still rubble. Somoza fled the country in July 1979, heading to Paraguay, which was ruled by fellow dictator Alfredo Stroessner. The next year Somoza was assassinated in Asunción by a commando team of political leftists. They shot a rocket-propelled grenade into Somoza's unarmored Mercedes, killing him instantly.

After fleeing the country, Somoza blamed the international Communist movement for his downfall. In truth, it was a mass, indigenous movement that toppled Somoza. The Sandinista leadership had ties to Cuba. But neither the Soviet Union nor the Nicaraguan Communist party played any role in Somoza's overthrow. As Salvadoran Communist leader Shafik Jorge Handal observed, "Latin America has had two great revolutions, those of Cuba and Nicaragua, in neither of which did Communists take the lead."[12] What outside assistance the Sandinistas received came from Latin American neighbors, like Costa Rica, Mexico, Panama, and Venezuela, who deplored Somoza's ruthlessness. In 1979, the Andean Pact nations—Bolivia, Colombia, Ecuador, Peru, and Venezuela—recognized the

A Sandinista soldier, carrying a U.S.-made M-16 rifle, stands by a toppled statue of Anastasio Somoza Debayle a few days after the Nicaraguan dictator fled the country on 17 July 1979. The Somoza family dominated Nicaragua for more than four decades, operating the country like a private hacienda. The Somozas closely cooperated with the United States during the Cold War, often permitting the CIA to use Nicaragua as training and staging ground for covert operations. The civil war that raged in the 1970s devastated the country and cost more than forty thousand Nicaraguans their lives, most at the hands of Somoza's National Guard. (Corbis Images)

Sandinistas as "legitimate combatants," granting the Sandinistas equivalent legal status to the Somoza regime.

Somoza also blamed President Jimmy Carter, who he smeared as a "Communist," for his downfall.[13] Unlike presidents going back to Franklin Roosevelt, Carter had not fawned over the Somoza clan. But Carter was neither a Communist nor was he naïve about international communism. Totalitarians of the left were as prone to violate human rights as were Latin American military dictators of South America. In a 1980 letter to Pope John Paul II (1978–2005), Carter noted that Central America's extreme left wanted to destroy the existing order and "replace it with a Marxist one which promises to be equally repressive and totalitarian."[14] The Carter administration hoped for a moderate solution to Nicaragua's civil war, not wanting its choices to be limited to either Somoza or the Sandinistas. The administration suspected the political leanings of key Sandinista leaders like Daniel Ortega Saavedra and Tomás Borge. As an NSC member noted in August 1978, "the United States needed to get in front of events and assemble a coalition government" to replace Somoza; otherwise, "the situation would polarize even further, increasing the probability of a Marxist victory."[15] The Carter administration found, however, that it could not direct the course of events in Nicaragua. Somoza fought to keep power, and Nicaraguans and the international community rejected a solution that would leave a reconstructed and reformed National Guard in charge of the country.

In accepting the Sandinista victory, the Carter administration chose not to resort to the interventionist policies pursued by previous Cold War administrations. The administration's actions could be readily compared, for example, to U.S. policies toward another small nation ruled by a long-time dictator. The Eisenhower and Kennedy administrations had aided and abetted assassins when Rafael Trujillo refused to leave the Dominican Republic. President Kennedy thereafter deployed U.S. air and sea power to bring about the coalitional government that the United States wanted. President Johnson dispatched U.S. marines into the Dominican Republic to forestall what he perceived as a Communist takeover of the government. President Carter kept, however, his commitment to human rights and the non-intervention principles of the OAS charter. He denied that international communism fomented revolution in Nicaragua, noting at a news conference that it was "a mistake for Americans to assume or to claim that every time an evolutionary change takes place, or even an abrupt change takes place in this hemisphere, that somehow it's the result of secret, massive Cuban intervention."[16] The administration reported to Congress that the Sandinistas were "an authentic Nicaraguan phenomenon" and that "the Sandinista movement represents a societal consensus that radical change was needed in Nicaragua." Shortly after Somoza fled, the new U.S. ambassador, Lawrence Pezzullo, arrived in Managua with a planeload of food and medical supplies and President Carter's personal expression of goodwill. Carter also secured a $75 million package of economic aid for Nicaragua from Congress. The administration professed that the United States had erred in 1959–1960 in not developing a cooperative relationship with Cuba. To be sure, Carter hedged his bets on the Sandinistas. He authorized covert spending, perhaps $1 million, to aid anti-Sandinista labor, press, and political organizations.[17]

THE SANDINISTAS

The Carter administration's judgment that the Sandinista movement was "an authentic Nicaraguan phenomenon" proved largely accurate both in its origins and subsequent evolution. The Sandinistas held power between 1979 and 1990, winning a big electoral victory in 1984 and suffering an election loss in 1990. Politically moderate members of the ruling coalition, like Violeta Chamorro and Edén Pastora, a courageous guerrilla fighter popularly known as *Commandante Cero* (Commander Zero), left the coalition, protesting the direction of the revolution. The ruling Sandinistas, headed by Daniel Ortega, consisted of a motley collection of political leftists—progressives, socialists, intellectual Marxists, and doctrinaire Communists. Ortega, who officially became president in 1984, and his supporters did not, however, attempt to transform Nicaragua into a Marxist-Leninist state or a facsimile of Castro's Cuba. Thomas C. Wright, a distinguished scholar of Latin American political history, has characterized the Nicaraguan Revolution has having an identity of its own. As Wright summarized, "led by Marxists, it was an anti-imperialist but capitalist revolution anchored in support of the lower and middle classes."[18] Nicaragua seemed to be evolving the way Mexico did after its revolution in 1910.

The Sandinistas substantially enlarged the role of the state in the economy, nationalizing the banks and confiscating the extensive holdings of the Somoza clan, which included land, factories, the national airline, construction firms, and real estate. The state sector rose from 15 percent of the economy under Anastasio Somoza to 45 percent by the mid-1980s. For the state to play a large role in the economy was normal throughout Latin America. In agriculture, the Sandinistas, responding to pressure from *campesinos* who wanted to farm individual plots, altered their plans to foster state agricultural cooperatives. The Sandinistas permitted both domestic and international investors to operate in Nicaragua. The Sandinistas ruled during a time when Communists around the world, like Deng Xiaoping (1978–87) in China and Mikhail Gorbachev (1985–91) in the Soviet Union, recognized the shortcomings of Communist economic theories. Even Fidel Castro advised the Sandinistas not to emulate the Cuban Revolution and allow a role for private entrepreneurs.[19]

The Sandinistas compiled a mixed record on issues of civil liberties and human rights. Immediately after taking power, they carried out five hundred to a thousand summary executions but thereafter abolished capital punishment. They dismantled the National Guard and built an enlarged military loyal to the Sandinista movement. The armed forces' new title was the "Sandinista People's Army." In creating a new military organization tied to revolution, the Sandinistas emulated what Castro and his followers had done after coming to power in 1959. Like the Cubans, the Sandinistas also established neighborhood "defense committees" to exercise "revolutionary vigilance," which was a euphemism for spying on neighbors. The Sandinistas borrowed a progressive human rights policy from the Cubans, launching health and literacy campaigns in the countryside. The Sandinistas claimed that they reduced illiteracy from 40 percent of the population to 13 percent in a decade. While improving the health and education of the poor, the Sandinistas needlessly harassed English-speaking blacks and indigenous people, especially the Moskito Indians, who resided along Nicaragua's Atlantic coastline. They also foolishly quarreled with and insulted Pope John Paul II, who visited Nicaragua. The pontiff preached that clergy should not engage in politics, although he reaffirmed his church's "preferential option for the poor." Despite the bombast and harassment of opponents by the Sandinistas, Nicaragua exhibited a pluralistic political system during the 1980s. Twenty-one political parties registered in the country, and numerous newspapers, magazines, and radio stations criticized the Sandinistas. International observers pronounced the 1984 national elections, in which 75 percent of registered voters participated, to be fair. Nicaragua under the Sandinistas resembled Mexico at mid-twentieth century—a country with a mixed economy, individual freedoms, and one political party (in Mexico's case, the Party of Revolutionary Institutions or PRI) that dominated the country. The allegation by U.S. officials that Sandinista Nicaragua was a "totalitarian" country like Communist East Germany was fatuous.[20]

The Sandinistas pledged to pursue a non-aligned foreign policy that respected the sovereignty of other nations. In fact, between 1979 and 1981, they meddled in El Salvador, aiding Salvadoran leftists. Nicaragua was also one of the few countries in the world that did not annually denounce the Soviet Union at the United Nations for its invasion of Afghanistan. The Sandinistas consulted closely with Fidel Castro. Cuban doctors and teachers came to Nicaragua to help with the health and literacy campaigns. Nicaragua also received significant economic and technical help from Western European countries. The Sandinistas opened commercial contacts with the Soviet bloc. Economic and military ties with Communist countries deepened, once the United States decided to attack Nicaragua. Nicaragua's historic economic dependence on the United States ended in the 1980s. But the relationship was severed by the U.S. decision to destroy the Nicaraguan economy.[21]

RONALD REAGAN AND CENTRAL AMERICA

President Ronald Reagan waged violent Cold War in Central America. Reagan and his foreign-policy team saw the world in apocalyptic terms. The Soviet Union was the "evil empire," fomenting turmoil and conflict throughout the world. As Reagan once famously asserted, "the Soviet Union underlies all the unrest that is going on. If they weren't engaged in this game of dominoes, there wouldn't be any hot spots in the world." Still following its blueprint for world domination, the Soviets had taken advantage of the post-Vietnam malaise of the United States to extend its reach to Vietnam, Cambodia, Laos, Afghanistan, Ethiopia, Zimbabwe, Angola, Mozambique, Grenada, Suriname, and Nicaragua. The Soviets backed their new influence with awesome military power, building a modern navy and rapidly expanding their nuclear forces. Reagan and his advisors warned that the Soviets had attained a "first-strike" capability. The Soviets allegedly could launch a nuclear strike against the United States, destroy U.S. nuclear forces in place, and "win" a nuclear war. To save itself and Western civilization, the United States needed to return to the prescriptions of NSC 68/2. The Reagan administration developed a five-year, $1.6 trillion spending plan to expand the U.S. naval forces and develop new intercontinental ballistic missiles. The president also pronounced his "Reagan Doctrine," promising to aid "freedom-fighters" around the world who resisted Communist subversion. The administration expanded the program developed by the Carter administration to assist Afghans who fought against the Soviet invaders.

The Reagan administration gave notice that the Soviet Union's grand design included subverting Latin America, the traditional alliance partner of the United States. "The Americas are under attack," bellowed the Committee of Santa Fe, five men who belonged to a conservative think tank, the Council for Inter-American Security. The committee's 1980 report claimed that Latin America was being penetrated by Soviet power, with the Caribbean rim and basin "spotted with Soviet surrogates and ringed with socialist states." The United States needed to dominate the region so it would be free to contest Soviet adventurism in Europe, Asia, and Africa. The committee further advised that the United States needed to show restraint in promoting internal reforms in Latin America.[22] President Carter had endangered U.S. national security by pushing human rights issues on the military dictators of South America. Members of the Committee of Santa Fe would join the Reagan foreign-policy team.

The paramount intellectual proponent of an aggressive policy in Latin America was Jeane J. Kirkpatrick, Reagan's ambassador to the United Nations. Kirkpatrick had caught Reagan's attention with her 1979 essay, "Dictatorships and Double Standards." She had denounced the Carter administration's abandonment of traditional U.S. allies like the Shāh of Iran and Anastasio Somoza. U.S. opposition to authoritarian rulers had inevitably led to totalitarian regimes like Islamic fundamentalists in Iran and the Sandinistas in Nicaragua. Kirkpatrick theorized that traditional, right-wing authoritarian regimes presented the possibility of evolving into open, democratic societies but that leftist totalitarian governments like the Communists would always be closed, repressive, and a threat to the United States. Kirkpatrick's theories were not grounded on an analysis of modern history. Even as she penned her essay, the People's Republic of China was transforming its socioeconomic system and drawing closer to the United States. Kirkpatrick also echoed the views of George Kennan, Edward Miller, Thomas Mann, and the Committee of Santa Fe in questioning whether Latin Americans could create humane societies. In a 1980 essay, she suggested that "traditionalist death squads" were rooted in El Salvador's political culture and could help transform brute violence into legitimate authority. Kirkpatrick was especially fond of Argentina's military rulers and *la guerra sucia*. She advised that Central Americans could learn valuable lessons on internal security from military regimes in the southern cone.[23] Her boss agreed with that assessment. In 1979, Reagan had glossed over the wholesale slaughter of Argentines, asserting: "Today, Argentina is at peace, the terrorist threat nearly eliminated. In the process of bringing stability to a terrorized nation of twenty-five million, a small number were caught in the crossfire, among them a few innocents." The first Latin American head of state that Reagan hosted in Washington was General Roberto Viola, the "president-designate" of Argentina's military regime. An Argentine court would subsequently sentence General Viola to seventeen years in prison for human rights violations during his presidency. Even after he left the presidency, Ronald Reagan continued to refer to human rights violations during the dirty war as "rumors."[24]

Analysts of Reagan's presidency argue that the overblown rhetoric should not be taken seriously, for Reagan pursued a prudent, cautious foreign policy when it came to contesting the Soviet Union and communism. When, for example, the Soviets demanded that Polish Communist authorities crush the trade union movement, Solidarnośc (Solidarity), led by Lech Walesa, Reagan advised citizens to light candles to show support for Walesa and his comrades. Like President Dwight Eisenhower during the Hungarian uprising of 1956, Reagan and his advisors understood that a military confrontation with the Soviet Union over its empire in Eastern Europe would have catastrophic consequences. Reagan's first secretary of state, Alexander M. Haig, Jr., a former close advisor to Richard Nixon, ordered the U.S. military to develop plans for an invasion of Cuba. Haig told Reagan at a NSC meeting that "you just give me the word and I'll turn that island into a fucking parking lot."[25] President Reagan demurred, however, for an invasion of Cuba would violate the 1962 accord that President John Kennedy struck with Nikita Khrushchev. The United States promised not to invade the island, if the Soviet removed their ballistic missiles from Cuba.

Restraint did not, however, characterize the Reagan administration's policy toward Central America. The administration was eager for domestic and international reasons for a victory over what it perceived as the international Communist movement. President Reagan "wanted to send a message to others in the world that there was a new management in the White House." The president told a U.S. audience that U.S. strength and integrity had to "be taken seriously—by friends and potential foes alike."[26] Reagan's director of the CIA, William J. Casey, offered that "I'm looking for a place to start rolling back the Communist empire." Central America presented the perfect opportunity. Given the global balance of power and the historic domination of Central America, the United States could act with impunity in the area. The region was also small and close. Secretary Haig advised: "Mr. President, this is one you can win." Defeating leftist guerrilla movements in El Salvador and Guatemala and overthrowing the Sandinistas in Nicaragua would wash away the bitter memories of failure in Vietnam. It would restore U.S. self-confidence, kicking away the so-called "Vietnam Syndrome." Reasserting U.S. hegemony in the traditional sphere of influence would also redeem U.S. global credibility. Elliot Abrams, who served as Assistant Secretary of State for Inter-American Affairs from 1985 to 1989, admitted that the United States had no significant tangible interests in Central America. It was a matter of international perception. Abrams asked, "If people see that the Americans are not going to move against the Sandinistas in their own backyard, what will they do ten thousand miles away?"[27]

In persuading the U.S. public to tend to its "backyard," the Reagan administration resorted to rhetoric not heard since the heyday of the Red Scare in the late 1940s and early 1950s. President Reagan resorted to the shop-worn "domino theory," predicting that Marxist victories in Nicaragua and El Salvador would lead to the dominos toppling both south and north—to South America and to Mexico. Secretary Haig testified to Congress that he would not label Soviet perfidy with the domino theory. The Soviets had "a priority target list, a hit list if you will, for the ultimate takeover of Central America." In a speech in 1983 to a joint session of Congress reminiscent of President Harry Truman's dramatic address in 1947 asking for emergency assistance for Greece and Turkey (Truman Doctrine), President Reagan proclaimed that "the national security of all the Americas is at stake in Central America," for "if we cannot defend ourselves there, we cannot expect to prevail elsewhere."[28]

A willful ignorance about Latin America informed the Reagan administration's decision to shed the blood of Central Americans. On 1 December 1982, President Reagan memorably toasted "the people of Bolivia" at a state dinner. The problem was that Reagan was in Brasília, not La Paz. It took a rare talent to confuse the futuristic capital of Brazil, set on a plateau in the interior of the country, with the ancient Bolivian capital situated at eleven thousand feet in the Andes Mountains. Reagan's gaffe was symptomatic of the administration's approach to the region. Ideological correctness meant more than professional competence. Elliot Abrams wanted "to be the first guy to reverse a Communist revolution."[29] Reagan's assistant secretaries for inter-American affairs, like Abrams and Thomas O. Enders, had no professional experience in Latin America, and Enders did not speak Spanish. Unfamiliarity with Latin America also characterized the people that Reagan appointed to be his ambassadors to Central America. Secretary Haig purged veteran foreign-service officers like Robert E. White (El Salvador) and Lawrence Pezzullo (Nicaragua), who argued for policies based on negotiations. President Reagan appointed Anthony C. E. Quainton to be his ambassador to Nicaragua. Quainton had never served in Latin America and spoke no Spanish. As one State Department officer noted, "It isn't embarrassing that the Secretary of State doesn't know anything about Central America. And it is only moderately embarrassing that the assistant secretary doesn't know very much. But it is very bad when the deputy assistant secretaries and even the office directors know so little."[30] Central Americans would pay a bloody price for this lack of knowledge.

WAR AGAINST THE SANDINISTAS

President Reagan attacked Nicaragua during his eight-year presidency. The standard administration line about the Sandinistas was that they were Marxist-Leninists who were dedicated to creating a totalitarian society at home and serving as surrogates for the Soviets and the Cubans abroad. Negotiations would be point-less, for the Sandinistas had enlisted in the campaign to subvert the United States and its allies. The Reagan administration made it clear from the outset that it would never release the $75 million in economic aid. Initially, the administration charged that they were withholding the aid because the Sandinistas funneled arms to leftists in El Salvador. In February 1981, the administration released a "White Paper," *Communist Interference in El Salvador*, which purportedly provided proof of a Sandinista conspiracy. Journalists demonstrated, however, that the documen-tary evidence offered was dubious and that Salvadoran leftists seemed to be armed with weapons manufactured in the United States. In any case, by mid-1981, State Department officials conceded that the arms flow to El Salvador had stopped.[31] President Reagan and his closest advisors gradually dropped that issue and began to insist that the United States would negotiate with the Sandinistas only after they "restored" democracy. Many failed to see the logic in that argument, for in the previous decades Nicaragua had experienced not democracy but tyranny under the Somoza family. The administration usually denied that it was trying to over-throw the Nicaraguan government. But in 1985 the blunt, relentless reporter Sam Donaldson of ABC News asked Reagan whether it was U.S. policy "to remove" the Sandinistas at a presidential news conference. Reagan answered, "Well, remove in the sense of its present structure, in which it is a Communist totalitarian state, and it is not a government chosen by the people." Pressed further to refine his circumlocutious answer, Reagan admitted that he wanted the Sandinistas to cry "Uncle" and that "you can say that we're trying to oust the Sandinistas by what we're saying."[32]

At his 21 February 1985 news conference, President Reagan confirmed what he had previously endorsed. In November 1981, Reagan approved National Security Decision Document (NSDD) No. 17, which authorized the CIA to orga-nize a military force of Nicaraguans to overthrow the Sandinistas. The Nicaraguan exiles came to be known as the "contras" (for *contra revolucionario*, the Spanish for "counterrevolutionary"). The contras assembled and trained in Honduras under the direction of Colonel Gustavo Alvarez Martínez, the commander of the National Police Academy and a virulent anti-Communist. Argentine military offi-cers trained the contras, until the collapse of the military dictatorship in Argentina in 1982–1983. The ubiquitous General Vernon Walters, who enjoyed the company of Latin America's military tyrants, had journeyed to Buenos Aires on behalf of the Reagan administration to facilitate Argentina's cooperation. Colonel Alvarez had also attended the military academy in Argentina. The initial contra force of five hundred would grow to over ten thousand through the 1980s. The senior military command of the contras was composed of former officers of the Somoza National Guard and was led by Colonel Enrique Bermúdez.[33] The Reagan administration's contra scheme resembled the PBSUCCESS operation against Guatemala in 1954. This was not, however, a covert operation. The content of NSDD 17 was disclosed to journalists in 1982. Throughout the 1980s, officers in the national security bureaucracy—the State and Defense Departments and the CIA—leaked Reagan administration decisions about Nicaragua to the press, because they judged the decisions to be both unwise and violations of both U.S. and international law.

The contras waged their form of "dirty war" against the Sandinistas and Nicaraguan citizens. The Reagan administration initially justified NSDD 17 by claiming that the mission of the contras was to interdict the arms flow to El Salvador. But the contras did not capture arms bound for El Salvador and did not coordinate operations with Salvadoran security forces. The Reagan administration later dubbed the contras as "freedom fighters," which was an ironic sobriquet for a military command that had a history of brutalizing Nicaraguans during the Somoza years. Indeed, murder, torture, rape, pillage, and burning became the *modus operandi* of the contras. Throughout the 1980s, the contras invaded Nicaragua. The contras were unsuccessful in holding territory or towns and suffered severe defeats when they engaged Sandinista regular forces. Whatever Nicaraguans thought of the Sandinistas, they opposed restoration of the savage rule they associated with the National Guard. The contras focused on attacking farms and villages and executing civilian public officials—mayors, justices of the peace, literacy volunteers, and nurses and doctors. The contra soldiers became infamous for kidnapping teenagers, dragooning the boys into the military and abusing the girls for their sexual pleasure. In 1985, *Newsweek* magazine published gruesome photos that depicted a man accused of being an informer forced by a contra patrol to dig his own grave with bare hands and lie down in it. The contras then slit his throat. When President Reagan was asked about the photo by Speaker of the House Thomas "Tip" O'Neill, he responded that the incident had been faked. Reagan consistently excoriated reports by international agencies of horrors in Nicaragua by labeling them "so-called atrocities."[34]

The United States aided and abetted the contras. Replaying the "make the Chilean economy scream" gambit, the Reagan administration successfully pressured commercial banks and international banks, like the World Bank and the Inter-American Development Bank, to deny Nicaragua credit. In 1985, the administration imposed a trade embargo on Nicaragua, much as the Eisenhower and Kennedy administrations had done to Cuba. The Nicaraguan economy went into depression and inflation soared out of control, hitting 33,000 percent in 1988. U.S. officials predictably blamed Sandinista mismanagement of the economy for the economic chaos. The administration also pressured non-militant, anti-Sandinista politicians not to participate in the 1984 elections. The administration wanted to defend its propaganda that Nicaragua was a totalitarian society.[35]

The Reagan administration also broke domestic and international laws in its campaign to destroy Nicaragua. In 1983–1984, U.S. commandos and contract agents of the CIA of Latin American heritage, known as "Unilaterally Controlled Latino Assets," or UCLAS, blew up oil storage tanks. The attack at a storage facility at the port of Corinto caused the loss of over three million gallons of fuel. More than one hundred people were injured, and twenty thousand had to be evacuated from Corinto. The UCLAS also participated in the mining of Nicaragua's harbors. In early 1984, ships from Japan, Panama, Liberia, the Netherlands, and the Soviet Union were damaged by mines.[36] Nicaragua filed a complaint about U.S. aggression with the International Court of Justice commonly known as the "World Court," the judicial organ of the United Nations. The Reagan administration chose to walk out of the court, denying its jurisdiction. As exemplified by the ideas of President Woodrow Wilson, the United States had historically been a strong proponent of international law and justice. In 1986, the World Court found the United States guilty on fifteen counts of illegally using force against Nicaragua and ordered Washington to pay $370 million in damages to Nicaragua. Other violations of international law by the United States and its contra allies included distributing a *Freedom Fighter's Manual*, a cartoon-format handbook for carrying out small acts of sabotage against the Nicaraguan government. Useful sabotage tactics included stuffing up toilet bowls, leaving the lights on to waste electricity, and building small incendiary bombs. The World Court also took note of a CIA manual for the contras, *Psychological Operations in Guerrilla Warfare*. Dubbed the "murder manual" after it was leaked to the press, it advised the contras to assassinate, or "neutralize" in CIA lingo, judges, police officers, and security officials after the local populations had been gathered in order "to take part in the act and formulate accusations against the oppressor."[37]

In addition to flaunting international law, the Reagan administration ignored public sentiments and violated the U.S. constitution. As measured in public opinion polls, U.S. citizens opposed President Reagan's wars in Central America. Citizens worried about sinking into another Vietnam-like quagmire. The mining of Nicaragua's waters and the shunting of the World Court embarrassed those who believed that the United States, as a world leader, had a responsibility to defend international law. U.S. citizens further thought it laughable the implication that impoverished, often barefoot Central Americans would invade the United States and spread communism throughout the homeland. Instead, citizens worried that warfare would lead the dispossessed of Central America to leave their countries and try to immigrate to the United States. An award-winning film, *El Norte* (1983), portrayed the horrific journey of two indigenous Guatemalans, a brother and sister, who flee violence in Guatemala and make their way to Los Angeles. By the mid-1980s, thirty thousand Central Americans were entering the United States each year. In the latter part of the twentieth century, 1.1 million Central Americans came to the United States.[38]

Reflecting popular anxieties about President Reagan's policies, Congress passed a series of laws in the 1980s that prohibited the administration from using public funds to finance an overthrow of the Sandinista government. Known as the "Boland amendments," the laws were sponsored by Representative Edward P. Boland (D-MA), the chair of the House Select Committee on Intelligence. At times, the Reagan administration beat back restrictions, securing, for example, $100 million from Congress in 1986 for the contras. Faced with public and congressional opposition to its policies, the administration sought money for the contras in devious and illegal ways. The administration transformed Honduras into a U.S. military base and transferred military aid for that country to the contras.

Honduras received an astounding $450 million in U.S. military aid in the 1980s. Administration officials asked wealthy, right-wing U.S. citizens to contribute to the contra cause. They also raised $45 million in cash in 1984–1985 from conservative allies—Israel, Saudi Arabia, and Taiwan. CIA Director William Casey proposed asking racist South Africa for financial help. The CIA worked with General Manuel Antonio Noriega (1983–89), the strongman of Panama and a narco-trafficker. Noriega, who had been on the CIA payroll for two decades, provided planes and pilots from his drug smuggling operations to move contra arms.[39] The Reagan administration also funded the contras by surreptitiously selling arms to Iran and using the proceeds of the sales for the contras. This scheme, which violated the Boland amendment, erupted into the "Iran-contra scandal." A special U.S. prosecutor subsequently indicted fourteen administration officials, including Secretary of Defense Caspar Weinberger, for violating U.S. statutes. Assistant Secretary of State for Inter-American Affairs Abrams pleaded guilty to two counts of misleading Congress. In 1986, Abrams had testified that he was unaware of secret U.S. efforts to aid the contras.

The most compelling argument that the Reagan administration had to offer in defending its claim that the Sandinista government threatened the national security of the United States was that the Soviet Union became a major arms supplier to Nicaragua. The Soviet Union's relationship with Nicaragua was initially tentative. It provided Nicaragua with World War II-era tanks and East German trucks that frequently broke down. As the contra war intensified, the military relationship between the Sandinistas and the Soviet Union deepened, with the Soviets providing up to $300 million a year in military aid, which included armed helicopters, in the mid-1980s. The Sandinistas built a forty-thousand-strong army that usually defeated the contras in pitched battles. The Soviet's support of Nicaragua, which also included substantial economic aid and shipments of oil, represented the only case, other than Cuba, in which the Soviet Union played a prominent role in Latin America during the Cold War. The Soviets, did not, for example, supply leftist guerrillas in either El Salvador or Guatemala.[40] Nonetheless, the Reagan administration screamed that military alliance proved that the Soviets intended to use Nicaragua as a base for Communist expansion and that they might replay the Cuban missile crisis, deploying offensive weapons systems in Nicaragua that would imperil the United States.

Analysts of Soviet foreign policy in Latin America have dismissed the idea that the Soviets had a "blueprint" in the 1980s for the domination of Latin America. Soviet leaders perceived aid to Nicaragua as a way of countering U.S. aid to the Afghan resistance movement. The United States violated the Soviet's sphere of influence, and the Soviets responded in kind. The Soviets refused to give President Daniel Ortega, who frequently traveled to Moscow, a security guarantee. A Soviet official privately admitted: "If the Americans invaded Nicaragua, what would we do? What could we do? Nothing." The Soviets pointed out that they were providing weapons to help Nicaragua defend itself from invasion. They permitted the Reagan administration to define what "offensive" weapons were, declining to supply Nicaragua with Soviet MIG fighters. The Soviets never contemplated placing nuclear-tipped missiles on Nicaraguan soil. The Soviets kept to the spirit of the Kennedy–Khrushchev agreement that ended the Cuban missile crisis.[41]

Nicaragua remained under attack through the 1980s. During the decade, Latin American nations both condemned the U.S. intervention and tried to find a solution to the violence. Whereas the Reagan administration publicly supported peace efforts by nations such as Colombia, Mexico, and Venezuela, it privately opposed and ridiculed the Latin Americans. Central Americans, led by President Oscar Arias Sánchez (1986–90, 2006–10) of Costa Rica, gradually convinced Nicaraguans to accept a negotiated settlement confirmed by a new election. President Arias, who was awarded the Nobel Prize for Peace, was aided by international developments. The Cold War ended, Soviet leader Mikhail Gorbachev curtailed Soviet international commitments, and the pragmatic George H. W. Bush replaced Ronald Reagan as president in 1989. Belying Jeane Kirkpatrick's depiction of them as totalitarians, the Sandinistas agreed to an election in 1990. The Bush administration covertly and openly funded an opposition coalition led by Violeta Barrios de Chamorro. In 1989–90, the CIA spent $11 million on Nicaraguan political groups. The National Endowment for Democracy, an agency funded by the U.S. Congress, provided an additional $11 million for opposition groups. The combined U.S. spending in Nicaragua was the equivalent of spending $1.6 billion on a U.S. election. Unsurprisingly, war-weary, exhausted Nicaraguans voted for Chamorro and the end to U.S. military intervention in their country. The Sandinista leadership accepted the results of the election. At the urging of former President Carter, who served as an international observer to the election, President Ortega made a gracious concession speech.[42]

The actions that flowed from NSDD 17 of 1981 destroyed Nicaragua. Forty-three thousand Nicaraguans perished during the contra war, and the economy declined by 50 percent. On a per capita basis, the death toll in Nicaragua was higher than in all U.S wars, including the Civil War, combined.[43] This death and destruction followed the appalling suffering that had taken place during the 1970s' uprising to overthrow Somoza and the Managua earthquake of 1972. Ronald Reagan had not succeeded in overthrowing the Sandinistas, forcing them to cry "Uncle." President Reagan had managed, however, to demolish Nicaragua.

DEATH IN EL SALVADOR

The Reagan administration, with the tacit backing of the U.S. Congress, also fostered madness, mayhem, and murder in tiny El Salvador. Injustice and repression had long characterized life in Latin America's smallest and most densely populated nation. In 1932, General Maximiliano Hernández Martínez (1931–44) directed *La Matanza* ("The Slaughter") of perhaps thirty thousand Salvadoran peasants, mainly indigenous people, who protested their hard lives working on coffee plantations. Included among the dead was Augustín Farabundo Martí, the Communist leader of the insurrection. *Los Catorce*, the elite network of families who dominated life in the country, thereafter were content to let military officers run the country while they exercised private power and privilege. The country was the land of "oligarchs and officers." The economic growth that Salvador experienced in the 1960s and 1970s helped undermine the traditional social structure. Professionals, merchants, laborers, and students formed associations and unions as ways of expressing their interests and demands. Urban groups rallied around José Napoleón Duarte, the mayor of San Salvador and a founder of the Christian Democratic Party. Calling for evolutionary change and reform, Duarte and his running mate, Guillermo Ungo, won the 1972 presidential election, but the military carried out massive voter fraud and blocked Duarte from assuming the presidency. In the countryside, desperate, landless peasants also organized. They were aided by Catholic priests, nuns, and lay workers who encouraged *campesinos* to pray together, organize, and discuss rural issues in Christian base communities or *comunidades de base*. El Salvador's rulers responded to the growing political activity with a new version of *La Matanza*. Paramilitary groups and death squads murdered citizens who organized peasants, workers, and students. Murder and torture became especially commonplace during the regime of General Carlos Humberto Romero (1977–79). His "Law for the Defense and Guarantee of Public Order" made it a crime to criticize the government.

The Kennedy administration had cultivated change in El Salvador in myriad ways. President Kennedy's call for freedom and social justice had inspired people like Duarte. The Alliance for Progress generated economic growth, and the Kennedy administration encouraged a Central American Common Market to spur trade and development. Salvador's elite had taken advantage of the export opportunities by expanding commercial agriculture and driving peasants off the land. The Kennedy administration had also enhanced the ability of the military rulers to control the population. The administration's anti-Communist policies included having the CIA and U.S. Special Forces help General José Alberto Medrano, the commander of the National Guard, develop counterinsurgency organizations. In particular, Medrano founded ORDEN, a national network of government informers and paramilitary groups, and ANESESAL, a centralized intelligence unit that coordinated the work of security forces. It was, in one scholar's words, a system of "enforcement terrorism." One of General Medrano's protégés was Major Roberto D'Aubuisson, who was popularly known as "Blowtorch Bob" for his favorite method of interrogation. U.S. Ambassador Robert White characterized D'Aubuisson as "pathological killer." Major D'Aubuisson became a leading figure in the right-wing party, Alianza Republicana Nacionalista (ARENA). ARENA, in Ambassador White's words, was "a violent fascist party modeled after the Nazis."[44]

Appalled by the mounting violence and alarmed about a growing, armed leftist insurgency, the Carter administration applauded the overthrow of the Romero regime on 15 October 1979. A junta consisting of two colonels and three civilians took power. In 1980, José Napoleón Duarte returned from exile and joined the junta. The administration pushed the junta to enact agrarian reform and to nationalize banking as a way of breaking the power of *Los Catorce*. The administration hoped that by backing Christian Democrats and social democrats it could isolate the extremists on the political left and right. The administration wanted to prevent a second Sandinista-style victory in Central America; it was certain that the ghastly repression of the military, paramilitary groups, and death squads would force the people into the hands of Communists. Reform to prevent radicalism had been a recurring Cold War policy of the United States. The Kennedy and Johnson administration had been stout supporters, for example, of the Christian Democrats in Chile in the 1960s.

The Carter administration's plans bore little fruit, as political violence intensified in El Salvador in 1980. The colonels decided to coalesce behind their reactionary superior officers, and civilians in the junta exercised no control over security forces. Perhaps eight thousand people were murdered, including 184 government officials who tried to carry out agrarian reform. A right-wing death squad assassinated Attorney General Mario Zamora, who tried to bring Christian Democrats and the political left together. Roberto D'Aubuisson orchestrated the murder of Archbishop Romero in his cathedral. The oligarchs and officers also closely observed the 1980 presidential election, hoping for a Ronald Reagan victory and the end of being hectored about "human rights." Wild celebrations greeted the news of Reagan's smashing electoral triumph in posh neighborhoods throughout Central America. Salvadoran conservatives interpreted Reagan's victory as a license to kill. On 27 November 1980, armed men wearing military-issued combat boots interrupted a meeting of the leaders of the Revolutionary Democratic Front (FDR), a broad coalition of left-wing civilian parties, and seized five leaders. The tortured and mutilated bodies of the politicians were found the next day dumped along a road outside San Salvador. In December, security forces murdered the four female missionaries from the United States. In early January 1981, in a restaurant in Salvador's Sheraton Hotel, soldiers murdered two U.S. citizens who worked for the American Institute for Free Labor Development. The AIFLD, an arm of the AFL-CIO, had worked with the CIA since the 1960s to promote anti-Communist labor and peasant organizations throughout Latin America. Salvador's rulers opposed any organization or association that empowered common people.[45]

Salvador's murderous criminals correctly predicted the new presidential administration's reaction to the horrors. Ronald Reagan observed that Salvador elites could not be expected to enact reforms in the middle of a civil war. The president also often suggested that guerrillas masquerading as rightists were responsible for most killings. Jeane Kirkpatrick defamed the murdered churchwomen, saying that "the nuns were not just nuns." She alleged that they were political activists who defended armed leftist insurgents. In fact, the churchwomen were Christian servants of the poor, doing religious and social welfare work. Secretary of State Haig joked about their death in congressional testimony and even suggested that they fired on security forces. Haig later modified his testimony about "pistol-packing nuns."[46] The administration's new ambassador in El Salvador, Deane Hinton, was a tough anti-Communist who dutifully denied that security forces perpetrated atrocities. Hinton was photographed giving an *abrazo* to Lt. Colonel Domingo

Monterrosa, the commander of the notorious Atlacatl Battalion that carried out massacres of peasants. But living amidst Salvador's madness affected Ambassador Hinton. In October 1982 he delivered a powerful speech to the American Chamber of Commerce in San Salvador. The ambassador's speech was well attended by the oligarchy of El Salvador. Hinton pointed out that thirty-thousand people had been "murdered, not killed in battle, murdered!" The ambassador asked: "Is it any wonder that much of the world is predisposed to believe the worst of a system which never brings to justice either those who perpetrate these acts or those who order them?" Ambassador Hinton earned a rebuke for his candor from the Reagan administration and was subsequently forced to resign.[47]

The Reagan administration argued that Cold War imperatives justified ignoring mass murder. Secretary Haig said in February 1981 that "our problem with El Salvador is external intervention in the internal affairs of a sovereign nation in this hemisphere, nothing more, nothing less." The Sandinistas, the Cubans, and the Soviets were allegedly sponsoring revolution in El Salvador as part of the master plan for world domination. As President Reagan pithily noted, "it is time the people of the United States realize that under the domino theory, we're the last domino."[48] El Salvador indeed had a formidable guerrilla army that numbered six thousand or more in the 1980s. In 1980, various armed leftist groups created a central organization, the Frente Farabundo Martí para la Liberación Nacional (FMLN), named after the peasant leader of 1932. Many FMLN leaders were Marxist-Leninists who admired the Cuban revolution. But allied to the FMLN were non-violent, non-Communist politicians from the Revolutionary Democratic Front, including Guillermo Ungo, the erstwhile ally of Duarte, and Rubén Zamora, the brother of the assassinated attorney general. In El Salvador to question what happened to a disappeared relative was to be characterized as a "terrorist." Advocating land reform or asserting the right to join a union in El Salvador earned a citizen the title of "Communist."

The Reagan administration's basic policy in El Salvador was to achieve a military victory over the guerrillas by building a powerful anti-Communist army. In March 1981, President Reagan approved $25 million in military aid. The $25 million represented more than the aggregate total that United States had granted to El Salvador's military during the Cold War, from 1946 to 1980. But the $25 million was only a down payment on what the Reagan administration intended for El Salvador. In the 1980s, El Salvador's military received approximately $1 billion in military aid from the United States. El Salvador had joined Israel as the major recipient of U.S. military aid. El Salvador's military grew from ten thousand to fifty thousand. Officers and men trained at U.S. war schools. The military was equipped with the latest military technology, including A-37 "Dragonfly" jet aircraft for bombing and AC-47 helicopter gunships for combat air support. The AC-47 helicopter, dubbed "Puff the Magic Dragon" during the Vietnam War, could fire eighteen thousand rounds per minute.[49] Despite its strength and firepower, El Salvador's military was unable to rout the armed insurgents. The guerrilla army of the FMLN was still intact in 1991.

Warfare exacted a costly toll on the people of El Salvador. At least seventy-five thousand citizens perished between 1979 and 1991. Over five hundred thousand Salvadorans fled the country, and another five hundred thousand were internally displaced. This death and suffering happened in a country of only five million people. There were battlefield deaths between the warring armies, and helpless citizens were caught in the crossfire. But the vast majority of the deaths, perhaps fifty thousand of them, came at the hands of the military and paramilitary groups and death squads associated with the military. To be sure, the FMLN committed atrocities. In 1985, for example, guerrillas killed off-duty U.S. marines sitting at an open-air café in San Salvador's *Zona Rosa* area and then sprayed the surrounding crowd with automatic fire. Urban commandos also kidnapped José Napoleón Duarte's daughter. But a U.N. "Truth Commission" reported in 1993 that El Salvador's security forces committed 85 percent of the assassinations and murders, whereas the U.N. commission attributed approximately 5 percent of the violence to the FMLN.[50] The U.N. report affirmed what international and domestic agencies, like Amnesty International and the Archdiocese of San Salvador, had been reporting throughout the 1980s. The Reagan administration argued that U.S. military aid, training, and influence would have the effect of curbing gross violations of human rights. One of the organizers of death squads, however, was Colonel Nicolás Carranza, the commander of the notorious Treasury Police and an ally of Roberto D'Aubuisson. U.S. diplomats referred to him as "fascist" and "the Gestapo." Colonel Carranza received $90,000 annually from the CIA to provide intelligence on the political left.[51]

The distinguished essayist and novelist Joan Didion wrote a short account, *Salvador*, after spending two harrowing weeks in country in 1982. She opened by observing that "terror is the given of the place." Words such as "hallucinatory," "nightmare," and "horror movie" conveyed her reaction to what she saw and experienced. "The dead and pieces of the dead" turned up every day in vacant lots, in the garbage thrown down ravines, in public rest rooms, in bus stations. Didion wrote in striking, haunting language that a visitor acquired a "special kind of practical information" about El Salvador. One learned "that vultures go first for the soft tissue, for the eyes, the exposed genitalia, the open mouth." One also learned that flesh deteriorated more rapidly than hair and "that a skull surrounded by a perfect corona of hair is a not uncommon sight in the body dumps." El Salvador's murderers favored mutilating or decapitating their victims. They wanted to limit the forensic evidence, and they wanted to heighten the terror for the living by leaving the victims unidentifiable. Their instruments of torture and death included tools used in slaughterhouses. El Salvador's security forces also made political points with their violence. As Didion noted, "one learns that an open mouth can be used to make a specific point, can be stuffed with something emblematic; stuffed, say with a penis, or, if the point has to do with a land title, stuffed with some of the dirt in question."[52]

The vast majority of the slaughtered lived in the countryside. The death squads worked for the land-owning oligarchy, and the military wanted to terrorize

A soldier in El Salvador's security forces photographed in the 1980s. An international commission established that the military and associated paramilitary forces ("State agents") were responsible for 85 percent of the seventy-five thousand deaths in the country's grisly civil war. The United States provided security forces with $1 billion in military aid in the 1980s. The soldier carries an M-16 semiautomatic rifle, which is manufactured in the United States. (Corbis Images)

campesinos to keep them from succoring the armed insurgents. The worst massacre took place in the remote village of El Mozote on 11 December 1981. The Atlacatl Battalion under the command of Lt. Colonel Monterrosa massacred more than eight hundred villagers. The Atlacatl Battalion, trained and equipped by the United States, was the pride of the U.S. military mission in El Salvador. Colonel Monterrosa had graduated from the School of the Americas in Panama. El Mozote was largely made up of apolitical evangelical Christians. The soldiers raped the young women and then murdered everyone. Among the dead were 195 children under the age of twelve. Soldiers tossed babies into the air and caught them on their bayonets. The soldiers wearied of hacking people to death and turned to their weapons. The shell casings left behind carried the stamp of a manufacturer in Lake City, Missouri. One resident, Rufina Amaya Márquez, escaped, hiding behind trees. She witnessed the decapitation of her husband and heard her son Cristino, 9, scream: "Mama, they're killing me. They've killed my sister. They're going to kill me." Rufina Amaya lost four children that day, including María Isabel, 8 months.[53]

The Reagan administration predictably denied the massacre at El Mozote. Ambassador Hinton and his staff used deceptive language in their reporting to Washington, neither explicitly confirming nor denying the massacre. Elliot Abrams, who headed the State Department's Human Rights section in the early 1980s, testified to a congressional committee that reports of a massacre were "not credible" and denounced the FMLN for publicizing the incident. U.S. officials were taking their cue from the president. In a televised address to the nation in 1984, Reagan asserted that violent security forces were "not part of the government." Administration officials privately conceded that government forces murdered and tortured. But they reasoned that the worst disaster that could befall human rights in El Salvador was a Communist victory. Defending El Salvador's government commanded the highest priority. As Abrams noted, "whatever you think of us from a human-rights point of view, what you think of us from a security point of view is determinative."[54] The oligarchs and officers grasped Abrams's insight, boasting to Joan Didion that the United States would never abandon them. As Didion put it, "anti-communism was seen as the bait the United States would always take."[55] The Atlacatl Battalion remained unreformed and unrepentant. In 1989, the battalion's soldiers executed six Jesuit priests, their housekeeper, and her daughter on the campus of *La Universidad Centroamericana* in San Salvador.

The U.S. public never approved of U.S. policy in El Salvador. But the Reagan administration showed greater political skill selling the war in El Salvador than the one in Nicaragua to U.S. legislators. U.S. officials marketed elections and José Napoleón Duarte. In 1982 and 1984, the CIA funneled a total $4 million dollars in El Salvador to facilitate first an election for a constituent assembly and then for the presidency. The covert money went to the Christian Democrats. The AIFLD gave $1 million in public money to unions that backed the Christian Democrats. The State Department footed the $10.5 million bill to pay for the presidential election. The administration's strategy was to persuade Congress that support for the government of El Salvador was support for democracy. The administration also wanted to put Duarte and reform-minded Christian Democrats in power and keep ARENA and especially Robert D'Aubuisson out of power. To the administration's dismay, ARENA won the majority of the votes in the 1982 elections, and D'Aubuisson became the leader of the constituent assembly. In 1984, however, Duarte won the presidency, defeating D'Aubuisson, and in 1985 the Christian Democrats gained control over El Salvador's legislature. Infuriated by the U.S. intervention, D'Aubuisson contemplated assassinating the U.S. ambassador in San Salvador.[56]

U.S. legislators found President Duarte (1984–89), who often travelled to Washington, a compelling figure. He was a courageous anti-Communist who favored land reform and social progress for El Salvador. He continued to function during the last year of his presidency, even though he had terminal liver cancer, dying in 1990. President Duarte brought back help for his country from

Washington. In addition to the $1 billion in military aid, El Salvador received $2.6 billion in economic aid during the 1980s. El Salvador ranked with Israel and Egypt as the largest recipients of U.S. economic assistance. U.S. legislators bought the democracy and reform arguments and the administration's dubious, periodic reports on human rights progress in El Salvador. Legislators also feared being branded with the hoary accusation of being "soft on communism." As Clement Zablocki (D-WI), the chair of the House Foreign Affairs Committee, admitted, "I certainly don't want to be accused of losing El Salvador by voting against more aid."[57]

The Reagan administration's marketing of democracy in El Salvador was filled with contradictions. Democracy demands more than elections. Democracy entails majority rule, respect for minority rights, peaceful transfers of power, and the promotion of a civic life, including freedom of speech and assembly. The political left did not participate in elections, because they justifiably feared being murdered if they campaigned openly. Impressive numbers of citizens participated in the 1982 and 1984 elections. But, as Joan Didion pointed out, a citizen's identity card indicated whether they had voted. El Salvador's security forces "encouraged" citizens to vote, knowing that high voter participation would lead to increased U.S. military aid.[58] President Duarte wielded little power once in office. ARENA politicians managed to gut land reform efforts, and security forces continued to terrorize *campesinos* who received titles to land. Security forces ignored President Duarte, even assassinating mayors who were Christian Democrats. The Reagan administration wanted President Duarte to exercise control over the military. The massive U.S. military aid program and the U.S. insistence on defeating the armed left inevitably reinforced the armed forces dominant role in the nation's life. The Christian Democrats also disappointed citizens. The colossal amount of money that the United States poured into El Salvador provided politicians with unending opportunities for graft and corruption. ARENA regained control of the legislature in 1988, and in 1989 ARENA's Alfredo Cristiani (1989–94) won the presidency.

As in Nicaragua, the war in El Salvador came to an unexpected end. The same international developments—the end of the Cold War, the Bush administration's pragmatism, the peace efforts of Costa Rica's President Arias—that facilitated the end of the war in Nicaragua played a similar role in El Salvador. Both the security forces and the armed left also gradually came to the conclusion that neither could defeat the other. The country could hardly take any more warfare. Beyond the human costs, the tiny country's ecosystem was collapsing. Ninety-four percent of the original forests, 80 percent of natural vegetation, and 77 percent of the arable soil had been damaged.[59] The United Nations, led by the outgoing secretary-general, Javier Pérez de Cuéllar (1981–91), a Peruvian, brokered an agreement. On 16 January 1992 in Mexico City, President Cristiani and the FMLN signed a peace accord to lay down arms and curb abuses. The FMLN received recognition as a legitimate political organization. A contingent of U.N. peacekeepers moved into El Salvador to oversee the peace. Throughout the 1980s, the Reagan administration opposed negotiations with the political left. It discouraged President Duarte's efforts to open a dialogue with the FMLN. Negotiations, not war, brought about peace in El Salvador and Nicaragua.

GENOCIDE IN GUATEMALA

The Reagan administration assisted the slaughter of the Mayan people. The political violence that had characterized life in Guatemala since the CIA intervention in 1954 took a gruesome turn in the 1980s under the regimes of General Romeo Lucas García (1978–82) and especially General Efraín Ríos Montt (1982–83). Almost eighteen thousand Guatemalans were murdered in 1982 alone. Various fact-finding and truth commissions reported in the late 1990s that of the two hundred thousand people who perished in political violence in the period from 1954 to 1996, over 80 percent were indigenous people. As in the cases of political violence in Argentina, Brazil, Chile, El Salvador, and elsewhere during the Cold War, state security forces or paramilitary groups associated with government leaders perpetrated most of the violence. The U.N. Truth Commission for Guatemala, which interviewed eleven thousand people, established that the political right bore responsibility for 93 percent of the deaths. The armed left caused 3 percent of the deaths.[60]

The Guatemalan armed forces decided to attack guerrilla forces, which numbered approximately six thousand, by eradicating Mayan villages and communities suspected of supporting guerrillas. The codename adopted for the ghastly policy was *Operación Sofía*. The Guatemalan military carried out massacres in 626 locales, including extermination campaigns in nearly six hundred rural Mayan communities. In the words of the Truth Commission, state agents "committed acts of genocide against groups of Mayan people." These conclusions were consistent with the classified reports that CIA agents were submitting to Washington. A secret CIA cable sent from Guatemala in February 1982 reported, for example, that the Guatemalan army was burning Mayan villages to the ground even though "the army has yet to encounter any major guerrilla force in the area." Guatemalan security forces employed the same terror tactics—rape, torture, body mutilation— favored by the military in El Salvador. The Guatemalan military's unique contribution to horror was to force the community to watch as they slit the stomachs of pregnant women or beat the women's bellies with rifle butts until they miscarried. These atrocities conveyed the symbolic and tangible message that the Mayan had no future in Guatemala.[61]

The 1980s seemed a propitious time to launch an offensive against the Mayan. Guatemala's elites resented the human rights policies of the Carter administration. The administration had suspended military aid and permitted only humanitarian economic assistance. Guatemalans celebrated Ronald Reagan's election, and two Guatemalan businessmen, who had donated $2 million to the Reagan campaign, met with the president-elect in December 1980 and denounced the human rights policies of President Carter. In a meeting in May 1981 with the Guatemalan foreign minister, Deputy Secretary of State William Clark, a confidant of the president, gave a sympathetic hearing to the Guatemalan request to be permitted "to do their own thing." The administration was unsuccessful in persuading Congress to resume military and economic aid. But it arranged for the sale of "non-lethal" equipment to Guatemala. For example, it licensed the sale of twenty-five unarmed Bell helicopters worth $25 million. Once they arrived in Guatemala, the helicopters were outfitted with weapons and used for military purposes. The Reagan administration also encouraged Israel to assist the Guatemalan military, and the Israelis built a munitions factory in the country.[62]

The Reagan administration initially blamed the political left for the violence. As the carnage mounted, however, administration officials adopted a "wait and see" policy toward the Guatemalan government. They hoped that the Guatemalan military waged war successfully, but did not want the United States associated with the abuses. Robert L. Jacobs, a State Department officer who served in the Bureau of Human Rights, blithely observed in October 1981 that "recent history is replete with examples where repression has been 'successful' in exorcising guerrilla threats to a regime's survival." Jacobs pointed to the recent "successful" repression in Argentina and Uruguay. Although not in favor of wholesale murder, Jacobs did not go so far as to recommend that the United States publicly condemn a policy that was tantamount to genocide. Not all U.S. officials were as sanguine about the slaughter of indigenous people. In January 1982, a political officer in the embassy in Guatemala City, Raymond J. González, protested that his government "should avoid condoning these illegal acts by its silence," adding "we become silent partners in the barbarous and criminal deeds of this government if we do not speak out." Ambassador Frederic Chapin accepted that González's protest of administration policy was a "cry of conscience." But the imperatives of the Cold War prevented the United States the "luxury" of protesting abuses of human rights.[63]

President Reagan could not, however, contain himself about Guatemala. He met Ríos Montt in Honduras in December 1982. He publicly praised the Guatemalan, calling him a man of great personal integrity and commitment" whose country was "confronting a brutal challenge from guerrillas armed and supported by others outside of Guatemala." In a session with journalists, Reagan added that Ríos Montt was dedicated to democracy and had received a "bum rap" from critics. The president indicated that he favored restoring military aid to Guatemala. The pleased Guatemalan leader joshed with the journalists, denying he was pursuing a "scorched-earth" policy. Instead, he directed a "scorched Communists" campaign.[64] Even as the two presidents spoke, Guatemalan commandos, members of the *Kabil* special operations force, were making their way into the community of Las Dos Eres. The Guatemalan army had prepared the *Kabiles* for savagery with training methods of extreme cruelty. The training included killing animals and then eating them raw and drinking their blood to demonstrate courage. The commandos murdered 162 people in Las Dos Eres, including 67 children. The commandos confessed to the Truth Commission that they had killed the younger children by grabbing hold of their legs and swinging them so their heads smashed against a wall.[65] As Kathryn Sikkink, a scholar of human rights, noted, President

Reagan's endorsement of Ríos Montt "was a gratuitous, thoughtless gesture made for a man guilty of mass murder of his population." Sikkink used "thoughtless" in the "manner suggested by Hannah Arendt, implying incapacity to tell right from wrong."[66] Arendt had developed her political theories through the study of totalitarian societies and monsters like Adolf Eichmann, the Nazi officer who organized the extermination of European Jewry.

Four years after Gabriel García Márquez delivered his memorable Nobel Prize address, Carlos Fuentes, another notable Latin American author, wrote about his region's suffering. The great Mexican novelist, the author of *La Muerte de Artemio Cruz* (1962), (*The Death of Artemio Cruz*) had lived for many years in the United States and admired its democratic achievements and cultural values. But Fuentes deplored the "arrogant and violent" policies of the United States in Latin America. Fuentes understood there was a Cold War. The spectacle of destruction served, however, only symbolic politics. Central Americans did not threaten U.S. national security. Reaffirming his love for U.S. society, Fuentes emphasized that "we will not confuse the United States and the Soviet Union, or indeed accept their moral equivalence." The Soviets pursued "coherent" policies, for they pursued "empire" both at home and abroad. The United States, on the other hand, "by acting like the Russians in its sphere of influence, becomes profoundly incoherent and hypocritical."[67]

Aftermath

L atin America and the United States have reacted in different ways to the end of the Cold War. For Latin Americans, coming to terms with the meaning of the Cold War has been an ongoing process that has stretched into the twenty-first century. Latin Americans have established commissions to establish the facts of what happened to their societies during the forty-five year confrontation between the United States and the Soviet Union. For more than two decades, Latin Americans have been looking to locate their dead and find their missing children. Latin Americans have also gradually concluded that they must prosecute the perpetrators of evil, if they are to achieve peace and closure in their societies. "*Nunca Más*" ("Never Again") has become a rallying cry in the region. The breaching of the Berlin Wall in November 1989 and the subsequent collapse of the Soviet Union in the summer of 1991 have not, however, prompted a similar pattern of reflection and soul-searching in the United States. The joy and satisfaction over the new-found freedom of Eastern Europeans, the unification of Germany, and the breakup of the Soviet Union has superseded any qualms about the hurt and pain inflicted upon Cold War bystanders. U.S. officials have issued scattered apologies for Cold War decisions that destroyed the lives of Latin Americans. But no agency of the U.S. government has conducted a systematic assessment of the U.S. role in Latin America during the Cold War. The United States also continued to pursue an atavistic Cold War policy—hostility toward Fidel Castro and the Cuban Revolution. However reluctantly, agencies like the CIA have gradually and incompletely complied with scholarly demands to release the documentary record on Cold War policies toward Latin America. The release of records has not, however, prompted a public discussion about the past. Discussion of the U.S. war in Latin America is largely confined to the scholarly community.

LATIN AMERICA AND COLD WAR HISTORY

Argentina, the home of *la guerra sucia*, has led the way in historical inquiry. The generals and admirals that had murdered thirty thousand Argentines left office in disgrace after the military debacle that was the war to liberate the Malvinas (Falkland Islands). In April 1982, Argentina's armed forces seized the Malvinas, which had been a possession of the United Kingdom for one hundred and fifty years. General Leopoldo Galtieri, the head of the latest military junta, ordered the action to fulfill long-held patriotic yearnings to restore Argentine sovereignty over the islands in the windy, cold South Atlantic. The military junta also hoped to distract the public from the military's mismanagement of the Argentine economy and the mounting protests over the dirty war. The United Kingdom, led by Prime Minister Margaret Thatcher, reacted in fury to Argentine aggression. Using combined air and sea power, British forces reasserted control over the islands in June 1982. British forces thrashed the Argentine armed forces, with a nuclear-powered British submarine torpedoing the World War II-vintage Argentine cruiser *General Belgrano*, sending over three hundred sailors to their death. General Galtieri had hoped for the tacit support of the Ronald Reagan administration in the war, calculating that the administration appreciated Argentina's training of anti-Communist forces in El Salvador and Nicaragua. The United States stuck by, however, its NATO ally and partner in World War I and II. Devastated by the embarrassing defeat and the military casualties, the Argentine public turned in fury against the junta. Galtieri resigned and was replaced by a caretaker general who promised elections. Argentina's anti-Communist military leaders had demonstrated to the world that their leadership skills and competence were limited to torturing and murdering defenseless civilians. In 1983, Argentines elected Raúl Alfonsín (1983–89) of the Radical Party as president. Alfonsín had upheld human rights and opposed military rule. Since the election of Alfonsín, Argentines have been able to maintain a constitutional system and civilian rule.

President Alfonsín named a *Comisión Nacional sobre la Desaparición de Personas* (National Commission on the Disappearance of Persons) or CONADEP to establish the truth about state terrorism in Argentina. In 1984, CONADEP, which was chaired by the renowned novelist and scientist Ernesto Sábato, issued its "report from hell," *Nunca Más*. The report documented 340 secret detention centers and 8,960 "disappeared" persons. The report further concluded that the number of disappeared was substantially higher than 8,960. *Nunca Más* opened with an allusion to the destruction of European Jewry, noting that "many of the events described in this report will be hard to believe. This is because the men and women of our nation have only heard of such horror in reports from distant places." CONADEP also indicted the military's anti-Communist rationales, their national security doctrines, labeling them as "totalitarian."[1] *Nunca Más* became an instant best-seller in Argentina. When it was republished in the mid-1990s in weekly installments, it sold two hundred thousand copies a week. *Nunca Más* served as an inspiration to other crusaders for human rights throughout Latin America. Chile, El Salvador, and Guatemala would issue similar reports in the 1990s on atrocities during the Cold War.[2] In Brazil, the Archdiocese of São Paulo, under the brave leadership of Cardinal Paulo Evarista Arns, published in 1985 its report on state-sponsored torture and murder in *Brasil: Nunca Mais* (*Brazil: Never Again*). *Nunca Mais* was based on a purloined copy of the Supreme Military

Tribunal's archive, which contained documents and photos produced by military courts against political prisoners.[3] As Argentines began the search for the *desaparecidos* in mass graves, they developed forensic skills in exhuming and identifying bodies. Argentine anthropologists thereafter assisted other nations in Latin America in recovering and identifying remains. Argentine scientists worked, for example, in establishing that a massacre occurred in El Mozote in El Salvador. President Alfonsín also paid homage to his friend and supporter, former President Jimmy Carter, by insisting that human rights issues be integrated into Argentine foreign policy.[4]

President Alfonsín authorized the prosecution of junta members (six generals and three admirals) who tyrannized Argentina from 1976 to 1982. The military leaders were unrepentant, with Admiral Emilio Massera claiming he had fought a "just war" against terrorism. The chief prosecutor labeled the military leaders as "criminals" who ordered the murder and torture of innocent civilians. A panel of judges in a federal appellate court found five of the junta members guilty and sentenced them to prison. General Jorge Videla and Admiral Massera received life sentences. Three of the four acquitted subsequently received prison sentences from military courts. Argentines, including the mothers and grandmothers of Plaza de Mayo, thereafter called for the prosecution of the military subordinates who had kidnapped, murdered, and tortured. Facing an increasingly mutinous and disloyal military, President Alfonsín decided to accept *punto final* (end point) and "due obedience" laws that would sharply curtail prosecutions. The due obedience law exempted military personnel below the rank of colonel from prosecution. The Argentine president reasoned that he had to prevent another military *golpe* and safeguard Argentine constitutionalism. Arguing that Argentina needed to move forward and focus on economic development, President Carlos Saúl Menem (1989–99), Alfonsín's successor, pardoned the convicted officers and those who had been indicted. Impunity had seemingly triumphed over justice in Argentina.

Domestic and international developments combined to lead Argentines from the late 1990s on to once again reassess their Cold War past. Argentines were left aghast, when, on 9 March 1995, Captain Adolfo Scilingo confessed on a popular television news show that he had participated in two of the weekly "death flights," dumping thirty living but drugged *desaparecidos* into the South Atlantic. A sixty-five-year old man, a sixteen-year-old boy, and two pregnant women in their early twenties were among the victims that Scilingo shoved out of the airplane. The articulate Scilingo, who was now conscience-stricken, appeared handsome, educated, socially adept, and, wearing a suit by Christian Dior, well groomed. Less visually appealing on television, but equally horrifying, was the torturer Julio Simón, known as "Julián the Turk." Simón, who attached a big swastika to his watch chain, was an opera fanatic and would listen to operatic music before commencing his torture sessions. He favored pushing sticks up the victim's anuses while shocking them with 220 volts of electricity. Speaking directly to the camera, the unrepentant Simón said "the norm was to kill everyone, and anyone kidnapped was tortured." He defended himself, asserting that he was fighting "terrorist hordes" and that "torture is eternal" and an "essential part of the human being." Such revelations, dubbed "the Scilingo effect," helped push Argentines into action. A new organization, the children of the murdered and disappeared, joined with the Plaza de Mayo women to agitate for justice. Jurists also challenged the constitutionality of pardons and legal immunities, citing such issues as the stolen children and the legal concept of *habeas corpus*.[5]

The Argentines received support in their quest for justice from the international legal community. Growing out of memories of the Holocaust, the principles of the Nuremburg trials, the adoption of the U.N. Declaration of Human Rights, and continued atrocities in places such as East Pakistan (Bangladesh), Cambodia, Guatemala, Uganda, Bosnia, and Rwanda, international lawyers and global leaders began to argue that there was "universal jurisdiction" for crimes against humanity. Belgium adopted a law in 1993 giving its legal system jurisdiction over war crimes anywhere in the world. Italian and Spanish jurists initiated extradition proceedings against Latin American military officers, charging that they had killed European nationals in countries such as Argentina, Chile, and Uruguay. Spanish judge Baltazar Garzón electrified the international legal community when in 1998 he demanded the arrest and extradition to Spain of General Augusto Pinochet of Chile on crimes of murder, torture, and genocide.[6] In 2005, Judge Garzón imposed a lengthy sentence on Captain Scilingo, who was residing in Spain, for the thirty murders he helped commit in the 1970s.

In the first decade of the twenty-first century, Argentine jurists pursued the criminals who waged *la guerra sucia*. In 2001, an Argentine federal judge ruled the *punto final* and due obedience laws unconstitutional, reasoning that they violated both Argentine and international law. The disappearance of persons was judged a crime against humanity and could not be amnestied. The court's judgment, which was upheld by Argentina's Supreme Court in 2005, received political support from President Néstor Kirchner (2003–07) and his successor and wife, Cristina Fernández de Kirchner (2007–). The young couple had been harassed during the years of military rule. The government decreed that the Navy Petty-Officers School of Mechanics (known by the Spanish initials as ESMA) in Buenos Aires would be transformed into a space for memory and the defense of human rights. More than five thousand Argentines had been confined in the ESMA torture center. Ninety percent of those never emerged alive from the military facility.

Both the prominent and the unpublicized perpetrators of murder and torture in Argentina faced justice. In 2002, General Galtieri was again indicted and put under house arrest; he died a few months later of a heart attack. In 2006, "Julián the Turk" (Julio Simón) received a twenty-five-year sentence for the torture of a disabled couple and the theft of their child. In 2008, Luciano Benjamín Menédez, the military commander who oversaw the notorious La Perla detention center in the city of Córdoba, received a life sentence for the kidnapping, torture, and murder of four political activists. In April 2010, an Argentine court convicted Reynaldo Bignone, a retired general and Argentina's last dictator (1982–83), for the kidnapping, torture, and murder of fifty-six people. Bignone, 82, received a twenty-five-year sentence. Human rights activists also celebrated the life sentence handed down in 2007 to the Reverend Christian von Wernich, a Roman Catholic priest. Father von Wernich was present at torture sessions, helping extract confessions, while at the same time offering consoling words to family members seeking their loved ones who had been kidnapped. The conviction forced both lay people and religious people to confront the Church's complicity in Argentina's sordid past.[7] Argentine religious leaders had not publicly opposed oppression, as they had in Brazil, Chile, and El Salvador.

International jurists also contributed to the movement for justice. Italian courts have an ongoing investigation of Operation Condor, the international terrorist network organized by Chile. In 1990, a jury in France convicted in absentia Navy Captain Alfredo Astiz for the disappearance of two French nuns. The nuns had been working with Argentine groups, including the Mothers of the Plaza de Mayo, in trying to learn about the fate of the disappeared. Captain Astiz, who was known as the "Angel of Death" for his youthful appearance, blonde hair, and ruthlessness, had infiltrated the peace groups, claiming that he had a brother who had also disappeared. In late 2009, Argentine jurists began the process of putting Captain Astiz on trial for murder. In 2008, Spanish authorities arrested a Dutch-Argentine airline pilot, Julio Alberto Poch, who flew planes used to throw

Reynaldo Bignone, a retired general and Argentina's last dictator (1982–83), fifth from left, awaits trial with other former military officers in Buenos Aires in November 2009. An Argentine court subsequently convicted Bignone and sentenced him to twenty-five years in prison for his role in the kidnapping, torture, and murder of Argentines during the "dirty war." (Corbis Images)

Argentines into the sea. In 2010, the Spanish High Court ordered the pilot's extradition to Argentina to face charges. As one scholar has noted, "time has not helped the criminals."[8]

The reunification of the perhaps five hundred kidnapped children with their grandparents has been a wrenching process for the victims. These were the children born in prison to abducted mothers who were subsequently murdered by the Argentine military. The grandmothers of the Plaza de Mayo have identified eighty-seven of the children, some of whom have integrated with their legitimate families and others of whom continue to live with the parents who raised them.[9] Journalist Roger Cohen of the *New York Times* and *International Herald Tribune* facilitated the discovery process when, in 1987, he identified twin boys living with an Argentine couple in Paraguay. Cohen's investigation and genetic testing confirmed that the couple were not the birth parents of the boys. Paraguay extradited the couple to Argentina, and the man was convicted of kidnapping and sent to jail in 1995. Revisiting the story in 2008, Cohen found that his good deed had not led to joy. Mistakes had been made in identifying the birth parents. The boys, now 30, had been left confused and unhappy by the process. Cohen could not find the twins, and they refused to talk to journalists. One boy reportedly carried a photo of his birth mother, whereas the other was inseparable from the woman who raised him. As Cohen noted, "the justice I had helped deliver had consisted, for them, of one broken home after another." Cohen asked himself whether the truth he had delivered to the twins was worth it. He answered: "For the dead, and Argentina, I say yes. For the twins, I don't know."[10]

Chile's movement from impunity to justice followed a path similar to Argentina's. The ruthless General Pinochet dominated political life in Chile until 1998, long after the Cold War had ended. Under mounting domestic and international pressure, Pinochet had agreed to hold a plebiscite in 1988, giving Chileans a choice on whether they wanted a continuation of one-man rule. The Reagan administration had surprisingly urged Pinochet to schedule a plebiscite. State Department officers wanted the administration to appear ideologically consistent—favoring elections in both Pinochet's Chile and the Sandinista's Nicaragua. Moreover, beginning in 1987, Democrats had regained control of Congress and were increasingly inclined to impose sanctions on Chile. The administration's new-found enthusiasm for democracy and human rights did not include President Reagan. The president informed an astonished George Shultz, the secretary of state, that "Pinochet saved Chile from communism; we should have him here on a state visit." The administration, through the National Endowment for Democracy, sent $1.6 billion to Chile to underwrite the costs of the plebiscite.[11] Chile's left and center political parties united in a political alliance known as the *Concertación* and urged Chileans to vote "no." The "no" vote triumphed by a decisive 55 to 43 percent. Pinochet agreed to relinquish the presidency, but he maintained substantial control. In 1978, he had declared a general amnesty for uniformed personnel. His constitution granted him the power to stay as commander-in-chief of the armed forces until 1998. The constitution also provided for non-elected senators, who were Pinochet's acolytes, to take seats in the Chilean legislature. In 1990, the glowering Pinochet draped the presidential sash over Patricio Aylwin of the Christian Democrats. After twenty-seven years of military rule, Chile had returned to free elections and constitutional processes.

President Aylwin (1990–94) and his successor, Eduardo Frei Ruiz-Tagle (1994–2000), the son of the former president, moved cautiously on human rights issues. The legacy of fear, a longing for social peace, and a desire for economic growth all hampered legal discoveries and the issuing of indictments. Aylwin appointed a National Commission on Truth and Reconciliation headed by a veteran politician from the Radical Party, Raúl Rettig. The Rettig Commission lacked subpoena power. It was authorized only to investigate deaths at the hands of state agents. It could not name perpetrators of crimes, and it could not investigate cases of arbitrary detention or of people who had been tortured but not murdered. Despite the restraints, the Rettig Commission provided a notable service to Chileans with its 1991 report. It documented over two thousand deaths and disappearances. Subsequent investigations raised the death toll to over three thousand. The commission rejected the Pinochet fantasy that the country had been at war after the overthrow of Salvador Allende and demonstrated that most of the dead were unarmed civilians, not armed guerrillas. Even as the commission took testimony, its work was aided by the discovery in June 1990 of a mass grave in Pisagua, a port city in northern Chile. Chileans gasped as they looked at the mummified faces of the disappeared on television and in newspaper photographs. General Pinochet denounced the Rettig Commission as a "sewer" and boasted that the armed forces took pride in saving the country from terrorism and international communism. The government thereafter provided compensation to the families of the executed and disappeared but did not challenge the 1978 amnesty law.[12] The only prominent Chilean officer prosecuted was Manuel Contreras of DINA who had overseen Operation Condor and the assassination of Orlando Letelier and Ronni Moffit in Washington in 1976. Pinochet had exempted that crime from his 1978 amnesty law, bowing to pressure from the Jimmy Carter administration. Contreras received, however, only a light sentence for his crime.

After 1998, Chileans began to engage directly with the past. General Pinochet stepped down as military commander, twenty-five years after he seized power, and took his seat in the legislature as "a senator for life." The audacious action infuriated the families of the victims and the hundreds of thousands of Chileans who had been arbitrarily detained or tortured. As a senator, Pinochet would also preserve his impunity. In September 1998, the cocky general travelled to London for a back operation. While there he had tea with his friend and fellow conservative, Lady Margaret Thatcher, stayed in a ritzy hotel, and shopped at Harrods, the upscale department store. Spain's Judge Garzón seized the moment. Armed with the extradition treaty that existed between Spain and the United Kingdom, Garzón issued a warrant for Pinochet's arrest. On 16 October 1998, British authorities arrested Pinochet, and he was kept under house arrest for the next sixteen months as the Spanish, British, and Chileans wrangled over the legal and jurisdictional issues. The British Foreign Office eventually shipped Pinochet home, ruling that he lacked the mental capacities to stand trial. Pinochet feigned illness, including dementia. But the once terrorized Chileans realized that their emperor no longer wore clothes. General Augusto Pinochet had become an epic international embarrassment.

After 2000, Pinochet would constantly find himself barraged with criminal cases and would lose his legal immunity and his senatorial seat. Chileans' fury mounted when they learned that Pinochet and his henchmen had stashed cash in banks around the world. Pinochet's secret bank accounts amounted to $28 million. As one scholar observed, Pinochet now appeared to erstwhile supporters "more like an old fashioned corrupt Caribbean-style dictator than the savior of Chile."[13] Claiming their client's ill health, lawyers kept Pinochet out of a Chilean jail. The dictator died in late 2006 at the age of ninety-one. Pinochet's military colleagues were not as fortunate. A Chilean judge, Juan Guzmán, successfully argued that the amnesty law did not exempt from prosecution those who had "disappeared" Chileans, because, under a writ of *habeas corpus*, the lack of a body meant that the kidnapping was an ongoing crime. Latin America's military dictatorships and death squads had thought they were clever when they "disappeared" victims or disfigured bodies beyond recognition. They were confident that they would never be prosecuted, because evidence no longer existed. By the end of 2006, more than one hundred Chileans, including numerous generals, had been convicted of disappearing Chileans. Manuel Contreras of Operation Condor received a life sentence in 2008 for the assassination of General Carlos Prats and his wife. President Michelle Bachelet called for the invalidation of the 1978 amnesty law, but Chile had not accomplished that goal as of 2010.[14] Chile accepted the jurisdiction of the International Criminal Court in 2009.

Beyond prosecuting its criminals, Chile took a variety of other measures to come to terms with its ghastly past. President Ricardo Lagos Escobar (2000–06), Chile's first socialist president since Allende, appointed a new commission, known as the Valech Commission, to listen to those who had been tortured. Over thirty-six thousand Chileans came forward to provide evidence of torture. The commission also identified over one thousand detention and torture centers.[15] The most notorious torture center, Villa Grimaldi, was transformed into a memorial for Pinochet's victims. Both President Bachelet and her mother had been tortured at Villa Grimaldi. Chile also erected a statue of Salvador Allende in the Plaza de la Constitución, near the presidential plaza, La Moneda. The statue carried the inscription of Allende's last public statement: "I have faith in Chile and her destiny." President Allende might think that faith was justified if he knew that his daughter, Isabel Allende Busi, served as the president of Chile's Chamber of Deputies.

As demonstrated in the cases of Argentina's missing children, the restoration of law and justice cannot erase the suffering that comes from memory. In 1980, the American Psychiatric Association defined "Post-Traumatic-Stress-Disorder" as a legitimate disease. At the time, it was popularly known in the United States as "Vietnam Syndrome." The psychiatrists were responding to the mental traumas experienced by U.S. veterans who had served in the horror that was the Vietnam War. Latin Americans also suffered from their Cold War. Steve Stern, a renowned scholar of Latin American history, has published remarkable interviews with Chileans of all political perspectives about their memories of the Pinochet era. Professor Stern conducted one interview, called the "memory tomb of the unknown soldier," with a frightened man, on the shoulder of a noisy highway outside of Santiago in the late 1990s. The man, who was given the pseudonym of Cristián, worried that General Pinochet, still the commander-in-chief, would overhear what he had to say. Cristián broke down as he told his story. Cristián, from a working class family, had been conscripted into the Chilean army as a teenager. In the weeks after the overthrow of Allende, his unit carried out terroristic break-ins and sweeps, known as *allanamientos*, of shantytown neighborhoods. In one home, Cristián's lieutenant smashed the butt of his rifle against the jaw of a small child who was petrified and wailing. When the mother responded, the lieutenant ordered another conscript to shoot the mother. Cristián's *compañero*, another conscript known as "Larita," refused to carry out the murder. The lieutenant took out his pistol and shot Larita in the head. Cristián was consumed by doubt and guilt over what he should have done. As one who became a father, he grieved for the child. His nightmares were filled with the vivid splattering of Larita's brains.[16]

The truth commissions in Argentina, Chile, and El Salvador documented atrocities and assigned responsibility for the carnage to the anti-Communist agents of the state. Analysts have noted, however, that these commissions avoided an extensive discussion of the political and social context in which the violence took place. Fears of another military *golpe* imposed caution on the fact finders. The multivolume study, *Guatemala: Memory of Silence* (1999), compiled by the Guatemalan Commission for Historical Clarification, broke from that circumspect approach. International pressure brought an end to the country's civil war in 1996. The United Nations designed the structure and composition of the Guatemalan commission. Beyond attributing to state security forces over 90 percent of Guatemala's two hundred thousand deaths, *Memory of Silence* explicitly repudiated "the theory of the two demons." The dead were not "collateral damage," having been caught in the crossfire between two warring armies. Agents of the state had targeted people because they were union leaders, rural organizers, and student activists who protested repression in Guatemala and wanted freedom and social justice. The military regimes also perpetrated racist, genocidal policies against the Mayan. The United States bore responsibility for the violence that swept over Guatemala for four decades. As the report noted, after the overthrow of President Jacobo Arbenz in 1954, "there was a rapid reduction in the opportunity for political expression." A "fundamentalist anti-communism" thereafter inspired legislation that "consolidated the restrictive and exclusionary nature of the political system." The Cold War policies of the United States received an enthusiastic welcome from elites and right-wing political groups in Guatemala. The United States backed military regimes and directed its military assistance "towards reinforcing the national intelligence apparatus and for training the officer corps in counterinsurgency techniques, key factors which had significant bearing on human rights violations during the armed confrontation." Indeed, the United States fostered "criminal counterinsurgency" with its anti-Soviet strategy in Latin America. The report further observed that Cuba had provided "political, logistical, instructional, and training support" to Guatemalan insurgents. But the report added that those sectors of the left imbued with Marxist ideology who adopted "the Cuban perspective of armed struggle" did so "in the context of an increasingly repressive State." [17]

Releasing historical analyses that interpret violence within a political and social context does not guarantee the pursuit of justice. President Alvaro Arzú, sitting next to his military commanders, showed no emotion as the head commissioner, Dr. Christian Tomushat of Germany, presented the report to a packed audience in Guatemala's National Theatre on 25 February 1999. President Arzú declined to step to the podium to accept *Memory of Silence*. A year before, the archdiocese of Guatemala City, led by Bishop Juan José Gerardi, released its four-volume study, *Guatemala: Nunca Mas* (1998), which recounted the military's atrocities against the Guatemalan people.[18] A few days after the release of the report, assailants bludgeoned to death Bishop Gerardi. The bishop's face was so disfigured that his corpse could be identified only by his episcopal ring.

Guatemala has not initiated a campaign to identify and prosecute its murderers and terrorists, although it did convict three mid-level military officers for the murder of Bishop Gerardi. As of 2010, Guatemala's most notorious figure, Efraín Ríos Montt, the former president, has not stood trial for overseeing the destruction of Mayan communities. In 1999, Rigoberta Menchú, the Guatemalan human rights activist and indigenous leader who received the Nobel Prize for Peace in 1992, filed charges of genocide against Ríos Montt in a Spanish court. The Spanish Constitutional Court ruled in 2005 that it could try those accused of crimes against humanity, even if the victims were not Spanish. A Spanish judge subsequently issued an international warrant for the arrest of Ríos Montt. Guatemala has refused, however, to extradite the former president, who has been a member of the Guatemalan Senate. The United Nations tried to help the beleaguered nation, setting up in 2007 the International Commission against Impunity in Guatemala to help a judiciary riddled with corruption. High levels of violence persisted in contemporary Guatemala. An average of sixteen murder victims turned up in Guatemala every day. Some victims were shot, some stabbed, some bludgeoned, and only about 3 percent of the cases were ever solved.[19]

Other Latin American countries have not fully confronted their Cold War past. Uruguay's truth commission documented 164 disappearances between 1973 and 1984 during the military dictatorship. But responding to political and military pressure, the commission declined to say that the practice of disappearing people was official policy.[20] In the 1980s, Uruguayans approved, both legislatively and via a plebiscite, amnesties for the military and leftist guerrillas. The amnesty applied only to crimes committed in Uruguay. Uruguayan authorities have prosecuted officers who participated in Operation Condor, such as General Gregorio Alvarez (1981–85), Uruguay's last dictator, who received a twenty-five-year sentence on 22 October 2009 for involvement in thirty-seven homicides and human rights violations. On 19 October 2009, Uruguay's Supreme Court declared the amnesty law for the military unconstitutional in reference to a specific case. But a week later, in a national election, voters again declined to overrule the amnesty laws via a constitutional amendment. In that same election, the leading vote getter for the presidency was José Mujica of the leftist Broad Front coalition. Now aged and plump, Mujica, a founder of the Tupamaro armed guerrilla movement, spent fourteen years in military prisons. Mujica won the runoff election in November and took office, as president, on 1 March 2010.

South America's most influential nation, Brazil, has not officially assessed the era of military dictatorship (1964–85). The study *Nunca Mais*, produced by the archdiocese of São Paulo, remains the most comprehensive assessment of murder and torture in Brazil. The military amnesty law of 1979 has not been repealed or declared unconstitutional by Brazilian courts. Brazilian authorities have not investigated deaths, disappearances, or torture during the military dictatorship. Brazil has shown remarkable economic growth in the twenty-first century, and Brazil has become a leading voice in global economic affairs, especially under the leadership of the working-class hero, President Luiz Inácio Lula da Silva (2002–10), known popularly as "Lula." During Lula's presidency, at least, Brazilians seemed intent on focusing on their bright future and not debating the dismal past of dictatorship. President Lula disappointed Brazil's human rights community by not establishing a truth commission to establish responsibility for military-era crimes. The able Brazilian leader was aware of the past. His minister of culture was Gilberto Gil, the internationally renowned recording artist who was forced into exile by the Brazilian military. The president's chief of staff was Dilma Rousseff. As a young woman, Rousseff resisted Brazilian military rule, was captured, and spent three years in prison on charges of participating in an armed militant group. Rousseff was tortured repeatedly with electric shocks. On 31 October 2010, Brazilian citizens elected Dilma Rousseff to the presidency of Brazil.

APOLOGIES

A noteworthy apology emanated from Latin America's historical thinking. In February 2009, the president of Guatemala, Alvaro Colom (2008-), apologized to Cuba on behalf of his country for having allowed the CIA to train Cuban exiles in Guatemala for the invasion of the Bay of Pigs. The Guatemalan leader officially asked for "forgiveness." On his official visit to Havana, Colom also awarded Guatemala's highest honor to Fidel Castro. A few days previously, Latin America's female presidents, Michelle Bachelet and Cristina Kirchner of Argentina, called on the old, ill Cuban *caudillo*. Their respective governments later released photographs of Castro with each of the presidents. The gestures by the Latin American presidents signaled the expected end of an era both for Castro and for the Cuban Revolution.

The end of the Cold War and the collapse of the Soviet Union brought dire economic times to Cuba. Cuba had become dependent on the Soviets' economic aid, receiving subsidized prices for oil imports and guaranteed prices for their exports, like sugar, to the Soviet bloc. The new Russia actually asked Cuba to pay back a $20 billion debt. In 1993, the Russians also withdrew the former Soviet infantry brigade that had been on the island since before the missile crisis of October 1962. The Cuban economy spiraled downward in the 1990s, declining by one-third. Communist Cuba had never broken the pre-revolutionary dependence on the sale of sugar for its economic solvency. It now had to compete on global markets without a Soviet or U.S. subsidy and continued to be denied access to the U.S. market by the trade embargo. Cuba looked to its past, trying to transform the island into a tourist destination. Tourists from Europe and Canada came, but so also did some of the ills of the pre-revolutionary past, such as prostitution. Cuba continued to blame the U.S. trade embargo for its poverty, unwilling to admit that the Communist system had been an economic failure everywhere in the world. In the twenty-first century, Cubans were poor and hungry. The country managed, however, to hold on to its gains in education and health. As measured by the widely respected Human Development Index compiled by the United Nations, Cuba was one of the leading nations in the Western Hemisphere in areas such as high literacy rates, access to education, life expectancy, and low infant mortality rates.[21]

In the post-Cold War era, Cuba had become an internationally insignificant country, where nostalgia reigned. In 1997, on the thirtieth anniversary of his death, the body of Ernesto Che Guevara was "discovered" buried under the runway at the airfield in Valle Grande, Bolivia. Bolivian authorities delivered Che's remains to Cubans who transported the remains back to Cuba. After a grand ceremony extolling Che's virtues, the Cubans returned the body to earth in Santa Clara. Troops commanded by Che had liberated the Cuban city in late 1958. Che had passed on to becoming an international symbol of romantic revolution. He was further associated with the optimistic times of the 1950s and 1960s. Forgotten was the pathetic, foolish mission that led to Che's death in Bolivia. Yearnings for the symbolic Che were highlighted by the release of two feature films about Guevara, *The Motorcycle Diaries* (2004) with the Mexican heartthrob, Gael García Bernal, and the four-hour epic, *Che* (2008), starring Benicio Del Toro. Web sites marketed Che memorabilia. T-shirts adorned with Che's visage were especially popular.[22] The noted U.S. folk singer, Richard Shindell, who lives in Buenos Aires, has highlighted the global phenomenon in his song of love and longing, *Che Guevara T-Shirt* (2004).

Latin Americans were not the only people issuing apologies for the Cold War in the Western Hemisphere. In 1990, Arthur M. Schlesinger, Jr., the famous historian and former aide to President John Kennedy, apologized in a public forum to the Guyanese leader, Cheddi Jagan, for the U.S. covert intervention in British Guiana (Guyana) in the 1960s. In Schlesinger's words, his beloved president had inflicted "a grave injustice" on Jagan. During the early 1960s, the United States had sponsored strikes and riots to destabilize the popularly elected government of Jagan. The United States feared that Jagan admired the Cuban Revolution. The ensuing political violence in the British colony took on ugly, racial tones with Afro-Guyanese attacking Indo-Guyanese and Indo-Guyanese retaliating. The Kennedy and Lyndon Johnson administrations also demanded that United Kingdom force Prime Minister Jagan from power, before granting the colony independence. In both 1964 and 1968, the CIA helped rig elections to ensure Jagan's defeat. The

U.S. man in Georgetown, Prime Minister Forbes Burnham (1964–85), an Afro-Guyanese leader, was a racist demagogue who persecuted the Indo-Guyanese majority, pilfered public funds, and reduced the country to absolute misery with his bizarre economic schemes. In 1992, Jagan finally had the free election that had been denied to him for decades. But it took extreme pressure from the State Department and especially the redoubtable Jimmy Carter, who oversaw the election, to force Burnham's political party to accept Jagan's victory. In one of the great ironies in the history of U.S. foreign relations, U.S. citizens helped put Cheddi Jagan and his party in power thirty years after Secretary of State Dean Rusk had declared that "it is not possible for us to put up with an independent British Guiana under Jagan." Prime Minister Jagan conducted friendly relations with the United States, but his administration was short-lived with Jagan dying of a heart attack in 1997 while seeking medical treatment at the Walter Reed Army Hospital in Washington, D.C. Guyana has preserved a democratic tradition but has been unable to escape its desperate poverty or surmount the racial tensions and hostilities between people of Indian and African heritages that were inflamed by the Cold War intervention.[23]

President Bill Clinton apologized for another Cold War intervention. In 1999, during a visit to Guatemala, after the release of *Memory of Silence*, Clinton observed that it was "imperative" that he address the report. In frank language, Clinton said: "For the United States, it is important that I state clearly that support for military forces or intelligence units which engage in violent and widespread repression of the kind described in the report was wrong, and the United States must not repeat that mistake." Secretary of State Colin Powell also suggested that there were Cold War activities that did not bring credit to the United States. In 2003, Secretary Powell addressed the U.S. role in the overthrow of Salvador Allende, noting "it is not a part of American history that we are proud of." The Chilean government of President Ricardo Lagos responded that it was pleased that the United States "now considers it was an error" to have supported the military *golpe* that overthrew President Allende.[24]

Although it did not issue an apology, the George H. W. Bush administration addressed another violation of international law perpetrated by the United States in its war in Latin America. In 1991, the administration struck an agreement with the new government of Violeta Chamorro to withdraw Nicaragua's suit against the United States in the International Court of Justice. The original 1984 finding of $370 million in damages for violating Nicaragua's sovereignty had ballooned to $17 billion with accrued interest and associated damage claims. On 12 September 1991, President Chamorro withdrew the suit. Two weeks later, the United States forgave $260 million in loans to Nicaragua. The settlement implied that the United States recognized that the 1984 judgment had legal meaning.

THE UNITED STATES AND COLD WAR HISTORY

Sporadic expressions of regret about the U.S. role in Latin America in the Cold War did not inspire demands for investigations and accountability. In the realm of public discourse, joy and satisfaction over the demise of the Soviet Union and the liberation of Eastern Europe crowded out thoughts about the dear prices that Latin Americans paid during the Cold War. Happy reenactments of the breaching of the Berlin Wall, as took place on 9 November 2009, the twentieth anniversary, sent the message that the West had acted nobly and bravely in confronting the Soviet Union and communism. Photographs of Chancellor Angela Merkel of Germany, Lech Walesa of Poland, and Mikhail Gorbachev of the former Soviet Union together in the new Berlin in a united Germany delivered the message that the Cold War was a "good war." Cold War regrets seemed to be saved for U.S. veterans of the Vietnam War, for not having received honor in their time and for their ongoing struggles to come to terms with their wartime memories of death and destruction.

Only the continuing presence of Henry Kissinger, Richard Nixon's sidekick, caused some to think about U.S. actions in Latin America. Kissinger enjoyed a position as a sage and thoughtful commentator on international affairs, who was consulted by influential journalists and asked to appear on high-toned public affairs television programs. But the iconoclastic public intellectual, Christopher Hitchens, has called for Kissinger to face war crimes trials for his decisions and policies, including his involvement in the assassination of General René Schneider of Chile.[25] Hitchens has a unique, multinational perspective. He was born in the United Kingdom and retained his British citizenship, but he lived in the United States and became a U.S. citizen. Kissinger has also faced calls from international jurists in Argentina and Chile to testify about his involvement with Operation Condor and the overthrow of Salvador Allende. Kissinger, through his lawyers, issued the vague response that he wished to "contribute what he can from his memory of those distant events." In his memoirs, Kissinger went to great lengths to absolve himself of responsibility for horrors in South America. Kissinger has also faced a little trouble abroad. In 2001 a French judge sent police officers to Kissinger's hotel in Paris to serve him with a request to answer questions about U.S. involvement in the Chilean *golpe*. French citizens had disappeared during the Pinochet era. Kissinger refused to respond to the subpoena, referred the matter to the Department of State, and flew on to Italy.[26]

One U.S. casualty of the Cold War in Latin America was the infamous School of Americas. By 2000, the school had trained over sixty thousand members of the Latin American military. An analysis of the Truth Commission for El Salvador report demonstrated that 75 percent of the military officers cited for involvement in major massacres in El Salvador had trained at the School of Americas. Other criminals who had studied at the school included Leopoldo Galtieri of Argentina and Efrain Ríos Montt of Guatemala. Roman Catholic peace activists, who opposed U.S. policies in Central America in the 1980s, had consistently called for the closing of the facility. In the 1990s, Representative Joseph Kennedy (D-MA), the son of the former attorney general and the nephew of President Kennedy, took up their cause. Representative Kennedy pressured the U.S. military to declassify training manuals used at the school. The manuals referred to tactics of false imprisonment, abuse of prisoners, torture, and the "neutralization" or assassination of suspects.

The Department of Defense discontinued the use of the manuals in 1996. Kennedy and his successors annually attempted to cut off funds for the school, finally succeeding in 1999. The Clinton administration closed the School of the Americas in 2000, but reopened it in January 2001 as the Western Hemisphere Institute for Security Cooperation. The new school, located at Ft. Benning in Georgia, claimed that it emphasized democracy and human rights to its military enrollees from Latin America.[27]

The United States has given haphazard assistance to the hunt for murderers and torturers who have fled their countries. In 2007, the human rights community hailed the arrest in the Washington, D.C., area and subsequent extradition to Argentina of Ernesto Guillermo Barreiro. Major Barreiro was the chief interrogator at the La Perla detention center in Córdoba. He fled to the United States in 2004, when President Kirchner revived prosecutions of war criminals. U.S. authorities arrested the Argentine fugitive on immigration charges. The U.S. legal system has not responded definitively, however, to the case of Luis Posada Carriles, a Cuban exile and former CIA asset who is wanted in Cuba and Venezuela on charges of masterminding the destruction a Cuban airliner in flight in 1976, killing seventy-three people. Twenty-four members of Cuba's national fencing team, as well as a Guyanese child, died in the explosion. Posada, who trained in explosives and sabotage at the School of the Americas in the 1960s, has denied involvement in the destruction of Cubana Airlines Flight 455, but he has tacitly admitted that he organized terrorist attacks on tourist facilities in Cuba in 1997 that killed and injured European tourists. Beyond fomenting violence against Cuba, Posada worked with the CIA in the 1980s assisting the contras of Nicaragua. Two men who confessed to planting explosives on Cubana Flight 455 have testified that they worked for Posada. Documentary evidence has also tied Posada to terrorism. Posada has lived freely in Miami since 2007, where he has support among anti-Castro exiles. In 2007, a federal judge in El Paso, Texas, dismissed immigration charges against Posada for illegally entering the United States in 2005.[28] In April 2009, the Justice Department of the new Barack Obama administration filed eleven new charges against Posada in federal court in El Paso, alleging he lied about the 1997 bombings and committed immigration fraud. As of mid-2010, Posada's jury trial was pending.

Luis Posada's ability to preserve his impunity pointed to the continuing Cold War between the United States and Cuba. The U.S. policy of hostility toward Castro's Cuba had barely changed between 1989 and 2010, even though Fidel Castro no longer dominated Cuba. In mid-2006, Castro had become seriously ill and transferred leadership to his brother, Raúl, in 2008. Public opinion polls demonstrated that U.S. citizens believed the non-recognition policy and the trade embargo were anachronistic, and U.S. exporters, especially farmers, were eager to sell their goods in Cuba. Their views were seconded by human rights activists in Cuba, who wanted democracy for the island. They argued that the continued "isolation of the people of Cuba benefits the most inflexible interests of its government, while any opening serves to inform and empower the Cuban people and helps to further strengthen our civil society." Much like the Mothers of the Plaza de

Mayo in Buenos Aires, a group of wives and mothers of political prisoners, known as the "Ladies in White" (*Damas de Blanco*), marched weekly after Sunday Mass in Havana. Their efforts combined with the good offices of the Archbishop of Havana, Cardinal Jaime Ortega, and the Spanish foreign ministry led to the release of five political prisoners in July 2010, with President Raúl Castro promising to set free an additional forty-seven dissidents in a few months. That would leave about 100 prisoners of conscience in Cuba.[29]

U.S. political leaders constantly worried, however, about the reaction of Cuban-Americans to a détente with Cuba. Political conservatives also had fond memories of the Cold War and did not mind seeing it continue. In 1996, the U.S. Congress tightened the trade embargo against Cuba with the Helms–Burton Act. In 1999–2000, U.S. citizens engaged in a hysterical debate over whether little Elián González should be returned to his father and communism in Cuba. The child had been found clinging to an inner tube off the coast of Ft. Lauderdale, Florida. Elián's mother had tried to escape Cuba, but she and ten others drowned when their boat capsized. The Clinton administration followed international and domestic law and returned the boy to his father. The intensity of the issue among Cuban-Americans was such, however, that the Justice Department had to send armed officers to retrieve the boy. An uncle, who had moved to the United States, had

The Ladies in White (*Las Damas de Blanco*) conduct their weekly march after Sunday mass in Havana to protest the imprisonment of human rights activists by the Cuban government. *Las Damas*, who were inspired by the Mothers of the Plaza de Mayo, began marching in 2003 after the Castro regime imprisoned seventy-five political dissidents. In 2005, the organization was awarded the Sakharov Prize for Freedom of Thought from the European Parliament. In mid-2010, the government of President Raúl Castro responded to the protests and the entreaties of the Roman Catholic Church and pledged to release some of the dissidents from jail. (Corbis Images)

become a hero among Cuban-Americans when he refused to obey a court order and relinquish Elián. The little boy was left terrified by the confrontation.[30]

The international community judged U.S. policy toward Cuba to be indefensible. An annual ritual at the United Nations was for the General Assembly to condemn the United States for its trade embargo against Cuba. The vote on the non-binding resolution in October 2009 had a typical result, with 187 nations in support, 3 opposed, and 2 abstaining. The United States could usually count on only Israel's support on this issue. In 2009, Palau also sided with the United States. In refusing to normalize relations with Cuba, the United States can fall back on a new feature of the Organization of American States. In 1992, the OAS unequivocally committed to democracy, permitting members by a two-thirds vote to suspend from the OAS any regime that overthrew a democratic government. OAS members had, however, diplomatic and economic relations with Cuba and joined in the U.N. vote condemning the United States.

Whereas the Cold War persisted with Cuba, the United States abandoned its Cold War concerns about Central America. El Salvador, Guatemala, and Nicaragua, the last theatres of the Cold War, were devastated countries. As measured on the 2009 U.N. Development Index of 182 countries, El Salvador ranked 106th, Guatemala ranked 122nd, and Nicaragua ranked 124th. The three counties had low per capita incomes and miserable records on the provision of health care and education to their people. Once the Cold War was over, the United States stopped focusing on the region. U.S. economic aid to Central America fell from $1.2 billion in 1985 to $167 million in 1996. The three countries depend on money sent home, *remesas*, from Central Americans who had migrated to the United States. An estimated 25 percent of El Salvador's population lived in the United States in 2009, and *remesas* accounted for 18 percent of the country's gross domestic product.[31] The U.S. prescription for Central America's economic health became trade, not aid. The United States has opened the U.S. market through the Central American Free Trade Agreement (CAFTA) (2005). The Dominican Republic, another impoverished country in which the United States waged Cold War, joined CAFTA. In one of the many ironies of Cold War history, Daniel Ortega of the Sandinistas was elected president of Nicaragua in late 2006, and in 2009 the voters of El Salvador elected Mauricio Funes of the FMLN to the presidency. The victory ended the rightist ARENA's two-decade-long domination of El Salvador's political life. Funes, a television journalist, had not fought with the FMLN in El Salvador's civil war. His brother, however, had been killed by the military.

One person who failed to notice that the United States no longer cared about the Cold War in Central America was General Manuel Antonio Noriega (1983–89), the despot of Panama. A month after the toppling of the Berlin Wall, President George H.W. Bush ordered U.S. troops into Panama to overthrow Noriega, seize him, and put him on trial in the United States. He was subsequently convicted in April 1992 of drug trafficking, racketeering, and money laundering and was incarcerated in a U.S. federal penitentiary until 2010. The United States thereafter extradited Noriega to France, where he received, in July 2010, a seven-year sentence for laundering drug money. Noriega, who trained at the School of the Americas, had been on the CIA payroll for two decades. He provided intelligence and aided the U.S. war against the Sandinistas. Under the spell of anticommunism, U.S. officials had overlooked the Panamanian's unlovely features—his ordering the murder of political opponents, his involvement in the international narcotics trade, and his perverted fondness for very young girls. Compared to the military murderers who had ruled Argentina, Brazil, Chile, and Uruguay, and the military butchers of El Salvador and Guatemala, General Noriega was, however, a minor tyrant. Human rights groups held Panamanian security forces responsible for twenty-two summary executions under Noriega's command between 1983 and 1988.[32] But the Cold War was over. The military intervention into Panama in December 1989 smacked of a return to the era of the Roosevelt Corollary. The United States was exercising "international police power" in the region. The United States vetoed a U.N. Security Council resolution deploring the invasion, although the General Assembly condemned the action. The United States was on the losing side of a 20–1 condemnation at the OAS.

The sharp reduction in economic aid to Central America and the military invasion of Panama further indicated that there would not be much official thinking or regretting about the Cold War in Latin America. In the public realm, debates over the issue of access to the documentary record have been the U.S. equivalent of a truth commission. Scholars have made progress on the opening the official record. In 2003, the Historical Office of the State Department released a volume in its *Foreign Relations of the United States* series on the U.S. intervention in Guatemala. This represented a redress of an appalling incident in the history of an esteemed series. In 1983, the Historical Office published a volume on Latin America, 1952–1954, which included a section on U.S. policy toward Guatemala. The documents did not demonstrate, however, that the United States had intervened in Guatemala. The Reagan administration had sharply restricted what the public could read about the nation's foreign policy past.[33] Scholars responded with both critical commentaries and legislative lobbying. The National Security Archive based at George Washington University became a relentless advocate for declassifying documents on the Cold War in Latin America.[34] The Clinton administration proved especially amenable to opening the record, authorizing major declassifications of records on U.S. policies toward El Salvador, Guatemala, and Honduras. In 1999, the administration, in response to the mounting international furor over General Pinochet, produced the Chile Declassification Project. The project yielded over twenty thousand documents on U.S. policies toward Chile from 1973 to 1990. The CIA has been recalcitrant in releasing documents. But in 2007, it disclosed the "Family Jewels," documents on top secret operations, including the CIA's collaboration with the Mafia in plots to kill Castro.[35] In 2009, the Historical Office released in electronic form a volume on U.S. relations with Latin America during the first administration of Richard Nixon. The electronic volume generated international publicity, because it demonstrated that President Nixon had asked Brazil's military government to enlist in the war against Salvador Allende. Isabel Allende called on Brazil to open archives that might shed light on any role it played in the overthrow of her father.[36] U.S. and Latin American citizens have not, however, gained complete access to the documentary record. The new electronic volume on Latin America did not offer documents on the Nixon administration's attitude toward military governments in Bolivia and Uruguay.

FINAL THOUGHTS

Explanations for the astonishing collapse of the Soviet empire in Eastern Europe and the demise of the Soviet Union and the international Communist movement were largely Eurocentric. Scholars agreed that the power of the West brought down the Soviet Union. They differed on whether to emphasize "hard" or "soft" power. One group focused on the military pressure that the United States brought to bear on the Soviets. Harry Truman and his advisors adopted the strategy of a "military power second to none" in NSC 68/2 and subsequent presidents, like John Kennedy and Ronald Reagan, intensified the pressure with massive expansions of U.S. nuclear and conventional forces. The Soviets ended up bankrupting their economy and society trying to match U.S. military power and lost their grip on their empire. Other analysts argued that the West undermined the Soviet system through its technology, its culture, and its ideas. Exchanges between the West and the East intensified after the Helsinki Accords of 1975. Leaders like Willy Brandt, the mayor of West Berlin, argued that tensions would be defused if Western citizens interacted on a daily basis with their counterparts in Communist countries. Russians and Eastern Europeans came to realize that their societies and lives were backward and boring. Mikhail Gorbachev had little choice but to make a useless effort to reform a tired, worn out system that had no possibility of competing with the vibrant West. The Soviet system imploded both at home and abroad.

The competing explanations for the events of 1989 made no mention of the Cold War in Latin America. Intervening in Guatemala, encouraging the Brazilian military to seize power, rigging elections in British Guiana and the Dominican Republic, teaching the latest methods of torture to the military and police of Latin America did not weaken the Soviet Union and lead to the liberation of Eastern Europeans. The Cuban missile crisis represented the one critical event in U.S.–Soviet relations during the region's Cold War. The confrontation would not have taken place, however, had the United States not waged war against Castro's Cuba in the preceding three years. A counterfactual argument can presumably be made that if the United States had not allied itself with reactionary groups, then Latin America would have turned leftward and the power and status of the Soviet Union would have been enhanced. The Cold War would have endured. The Soviet Union would still be with us. Eastern Europeans would still be slaves. This argument assumes that the power of the Soviet Union was infinite and that it could direct the course of history. Such reasoning also falsely equates revolutionary nationalism, Marxism, socialism, and communism with the Soviet Union. Implicit in such reasoning is also the patronizing, condescending assumption that left-leaning Latin Americans in power would be capable of making only once choice—an alliance with the Soviet Union. Latin Americans have always been motivated by their unique national identities, their culture, their religion, and their sense of their region's place in history.

The United States waged Cold War in Latin America because it judged that communism in the region, however loosely and broadly defined, threatened U.S. national security, impeded the U.S. ability to act elsewhere, and would incite a nasty domestic political debate at home. The U.S. war in Latin America had symbolic elements. The United States also practiced sphere-of-influence politics in the international arena. Latin America was in the "backyard" of the United States. The United States had the power to act with impunity. Since the late nineteenth century, inter-American relations have fulfilled the well-known reflection of Thucydides on international relations—large nations do what they wish, while small nations accept what they must.

Realpolitik alone cannot explain, much less justify, what happened in Latin America during the Cold War. The horror that beset big countries like Argentina and little ones like El Salvador have left scholars of international affairs aghast. The United States undermined constitutional systems, overthrew popularly elected governments, rigged elections, and supplied, trained, coddled, and excused barbarians who tortured, kidnapped, murdered, and "disappeared" Latin Americans. The United States allied with groups and individuals who stole babies. U.S. officials rationalized this criminal behavior, because they had a profound contempt for Latin American thought, society, and culture. Disdain for the people and the region ran through George Kennan right through to Jeane Kirkpatrick and Ronald Reagan. President Jimmy Carter and a few thoughtful diplomatic officials, such as F. Allan "Tex" Harris and Viron Vaky of the State Department, rose above the ethnocentrism and racism. But officers in the State Department, the CIA, and the U.S. military adopted the prejudices of their superiors in the White House and the national security bureaucracy.

To be sure, Latin American reactionaries, not U.S. officials, usually inflicted the hurt and pain on union organizers, student leaders, advocates for the disabled, and *campesinos*. But scholars can exhaust themselves attempting to parse out the domestic and foreign dimensions of the violence and terror.[37] The report *Guatemala: Memory of Silence* reasoned cogently when it found that the anti-Communist philosophies and policies of the United States "fell on fertile ground in Guatemala" and throughout Latin America. Through its Cold War words and actions, the United States sent clear signals to Latin American authorities what they had to do to defeat communism and protect the United States. Armed groups in Latin America received those signals and resorted to political terror to preserve and protect their own power and the elite socioeconomic groups that they served. Put another way, Latin American conservatives developed their own anti-Communist and national security issues. These doctrines coincided with the perspectives of the powerful officials who resided in Washington.[38]

Only small numbers of U.S. citizens are aware of the dimensions of the Cold War that the United States waged in Latin America. The charitable organization

The white scarf of the Mothers of the Plaza de Mayo has become a symbol of the movement for international human rights. (Stephen G. Rabe)

Physicians for Human Rights, headquartered in Cambridge, Massachusetts, has been working with *Pro Búsqueda de Niñas y Niños Desaparecidos*, the association that reunited Suzanne Marie Berghaus with her birth parents in El Salvador. The physicians arrange DNA testing to help identify children. An estimated 2,300 children were adopted by U.S. families. The children were either forcibly taken by the military or were orphaned when their parents were murdered or "disappeared." The DNA testing has helped confirm the identities of over three hundred children.[39] The good doctors have been doing their part in fulfilling the insight of Milan Kundera, the novelist who fled Communist Czechoslovakia, that "the struggle of man against power is the struggle of memory against forgetting."

Notes

ABBREVIATIONS

In addition to abbreviations used in the text, the following abbreviations appear in the endnotes.

DSB	Department of State Bulletin
FRUS	Foreign Relations of the United States
JFK	John F. Kennedy
LBJ	Lyndon Baines Johnson
PPP	Public Papers of the President

INTRODUCTION

1. Melvyn P. Leffler, *For the Soul of Mankind: The United States, the Soviet Union, and the Cold War* (New York: Hill and Wang, 2007).
2. Marc Lacey, "A Daughter Stolen in Wartime Returns to El Salvador," *New York Times*, 5 April 2007.
3. Piero Gleijeses, *Conflicting Missions: Havana, Washington, and Africa, 1959–1976* (Chapel Hill: University of North Carolina Press, 2002).
4. Aide to Dulles, quoted in Stephen G. Rabe, *The Road to OPEC: United States Relations with Venezuela, 1919–1976* (Austin: University of Texas Press, 1982), 126.
5. Vaky to Assistant Secretary of State Covey T. Oliver, "Guatemala and Counter-terror," 29 March 1968, *FRUS, 1964–1968* 31: *South and Central America; Mexico* (Washington, DC: Government Printing Office, 2004), 237–41; Ambassador Mein to Oliver, 27 February 1969, ibid., 227–34.
6. Greg Grandin, *The Last Colonial Massacre: Latin America in the Cold War* (Chicago: University of Chicago Press, 2004), 94–101. See also Tina Rosenberg, *Children of Cain: Violence and the Violent in Latin America* (New York: William Morrow, 1991), 17–19.
7. Gilbert M. Joseph and Daniela Spenser, eds., *In from the Cold: Latin America's New Encounter with the Cold War* (Durham: Duke University Press, 2008); Max Paul Friedman, "Retiring the Puppets, Bringing Latin America Back In: Recent Scholarship on United States–Latin American Relations," *Diplomatic History* 27 (November 2003): 621–36.

8. Reagan administration official, quoted in Thomas Carothers, *In the Name of Democracy: U.S. Policy toward Latin America in the Reagan Years* (Berkeley: University of California Press, 1991), 59. For defenses of the "two demons" thesis see Jorge Castañeda, *Utopia Unarmed: The Latin American Left after the Cold War* (New York: Alfred A. Knopf, 1993), 5, 51–112; David Stoll, *Between Two Armies in the Ixil Towns of Guatemala* (New York, Columbia University Press, 1993); David Stoll, *Rigoberta Menchú and the Story of all Poor Guatemalans* (Boulder, CO: Westview Press, 1999), 141–55; Hal Brands, *Latin America's Cold War* (Cambridge, MA: Harvard University Press, 2010), 126–28.

9. Jeffrey L. Gould, "Solidarity under Siege: The Latin American Left, 1968," *American Historical Review* 114 (April 2009): 348–75; Carothers, *In the Name of Democracy*, 59; J. Patrice McSherry, *Predatory States: Operation Condor and Covert War in Latin America* (Lanham, MD: Rowman & Littlefield, 2005), 27–28; Rosenberg, *Children of Cain*, 112–17.

10. Deputy Chief of Mission in Chile, Joseph John Jova, to Assistant Secretary of State Thomas C. Mann, 5 May 1964, *FRUS, 1964–1968* 31: *South and Central America; Mexico*: 568, fn #3.

11. Mark Danner, *The Massacre at El Mozote: A Parable of the Cold War* (New York: Vintage Books, 1993).

12. 4 December 1982, *PPP: Ronald Reagan, 1982* II: 1562–66.

13. Alan McPherson, *Intimate Ties, Bitter Struggles: The United States and Latin America since 1945* (Washington, DC: Potomac Books, 2006).

14. Michael Grow, *U.S. Presidents and Latin American Interventions: Pursuing Regime Change in the Cold War* (Lawrence: University Press of Kansas, 2008), xiii.

CHAPTER 1

1. Odd Arne Westad, *The Global Cold War* (New York: Cambridge University Press, 2007), 396–97.

2. James William Park, *Latin American Underdevelopment: A History of Perspectives in the United States* (Baton Rouge: Louisiana State University Press, 1995), 7–62.

3. Letter of Adams, 28 April 1823, in Robert H. Holden and Eric Zolov, eds., *Latin America and the United States: A Documentary History* (New York: Oxford University Press, 2000), 7–11.

4. *The Sentinel: Newsletter of SunAmerica Securities*, 28 February 1994, 1–2.

5. Rabe, *Road to OPEC*, 7–8.

6. Louis A. Pérez, Jr., *The War of 1898: The United States and Cuba in History and Historiography* (Chapel Hill: University of North Carolina Press, 1998), 1–22, 80.

7. Wood quoted in Lars Schoultz, *Beneath the United States: A History of U.S. Policy toward Latin America* (Cambridge, MA: Harvard University Press, 1998), 151.

8. David F. Healy, *Drive to Hegemony: The United States in the Caribbean, 1898–1917* (Madison: University of Wisconsin Press, 1988), 106–09.

9. Harold Molineu, *U.S. Policy toward Latin America: From Regionalism to Globalism* (Boulder, CO: Westview Press, 1986), 36; Tony Smith, *The Pattern of Imperialism: The United States, Great Britain, and the Late-Industrializing World since 1815* (New York: Cambridge University Press, 19181), 6–7; Norman Etherington, *Theories of Imperialism: War, Conquest, and Capital* (Totowa, NJ: Barnes and Noble, 1984), 278–80.

10. Walter LaFeber, "The Evolution of the Monroe Doctrine from Monroe to Reagan," in *Redefining the Past: Essays in Diplomatic History in Honor of William Appleman Williams*, ed. Lloyd C. Gardner (Corvallis: Oregon State University Press, 1986), 139–40.

11. Walter LaFeber, *The Panama Canal: The Crisis in Historical Perspective*, updated edition (New York: Oxford University Press, 1989), 23–70.

12. Root quoted in Walter LaFeber, *Inevitable Revolutions: The United States in Central America* (New York: Oxford University Press, 1983), 37.

13. Stimson quoted in Hans Schmidt, *The United States Occupation of Haiti, 1915–1934* (New Brunswick, NJ: Rutgers University Press, 1995), 231.

14. Rabe, *Road to OPEC*, 9–13.

15. Lester D. Langley, *The Banana Wars: An Inner History of American Empire, 1900–1934* (Lexington: University of Kentucky Press, 1983), 34–42.

16. Louis A. Pérez, Jr., "Intervention, Hegemony, and Dependency: The United States in the circum-Caribbean, 1898–1980," *Pacific Historical Review* 51 (May 1982): 181.

17. Root, quoted in LaFeber, *Inevitable Revolutions*, 36. See also Langley, *Banana Wars*, 1–8, and Louis A. Pérez, Jr., *Cuba in the American Imagination: Metaphor and the Imperial Ethos* (Chapel Hill: University of North Carolina Press, 2008), 1–11.

18. For statistics see Rabe, *Road to OPEC*, 193–95.

19. Wilson speech, 27 October 1913, in Holden and Zolov, *Latin America and the United States*, 110–12.

20. Schmidt, *United States Occupation of Haiti*, 82–206.

21. U.S. officials quoted in Langley, *Banana Wars*, 123–37. For a fine analysis of U.S. paternalism and racism in Haiti, see Mary A. Renda, *Taking Haiti: Military Occupation and the Culture of Imperialism, 1915–1940* (Chapel Hill: University of North Carolina Press, 2001), 124–81.

22. Bruce J. Calder, *The Impact of Intervention: The Dominican Republic during the U.S. Occupation of 1916–1924* (Austin: University of Texas Press, 1984), 49–62; Eric Paul Rooda, *The Dictator Next Door: The Good Neighbor Policy and the Trujillo Regime in the Dominican Republic, 1930–1945* (Durham, NC: Duke University Press, 1998), 21–22.

23. Rabe, *Road to OPEC*, 22–42.

24. Robert N. Seidel, "American Reformers Abroad: The Kemmerer Missions in South America, 1923–1931," and Barry Eichengreen, "House Calls of the Money Doctor: The Kemmerer Missions to Latin America, 1917–1931," both in *Money Doctors, Foreign Debts, and Economic Reforms in Latin America from the 1890s to the Present*, ed. Paul W. Drake (Wilmington, DE: Scholarly Resources, 1994), 86–132.

25. Jules R. Benjamin, *The United States and Cuba: Hegemony and Dependent Development, 1880–1934* (Pittsburgh: University of Pittsburgh Press, 1977), 171–85; Louis A. Pérez, Jr., *Cuba Under the Platt Amendment, 1902–1934* (Pittsburgh: University of Pittsburgh Press, 1986), 301–32; Raymond H. Pulley, " The United States and the Trujillo Dictatorship, 1933–1940: The High Price of Caribbean Stability," *Caribbean Studies* 5 (October 1965): 22–31.

26. Michael J. Francis, *The Limits of Hegemony: United States Relations with Argentina and Chile during World War II* (Notre Dame, IN: University of Notre Dame Press, 1977), 102–44.

27. Max Paul Friedman, *Nazis and Good Neighbors: The United States Campaign against the Germans of Latin America in World War II* (New York: Cambridge University Press, 2003), 3–10.

28. Leslie Bethell and Ian Roxborough, "Introduction," in *Latin American between the Second World War and the Cold War, 1944–1948*, ed. Leslie Bethell and Ian Roxborough (Cambridge: Cambridge University Press, 2002), 1–11.

29. Molineu, *U.S. Policy toward Latin America*, 13–15.

30. Santos quoted in Bradley Lynn Coleman, *Colombia and the United States: The Making of an Inter-American Alliance* (Kent, OH: Kent State University Press, 2008), 11.

31. Bryce Wood, *The Dismantling of the Good Neighbor Policy* (Austin: University of Texas Press, 1985), ix–xiv; Bryce Wood, *The Making of the Good Neighbor Policy* (New York: W. W. Norton, 1961). For a critique of Wood's thesis, see Friedman, *Nazis and Good Neighbors*, 227–35.

CHAPTER 2

1. George F. Kennan, *Memoirs, 1925–1950* (New York: Bantam Books, 1967), 502–10.

2. Memorandum by the Counselor of the Department of State (George Kennan) to the Secretary of State, 29 March 1950, *FRUS, 1950* 2: *United Nations; The Western Hemisphere* (Washington, DC: Government Printing Office, 1976): 598–624.

3. Roger R. Trask, "George F. Kennan's Report on Latin America (1950)," *Diplomatic History* 2 (Summer 1978): 307–12.

4. Jane Mayer, "The Big Idea: A Doctrine Passes," *The New Yorker*, 14 & 21 October 2002, 70; Tim Weiner and Barbara Crossette, "George Kennan Dies at 101: Leading Strategist of Cold War, *New York Times*, 18 March 2005.

5. LaFeber, "Evolution of the Monroe Doctrine," 139–40; Gaddis Smith, *The Last Years of the Monroe Doctrine, 1945–1993* (New York: Hill & Wang, 1994), 68–72.

6. Leslie Bethell and Ian Roxborough, "The Impact of the Cold War on Latin America," in *Origins of the Cold War: An International History*, 2ⁿᵈ ed., ed. Melvyn P. Leffler and David S. Painter (New York: Routledge, 2005), 299–303.

7. Thomas M. Leonard, "Central America: On the Periphery," in *Latin America during World War II*, ed. Thomas M. Leonard and John F. Bratzel (Lanham, MD: Rowman & Littlefield, 2007), 36–53.

8. Joseph Smith, "Brazil: Benefits of Cooperation," in Leonard and Bratzel, *Latin America during World War II*, 154–59.

9. Coleman, *Colombia and the United States*, 38.

10. Bethell and Roxborough, "Impact of the Cold War," 299–316.

11. Smith, *Last Years of the Monroe Doctrine*, 51–52.

12. Truman, quoted in ibid., 67; Robert L. Beisner, *Dean Acheson: A Life in the Cold War* ((New York: Oxford, 2006), 568.

13. Stephen G. Rabe, "The Elusive Conference: United States Economic Relations with Latin America, 1945–1952," *Diplomatic History* 2 (Summer 1978): 279–94.

14. Stephen G. Rabe, *Eisenhower and Latin America: The Foreign Policy of Anticommunism* (Chapel Hill: University of North Carolina Press, 1988), 15–17.

15. Stanley Hilton, "The United States, Brazil, and the Cold War: End of the Special Relationship," *Journal of American History* 68 (December 1981): 604.

16. Wood, *Dismantling of the Good Neighbor Policy*, 136; Roger R. Trask, "The Impact of the Cold War on United States–Latin American Relations, 1945–1949," *Diplomatic History* 1 (Summer 1977): 271–84; Bethell and Roxborough, "Impact of the Cold War," 307–15.

17. Greg Grandin, "Off the Beach: The United States, Latin America, and the Cold War," in *A Companion to Post-1945 America*, ed. Jean-Christophe Agnew and Roy Rosenzweig (Malden, MA: Blackwell, 2002), 431–34.

18. Thomas E. Skidmore, "Studying the History of Latin America: A Case of Hemispheric Convergence," *Latin American Research Review*, No. 1 (1998): 113.

19. Rabe, *Road to OPEC*, 94–116. See also Steven Schwartzberg, *Democracy and U.S. Policy in Latin America during the Truman Years* (Gainesville: University Press of Florida, 2003), 125–67.

20. NSC 16, in Paper Prepared by Policy Planning Staff (PPS–26), 22 March 1948, *FRUS, 1948* 9: *The Western Hemisphere* (Washington, DC: Government Printing Office, 1972): 196; NSC 7, quoted in Trask, "Impact of the Cold War," 280.

21. Paper Prepared by Policy Planning Staff (PPS–26), 22 March 1948, *FRUS, 1948* 9: 194–201.

22. Bethell and Roxborough, "Impact of the Cold War," 304–05; Skidmore, "Studying the History of Latin America," 119.

23. Beisner, *Dean Acheson*, 569–72; memorandum by Miller to Halle, 7 November 1950, *FRUS 1950* 2: 625–28; "Y" (Louis Halle), "On a Certain Impatience with Latin America," *Foreign Affairs* 28 (July 1950): 565–79.

24. Miller quoted in Rabe, *Eisenhower and Latin America*, 20–21.

25. Miller, "Non-Intervention and Collective Responsibility in the Americas," *DSB* 22 (15 May 1950): 768–70.

26. Stephen G. Rabe, "The Johnson Doctrine," *Presidential Studies Quarterly* 36 (March 2006): 48–58; LaFeber, *Inevitable Revolutions*, 94–95.

27. Stephen G. Rabe, "Inter-American Military Cooperation, 1944–1951," *World Affairs* 137 (Fall 1974): 132–49.

28. Report by National Security Council to President, NSC 56/2, 18 May 1950, *FRUS, 1950* 1: *National Security Affairs; Foreign Economic Policy* (Washington, DC: Government Printing Office, 1977): 628–37.

29. Brazilian foreign minister quoted in Hilton, "United States, Brazil, and the Cold War," 609.

30. Rabe, *Eisenhower and Latin America*, 6.

CHAPTER 3

1. Grandin, *Last Colonial Massacre*, 32.

2. Grow, *U.S. Presidents and Latin American Interventions*, 2.

3. Jason M. Colby, " 'Banana Growing and Negro Management': Race, Labor, and Jim Crow Colonialism in Guatemala, 1884–1930," *Diplomatic History* 30 (September 2006): 595–621.

4. Memorandum from King to Frank Wisner of CIA, 11 January 1952, *FRUS, 1952–1954, Guatemala* (Washington, DC: Government Printing Office, 2003), 2–4; CIA to CIA Station, 26 January 1952, ibid, 6.

5. Patterson, quoted in Richard H. Immerman, *The CIA in Guatemala: The Foreign Policy of Intervention* (Austin: University of Texas Press, 1982), 102.

6. Nick Cullather, *Secret History: The CIA's Classified Account of Its Operations in Guatemala, 1952–1954* (Stanford: Stanford University Press, 1999), 22–26.

7. Rabe, *Eisenhower and Latin America*, 44–46.

8. Memorandum from Western Hemisphere Division of CIA to Wisner, 9 July 1952, *FRUS, 1952-1954, Guatemala*, 20-22.

9. Memorandum from Western Hemisphere Division of CIA to Richard Helms of CIA, with attachment, 17 March 1952, ibid, 13-16.

10. Telegram from CIA Station to CIA, 12 September 1952, ibid, 26-27; memorandum on Trujillo from Jacob R. Seekford, CIA, to King, 18 September 1952, ibid, 27.

11. Beisner, *Dean Acheson*, 576-84.

12. Memorandum of CIA meeting with Miller and Mann, 8 October 1952, *FRUS, 1952-1954, Guatemala*, 31.

13. Miller quoted in CIA memorandum for record, 8 October 1952, ibid, 33-35.

14. CIA report, 8 October 1952, ibid, 29-30.

15. Beisner, *Dean Acheson*, 584-86.

16. CIA memorandum, Seekford to King, 28 October 1952, *FRUS, 1952-1954, Guatemala*, 46-47; CIA report, 1 December 1952, ibid, 50-55; Cullather, *Secret History*, 27-33.

17. Rabe, *Eisenhower and Latin America*, 31-32.

18. Ibid, 32-33.

19. Memorandum for record by Dulles, 8 March 1953, *FRUS, 1952-1954, Guatemala*, 79-80.

20. Halle to Robert Bowie, Director of Policy Planning Staff, 28 May 1954, *FRUS, 1952-1954* 4: *The American Republics* (Washington, DC: Government Printing Office, 1983): 1139-49; draft policy paper prepared in Bureau of Inter-American Affairs, 19 August 1953, ibid, 1083.

21. Memorandum for record by Dulles, 8 March 1953, *FRUS, 1952-1954, Guatemala*, 79-80; CIA memorandum for record on briefing of Ambassador Peurifoy, 1 September 1953, ibid, 93-94.

22. Stephen Schlesinger and Stephen Kinzer, *Bitter Fruit: The Untold Story of the American Coup in Guatemala* (Garden City, NY: Anchor Books, 1983), 106-07, 203.

23. State Department intelligence report, 5 March 1953, *FRUS, 1952-1954, Guatemala*, 70-78; Dulles quoted in Rabe, *Eisenhower and Latin America*, 58.

24. State Department intelligence report, 1 January 1953, *FRUS, 1952-1954, Guatemala*, 56-66; paper prepared in PBSUCCESS headquarters on "Communism in Central America," 21 April 1954, ibid, 239-43.

25. CIA to CIA station in Guatemala, 30 June 1954, ibid, 408-09; Cullather, *Secret History*, 106-07;

26. Peurifoy to State Department, 17 December 1953, *FRUS, 1952-1954* 4: 1091-93.

27. Piero Gleijeses, *Shattered Hope: The Guatemalan Revolution and the United States, 1944-1954* (Princeton: Princeton University Press, 1991), 137-48.

28. Cullather, *Secret History*, 77-82.

29. Dulles quoted in Rabe, *Eisenhower and Latin America*, 57.

30. Edward T. Brett, *The U.S. Catholic Press on Central America: From Cold War Anticommunism to Social Justice* (Notre Dame: University of Notre Dame Press, 2003), 16-20; E. Howard Hunt, *American Spy: My Secret History in the CIA, Watergate, and Beyond* (Hoboken, NJ: John Wiley and Sons, 2007), 70-84.

31. Memorandum for record on weekly PBSUCCESS meeting, 9 March 1954, *FRUS, 1952-1954, Guatemala*, 214-17; paper prepared in PBSUCCESS headquarters, undated, ibid, 274-76; telegram from PBSUCCESS headquarters to CIA station in Guatemala, 30 January 1954, ibid, 177-79.

32. Cullather, *Secret History*, 57–62.

33. PBSUCCESS headquarters to CIA, 19 February 1954, *FRUS, 1952–1954, Guatemala*, 196–97; CIA station to PBSUCCESS headquarters, 11 May 1954, ibid, 280.

34. PBSUCCESS headquarters to CIA, 31 January 1954, ibid, 183–84; CIA memorandum for record on Calligeris (Castillo Armas), 14 May 1954, ibid, 282–85.

35. Memorandum for record by King of CIA, 11 September 1953, 102–09, ibid; Ambassador Peurifoy to Assistant Secretary of State for Inter-American Affairs John Moors Cabot, 28 December 1953, ibid, 159–61.

36. Wisner of CIA to Helms of CIA, 19 November 1953, ibid, 144–46; Wisner of CIA to CIA Director Dulles, 24 April 1954, ibid, 251–60.

37. Tim Weiner, *Legacy of Ashes: The History of the CIA* (New York: Doubleday, 2007), 93–104; Max Holland, "Private Sources of U.S. Foreign Policy: William Pawley and the 1954 Coup d'Etat in Guatemala," *Journal of Cold War Studies* 7 (Fall 2005): 58–63.

38. Cullather, *Secret History*, 95–104; Rabe, *Eisenhower and Latin America*, 56.

39. Ibid, 60–61.

40. Stephen G. Rabe, "The Johnson (Eisenhower?) Doctrine for Latin America," *Diplomatic History* 9 (Winter 1985): 94–100; Lars Schoultz, *That Infernal Little Cuban Republic: The United States and the Cuban Revolution* (Chapel Hill: University of North Carolina Press, 2009), 55–57; Rabe, *Eisenhower and Latin America*, 39–40.

41. Weiner, *Legacy of Ashes*, 108–09.

42. Mark T. Hove, "The Arbenz Factor: Salvador Allende, U.S.–Chilean Relations, and the 1954 U.S. Intervention in Guatemala," *Diplomatic History* 31 (September 2007): 623–63.

43. Ibid, 658–63.

44. Paul J. Dosal, *Commandante Che: Guerilla Soldier, Commander, and Strategist, 1956–1967* (University Park: Pennsylvania State University Press, 2003), 23–43.

45. Grandin, *Last Colonial Massacre*, 66.

46. Note for the files, "Disposal List," 1 June 1954, *FRUS, 1952–1954, Guatemala*, 302; Cullather, *Secret History*, 137–42; Grandin, *Last Colonial Massacre*, 66–69.

47. Ibid, 66.

48. Jim Handy, *Revolution in the Countryside: Rural Conflict and Agrarian Reform in Guatemala, 1944–1954* (Chapel Hill: University of North Carolina Press, 1994), 192–207; Rabe, *Eisenhower and Latin America*, 61.

49. Stephen M. Streeter, *Managing the Counterrevolution: The United States and Guatemala, 1954–1961* (Athens: The University of Ohio Press, 2000), 137.

50. Phillips quoted in Rabe, *Eisenhower and Latin America*, 62.

51. Immerman, *CIA in Guatemala*, 201; the conclusion and recommendations of the Truth Commission report, *Guatemala: Memory of Silence* (1999), can be found in http://shr.aaas.org/guatemala/ceh/report/english/toc.html.

52. Streeter, *Managing the Counterrevolution*, 210–38.

53. Stephen G. Rabe, *The Most Dangerous Area in the World: John F. Kennedy Confronts Communist Revolution in Latin America* (Chapel Hill: University of North Carolina Press, 1999), 71–77.

54. Ibid, 76; *Guatemala: Memory of Silence* (1999) in http://shr.aaas.org/guatemala/ceh/report/english/toc.html.

55. Grandin, *Last Colonial Massacre*, 97–102.

56. Ibid, 99.

57. Gleijeses quoted in "Afterword: The Culture of Fear," in Cullather, *Secret History*, xix–xxxii.

CHAPTER 4

1. Paul J. Dosal, *Comandante Che: Guerrilla Soldier, Commander, and Strategist, 1956–1967* (University Park: Pennsylvania State University Press, 2003), 1–22; Thomas C. Wright, *Latin America in the Era of the Cuban Revolution*, Revised Edition (Westport, CT: Praeger, 2001), 16–18.

2. Ramón Eduardo Ruiz, *Cuba: The Making of a Revolution* (New York: W.W. Norton, 1970), 133–40; Thomas G. Paterson, *Contesting Castro: The United States and the Triumph of the Cuban Revolution* (New York: Oxford University Press, 1994), 74–80; Samuel Farber, *The Origins of the Cuban Revolution Reconsidered* (Chapel Hill: University of North Carolina Press, 2006), 63–68.

3. Castro quoted in Schoultz, *That Infernal Little Cuban Republic*, 82.

4. Farber, *Origins of the Cuban Revolution*, 7–22.

5. Schoultz, *That Infernal Little Cuban Republic*, 121–24.

6. Farber, *Origins of the Cuban Revolution*, 63.

7. Ibid, 142–54.

8. Rabe, *Eisenhower and Latin America*, 171.

9. James G. Blight and Philip Brenner, *Sad and Luminous Days: Cuba's Struggle with the Superpowers after the Missile Crisis* (Lanham, MD: Rowman & Littlefield, 2007), 73–146; Dosal, *Comandante Che*, 182–89; Rabe, *Most Dangerous Area*, 135–41.

10. Rabe, *Road to OPEC*, 139–54; Stephen G. Rabe, "The Caribbean Triangle: Betancourt, Castro, and Trujillo and U.S. Foreign Policy, 1958–1963 in *Empire and Revolution: The United States and the Third World since 1945*, ed. Peter L. Hahn and Mary Ann Heiss (Columbus: Ohio State University Press, 2001), 48–70.

11. Piero Gleijeses, *Conflicting Missions: Havana, Washington, and Africa, 1959–1976* (Chapel Hill: University of North Carolina Press, 2002), 5–222, 373–79; Blight and Brenner, *Sad and Luminous Days*, 104–05.

12. Blight and Brenner, *Sad and Luminous Days*, 73–119.

13. Ibid. 129–45; National Intelligence Estimate (NIE), "Prospects for Argentina," 9 June 1965, *FRUS, 1964–1968* 31: 293–95; editorial note on President Johnson's conversation with Kosygin and subsequent Johnson conversation with President Eisenhower, 25 June 1967, ibid, 146; Rabe, *Most Dangerous Area*, 135–41.

14. Wright, *Latin America in the Era of the Cuban Revolution*, 29–36.

15. Paterson, *Contesting Castro*, 195–237.

16. Rabe, *Eisenhower and Latin America*, 127–29; Jeffrey J. Safford, "The Nixon–Castro Meeting of 19 April 1959, *Diplomatic History* 4 (Fall 1980): 425–31.

17. Rabe, *Eisenhower and Latin America*, 129–30; Schoultz, *That Infernal Little Cuban Republic*, 116–17.

18. CIA memorandum, "Johnny Roselli," not dated, pp. 12–16, and Howard J. Osborn, Director of Security, to CIA Director, "Johnny Roselli," 19 November 1970, pp. 44–48, both in CIA "Family Jewels" Project on Freedom of Information Act, Web site: http://www/foia.cia.gov.

19. Rabe, *Eisenhower and Latin America*, 170–71.

20. Schoultz, *That Infernal Little Cuban Republic*, 146–48.

21. CIA papers on Cuba prepared by Bissell, 17 February 1961, 11 March 1961, and 15 March 1961, all in *FRUS, 1961–1963* 10: *Cuba, 1961–1962* (Washington, DC: Government Printing Office, 1997): 102–09, 137–42, 145–48.

22. Schlesinger to president, 5 April 1961 and 10 April 1961, ibid, 186–89, 196–203; Howard Jones, *The Bay of Pigs* (New York: Oxford University Press, 2008), 65.

23. Memorandum prepared in CIA to General Maxwell D. Taylor on report of Colonel Hawkins prepared on 13 April 1961, 26 April 1961, *FRUS, 1961–1963* 10: 221–22.

24. Scholutz, *That Infernal Little Cuba Republic*, 148; Jones, *Bay of Pigs*, 72–74.

25. Peter Kornbluh, ed., *Bay of Pigs Declassified: The Secret CIA Report on the Invasion of Cuba* (New York: Free Press, 1998), 10–12.

26. Actions and notes of 483rd meeting of NSC, 5 May 1961, *FRUS, 1961–1963* 10: 476–83; Robert Kennedy, quoted in memorandum from Helms of CIA to CIA Director John McCone, 19 January 1962, ibid, 719–20; Don Bohning, *The Castro Obsession: U.S. Covert Operations against Cuba, 1959–1965* (Washington, DC: Potomac Books, 2006), 79–85.

27. Interagency Task Force on Cuba, paper for NSC, 4 May 1961, *FRUS, 1961–1963* 10: 459–75.

28. Rabe, *Most Dangerous Area*, 32.

29. Memorandum from Sherman Kent, Chair of the Board of National Estimates, to CIA Director Dulles, 3 November 1961, *FRUS, 1961–1963* 10: 668–72; "The Cuba Project," program review by Lansdale, 18 January 1962, ibid, 710–18; Blight and Brenner, *Sad and Luminous Days*, 17.

30. Anna Kasten Nelson, "Operation Northwoods and the Covert War against Cuba, 1961–1963," *Cuban Studies* 32 (2002): 145–54. For Robert Kennedy's scheme to attack Guantánamo, see memorandum of discussion in Secretary of State Dean Rusk's office, 21 August 1962, *FRUS, 1961–1963* 10: 947–49.

31. Jones, *Bay of Pigs*, 5, 12, 49.

32. Memorandum of record for Robert Kennedy on CIA briefing, 14 May 1962, *FRUS, 1961–1963* 10: 807–09; memorandum for record prepared by Thomas A. Parrott, assistant to General Maxwell Taylor, on president's interest in Castro's removal, 5 October 1961, ibid, 659–60; Arthur M. Schlesinger, Jr., *Robert Kennedy and His Times* (Boston: Houghton Mifflin, 1978), 498; Helms, quoted in Weiner, *Legacy of Ashes*, 187.

33. Seymour Hersh, *The Dark Side of Camelot* (Boston: Little, Brown, 1997), 268–93.

34. Kennedy, quoted in Ernest R. May and Philip D. Zelikow, eds., *The Kennedy Tapes: Inside the White House during the Cuban Missile Crisis* (Cambridge, MA: Belknap Press of Harvard University, 1997), 107; McNamara, quoted in Blight and Brenner, *Sad and Luminous Days*, 17; Schoultz, *That Infernal Little Cuban Republic*, 186.

35. Two excellent accounts are Alexsandr Fursenko and Timothy Naftali, *"One Hell of a Gamble": Khrushchev, Castro, and Kennedy, 1958–1964* (New York: W.W. Norton, 1997) and Don Munton and David Welch, *The Cuban Missile Crisis: A Concise History* (New York: Oxford University Press, 2007).

36. Blight and Brenner, *Sad and Luminous Days*, 73–119.

37. Stephen G. Rabe, "After the Missiles of October: John F. Kennedy and Cuba, November 1962 to November 1963," *Presidential Studies Quarterly* 30 (December 2000): 714–26.

38. Memorandum for record of White House meeting on Cuba, 19 June 1963, *FRUS, 1961–1963* 11: *Cuban Missile Crisis and Aftermath* (Washington, DC: Government Printing Office, 1996): 837–38; CIA memorandum of record of meeting of 12 November

1963 to review Cuban program, *FRUS, 1961–1963, Microfiche Supplement*, 10–12: (Washington, DC: Government Printing Office, 1998): 718.

39. Rabe, "After the Missiles of October," 722–23. See also Gleijeses, *Conflicting Missions*, 23.

40. Weiner, *Legacy of Ashes*, 207–09; Kennedy speech in *DSB* 49 (9 December 1963): 900–04; Hersh, *Dark Side of Camelot*, 440. Hersh's assertion about the intention of Kennedy's speech is supported by documentary record in memorandum of meeting with President Johnson, 19 December 1963, *FRUS, 1961–1963* 11: 904–09.

41. Robert Dallek, *An Unfinished Life: John F. Kennedy, 1917–1963* (Boston: Little, Brown, 2003), 709; Rabe, "After the Missiles of October," 723–24.

42. Johnson quoted in Schoultz, *That Infernal Little Cuban Republic*, 214.

43. Editorial note on Secretary Rusk meetings with European ambassadors, 15 September 1964, *FRUS, 1964–1968* 32: *Dominican Republic; Cuba; Haiti; Guyana* (Washington, DC: Government Printing Office, 2005): 684; memorandum of conversation between Undersecretary of State George Ball and British Ambassador David Ormsby Gore, 7 February 1964, ibid, 577; White House meeting with British prime minister, 12 February 1964, ibid, 594–97.

44. Memorandum of meeting with President Johnson, 19 December 1963, *FRUS, 1961–1963* 11: 904–09. On the 1964 dispute over water supplies, see Jana K. Lipman, *Guantánamo: A Working Class History between Empire and Revolution* (Berkeley: University of California Press, 2009), 181–90.

45. Johnson quoted in editorial note on meeting between Johnson and CIA Director John McCone, 27 December 1963, *FRUS, 1961–1963* 11: 911 and in Bohning, *Castro Obsession*, 177.

46. Telephone conversation between Johnson and Assistant Secretary of State Mann, 11 June 1964, *FRUS, 1964–1968* 32: 658–60; Mann to Secretary of State Rusk, 14 July 1964, ibid., 734–36.

47. Dosal, *Comandante Che*, 188–94.

48. Ibid, 209, 264; Wright, *Latin America in the Era of the Cuban Revolution*, 80–87.

49. Rabe, *Most Dangerous Area*, 130–31.

50. Memorandum by Richard Helms, CIA Director, on "Capture and Execution of Ernesto 'Che' Guevara," 11 October 1967, *FRUS, 1964–1968* 31: 381–82 with footnotes; Dosal, *Comandante Che*, 277–303. See also Henry Ryan Butterfield, *The Fall of Che Guevara: A Story of Soldiers, Spies, and Diplomats* (New York: Oxford University Press, 1999).

51. Rabe, *Most Dangerous Area*, 135–39; NIE, "The Potential for Revolution in Latin America," 28 March 1968, *FRUS, 1964–1968* 31: 170–72.

52. Blight and Brenner, *Sad and Luminous Days*, 141–45.

CHAPTER 5

1. *DSB* 44 (3 April 1961): 471–74.

2. Jeffrey F. Taffett, *Foreign Aid as Foreign Policy: The Alliance for Progress in Latin America* (New York: Routledge, 2007), 11–27, 205–23.

3. *DSB* 44 (3 April 1961): 471–74.

4. Memorandum of conversation between Kennedy and Prime Minister Harold Macmillan, 30 June 1963, *FRUS, 1961–1963* 12: *American Republics* (Washington, DC: Government Printing Office, 1996): 607–09.

5. Rabe, *Most Dangerous Area*, 22–23.

6. Bevan Sewall, "A Perfect (Free–Market) World? Economics, the Eisenhower Administration, and the Soviet Economic Offensive in Latin America," *Diplomatic History* 32 (November 2008): 841–68; Taffett, *Foreign Aid as Foreign Policy*, 11–27; Rabe, *Most Dangerous Area*, 9–33.

7. William Taubman, *Khrushchev: The Man and His Era* (New York: W.W. Norton, 2003), 487–88; Michael R. Beschloss, *The Crisis Years: Kennedy and Khrushchev, 1960–1963* (New York: Edward Burlingame Books, 1991), 60–61.

8. Lincoln Gordon, "US–Brazilian Reprise," *Journal of Inter-American Studies and World Affairs* 32 (Summer 1990):168.

9. Kennedy quoted in "Report on Berlin Crisis," 25 July 1961, *PPP: JFK, 1961*, 441–45; Rusk quoted in Rabe, *Most Dangerous Area*, 21.

10. Memorandum of conversation between Rusk and Argentine diplomats, 18 January 1962, *FRUS, 1961–1963* 12: *American Republics*: 292–94.

11. Kennedy quoted in Rabe, *Most Dangerous Area*, 19–20.

12. Arthur M. Schlesinger, Jr., *A Thousand Days: John F. Kennedy in the White House* (Boston: Houghton Mifflin, 1965), 773.

13. Michael E. Latham, *Modernization as Ideology: American Social Science and "Nation Building" in the Kennedy Era* (Chapel Hill: University of North Carolina Press, 2000), 1–108.

14. Arthur M. Schlesinger, Jr., "The Alliance for Progress: A Retrospective," in Ronald G. Hellman and H. Jon Rosenbaum, eds., *Latin America: The Search for a New International Role* (New York, Halsted Press, 1975), 57–92.

15. Rabe, *Most Dangerous Area*, 17.

16. Kennedy speech in Miami, 18 November 1963, *DSB* 49 (9 December 1963): 900–04.

17. Robert Packenham, *Liberal America and the Third World: Political Development Ideas and Social Science* (Princeton: Princeton University Press, 1973), 34–35, 59–75, 111–60; Tony Smith, *America's Mission: The United States and the Worldwide Struggle for Democracy in the Twentieth Century* (Princeton: Princeton University Press, 1994), 18, 217–27.

18. Rabe, *Most Dangerous Area*, 148–72; Taffett, *Foreign Aid as Foreign Policy*, 40–41.

19. Rabe, *Road to OPEC*, 139–67.

20. Rabe, *Most Dangerous Area*, 162–64; Taffett, *Foreign Aid as Foreign Policy*, 51.

21. James F. Siekmeier, "A Sacrificial Llama? The Expulsion of the Peace Corps from Bolivia in 1971," *Pacific Historical Review* 69 (February 2000): 65–87.

22. Rabe, *Most Dangerous Area*, 164–67.

23. Stephen G. Rabe, *U.S. Intervention in British Guiana: A Cold War Story* (Chapel Hill: University of North Carolina Press, 2005), 124–38.

24. Rabe, *Most Dangerous Area*, 34–40.

25. Schlesinger, *Thousand Days*, 769.

26. Rabe, *Most Dangerous Area*, 41–48.

27. Ibid, 47; telephone conversation between Johnson and Mann, 27 April 1965, *FRUS, 1964–1968*, 32: 63–66; Alan McPherson, "Misled by Himself: What the Johnson Tapes Reveal about the Dominican Intervention of 1965," *Latin American Research Review* 38, No.2: 130, 133.

28. Memorandum of meeting between State Department and CIA officials, 14 April 1965, *FRUS, 1964–1968* 32: 57–58.

29. McPherson, "Misled by Himself," 141–44.

30. Johnson, address to nation, 2 May 1965, *PPP: LBJ*, 1965, 469–75.

31. Randall B. Woods, "Conflicted Hegemon: LBJ and the Dominican Republic," *Diplomatic History* 32 (November 2008): 749–66.

32. Ibid, 753; McPherson, "Misled by Himself," 137.

33. Stephen G. Rabe, "The Johnson Doctrine," *Presidential Studies Quarterly* 36 (March 2006): 48–58.

34. Taffett, *Foreign Aid as Foreign Policy*, 138; McPherson, "Misled by Himself," 136.

35. Valenti's notes of meeting in White House Cabinet Room, 30 April 1965, *FRUS, 1964–1968* 32: 100–02.

36. Russell Crandall, *Gunboat Democracy: U.S. Interventions in the Dominican Republic, Grenada, and Panama* (Lanham, MD: Rowman & Littlefield, 2006), 35–103; Alan McPherson, "How to Intervene and Get Out," *History News Service*, 29 March 2005. Available from http://www.h-net.org/~hns/articles/2005/032905a.html (McPherson no longer stands by his characterization of the 1966 election, because of the release of new documents); General Bruce Palmer, Jr., *Intervention in the Caribbean: The Dominican Crisis of 1965* (Lexington: University of Kentucky Press, 1989), 133–34.

37. McPherson, "Misled by Himself," 136.

38. Taffett, *Foreign Aid as Foreign Policy*, 123–47.

39. Editorial note on U.S. covert program in Dominican Republic in 1966, *FRUS, 1964–1968* 32: 357–58; memorandum from Helms to Desmond Fitzgerald of CIA, 29 December 1965, ibid, 358–62; memorandum prepared for the 303 Committee, 11 January 1966, ibid, 368–71.

40. Circular telegram from State Department to embassies in American Republics, 11 May 1966, ibid, 412–13.

41. NIE on Dominican Republic, 28 April 1966, ibid, 398–99.

42. Eric Thomas Chester, *Rag-Tags, Scum, Riff-Raff, and Commies: The U.S. Intervention in the Dominican Republic, 1965–1966* (New York: Monthly Review Press, 2001) 283–89.

43. Memorandums prepared for the 303 Committee, 17 March 1967 and 5 June 1968, *FRUS, 1964–1968* 32: 930–35, 951–54; Rabe, *U.S. Intervention in British Guiana*, 139–62.

44. NIE, 25 September 1969, *FRUS, 1969–1976* E-10: *Documents on the American Republics, 1969–1972* (Washington, DC: Government Printing Office, 2009): document 271. Volume available at http://www.history.state.gov/historicaldocuments/frus1969-76ve10.

45. Chester, *Rag-Tags*, 272–78.

46. State Department paper, "Guidelines of U.S. Policy and Operations, Brazil," 7 February 1963, *FRUS, 1961–1963* 12: 488–90; Kennedy conversation with Brazilian Foreign Minister, 13 March 1963, ibid., 500–503; Mann quoted in Taffett, *Foreign Aid as Foreign Policy*, 118.

47. Ambassador Lincoln Gordon to State Department on conversation with President Goulart, 21 October 1961, *FRUS, 1961–1963* 12: 448–50.

48. Cabot quoted in Rabe, *Most Dangerous Area*, 65.

49. Memorandum of conversation between Kennedy and Brazilian Finance Minister, 15 May 1961, *FRUS, 1961–1963* 12: 435–36.

50. Ambassador Gordon's views in W. Michael Weis, *Cold Warriors and Coups d'Etat: Brazilian–American Relations, 1945–1964* (Albuquerque: University of New Mexico Press, 1993), 149–66.

51. Memorandum of conversation between Kennedy and Kubitschek, 13 December 1962, *FRUS, 1961–1963* 12: *American Republics*: 117–25; Rabe, *Most Dangerous Area*, 67–68.

52. Jan Knippers Black, *United State Penetration of Brazil* (Philadelphia: University of Pennsylvania Press), 1977; Ruth Leacock, *Requiem for Revolution: The United States and Brazil, 1961–1969* (Kent, OH: Kent State University Press, 1990); Phyllis R. Parker, *Brazil and the Quiet Intervention, 1964* (Austin: University of Texas Press, 1979); Weis, *Cold Warriors and Coups d'Etat*; Taffett, *Foreign Aid as Foreign Policy*, 110–11.

53. Parker, *Quiet Intervention*, 62–63.

54. President Johnson's telephone conversation with George Ball and Thomas Mann, 31 March 1964, can be accessed through the web site http://www.gwu.edu/~nsarchiv/NSAEBB/NSAEBB118/index.htm.

55. Taffett, *Foreign Aid as Foreign Policy*, 117–20.

56. Virginia Langland, "Birth Control Pills and Molotov Cocktails: Reading Sex and Revolution in 1968 Brazil," in *In from the Cold: Latin America's New Encounter with the Cold War*, ed. Gilbert M. Joseph and Daniela Spenser (Durham: Duke University Press, 2008), 308–49.

57. Gould, "Solidarity under Siege," 358.

58. Castañeda, *Utopia Unarmed*; Stoll, *Between Two Armies*; Brands,"Latin America's Cold War." For an incisive critique of their position, see Gould, "Solidarity under Siege," 348–75.

59. Thomas E. Skidmore, *Brazil: Five Centuries of Change* (New York: Oxford University Press, 1999), 164–66.

60. Embassy in Argentina to State Department, 8 June 1966, *FRUS, 1964–1968* 31: 303–05.

61. Jeffrey J. Ryan, "Turning on Their Masters: State Terrorism and Unlearning Democracy in Uruguay," in *When States Kill: Latin America, the U.S., and Technologies of Terror*, ed. Cecilia Menjívar and Néstor Rodríguez (Austin: University of Texas Press, 2005), 278–301.

62. State Department to Embassy in Brazil, 25 December 1968, *FRUS, 1964–1968* 31: 534–37; Rabe, *Most Dangerous Area*, 70.

63. Martha K. Huggins, *Political Policing: The United States and Latin America* (Durham: Duke University Press, 1998), 99–204; Jeremy Kuzmarov, "Modernizing Repression: Police Training, Political Violence, and Nation-Building in the 'American Century,'" *Diplomatic History* 33 (April 2009): 199–209; Gould, "Solidarity under Siege," 372.

64. Huggins, *Political Policing*, 166–67.

65. Joan Dassin, ed., *Torture in Brazil: A Report by the Archdiocese of São Paulo*, Translated by Jaime Wright (New York: Vintage Books, 1986), xxv–xxvi.

CHAPTER 6

1. Remarks to news media executives, Kansas City, Missouri, 6 July 1971, *PPP: Richard Nixon, 1971*.

2. Conversation between Nixon, MacArthur and General Alexander Haig, 8 April 1971, *FRUS, 1969–1976* E-4: *Documents on Iran and Iraq, 1969–1972* (Washington: Government Printing Office, 2006): document 122. Professor Douglas Little of Clark University alerted me to this conversation.

3. Nixon conversation with Finch, 30 September 1971, *FRUS, 1969–1976* E-10: document 50.

4. Robert Dallek, *Nixon and Kissinger: Partners in Power* (New York: HarperCollins, 2007), 227.

5. National Security Study Memorandum (NSSM) 15, 3 February 1969, *FRUS, 1969–1976* E-10: document 1.

6. Nelson Rockefeller, *The Rockefeller Report on the Americas* (Chicago: Quadrangle Books, 1969).

7. Study prepared in response to NSSM 15, 5 July 1969, *FRUS, 1969–1976* E-10: document 4; minutes of NSC Review Group meeting, 9 October 1969, ibid, document 12; minutes of NSC meeting, 15 October 1969, ibid, document 14.

8. Vaky to Kissinger, 1 January 1970, ibid, document 21.

9. 31 October 1969 address, *DSB* (17 November 1969), 409–14.

10. Vaky to Kissinger, 1 January 1970, *FRUS, 1969–1976* E-10: document 21; Taffett, *Foreign Aid as Foreign Policy*, 185–94.

11. Memorandum from Finch to Nixon, undated but January 1971, *FRUS, 1969–1976* E-10: document 52.

12. Dallek, *Kissinger and Nixon*, 228–29; Seymour M. Hersh, *The Price of Power: Kissinger in the Nixon White House* (New York: Summit Books, 1983), 263; Mark Atwood Lawrence, "History from Below: The United States and Latin America in the Nixon Years," in *Nixon in the World: American Foreign Relations, 1969–1977*, ed. Fredrik Logevall and Andrew Preston (New York: Oxford University Press, 2008), 269–77.

13. Ibid, 269.

14. Nixon handwritten note on Kissinger memorandum to Nixon on economic aid to Latin America, 7 May 1969, *FRUS, 1969–1976* E-10: document 2; conversation between Nixon and Finch, 30 September 1971, ibid, document 50; Nixon to Connally, 6 June 1972, ibid, document 53.

15. Conversation between Nixon, Kissinger, Haldeman, Haig, and CIA Director Richard Helms, 5 March 1971, ibid, document 36.

16. Conversation between Nixon and Finch, 30 September 1971, ibid, document 50.

17. Conversation between Nixon, Kissinger, and Connally, 11 June 1971, ibid, document 43.

18. Rabe, *Eisenhower and Latin America*, 85–86.

19. Minutes of NSC meeting, 15 October 1969, *FRUS, 1969–1976* E-10: document 14.

20. Walters to Kissinger, undated but December 1968, ibid, document 116.

21. Kristian Gustafson, *Hostile Intent: U.S. Covert Operations in Chile, 1964–1974* (Washington: Potomac Books, 2007), 222–24; Jonathan Haslam, *The Nixon Administration and the Death of Allende's Chile: A Case of Assisted Suicide* (London, Verso, 2005), 219.

22. Walters to Kissinger, 3 November 1970, *FRUS, 1969–1976* E-10: document 30.

23. Official quoted is Viron Vaky in his covering memorandum contained in Kissinger to Nixon, 15 April 1970, ibid, document 127.

24. Memorandum of meeting between Nixon and Rountree, 14 December 1970, ibid, document 134.

25. Memorandum of meeting between Nixon and Brazilian president, 7 December 1971, ibid, document 141.

26. Memorandum of meeting between NSC and Brazilian president, 8 December 1971, ibid, document 141; Walters to Kissinger, undated but December 1971, ibid, document 144.

27. Memorandum of discussions between Nixon and Brazilian president, 9 December 1971, ibid, document 143. On Nixon's comment to Prime Minister Heath, see editorial

notes to memorandum from CIA Acting Director Robert E. Cushman, Jr. to Kissinger, 29 December 1971, ibid, document 145; Hal Brands, "Third World Politics in an Age of Global Turmoil: The Latin American Challenge to U.S. and Western Hegemony, 1965–1975," *Diplomatic History* 32 (January 2008): 130–31.

28. Memorandum of discussions between Nixon and Brazilian president, 9 December 1971, *FRUS, 1969–1976* E-10: document 143.
29. Taffett, *Foreign Aid as Foreign Policy*, 67–75.
30. Rabe, *Most Dangerous Area*, 109–16.
31. Taffett, *Foreign Aid as Foreign Policy*, 76–77.
32. Joseph John Jova, U.S. embassy in Santiago, to Assistant Secretary Mann on conversations with Frei, 5 May 1964, *FRUS, 1964–1968* 31: 568–70.
33. Rabe, *Most Dangerous Area*, 114–15.
34. Editorial note on memorandum by Peter Jessup of 303 Committee to NSC advisor Bundy, 23 July 1964, *FRUS, 1964–1968* 31: 582–83.
35. Haslam, *Nixon Administration and the Death of Chile*, 13–14.
36. Margaret Power, "The Engendering of Anticommunism and Fear in Chile's 1964 Presidential Election," *Diplomatic History* 32 (November 2008): 931–53.
37. CIA memorandum, "Chilean Election Forecast," 1 September 1964, *FRUS, 1964–1968* 31: 589–91.
38. Taffett, *Foreign Aid as Foreign Policy*, 81–93.
39. CIA headquarters to station in Santiago, 27 September 1970, in Peter Kornbluh, *The Pinochet File: A Declassified Dossier on Atrocity and Accountability* (New York: The New Press, 2003), 50–56.
40. Grow, *U.S. Presidents and Latin American Interventions*, 93, 98.
41. Kornbluh, *Pinochet File*, xvi–xvii.
42. Gustafson, *Hostile Intent*, 88–105.
43. Handwritten notes by Helms on meeting with Nixon, 15 September 1970, reproduced in Kornbluh, *Pinochet File*, 36.
44. Gustafson, *Hostile Intent*, 102; Dallek, *Nixon and Kissinger*, 231–32.
45. Minutes of 40 Committee meeting, 8 September 1970, in Kornbluh, *Pinochet File*, 45; conversation between Nixon and Kissinger, 11 June 1971, *FRUS, 1969–1976* E-10: document 42.
46. Lawrence, "History from Below," 277; Haslam, *Nixon Administration and the Death of Allende's Chile*, 55–56.
47. Conversation between Nixon and CIA Director Helms, 5 March 1971, *FRUS, 1969–1976* E-10: document 36.
48. Kornbluh, *Pinochet File*, 11–22.
49. Ibid, 22–35.
50. Dallek, *Nixon and Kissinger*, 236–38.
51. Gustafson, *Hostile Intent*, 140.
52. Nicola Miller, *Soviet Relations with Latin America, 1959–1987* (Cambridge: Cambridge University Press, 1989), 127–47.
53. Haslam, *Nixon Administration and the Death of Allende's Chile*, 79–157.
54. Memorandum of conversation of NSC meeting, 6 November 1970 and National Security Decision Memorandum 93, 9 November 1970, both in Kornbluh, *Pinochet File*, 116–23.
55. Dallek, *Nixon and Kissinger*, 239; Lawrence, "History from Below," 277.

56. U.S. Congress, Senate, Select Committee to Study Governmental Operations with Respect to Intelligence Activities, *Covert Action in Chile, 1963-1973*, 94th Congress, 1st session (Washington: Government Printing Office, 1975), 33-35; Kornbluh, *Pinochet File*, 84.

57. Kissinger quoted in Anand Toprani and Richard A. Moss, "Filling the Three-Year Gap: Nixon, Allende, and the White House Tapes, 1971-73," Unpublished paper, 2010 (in author's possession). The conversations took place in Nixon's hideaway office in the Executive Office Building on 6 April 1971 (Conversation No. 245-6) and in the Oval Office on 11 June 1971 (Conversation 517-4). I thank Professors Toprani and Moss for permitting me to read their research.

58. Senate Select Committee, *Covert Action in Chile*, 31; Haslam, *Nixon Administration and the Death of Allende's Chile*, 122-57, 130, 141, 193; Rabe, *U.S. Intervention in British Guiana*, 101, 113, 149-50.

59. CIA reports on Pinochet, 6 August 1971 and 27 September 1972, both in Kornbluh, *Pinochet File*, 134-37; Senate Select Committee, *Covert Action in Chile*, 34; Lesley Gill, *The School of the Americas: Military Training and Political Violence in the Americas* (Durham: Duke University Press, 2004), 79-80.

60. Haslam, *Nixon Administration and the Death of Allende's Chile*, 169-70, 182, 219.

61. *New York Times*, 28 May 2004; Dallek, *Nixon and Kissinger*, 511-12.

62. Ibid, 515.

63. Kornbluh, *Pinochet File*, 201-03.

64. Ibid, 203-6; Gill, *School of the Americas*, 79-80.

65. Thomas C. Wright, *State Terrorism in Latin America: Chile, Argentina, and International Human Rights* (Lanham, MD: Rowman & Littlefield, 2007), 65-66, 213; Luz Arce, *The Inferno: A Story of Terror and Survival in Chile*. Translated by Stacey Alba Skar (Madison: University of Wisconsin Press, 2004), 38-40. Mary Helen Spooner, *Soldiers in a Narrow Land: The Pinochet Regime in Chile* (Berkeley: University of California Press, 1999), 49-82.

66. Brian Loveman and Elizabeth Lira, "Truth, Justice, Reconciliation, and Impunity as Historical Themes: Chile, 1814-2006," *Radical History* 97 (Winter 2007): 61-70; Steve J. Stern, *Remembering Pinochet's Chile: On the Eve of London, 1998* (Durham: Duke University Press, 2004), xxi, 158-61.

67. Wright, *State Terrorism*, 59-61; Wright, *Latin America in the Era of the Cuban Revolution*, 158.

68. Wright, *State Terrorism*, 60-65; Jonathan Kandell, "Augusto Pinochet, 91, Dictator Who Ruled by Terror in Chile Dies," *New York Times*, 11 December 2006, 1, 27.

69. Wright, *State Terrorism*, 66.

70. John Dinges, *The Condor Years: How Pinochet and His Allies Brought Terrorism to Three Continents* (New York: The New Press, 2004), 10-125; McSherry, *Predatory States*.

71. John Dinges and Saul Landau, *Assassination on Embassy Row* (New York: Pantheon Books, 1980), 207-27.

72. Kornbluh, *Pinochet File*, 201-33.

73. Memorandum of conversation between Kissinger and Pinochet, 8 June 1976, in ibid, 256-65.

74. Ibid, 207-16; Wright, *State Terrorism*, 71-72.

75. Dinges, *Condor Years*, 184-98; McSherry, *Predatory States*, 107-08.

76. Memorandum from Haig to President Nixon on financial assistance for Argentina, 14 July 1971, *FRUS, 1969-1976* E-10: document 69; backchannel message from Ambassador John Davis Lodge to State Department, 31 August 1971, ibid, document 72.

77. Memorandum of conversation between Kissinger and Guzzetti, 10 June 1976, in Southern Cone Documentation Project of the National Security Archive, Washington, http://www.gwu.edu/~nsarchiv/NSAEBB/NSAEBB133/index.htm; Jeremi Suri, *Henry Kissinger and the American Century* (Cambridge, MA: Belknap Press of Harvard University, 2009), 239–42; Dinges, *Condor Years*, 199–206; Brands, "Third World Politics in an Age of Global Turmoil," 132.

78. Wright, *State Terrorism*, 99–118; Jacobo Timerman, *Prisoner without a Name, Cell without a Number*, translated by Tony Talbot (Madison: University of Wisconsin Press, 2002).

CHAPTER 7

1. Nobel Lecture, "The Solitude of Latin America," by Gabriel García Márquez, 8 December 1982, available at Web site: http://nobelprize.org/nobel_prizes/literature/laureates/1982/marquez-lecture-e.html.

2. Lars Schoultz, *Human Rights and United States Policy toward Latin America* (Princeton: Princeton University Press, 1981), 179–80.

3. Ibid, 113–15; David F. Schmitz and Vanessa Walker, "Jimmy Carter and the Foreign Policy of Human Rights: The Development of a Post–Cold War Foreign Policy," *Diplomatic History* 28 (January 2004): 113–43.

4. Kathryn Sikkink, *Mixed Signals: U.S. Human Rights Policy and Latin America* (Ithaca: Cornell University Press, 2004), 106–22. For a report on Elida Messina's abduction, see telegram, Ambassador Hill to State Department, 27 May 1976, on Web site http://www.desclasificados.com.ar/index.php?ref=http://www.desclasificados.com.ar/i.php?i=4447.

5. Sikkink, *Mixed Signals*, 122–47; Schoultz, *Human Rights*, 172, 214–15.

6. Wright, *State Terrorism*, 118–25; Sikkink, *Mixed Signals*, 80–105, 121–47; Schoultz, *Human Rights*, 363; Timerman, *Prisoner without a Name*.

7. Schoultz, *Human Rights*, 112, 116–17, Sikkink, *Mixed Signals*, 132–34.

8. William H. Durham, *Scarcity and Survival in Central America: Ecological Origins of the Soccer War* (Stanford: Stanford University Press, 1979), 21–62, 159–73; Robert G. Williams, *Export Agriculture and the Crisis in Central America* (Chapel Hill: University of North Carolina Press, 1986), 77, 99, 155–65; Rabe, *Most Dangerous Area*, 157–60.

9. Gill, *School of the Americas*, 75–78.

10. Wright, *State Terrorism*, 117–18.

11. Walter LaFeber, *Inevitable Revolutions: The United States in Central America* (New York: W.W. Norton, 1983), 219–26, 250–52; Edward T. Brett, *The U.S. Catholic Press on Central America: From Cold War Anticommunism to Social Justice* (Notre Dame, IN: University of Notre Dame Press, 2003), 35–122.

12. Cole Blasier, *The Giant's Rival: The USSR and Latin America*, rev. ed. (Pittsburgh: University of Pittsburgh Press, 1987), 140.

13. Anastasio Somoza, as told to Jack Cox, *Nicaragua Betrayed* (Boston: Western Islands, 1980).

14. Letter to Pope John Paul II, quoted in John A. Soares, Jr., "Strategy, Ideology, and Human Rights: Jimmy Carter Confronts the Left in Central America, 1979-1981," *Journal of Cold War Studies* 8 (Fall 2006): 66.

15. Robert A. Pastor, *Condemned to Repetition: The United States and Nicaragua* (Princeton: Princeton University Press, 1987), 79.

16. News conference, 25 July 1979, *PPP: Jimmy Carter, 1979*, 1307.

17. Soares, "Strategy, Ideology, and Human Rights," 71–77, 89–91; Schmitz and Walker, "Jimmy Carter and the Foreign Policy of Human Rights," 141–43.

18. Wright, *Latin America in the Era of the Cuban Revolution*, 183.

19. Ibid, 180–83; Laura J. Enríquez, *Harvesting Change: Labor and Agrarian Reform in Nicaragua, 1979–1990* (Chapel Hill: University of North Carolina Press, 1991), 83–120; Pastor, *Condemned to Repetition*, 6.

20. Ilja A. Luciak, "Democracy and Revolution in Nicaragua," in *Understanding the Central American Crisis: Sources of Conflict, U.S. Policy, and Options for Peace*, ed. Kenneth M. Coleman and George C. Herring (Wilmington, DE: SR Books, 1991), 77–107; Wright, *Latin America in the Era of the Cuban Revolution*, 177–83.

21. Blasier, *The Giant's Rival*, 144–53; Nicola Miller, *Soviet Relations with Latin America, 1959–1987* (Cambridge: Cambridge University Press, 1989), 188–216.

22. The Committee of Santa Fe, *A New Inter-American Policy for the Eighties* (Washington: Council for Inter-American Security, 1980), 52–53.

23. Jeane J. Kirkpatrick, *Dictatorships and Double Standards: Rationalism and Reason in Politics* (New York: American Enterprise Institute and Simon & Schuster, 1982), 23–52; William M. LeoGrande, *Our Own Backyard: The United States in Central America, 1977–1992* (Chapel Hill: University of North Carolina Press, 1998), 291; Greg Grandin, *Empire's Workshop: Latin America, the United States, and the Rise of the New Imperialism* (New York: Henry Holt, 2007), 69–86.

24. Sikkink, *Mixed Signals*, 152–55; LeoGrande, *Our Own Backyard*, 292.

25. Schoultz, *That Infernal Little Cuban Republic*, 366–69.

26. Ronald Reagan, *An American Life* (New York: Simon & Schuster, 1990), 266–67; Grow *U.S. Presidents and Latin American Interventions*, 125.

27. LeoGrande, *Our Own Backyard*, 283; Grow *U.S. Presidents and Latin American Interventions*, 125–28.

28. *PPP: Ronald Reagan, 1983*, 605–07.

29. LeoGrande, *Our Own Backyard*, 444.

30. Ibid, 77–80.

31. Carothers, *In the Name of Democracy*, 82–84; LeoGrande, *Our Own Backyard*, 86–88, 106–09.

32. *PPP: Ronald Reagan, 1985* I: 200; Carothers, *In the Name of Democracy*, 97–98.

33. LeoGrande, *Our Own Backyard*, 116, 143–46; Ariel C. Armony, "Transnationalizing the Dirty War: Argentina in Central America," in *In from the Cold*, ed. Joseph and Spenser, 134–68.

34. "Execution in the Jungle," *Newsweek*, 29 April, 1985; LeoGrande, *Our Own Backyard*, 413–16.

35. LeoGrande, *Our Own Backyard*, 429–31, 442, 449.

36. Bob Woodward, *Veil: The Secret Wars of the CIA, 1981–1987* (New York: Simon & Schuster, 1987), 281–81, 320–38.

37. For excerpts of the *Freedom Fighter's Manual* and the International Court of Justice's ruling, see Holden and Zolov, eds., *Latin America and the United States*, 297–303; LeoGrande, *Our Own Backyard*, 363–64.

38. Jennifer H. Lundquist and Douglas Massey, "Politics or Economics? International Migration during the Nicaraguan Contra War," *Journal of Latin American Studies* 37 (February 2005): 29–53.

39. LeoGrande, *Our Own Backyard*, 391–93. For data on U.S. military and economic aid to Central America, see John A. Booth, "Central America and the United States: Cycles of Containment and Response," in *United States Policy in Latin America: A Decade of Crisis and Challenge*, ed. John D. Martz (Lincoln: University of Nebraska Press, 1995), 191–92.

40. Blasier, *The Giant's Rival*, 143.

41. Miller, *Soviet Relations with Latin America*, 188–216.

42. Robert A. Pastor, "George Bush and Latin America: The Pragmatic Style and the Regionalist Option," in *Eagle in a New World: American Grand Strategy in the Post-Cold War Era*, ed. Kenneth A. Oye, Robert J. Lieber, and Donald Rothchild (New York: HarperCollins Publishers, 1992), 361–71; Carothers, *In the Name of Democracy*, 92–95; LeoGrande, *Our Own Backyard*, 560–61.

43. Carothers, *In the Name of Democracy*, 107.

44. Grandin, *Empire's Workshop*, 95–96, 103; Aldo A. Lauria-Santiago, "The Culture and Politics of State Terror and Repression in El Salvador," in *When States Kill*, ed. Menjívar and Rodríguez, 97.

45. LeoGrande, *Our Own Backyard*, 38–71, 166–67.

46. Ibid, 63–64; Carothers, *In the Name of Democracy*, 22, 266 n. 9.

47. LeoGrande, *Our Own Backyard*, 178–80, 195.

48. Carothers, *In the Name of Democracy*, 16; LeoGrande, *Our Own Backyard*, 147.

49. Booth, "Central America and the United States," 191–92, 200–01; LeoGrande, *Our Own Backyard*, 265–66.

50. *Report of the UN Truth Commission on El Salvador*, 1 April 1993, in http://www.aprodeh.org.pe/desc/documentos_unctad/equipo_Nizkor.pdf.

51. LeoGrande, *Our Own Backyard*, 234.

52. Joan Didion, *Salvador* (New York: Simon & Schuster, 1983), 13–19; Lauria-Santiago, "Culture and Politics of State Terror," 98–100.

53. Danner, *Massacre at El Mozote*, 3–84.

54. Ibid, 110–39.

55. Didion, *Salvador*, 95.

56. Carothers, *In the Name of Democracy*, 30–43; LeoGrande, *Our Own Backyard*, 160, 249–50.

57. Ibid, 215.

58. Didion, *Salvador*, 90–95.

59. McPherson, *Intimate Ties, Bitter Struggles*, 101.

60. *Report of Truth Commission: Commission for Historical Clarification*, February 1999, in http://shr.aaas.org/guatemala/ceh/report/english/toc.html.

61. Ibid; M. Gabriela Torres, "Bloody Deeds/*Hechos Sangrientos*: Reading Guatemala's Record of Political Violence in Cadaver Reports," in *When States Kill*, ed. Menjívar and Rodríguez, 143–69; Daniel Wilkinson, *Silence on the Mountain: Stories of Terror, Betrayal, and Forgetting in Guatemala* (Boston: Houghton Mifflin, 2002), 210, 310, 327–28; Daniel Jonah Goldhagen, *Worse than War: Genocide, Eliminationism, and the Ongoing Assault on Humanity* (New York: Public Affairs, 2009), 179, 181, 336–37, 431, 469–70.

62. Sikkink, *Mixed Signals*, 159–61; Carothers, *In the Name of Democracy*, 61–63; Wilkinson, *Silence on the Mountain*, 328; Jacobs quoted in his 5 October 1981 memorandum, "Guatemala: What Next?" Memorandum can be found as Document 18 on the

National Security Archives Web site on the "Guatemalan Military: What the U.S. Files Reveal," Volume 2, Documents: http://www.gwu.edu/~nsarchiv/NSAEBB/NSAEBB32/vol2.html.

63. Sikkink, *Mixed Signals*, 164.

64. 4 December 1982, *PPP: Ronald Reagan, 1982* II: 1562–66; Wilkinson, *Silence on the Mountain*, 327.

65. Ibid, 327–28; *Report of Truth Commission: Commission for Historical Clarification* in http://shr.aaas.org/guatemala/ceh/report/english/toc.html.

66. Sikkink, *Mixed Signals*, 168.

67. Carlos Fuentes, "Land of Jekyll and Hyde, "*The Nation* 242 (22 March 1986): 334–37. Alan McPherson in *Intimate Ties, Bitter Struggles*, 99, pointed me to this essay. For the impact of the Cold War on the thinking and writing of Latin America's major literary figures, see Jean Franco, *The Decline and Fall of the Lettered City: Latin America in the Cold War* (Cambridge: Harvard University Press, 2002).

AFTERMATH

1. For an English translation, see *Nunca Más: The Report of the National Commission of the Disappeared*, with an introduction by Ronald Dworkin (New York: Farrar Straus Giroux, 1986).

2. For a critical review of the reports, see Greg Grandin, "The Instruction of a Great Catastrophe: Truth Commissions, National History, and State Formation in Argentina, Chile, and Guatemala," *American Historical Review* 110 (February 2005): 46–67.

3. Dassin, ed., *Torture in Brazil*, ix–ixx.

4. Wright, *State Terrorism*, 141–51; Danner, *Massacre at El Mozote*, 155–61.

5. Marguerite Feitlowitz, *A Lexicon of Terror: Argentina and the Legacies of Torture* (New York: Oxford University Press, 1998), 79–81, 193–255; Wright, *State Terrorism*, 151–69.

6. Silvia Borzutzky, "The Politics of Impunity: The Cold War, State Terror, Trauma, Trials and Reparations in Argentina and Chile," *Latin America Research Review* 42 (February 2007): 167–85.

7. *New York Times*, 17 September 2007, A4; ibid, 10 October 2007, A5; Feitlowitz, *Lexicon of Terror*, 219–23.

8. Borzutzky, "Politics of Impunity," 180. For the Astiz case, see Rosenberg, *Children of Cain*, 95–106, 140–41 and "Former Argentine Navy Officer to Be Tried in Torture Deaths," *New York Times*, 13 December 2009, A13.

9. The *abuelas* (grandmothers) of the Plaza de Mayo have a Web site: http://www.abuelas.org.ar/english/history.htm.

10. Roger Cohen, "Lost Children, Lost Truths," *New York Times*, 13 January 2008.

11. Carothers, *In the Name of Democracy*, 150–63; Morris Morley and Chris McGillon, "Soldiering on: The Reagan Administration and Redemocratisation in Chile, 1983–1986," *Bulletin of Latin American Research* 25 (January 2006): 1–22.

12. Brian Loveman and Elizabeth Lira, "Truth, Justice, Reconciliation, and Impunity as Historical Themes: Chile, 1814–2006," *Radical History Review* 97 (Winter 2007): 61–64.

13. Wright, *State Terrorism*, 212.

14. "Chile's Leader Attacks Amnesty for Pinochet-Era Crimes," *New York Times*, 24 December 2006, A3; Antonius C.G.M. Robben, "State Terror in the Netherworld: Disappearance and Reburial in Argentina," in *Death, Mourning and Burial: A*

Cross-Cultural Reader, edited Antonius C.G.M. Robben (Malden, MA: Blackwell Publishing, 2004), 134–48.

15. Loveman and Lira, "Truth, Justice, Reconciliation," 66–68.

16. Stern, *Remembering Pinochet's Chile*, 134–42.

17. An English translation of the conclusion of *Memory of Silence* can be found at the Web site http://shr.aaas.org/guatemala/ceh/report/english/toc.html; Elizabeth Oglesby, "Educating Citizens in Postwar Guatemala: Historical Memory, Genocide, and the Culture of Peace," *Radical History Review* 97 (Winter 2007): 77–98.

18. For Bishop Gerardi's murder, see *Francisco Goldman, The Art of Political Murder: Who Killed the Bishop?* (New York: Grove Press, 2008).

19. *New York Times*, 22 May 2009, A4; Elisabeth Malkin, "Political Struggle Lays Bare the Frailty of Guatemala's Justice System Experiment," ibid, 4 July 2010, 4; Goldhagen, *Worse than War*, 582–85. For Rigoberta Menchú's famous account of her life and the terror in Guatemala, see *I, Rigoberta Menchú: An Indian Woman in Guatemala*, edited and introduced by Elisabeth Burgos-Debray, translated by Ann Wright (London: Verso: 1984).

20. Wright, *State Terrorism*, 187–88.

21. The United Nations has a useful Web site for the Human Development Index: http://hdr.undp.org/en/statistics/.

22. Wright, *Latin America in the Era of the Cuban Revolution*, 187. For a discussion of the symbolic power of Che Guevara in contemporary life, see Michael Casey, *Che's Afterlife: The Legacy of an Image* (New York: Vintage Books, 2009).

23. Rabe, *U.S. Intervention in British Guiana*, 75–173.

24. Clinton quoted in Sikkink, *Mixed Signals*, 181; David Scott Palmer, *U.S. Relations with Latin America during the Clinton Years* (Gainesville: University Press of Florida, 2006), 30; Powell quoted in *New York Times*, February 25 February, 2003, A10.

25. Christoper Hitchens, *The Trial of Henry Kissinger* (London: Verso, 2001).

26. "A Door Opens for Legal Actions in Chilean Coup, Kissinger Is Numbered among the Hunted," *New York Times*, 28 March 2002, A10.

27. Sikkink, *Mixed Signals*, 202–05.

28. Daniel P. Erikson, *The Cuba Wars: Fidel Castro, the United States, and the Next Revolution* (New York: Bloomsbury Press, 2008), 176–83; "Venezuela Will Push U.S. to Hand Over Man Tied to Plane Bombing," *New York Times*, 23 January 2009, A5.

29. "Cuba: Dissidents Support U.S. Bill," *New York Times*, 11 June 2010, A10; Marc Lacey, "Cuba Releases Five Prisoners and Promises to Free More," *New York Times*, 8 July 2010, A12.

30. Schoultz, *That Infernal Little Cuban Republic*, 419–567; Erikson, *Cuba Wars*, 27–53.

31. McPherson, *Intimate Ties, Bitter Struggles*, 110; Human Development Index: http://hdr.undp.org/en/statistics/; "Elections in El Salvador Invoke Rivalries of Civil War Years," *New York Times*, 12 March 2009, A6.

32. John Dinges, *Our Man in Panama: The Shrewd Rise and Brutal Fall of Manuel Noriega* (New York: Random House, 1991); Sikkink, *Mixed Signals*, 183–84; David Jolly, "French Court Sentences Noriega to 7 Years," *New York Times*, 8 July 2010, A12.

33. Stephen G. Rabe, "The U.S. Intervention in Guatemala: The Documentary Record," *Diplomatic History* 28 (November 2004): 785–90.

34. Thomas S. Blanton, "Recovering the Memory of the Cold War: Forensic History and Latin America," in *In from the Cold*, ed. Joseph and Spencer, 47–73.

35. CIA "Family Jewels" Project on Freedom of Information Act (FOIA) Web site: http://www.foia.cia.gov.

36. "Memos Show Nixon's Bid to Enlist Brazil in Coup," *New York Times*, 17 August 2009, A7; ibid, 19 August 2009, A9.

37. Gilbert M. Joseph, "What We Know and Should Know: Bringing Latin America More Meaningfully into Cold War Studies," in *In from the Cold War*, ed. Joseph and Spenser, 3–46.

38. *Guatemala: Memory of Silence*, on Web site: http://shr.aaas.org/guatemala/ceh/report/english/toc.html. See also Borzutzky, "Politics of Impunity," 184; Sikkink, *Mixed Signals*, 204; Cecilia Menjívar and Néstor Rodríguez, "State Terror in the U.S.–Latin American Interstate Regime," in *When States Kill*, ed. Menjívar and Rodríguez, 3–22.

39. The Physicians for Human Rights have a Web site: http://physiciansforhumanrights.org/forensic/pro-busqueda.html

Recommendations for Further Reading and Research

First off, if you are interested in pursuing any of the topics or issues raised in my study on U.S. policies toward Latin America during the Cold War, you can contact me by either writing or sending me an Email inquiry. I have been offering bibliographic advice to colleagues, students, and citizens for over thirty years now. I do not consider this an imposition. It is my job.

Stephen G. Rabe
Arts and Humanities Endowed Chair
MS JO 31
University of Texas at Dallas
800 West Campbell Road
Richardson, TX 75080
USA
Email: rabe@utdallas.edu

What I have included here is a select list of recommendations for further reading. I have chosen what I consider the freshest and most accessible and compelling books. I have not included articles, although you can find many articles cited in the footnotes. On the assumption that most readers of *The Killing Zone* are relatively new to the fields of U.S. foreign relations, inter-American relations, and Latin American history, I have limited the citations to secondary sources and to books in English. After offering sections on "Bibliographic Guides and General Interpretations" and then "Cold War History," I list and comment on works by the chapter sequence in the book.

BIBLIOGRAPHIC GUIDES AND GENERAL INTERPRETATIONS

In order of date of publication, the following bibliographies, documentary collections, and encyclopedias introduce one to the vast literature on U.S. foreign relations and inter-American relations.

Robert L. Beisner, ed. *American Foreign Relations since 1600: A Guide to the Literature.* 2nd ed. 2 vols. Santa Barbara, CA: ABC-Clio, 2003. This great bibliography has been updated since 2006. Your library may have access to the updated online version. If not, contact: http://ebooks.abc-clio.com/main.aspx?isbn=9781851099504&webSiteCode= EBOOKS_PROD

See also:

Robert Holden and Eric Zolov, eds. *Latin America and the United States: A Documentary History.* New York: Oxford University Press, 2000.

Bruce W. Jentleson and Thomas G. Paterson, eds. *Encyclopedia of U.S. Foreign Relations.* 4 vols. New York: Oxford University Press, 1997.

Richard Dean Burns, ed. *Guide to American Foreign Relations since 1700.* Santa Barbara, CA: ABC-Clio, 1983.

Michael Meyer, ed. *Supplement to a Bibliography of United States–Latin American Relations since 1810.* Lincoln: University of Nebraska Press, 1979.

David F. Trask, et al., eds. *A Bibliography of United States–Latin American Relations since 1810.* Lincoln: University of Nebraska Press, 1968.

Beyond providing factual information, textbooks and surveys can be excellent sources for bibliographic advice. The following textbooks are by scholars whose primary training was in Latin American studies.

Brian Loveman. *American Foreign Policy and the Western Hemisphere since 1776.* Chapel Hill: University of North Carolina Press, 2010.

Thomas E. Skidmore, Peter H. Smith, and James N. Green. *Modern Latin America.* 7th ed. New York: Oxford University Press, 2009.

Gregory Weeks. *U.S. and Latin American Relations.* New York: Pearson Education, 2008.

Thomas F. O'Brien. *Making the Americas: The United States and Latin America from the Age of Revolutions to the Era of Globalization.* Albuquerque: University of New Mexico Press, 2007.

Peter H. Smith. *Talons of the Eagle: The United States, Latin America, and the World.* 3rd ed. New York: Oxford University Press, 2007.

Don M. Coerver and Linda B. Hall. *Tangled Destinies: Latin America and the United States.* Albuquerque: University of New Mexico Press, 1999.

Lars Schoultz. *Beneath the United States: A History of U.S. Policy toward Latin America.* Cambridge, MA: Harvard University Press, 1997.

John H. Coatsworth. *Central America and the United States: The Colossus and the Clients.* New York: Twayne, 1997.

These textbook and survey authors received their training primarily in the field of U.S. foreign relations or U.S. foreign policy.

Lester D. Langley. *America and the Americas: The United States in the Western Hemisphere.* 2nd ed. Athens: University of Georgia Press, 2010.

Kyle Longley. *In the Eagle's Shadow: The United States and Latin America.* 2nd ed. Wheeling, IL: Harlan Davidson, 2009.

Mark T. Gilderhus. *The Second Century: U.S.–Latin American Relations since 1889.* Wilmington, DE: Scholarly Resources, 2000.

Walter LaFeber. *Inevitable Revolutions: The United States in Central America*. 2nd rev. ed. New York: W.W. Norton, 1993.

Thomas M. Leonard. *Central America and the United States: The Search for Stability*. Athens: University of Georgia Press, 1991.

Harold Molineu. *U.S. Policy toward Latin America: From Regionalism to Globalism*. Boulder, CO: Westview Press, 1986.

Major journals review books and note articles recently published in the field of U.S. relations with Latin America. One should consult the *Hispanic American Historical Review*, the *Journal of Latin American Studies*, the *Latin American Research Review*, the *Journal of Latin American Studies and World Affairs*, the *American Historical Review*, and the *Journal of American History*, among others.

The leading journal for historians of U.S. foreign relations is *Diplomatic History*. The Society for Historians of American Foreign Relations (SHAFR) publishes the journal and offers members a variety of valuable educational and research services. Membership costs are modest for all, especially students. SHAFR's Web site is www.shafr.org. Many of the books reviewed and articles published in *Diplomatic History* are debated on the Web site H-DIPLO (http://www.h-net.org/~diplo/).

COLD WAR HISTORY

The literature on the history of the Soviet–American confrontation, the Cold War, is vast. I have been influenced by the following overviews, which ask hard questions about policies pursued by both sides. John L. Gaddis, the author of the last book listed, is often identified as one who primarily blames the Soviet Union for the tragedies of the Cold War. Gaddis concedes, however, that the West victimized some people in the Western Hemisphere, such as the people of British Guiana (Guyana).

Walter LaFeber. *America, Russia, and the Cold War, 1945–2006*. 10th ed. New York: McGraw Hill, 2006.

Melvyn P. Leffler. *For the Soul of Mankind: The United States, the Soviet Union, and the Cold War*. New York: Hill & Wang, 2008.

Thomas G. Paterson. *On Every Front: The Making and Unmaking of the Cold War*. Rev. ed. New York: W. W. Norton, 1993.

Odd Arne Westad. *The Global Cold War: Third World Interventions and the Making of the Cold War*. Cambridge, UK: Cambridge University Press, 2005.

John L. Gaddis. *We Now Know: Rethinking Cold War History*. New York: Oxford University Press, 1998.

The following books provide overviews of U.S. policies toward Latin America and developments in Latin America during the Cold War from a variety of perspectives.

Michael Grow. *U.S. Presidents and Latin American Interventions: Pursuing Regime Change in the Cold War*. Lawrence: University Press of Kansas, 2008.

Gil Joseph and Daniela Spenser, eds. *In from the Cold: Latin America's New Encounter with the Cold War*. Durham: Duke University Press, 2008.

Alan McPherson. *Intimate Ties, Bitter Struggles: The United States and Latin America since 1945*. Washington, DC: Potomac Books, 2006.

Gaddis Smith. *The Last Years of the Monroe Doctrine, 1945–1993*. New York: Hill & Wang, 1994.

Thomas C. Wright. *Latin America in the Era of the Cuban Revolution*. Rev. ed. New York: Praeger, 2000.

CHAPTER 1: ROOTS OF COLD WAR INTERVENTIONS

This chapter explores four major topics: U.S. attitudes toward Latin Americans in the nineteenth and early twentieth centuries; the course, conduct, and impact of U.S. interventions in the Caribbean and Central America; the development of the Good Neighbor policy; and wartime developments. Books than enlightened me on perceptions of Latin American thought, society, and culture by U.S. citizens and policy makers include those listed below.

Michael H. Hunt. *Ideology and U.S. Foreign Policy*. New Haven: Yale University Press, 1987.

John J. Johnson. *Latin America in Caricature*. Austin: University of Texas Press, 1980.

James William Park. *Latin American Underdevelopment: A History of Perspectives in the United States*. Baton Rouge: Louisiana State University Press, 1995.

Louis A. Pérez, Jr. *Cuba in the American Imagination: Metaphor and the Imperial Ethos*. Chapel Hill: University of North Carolina Press, 2008.

Historians have been very busy over the past decades probing the meaning of U.S. interventions in Latin America during the first part of the twentieth century. A good place to start would be with the following books. The studies by Bruce Calder and Hans Schmidt are especially strong.

Bruce J. Calder. *The Impact of Intervention: The Dominican Republic during the U.S. Occupation, 1916–1924*. Austin: University of Texas Press, 1984.

Paul W. Drake, ed. *Money Doctors, Foreign Debts, and Economic Reforms in Latin America from the 1890s to the Present*. Wilmington, DE: Scholarly Resources, 1994.

David F. Healy. *Drive to Hegemony: The United States in the Caribbean, 1898–1917*. Madison: University of Wisconsin Press, 1988.

Walter LaFeber. *The Panama Canal: The Crisis in Historical Perspective*. Updated ed. New York: Oxford University Press, 1989.

Lester D. Langley. *The Banana Wars: An Inner History of American Empire, 1900–1934*. Lexington: University of Kentucky Press, 1983.

Louis A. Pérez, Jr. *Cuba under the Platt Amendment, 1902–1934*. Pittsburgh: University of Pittsburgh Press, 1986.

Louis A. Pérez, Jr. *The War of 1898: The United States and Cuba in History and Historiography*. Chapel Hill: University of North Carolina Press, 1998.

Stephen G. Rabe. *The Road to OPEC: United States Relations with Venezuela, 1919–1976*. Austin: University of Texas Press, 1982.

Mary A. Renda. *Taking Haiti: Military Occupation and the Culture of Imperialism, 1915–1940*. Chapel Hill: University of North Carolina Press, 2001.

Hans Schmidt. *The United States Occupation of Haiti, 1915–1934*. New Brunswick, NJ: Rutgers University Press, 1995.

On the Good Neighbor policy and the policy of non-intervention, the following books would be a good place to start. Bryce Woods wrote the classic study.

Fredrick B. Pike. *FDR's Good Neighbor Policy: Sixty Years of Generally Gentle Chaos*. Austin: University of Texas Press, 1995.

Eric Paul Rooda. *The Dictator Next Door: The Good Neighbor Policy and the Trujillo Regime in the Dominican Republic, 1930–1945*. Durham: Duke University Press, 1998.

David F. Schmitz. *Thank God They're on Our Side: The United States and Right-Wing Dictatorships, 1921–1965*. Chapel Hill: University of North Carolina Press, 1999.

Bryce Wood. *The Making of the Good Neighbor Policy*. New York: W. W. Norton, 1961.

During World War II, the United States developed a global perspective and altered its view of the significance of relations with Latin America and other Western Hemisphere nations. Major political and socioeconomic changes marked Latin America during the war.

Leslie Bethell and Ian Roxborough, eds. *Latin American between the Second World War and the Cold War, 1944–1948*. Cambridge: Cambridge University Press, 2002.

Michael J. Francis. *The Limits of Hegemony: United States Relations with Argentina and Chile during World War II*. Notre Dame, IN: University of Notre Dame Press, 1977.

Max Paul Friedman. *Nazis and Good Neighbors: The United States Campaign against the Germans of Latin America in World War II*. New York: Cambridge University Press, 2003.

Thomas M. Leonard and James F.Bratzel, eds. *Latin America during World War II*. Lanham, MD: Rowman & Littlefield, 2007.

Harvey R. Neptune. *Caliban and the Yankees: Trinidad and the United States Occupation*. Chapel Hill: University of North Carolina Press, 2007.

CHAPTER 2: THE KENNAN COROLLARY

There has not been extensive work on U.S. relations with Latin America during the early Cold War and the Harry S. Truman administration. Many of the authors already listed—Gaddis Smith, Leslie Bethell, and Ian Roxborough, for examples—cover the period. Steven Schwartzberg is an author who has focused on the Truman administration. But his study does not always ask hard, analytic questions, and he largely ignores the Truman administration's plans to destabilize Guatemala. Bryce Woods sees a dramatic change in the U.S. approach to Latin America from President Franklin Roosevelt to Truman and then President Dwight Eisenhower.

Bradley Lynn Coleman. *Colombia and the United States: The Making of an Inter-American Alliance*. Kent, OH: Kent State University Press, 2008.

Gerald K. Haines. *The Americanization of Brazil: A Study of U.S. Cold War Diplomacy in the Third World, 1945–1954*. Wilmington, DE: Scholarly Resources, 1989.

Steven Schwartzberg. *Democracy and U.S. Policy in Latin America during the Truman Years*. Gainesville: University of Florida Press, 2003.

Bryce Wood. *The Dismantling of the Good Neighbor Policy*. Austin: University of Texas Press, 1985.

CHAPTER 3: GUATEMALA—THE MOTHER OF INTERVENTIONS

Students, the educated public, and scholars have available to them a very complete record of the U.S. intervention in Guatemala. I have listed the major studies as they appeared. Over time, the records of the intervention in Guatemala were declassified by various agencies of the U.S. government.

Stephen Schlesinger and Stephen Kinzer. *Bitter Fruit: The Untold Story of the American Coup in Guatemala*. Garden City, NY: Anchor Books, 1982.
Richard H. Immerman. The *CIA in Guatemala: The Foreign Policy of Intervention*. Austin: University of Texas Press, 1982.
Piero Gleijeses. *Shattered Hope: The Guatemalan Revolution and the United States, 1944–1954*. Princeton: Princeton University Press, 1991.
Nick Cullather. *Secret History: The CIA's Classified Account of Its Operations in Guatemala, 1952–1954*. Stanford: Stanford University Press, 1999.

It is also necessary to analyze the U.S. intervention in Guatemala from a Guatemalan perspective and to explore what happened to Guatemala after the overthrow of the constitutional government.

Greg Grandin. *The Last Colonial Massacre: Latin America in the Cold War*. Chicago: University of Chicago Press, 2004.
Jim Handy. *Revolution in the Countryside: Rural Conflict and Agrarian Reform in Guatemala, 1944–1954*. Chapel Hill: University of North Carolina Press, 1994.
Stephen M. Streeter. *Managing the Counterrevolution: The United States and Guatemala, 1954–1961*. Athens: University of Ohio Press, 2000.

President Eisenhower's approach to Latin American nations other than Guatemala can be pursued in the works listed below.

Michael D. Gambone, *Eisenhower, Somoza, and the Cold War in Nicaragua, 1953–1961*. Westport, CT: Praeger, 1997.
Stephen G. Rabe. *Eisenhower and Latin America: The Foreign Policy of Anticommunism*. Chapel Hill: University of North Carolina Press, 1988.

After the overthrow of President Arbenz, U.S. investigators searched in vain for connections between Guatemalan leftists and the Soviet Union. Scholars who have analyzed the Soviet Union's policies in Latin America have noted that the Soviet Union played a minimal role in the region other than its alliance with Fidel Castro's Cuba.

Cole Blasier. *The Giant's Rival: The USSR and Latin America*. Rev. ed. Pittsburgh: University of Pittsburgh Press, 1987.
Nicola Miller. *Soviet Relations with Latin America, 1959–1987*. Cambridge, UK: Cambridge University Press, 1989.
Ilya Prizel. *Latin America through Soviet Eyes: The Evolution of Soviet Perceptions during the Brezhnev Era, 1964–1982*. Cambridge, UK: Cambridge University Press, 1990.

CHAPTER 4: WAR AGAINST CUBA

U.S. officials and citizens have been obsessed with Fidel Castro and the Cuban Revolution for more than fifty years. The literature on Cuba and its leader is predictably voluminous. The books listed below are a good place start on the origins of the Cuban Revolution.

Samuel Farber. *The Origins of the Cuban Revolution Reconsidered*. Chapel Hill: University of North Carolina Press, 2006.

Ramón Eduardo Ruiz. *Cuba: The Making of a Revolution*. New York: W. W. Norton, 1970.

Hugh Thomas. *Cuba: The Pursuit of Freedom*. New York: Harper & Row, 1971.

It is difficult to find a balanced study of Fidel Castro. The studies by Quirk and Szulc are quite critical of the Cuban revolutionary, whereas the interviews conducted by Lockwood are favorable toward Castro.

Lee Lockwood. *Castro's Cuba, Cuba's Fidel*. New York: Vintage, 1969.

Robert E. Quirk. *Fidel Castro*. New York: W. W. Norton, 1993.

Tad Szulc. *Fidel: A Critical Portrait*. New York: Morrow, 1986.

Compared to studies on Fidel Castro, biographies on Ernesto "Che" Guevara are more nuanced and analytical.

Jon Lee Anderson, *Che Guevara: A Revolutionary Life*. New York: Grove Press, 1997.

Jorge C. Castañeda. *Compañero: The Life and Death of Che Guevara*. Translated by Marina Castañeda. New York: Knopf, 1997.

Paul J. Dosal, *Commandante Che: Guerrilla Soldier, Commander, and Strategist, 1956–1967*. University Park: Pennsylvania State University Press, 2003.

Revolutionary Cuba allied with the Soviet Union during the Cold War. But Cuba's relationship with the Communist superpower was often strained.

James G. Blight and Philip Brenner. *Sad and Luminous Days: Cuba's Struggle with the Superpowers after the Missile Crisis*. Lanham, MD: Rowman & Littlefield, 2007.

Piero Gleijeses. *Conflicting Missions: Havana, Washington, and Africa, 1959–1976*. Chapel Hill: University of North Carolina Press, 2002.

On the perpetual U.S. war against revolutionary Cuba, the best place to start is with Lars Schoultz's massive history. I thereafter list major works in the order of key events: opposition to Castro in the 1950s; the Bay of Pigs; Operation Mongoose; the Cuban Missile Crisis; the hunt for Che Guevara; and post-1960s relations.

Lars Schoultz. *That Infernal Little Cuban Republic: The United States and the Cuban Revolution*. Chapel Hill: University of North Carolina Press, 2009.

Thomas G. Paterson. *Contesting Castro: The United States and the Triumph of the Cuban Revolution*. New York: Oxford University Press, 1994.

Peter Kornbluh, ed. *Bay of Pigs Declassified: The Secret CIA Report on the Invasion of Cuba*. New York: New Press, 1998.

Howard Jones. *Bay of Pigs*. New York: Oxford University Press, 2008.

Don Bohning. *The Castro Obsession: U.S. Covert Operations against Cuba, 1959–1965*. Washington, DC: Potomac Books, 2006.

Alexsandr Fursenko and Timothy Naftali. *"One Hell of a Gamble": Khrushchev, Castro, and Kennedy, 1958–1964*. New York: W. W. Norton, 1997.

Don Munton and David Welch. *The Cuban Missile Crisis: A Concise History*. New York: Oxford University Press, 2007.

Henry Ryan Butterfield. *The Fall of Che Guevara: A Story of Soldiers, Spies, and Diplomats*. New York: Oxford University Press, 1999.

Esteban Morales Dominguez and Gary Prevost, eds. *United States–Cuban Relations: A Critical History*. Lanham, MD: Lexington Books, 2008.

Daniel P. Erikson, *The Cuba Wars: Fidel Castro, the United States, and the Next Revolution*. New York: Bloomsbury Press, 2008.

CHAPTER 5: NO MORE CUBAS—THE KENNEDY AND JOHNSON DOCTRINES

The John F. Kennedy and Lyndon Johnson administrations wanted to fight radicalism, communism, and the Cuban Revolution through development and "modernization." The grand economic aid program, the Alliance for Progress, the "Marshall Plan for Latin America," failed, however, to achieve U.S. goals in the region. The Alliance for Progress is analyzed in the following works.

Michael E. Latham. *Modernization as Ideology: American Social Science and "Nation Building" in the Kennedy Era*. Chapel Hill: University of North Carolina Press, 2000.

Robert Packenham. *Liberal America and the Third World: Political Development Ideas and Social Science*. Princeton: Princeton University Press, 1973.

Stephen G. Rabe. *The Most Dangerous Area in the World: John F. Kennedy Confronts Communist Revolution in Latin America*. Chapel Hill: University of North Carolina Press, 1999.

Jeffrey F. Taffett. *Foreign Aid as Foreign Policy: The Alliance for Progress in Latin America*. New York: Routledge, 2007.

When modernization schemes failed to create sturdy, self-reliant, anti-Communist states in Latin America, the Kennedy and Johnson administrations turned to covert interventions and the training of Latin American military and police officers. Before examining the U.S. covert interventions in British Guiana and Brazil and the invasion of the Dominican Republic, a student might want to examine books about the CIA and military and police training. Agee was a former CIA operative who turned against the agency and went into exile in Cuba.

Philip Agee. *Inside the Company: CIA Diary*. New York: Stonehill Publishing, 1975.

Tim Weiner. *Legacy of Ashes: The History of the CIA*. New York: Doubleday, 2007.

Lesley Gill. *The School of the Americas: Military Training and Political Violence in the Americas*. Durham: Duke University Press, 2004.

Martha K. Huggins. *Political Policing: The United States and Latin America*. Durham: Duke University Press, 1998.

At present, my book is the only study that focuses on the U.S. intervention in British Guiana. Colin Palmer, a distinguished historian of the Caribbean, has written a new analysis of Cheddi Jagan.

Stephen G. Rabe, *U.S. Intervention in British Guiana: A Cold War Story*. Chapel Hill: University of North Carolina Press, 2005.

Colin Palmer. *The Politics of Power: Cheddi Jagan, Great Britain, the United States, and the Struggle for British Guiana*. Chapel Hill: University of North Carolina Press, 2010.

Four authors have provided an excellent understanding of the "quiet" U.S. intervention in Brazil from 1962 to 1964. Before perusing these studies, one might investigate Thomas Skidmore's fine account of Brazilian history.

Thomas E. Skidmore. *Brazil: Five Centuries of Change*. 2nd ed. New York: Oxford University Press, 2009.

Jan Knippers Black. *United States Penetration of Brazil*. Philadelphia: University of Pennsylvania Press, 1977.

Ruth Leacock. *Requiem for Revolution: The United States and Brazil, 1961–1969*. Kent, OH: Kent State University Press, 1990.

Phyllis R. Parker. *Brazil and the Quiet Intervention*. Austin: University of Texas Press, 1979.

W. Michael Weis. *Cold Warriors and Coups d'Etat: Brazilian–American Relations, 1946–1964*. Albuquerque: University of New Mexico Press, 1993.

The scholarly community still lacks an analysis of the U.S. invasion of the Dominican Republic that incorporates recently declassified material and new methodologies in the history of U.S. foreign relations. The studies by Gleijeses and Lowenthal are dated but useful. Chester offers intriguing insights.

Piero Gleijeses. *The Dominican Crisis: The 1965 Constitutionalist Revolt and American Intervention*. Baltimore: Johns Hopkins University Press, 1978.

Abraham F. Lowenthal. *The Dominican Intervention*. Cambridge, MA: Harvard University Press, 1972.

Eric Thomas Chester, *Rag-Tags, Scum, Riff-Raff, and Commies: The U.S. Intervention in the Dominican Republic, 1965–1966*. New York: Monthly Review Press, 2001.

CHAPTER 6: MILITARY DICTATORS— COLD WAR ALLIES

No historian has yet produced a comprehensive study of the Latin American policy of the Richard M. Nixon administration. The declassification of State Department and National Security Council records, Henry Kissinger's telephone conversations, and President Nixon's taped conversations in the Oval Office of the White House make such a study feasible. For the time being, a student might consult general histories of Nixon's foreign policy. The edited work by Logevall and Preston contains an essay by Mark Lawrence on Nixon and Latin America.

Robert Dallek. *Nixon and Kissinger: Partners in Power*. New York: HarperCollins, 2007.

Jussi M. Hanhimäki. *Flawed Architect: Henry Kissinger and American Foreign Policy*. New York: Oxford University Press, 2004.

Fredrik Logevall and Andrew Preston, eds. *Nixon in the World: American Foreign Relations, 1969–1977*. New York: Oxford University Press, 2008.

Jeremi Suri. *Henry Kissinger and the American Century*. Cambridge, MA: Belknap Press of
    Harvard University, 2009.

Before investigating the U.S. intervention in Chile and U.S. relations with the Argentine
military, it would be best to gain some insight into Chilean and Argentine history.

Brian Loveman. *Chile: The Legacy of Hispanic Capitalism*. New York: Oxford University
    Press, 2001.
Luis Alberto Romero. *A History of Argentina in the Twentieth Century*. University Park:
    Pennsylvania State University Press, 2002.

The U.S. intervention in Chile is the one case study of the Nixon administration's policy
toward Latin America that is well documented. President Bill Clinton ordered the declassification of more than twenty thousand documents on U.S. policy toward Chile. These documents are available via the Internet. The documents for the National Security council, for
example, are at http://foia.state.gov/SearchColls/NSC.asp. For the CIA, the Web site would
be http://foia.state.gov/SearchColls/CIA.asp. These documents inform many of the studies
listed. Kornbluh's book is the best place to start an investigation of the U.S. intervention.

Kristian Gustafson. *Hostile Intent: U.S. Covert Operations in Chile, 1964–1974*. Washington,
    DC: Potomac Books, 2007.
Jonathan Haslam. *The Nixon Administration and the Death of Allende's Chile: A Case of
    Assisted Suicide*. London: Verso, 2005.
Peter Kornbluh. *The Pinochet File: A Declassified Dossier of Atrocity and Accountability*.
    New York: The New Press, 2003.

General Augusto Pinochet and other South American military dictators spread murder and terror throughout the continent and sponsored international terrorism through
Operation Condor. Thomas Wright's book is especially compelling in detailing the atrocities ordered by the military dictators.

John Dinges, *The Condor Years: How Pinochet and His Allies Brought Terrorism to Three
    Continents*. New York: The New Press, 2004.
John Dinges and Saul Landau. *Assassination on Embassy Row*. New York: Pantheon Books,
    1980.
J. Patrice McSherry. *Predatory States: Operation Condor and Covert War in Latin America*.
    Lanham, MD: Rowman & Littlefield, 2005.
Thomas C. Wright. *State Terrorism in Latin America: Chile, Argentina, and International
    Human Rights*. Lanham, MD: Rowman & Littlefield, 2007.

Survivors of the horrors of torture, rape, and degradation in countries such as Argentina
and Chile have written about their experiences. The accounts by Arce and Timerman make
for grim reading. Cooper, a U.S. citizen, was in Chile when Pinochet seized power and was
a witness to the enveloping terror.

Luz Arce. *The Inferno: A Story of Terror and Survival in Chile*. Translated by Stacey Alba
    Skar. Madison: University of Wisconsin Press, 2004.

Marc Cooper. *Pinochet and Me*. London: Verso, 2001.

Jacobo Timerman. *Prisoner without a Name, Cell without a Number*. Translated by Tony Talbot. Madison: University of Wisconsin Press, 2002.

CHAPTER 7: COLD WAR HORRORS— CENTRAL AMERICA

Chapter 7 first surveys the human rights initiatives of President Jimmy Carter and then analyzes the Ronald Reagan administration's war against political leftists in Nicaragua, El Salvador, and Guatemala. The studies by Schoultz and Sikkink on Carter's policies are both outstanding. Pastor, who served on the National Security Council, provides a detached view of Carter's policies in Central America.

Lars Schoultz. *Human Rights and United States Policy toward Latin America*. Princeton: Princeton University Press, 1981.

Kathyrn Sikkink. *Mixed Signals: U.S. Human Rights Policy and Latin America*. Ithaca: Cornell University Press, 2004.

Robert A. Pastor. *Condemned to Repetition: The United States and Nicaragua*. Princeton: Princeton: University Press, 1987.

Gaining insight into the people and culture of Central America is an essential first task before embarking on an investigation of U.S. policies in the region between 1979 and 1989.

John A. Booth, Christine J. Wade, and Thomas W. Walker. *Understanding Central America: Global Forces, Rebellion, and Change*. 5th ed. Boulder, CO : Westview Press, 2009.

Ralph Lee Wooward, Jr. *Central America: A Nation Divided*. 3rd ed. New York: Oxford University Press, 1999.

My friend Tom Leonard once calculated that, from 1979 to 1992, over nine hundred books appeared purporting to explain the Central American crisis. A student might begin with the aforementioned surveys (in the **Bibliographic Guides and General Interpretations** section) by Coatsworth, *Central America and the United States* (1997); LaFeber, *Inevitable Revolutions* (1993); and Leonard, *Central America and the United States* (1991). Three studies on the Reagan administration's approach are listed. LeoGrande's massive tome is the best and most comprehensive history of the policy debates that erupted within the United States during the Central American crisis.

Thomas Carothers. *In the Name of Democracy: U.S. Policy toward Latin America in the Reagan Years*. Berkeley: University of California Press, 1991.

Greg Grandin. *Empire's Workshop: Latin America, the United States, and the Rise of the New Imperialism*. New York: Henry Holt, 2007.

William M. LeoGrande. *Our Own Backyard: The United States in Central America, 1977–1992*. Chapel Hill: University of North Carolina Press, 1992.

The following books convey some of the horrors that Central Americans were subjected to in the 1980s.

Mark Danner. *The Massacre at El Mozote: A Parable of the Cold War.* New York: Vintage Books, 1994.

Joan Didion. *Salvador.* New York: Simon & Schuster, 1983.

Cecilia Menjívar and Néstor Rodríguez, eds. *When States Kill: Latin America, the U.S., and Technologies of Terror.* Austin: University of Texas Press, 2005.

Daniel Wilkinson. *Silence on the Mountain: Stories of Terror, Betrayal, and Forgetting in Guatemala.* Boston: Houghton Mifflin, 2002.

AFTERMATH

In the post–Cold War period, governments, international agencies, and non-governmental organizations like the Roman Catholic Church have produced compelling, credible reports on the ghastly violations of human rights in countries such as Argentina, Brazil, Chile, El Salvador, and Guatemala. Some of these reports, or at least their conclusions, can be read in English in book form or on the Internet.

Archdiocese of São Paulo. *Torture in Brazil.* Translated by Jaime Wright. Edited and with an Introduction by Joan Dassin. New York: Vintage Books, 1986.

Argentine National Commission on the Disappeared. *Nunca Más.* With an Introduction by Ronald Dworkin. New York: Farrar Strauss Giroux, 1986.

Commission on the Truth for El Salvador. *From Madness to Hope: The Twelve Year War in El Salvador.* 1993. http://www.usip.org/files/file/ElSalvador-Report.pdf

Guatemalan Commission for Historical Clarification. *Guatemala: Memory of Silence.* 1999. An English translation of the conclusion of *Memory of Silence* can be found at the Web site http://shr.aaas.org/guatemala/ceh/report/english/toc.html

Scholars and journalists have also been interviewing the victims of the Cold War and those who perpetrated the atrocities. Goldhagen, a renowned scholar on the Holocaust and the destruction of European Jewry, interprets what happened in countries such as Argentina and Guatemala within the context of the atrocities committed by the Nazis. Steve Sterns's work on memory in Chile after Pinochet is truly amazing and vital.

Marguerite Feitlowitz. *A Lexicon of Terror: Argentina and the Legacies of Torture.* New York: Oxford University Press, 1998.

Daniel Jonah Goldhagen. *Worse than War: Genocide, Eliminationism, and the Ongoing Assault on Humanity.* New York: Public Affairs, 2009.

Matilde Mellibovsky. *Circle of Love over Death: Testimonies of the Mothers of the Plaza de Mayo.* Translated by Marie and Matthew Poser. Willimantic, CT: Curbstone Press, 1997.

Tina Rosenberg. *Children of Cain: Violence and the Violent in Latin America.* New York: William Morrow, 1991.

Steve J. Stern. *Remembering Pinochet's Chile: On the Eve of London, 1998.* Durham: Duke University Press, 2004.

Steve J. Stern. *Reckoning with Pinochet: The Memory Question in Democratic Chile, 1989–2006.* Durham: Duke University Press, 2010.

Index